D0918566

IDEAS IN CONTEXT

CHRISTIAN HUMANISM
AND THE
PURITAN SOCIAL ORDER

IDEAS IN CONTEXT

Edited by Wolf Lepenies, Richard Rorty, J. B. Schneewind
and Quentin Skinner

The books in this series will discuss the emergence of intellectual traditions and of related new disciplines. The procedures, aims and vocabularies that were generated will be set in the context of the alternatives available within the contemporary frameworks of ideas and institutions. Through detailed studies of the evolution of such traditions, and their modification by different audiences, it is hoped that a new picture will form of the development of ideas in their concrete contexts. By this means, artificial distinctions between the history of philosophy, of the various sciences, of society and politics, and of literature may be seen to dissolve.

This series is published with the support of the Exxon Education Foundation

CHRISTIAN HUMANISM
AND THE
PURITAN SOCIAL ORDER

MARGO TODD

*Department of History,
Vanderbilt University*

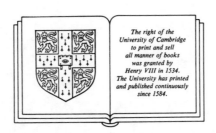

The right of the
University of Cambridge
to print and sell
all manner of books
was granted by
Henry VIII in 1534.
The University has printed
and published continuously
since 1584.

CAMBRIDGE UNIVERSITY PRESS

CAMBRIDGE
NEW YORK   NEW ROCHELLE
MELBOURNE   SYDNEY

Published by the Press Syndicate of the University of Cambridge
The Pitt Building, Trumpington Street, Cambridge CB2 1RP
32 East 57th Street, New York, NY 10022, USA
10 Stamford Road, Oakleigh, Melbourne 3166, Australia

First published 1987

Printed in Great Britain at the University Press, Cambridge

Todd, Margo
Christian humanism and the Puritan social
order. – (Ideas in context).
1. Puritans – England – History
2. Humanism – History
I. Title   II. Series
285′.9′0942   BX9334.2

Library of Congress cataloguing in publication data
Todd, Margo.
Christian humanism and the Puritan social order
(Ideas in context)
Bibliography
1. Puritans – Historiography.   2. Sociology, Christian.
3. Humanism.   I. Title.   II. Series.
BX9322.T62   1987   285′.9   87–6644

ISBN 0 521 33129 3

CONTENTS

For Charles, Jesse and Adam

PREFACE

I have incurred many debts during the course of research for this study. The greatest of all I owe to my mentor, Derek Hirst, who has been unstinting with his time, generous with his suggestions, incisive in his criticism, and consistent in his encouragement of this project since its genesis several years ago in his seminar in Stuart history at Washington University. His own zeal for research and for the reassessment of traditional interpretations has been an unfailing source of inspiration. J. H. Hexter has provided many useful suggestions, and to his own work goes the credit for stimulating my early thinking about the similarities between protestant and Christian humanist social thought. Early drafts of all or parts of the study were kindly read by Quentin Skinner, H. C. Porter, James McConica and J. H. Plumb, and the final version has benefited greatly from their insights; had I trod more carefully in the paths they indicated, I would doubtless have avoided the errors that remain. For valuable research suggestions early in the process I am grateful to George Huppert, Nicholas Tyacke and Conrad Russell, and conversations with Peter Lake and Jacqueline Levy proved more formative than they may have known.

Research for this study was made possible by fellowships and a travel grant from the Department of History at Washington University, and by a summer research fellowship from the Vanderbilt University Research Council. A year's leave from teaching responsibilities at Vanderbilt provided opportunity to write and revise; however, the preceding years of teaching also played their part in the final production – the fresh perspective of undergraduate queries may have a more critical role than we generally acknowledge in refining our interpretations.

To the staffs of the British Library, the Bodleian Library, the

Cambridge University Library, the Lambeth Palace Library and the Trinity College Library in Dublin I wish to express my appreciation of many courtesies. I am also indebted to the Masters and Fellows of the Queen's College and Balliol College, Oxford, and of Emmanuel, Pembroke, St. John's, Sidney Sussex and Trinity Colleges, Cambridge, and to the President and Fellows of Queens' College, Cambridge, for access to manuscripts in their possession. The college librarians were unfailing in their patience and helpfulness.

Portions of chapter 4 were previously published as 'Humanists, Puritans, and the Spiritualized Household' in *Church History* 49 (1980). I am grateful to the American Society of Church History for permission to reprint this material.

Finally, for the patience and selflessness of my husband during these years of research and writing, I have admiration as well as gratitude. But for his steady encouragement and unwavering faith, I might have followed an easier, but less interesting, route. To my sons, so young to have lived so long with Erasmus, thanks.

As for the work that follows, I am inclined to echo Thomas Gataker's preface to his own first book. He told his reader in 1619, 'Defects in it (I know) there can not but be many. Of thee (whosoever thou art) I desire but to find an unpartial reader, a judicious discusser, and a charitable censurer.'

ABBREVIATIONS

Add.   Additional
BL   British Library
Bodl.   Bodleian Library
CH   *Church History*
Coll.   *The Colloquies of Erasmus*, tr. Craig R. Thompson (Chicago, 1965)
CSPD   *Calendar of State Papers, Domestic*
CUL   Cambridge University Library
CWE   *Collected Works of Erasmus* (Toronto, 1974–)
DNB   *Dictionary of National Biography*
EHR   *English Historical Review*
F&R   *Acts and Ordinances of the Interregnum, 1642–1660*, ed. C. H. Firth and R. S. Rait (1911)
Harl.   Harleian
HJ   *The Historical Journal*
HLQ   *Huntington Library Quarterly*
HMC   *Historical Manuscripts Commission Reports*
JBS   *Journal of British Studies*
JEH   *Journal of Ecclesiastical History*
JHI   *Journal of the History of Ideas*
JMH   *Journal of Modern History*
NYRB   *New York Review of Books*
P&P   *Past and Present*
PRO   *Public Record Office*
Rawl.   *Rawlinson*
SCJ   *Sixteenth Century Journal*
SP   State Papers
STC   A. W. Pollard and G. R. Redgrave, *A Short-Title Catalogue of Books Printed in England . . . 1475–1640* (1926)

TCD   Trinity College, Dublin
TED   *Tudor Economic Documents*, ed. R. H. Tawney and Eileen Power (1924)
TRHS   *Transactions of the Royal Historical Society*
Trin.   Trinity College, Cambridge

Spelling, punctuation and capitalization have been modernized except in titles of published works, and titles of contemporary publications have been shortened except where the verbiage adds to the description of the work or is otherwise of interest. For the reader's convenience, modern English translations of works originally published in Latin are quoted wherever possible. Where good modern translations are not available, or where sixteenth-century translations are of particular significance, contemporary translations published in England are cited. Place of publication is London unless otherwise stated. All dates are Old Style, but the year is held to begin on 1 January.

1

Introduction:
the demythologizing of puritanism

The historiographical problem of puritanism has now reached epic proportions. While some historians carry on the old debate about precisely what constellation of beliefs constitutes 'puritanism', others now question whether the concept exists at all.[1] While some go on to attach the puritan label even to bishops, others are able to talk about people traditionally regarded by everyone as puritans without even using the word.[2] The most extreme revisionists deny that either puritans or puritanism had anything to do with the conflict of the 1640s; others, however, have resurrected the notion of a Puritan Revolution.[3] While advocates of the latter view find elements of radicalism in puritan thought, others have shown puritans to have been upholders of the established order in church and state.[4]

[1] Recent contributors to the literature on definition include Peter Lake, *Moderate Puritans and the Elizabethan Church* (Cambridge, 1982); William Hunt, *The Puritan Moment: The Coming of Revolution in an English County* (Cambridge, Mass., 1983); Paul Christianson, 'Reformers and the Church of England under Elizabeth I and the Early Stuarts,' *JEH* 31 (1980), 463–82; Patrick Collinson, 'A Comment: Concerning the name Puritan', *JEH*, 31 (1980), 483–8; and Richard Greaves, *Society and Religion in Elizabethan England* (Minneapolis, 1981). Among those denying any meaning to 'puritanism' is Michael Findlayson, *Historians, Puritanism, and the English Revolution: The Religious Factor in English Politics before and after the Interregnum* (Toronto, 1983).

[2] Lake, 'Matthew Hutton: A Puritan Bishop?', *History*, 64 (1979), 182–204; *cf.* C. M. Dent, *Protestant Reformers in Elizabethan Oxford* (Oxford, 1983).

[3] Findlayson, ch. 3. *cf.* Hunt, *passim*; B. Reay, 'Radicalism and Religion in the English Revolution,' *Radical Religion in the English Revolution*, ed. J. F. McGregor and B. Reay (Oxford, 1984), 1–21; John Morrill, *Cheshire 1630–1660* (Oxford, 1974), *Reactions to the English Civil War* (New York, 1983), Introduction, 'The Religious Context of the English Civil War,' *TRHS*, 5th ser., 34 (1984), 155–78, esp. pp. 170ff, and 'Sir William Brereton and England's Wars of Religion,' *JBS* 24 (1985), 311–32; and Anthony Fletcher, *The Outbreak of the English Civil War* (London, 1981).

[4] Hunt, chs. 8–10; Reay, p. 2; and Christopher Hill, *The World Turned Upside Down* (1972), *Milton and the English Revolution* (1977), and *The Experience of Defeat* (1984). On the other side, see Patrick Collinson, *The Religion of Protestants* (Oxford, 1982) and 'The Early Dissenting Tradition,' *Godly People* (1983), 526–62.

The debate during the past decade has been intense and sometimes bitter, and resolution of some of the most basic questions seems as illusory as ever.

Fortunately, however, the historiographic conflict has not been without positive results. It has managed to bring us closer to understanding who puritans were and how they acted. Even those historians who have ceased using the term still talk about the people who we have always thought were puritans and have taught us a good deal about them. As the polemical dust clears, it is becoming evident that some old and weakly-founded constructs have been quite properly demolished, and new interpretations based on manuscript evidence and the discoveries of local historians have been erected to good effect.

The biggest step forward has been the move to put puritans back into the protestant mainstream of Elizabethan and early Stuart England.[5] Puritans are increasingly being depicted not as an alienated opposition group but as part of the established order, functioning as magistrates and ministers to establish the protestantism of which they were the best representatives. Far from being a seething revolutionary substratum of the Church of England, they comprised a sort of 'moral majority' within it, the 'sharp cutting edge of an evangelical Protestantism.'[6] Of course, whether puritans were sufficiently entrenched within mainline protestantism to render meaningless their distinctively 'puritan' identity is at least questionable. The fact that historians who repudiate 'puritan' wind up substituting for it terms like 'advanced protestant' and 'precisionist' and 'evangelical' is suggestive, and as Peter Lake has been at pains to show us, the 'godly', however moderate, certainly recognized each other in the midst of the 'mere Prayer Book protestants' who comprised the bulk of their church.[7] But setting aside for the moment the question of taxonomy, the least that can be said about accomplishments thus far is that Elizabethan and Jacobean puritanism is no

---

[5] The achievement especially of Collinson in *The Religion of Protestants* and 'Early Dissenting Tradition.' See also Paul Christianson, *Reformers and Babylon* (Toronto, 1978).

[6] Collinson, *Religion of Protestants*, esp. ch. 4, 'A Comment' (the oft-quoted 'moral majority' appears on p. 485), and 'Early Dissenting Tradition,' pp. 534–5, on the 'widespread social entrenchment of puritanism in Jacobean England'; Lake, 'Puritan Identities,' *JEH* 35 (1984), 112–23, p. 113; Christianson, *Reformers and Babylon, passim*; Morrill, 'Religious Context', p. 162.

[7] Dent uses 'advanced protestant,' 'radical' and 'reformer'; Morrill, *Reactions*, Introduction (p. 15) uses 'advanced Protestants (or Puritan, if you will)'; Mary Fulbrook, *Piety and Politics: Religion and the Rise of Absolutism in England, Wurtemberg and Prussia* (Cambridge, 1983), uses 'precisionist,' although she retains 'puritan' as well; Lake's *Moderate Puritans* leans toward 'evangelical.'

longer welded immovably to revolutionary opposition to the establishment, and this recognition has been an undeniable boon to the study of puritans. It has broadened our perspective on and therefore our understanding of puritans by drawing our attention to the likes of Chaderton and Hutton, along with Field and Perkins, to episcopally-approved lectures by combination, along with covert classes, and to the cooperation of bishops and godly magistrates in the enforcement of sabbatarianism and the reformation of manners.[8] Puritans have been removed from their historiographic box and examined within the context of the church and political order of which they were in fact very much a part.

The problem with all of this, of course, is that in 1642 these bastions of order took up arms against their king; in 1645 the godly representatives of the people tried and executed the Archbishop of Canterbury; and in 1649 these bulwarks of magistracy and ministry launched an experiment in republicanism and congregationalism. The consensus that Patrick Collinson has described for the Jacobean period broke down in the next reign, and until it becomes clear how the conservative, godly magistrates and ministers of Stuart England managed so radically to re-channel English politics and society in the 1640s, historians are not rid of the puritan problem.

One area generally neglected by recent studies, an area potentially crucial to understanding what happened in the 1640s, is that of puritan social and political thought. The focus of late has been more on activities than on ideas,[9] perhaps in unconscious compensation for the frequently misguided treatment of puritans by intellectual historians and political scientists in the 1960s and 1970s. We now know more than ever about what puritans did, as urban magistrates and churchwardens and clergymen and gentlemen, but the theoretical underpinning for their actions has received scant attention of late. There has been virtually no systematic re-evaluation of the origins and nature of puritan social thought and its political ramifications. To the extent that studies focused on puritanism and society have been produced, their conclusions seem to have very little to do with the new, broader view of puritans as part of the mainstream; they simply repeat old orthodoxies. Students who wish to examine puritan social thought are left with the interpretations of the old

---

[8] Lake, *Moderate Puritans*; Collinson, *Religion of Protestants*, chs. 3 and 4, and *Godly People*; Kenneth Parker, 'Thomas Rogers and the English Sabbath: The Case for a Reappraisal,' *CH*, 53 (1984), 332–47.

[9] The exception of theological studies should be noted: R. T. Kendall, *Calvin and English Calvinism to 1649* (Oxford, 1979); Dewey Wallace, *Puritans and Predestination: Grace in English Protestant Theology, 1525–1695* (Chapel Hill, NC, 1982).

masters, complete with misconceptions. Among the gravest of these is the old myth that there was a distinctly puritan social theory, a new view of social order peculiar to the hotter sort of protestants. The myth has puritans as intellectual innovators – genuine creators, breathing their spiritual zeal on theological dust, as it were, to bring into being an original body of social thought that distinguished them from their contemporaries, both protestant and Catholic. In the context of the broad religious consensus that has been demonstrated for Elizabethan and Jacobean England, this account looks odd indeed, but it remains the going version for students of social theory and continues to shape accounts of the Civil War. Clearly, some review and re-evaluation is in order.

The historiography of puritan social thought from Weber and Tawney to Hill and Walzer has attributed to protestant religious zealots a degree of originality of thought rarely assigned to and almost never deserved by any intellectual movement.[10] While puritan intentions have been disputed and the precise nature of their social ethic variously interpreted, there is agreement among these historians that the social order to which puritans aspired represented a drastic and distinctively protestant break with the immediate past. Where intellectual debts are acknowledged, they are credited to continental Calvinist theology and to the Bible. But even where the puritan outlook has been broadened into the Protestant Mind, there is no suggestion that the social theorists of Elizabethan and early Stuart England built on any but thoroughly Reformed foundations.[11] Students are thus presented with a view of puritanism which, given modern veneration for creativity and innovative thinking, amounts to little less than secular hagiography.

Christopher Hill, of course, is master of them all. His voluminous and erudite output has given us a view of zealous Elizabethan and early Stuart Calvinists as the generators of a progressive and ultimately revolutionary theory of social order. Hill and his followers have puritan social thought rising phoenix-like from the ashes of medieval social and intellectual stagnation to ignite the Civil

---

[10] Max Weber, 'Die protestantische ethik und der geist des kapitalismus,' in *Gesammelte aufsätze zur religionssoziologie* (Tubingen, 1922); R. H. Tawney, *Religion and the Rise of Capitalism* (New York, 1926); William Haller, *The Rise of Puritanism* (New York, 1938); *cf.* Charles H. George, 'Social Interpretation of English Puritanism,' *JMH*, 25 (1953), 327–42; Christopher Hill, *Intellectual Origins of the English Revolution* (Oxford, 1965), *Puritanism and Revolution* (1958), *Society and Puritanism* (New York, 1964); Michael Walzer, *The Revolution of the Saints* (New York, 1972).

[11] Charles H. and Katherine George, *The Protestant Mind of the English Reformation* (Princeton, 1961).

War and usher in a new, bourgeois social system in seventeenth-century England. Stressing the peculiar appeal of the Calvinist ethic to the 'industrious sort', Hill portrays a rising bourgeoisie of late sixteenth- and early seventeenth-century England seizing upon such Calvinist precepts as the priesthood of believers, the evident election of the godly and the eventual triumph of the saints as an ideological means of transforming the medieval social stasis which they had inherited into a progressive, sober, hard-working, definitely middle-class order. According to Hill, 'Men's ideas were blurred in the sixteenth century, traditional attitudes outliving the social environment which had given them birth.' It was puritans who took up the challenge of stagnant values in a changing society and, on the basis of purely protestant assumptions, produced 'a new pattern of social discipline.'[12] To the protestant Reformation generally, and to puritanism in particular, Hill attributes an incredibly broad spectrum of social and intellectual creativity. From the Elizabethan poor laws to the Scientific Revolution to the Civil War, change in sixteenth- and seventeenth-century England is traced to the 'hotter sort' of protestants.[13]

Among the most significant changes thus inaugurated, Hill identifies the phenomenon which he calls the spiritualization of the household. Puritans are seen as the creators of an exalted notion of the family as the fundamental spiritual unit of society. The family as a 'little commonwealth' is set against traditional forms of order and relationship; as a 'little church', it challenges the authority of the ecclesiastical hierarchy. The concomitants of the doctrine – an exaltation of the marriage relationship, a demand for household religious education and discipline, and a slight but noteworthy elevation of the position of women within the household – are clearly attributed to protestant theology in the hands of zealous English practitioners. Nor is Hill alone in his assertion that it was puritanism which gave rise to this phenomenon: while his is the clearest and most extensive treatment of it, he has both predecessors and followers.[14] Rarely is it suggested that puritans might

---

[12] Hill, *Puritanism and Revolution*, pp. 222–3; *Society and Puritanism, passim*.

[13] On the Scientific Revolution, *Intellectual Origins*, pp. 22, 34–61, and 'Puritanism, capitalism and the scientific revolution,' in *The Intellectual Revolution of the Seventeenth Century*, ed. Charles Webster (1974), pp. 243–53; *cf.* Charles Webster, *The Great Instauration: Science, Medicine and Reform 1626–1660* (New York, 1975).

[14] Hill, *Society and Puritanism*, pp. 443–81; Chilton Powell, *English Domestic Relations, 1487–1653* (New York, 1917), pp. 129, 147 *et passim*; Louis B. Wright, *Middle-Class Culture in Elizabethan England* (Chapel Hill, 1935), pp. 201–27; Levin L. Schücking, *The Puritan Family* (tr. B. Battershaw, New York, 1970), *passim*; Keith Thomas, 'Women and the Civil War Sects', *P&P*, 13 (1958), 42–62; Walzer, pp. 183–98; and most recently, Greaves, *Society and Religion*, ch. 7 and pp. 737–67.

have gone beyond the Bible or their Reformed heritage for their ideas.

Hill and others have similarly traced to the Calvinist doctrine of calling the insistence of puritans on the obliteration of idleness and of the indiscriminate charity which fostered it as the solution to the problem of poverty. Hill finds 'the very closest connection between the protestant ideology of hard work and the economic needs of English society.' Puritans, as 'a class for whom the accumulation of capital had become an absolute good in itself', accordingly preached a morality in which 'humanitarianism was irrelevant.' Alms were to be carefully administered to train and employ the poor and set 'lusty beggars' on forced work; only thus would the godly prosper and the commonwealth be reformed.[15] Other historians have quarreled with this interpretation of the puritan attitude toward wealth and property, and local historians have unearthed many examples of puritan charity. At least one study has suggested that whatever puritan conceptions were, they were shared by Anglicans, but an historiographical consensus exists on the *protestant* generation of these ideas.[16]

In parallel fashion, Michael Walzer has attributed to puritanism the beginnings of the end of the Great Chain of Being, that medieval doctrine of the cosmos as a natural, static hierarchy of orders and degrees. The arbitrary God of the Calvinists, we are told, establishes his own omnipotence by leveling the cosmos and destroying the intermediary powers of angels, saints, bishops, and kings. Degree in the kingdom of the elect now depends on behavior, rather than on being, and order in the commonwealth is to be achieved not by enforcing obedience to constituted hierarchical authority, but by informing and disciplining the individual conscience.[17]

[15] Hill, *Society and Puritanism*, pp. 276, 287, 292; *Puritanism and Revolution*, pp. 215–38; *The World Turned Upside-Down* (New York, 1972), pp. 32–3.
[16] V. Kiernan, 'Puritans and the Poor,' *P&P*, 3 (1953), 45–53 (*cf.* Hill's response, pp. 53–4); Timothy H. Breen, 'The Non-Existent Controversy: Puritan and Anglican Attitudes on Work and Wealth, 1600–1640,' *CH*, 35 (1966), 273–87; W. K. Jordan, *Philanthropy in England, 1480–1660* (New York, 1959), pp. 151ff. George, *Protestant Mind*, p. 155, sees the protestant view of charity as the assertion of brotherhood. Greaves contrasts Anglican suspicion of wealth with puritan receptivity of 'the idea that prosperity could be a reward of godliness' (p. 751), although he notes Anglican and puritan similarity on many aspects of poor relief (e.g. pp. 572, 575). William Hunt provides abundant examples of puritan charity in Essex; however, he is not interested in the generation of the puritan ideology of poor relief (chs. 6 and 10). Paul Slack does note briefly in 'Poverty and Social Regulation in Elizabethan England,' *The Reign of Elizabeth I* (Athens, Georgia, 1985), 221–37, p. 236, that Elizabethan governors were 'anxious to prove their humanist credentials with a little social engineering in the interests of the commonwealth,' but on the same page he remarks that the 'new ideological input in Elizabeth's reign ... came from Protestant religious enthusiasm.'
[17] Walzer, *passim*; cf. Hill, *Intellectual Origins*, pp. 293–4; Hunt, p. 250, says of the Warwick/Barrington circle in the 1630s, 'their puritanism provided them with a

The radical implications of these and other elements of puritan social thought are readily apparent, and however staid and conservative the moderate puritans of recent accounts appear, the evidence produced by the authors of the old orthodoxy, and the evidence of the war itself, demand that we take another look. Furthermore, suggestions of puritan radicalism are not confined to a past generation of historians. Not only has Hill's own productivity not waned in retirement – the revivers of the 'Puritan Revolution' will not let the question rest. Hunt's Essex puritans were certainly in opposition to Crown and Canterbury by the mid-1620s, and it does not seem far-fetched to identify them with 'the aggressive, reformative, and hence socially disruptive aspects of zealous Protestantism' which he finds in Essex and defines as 'puritanism'.[18] The fact that Collinson devotes a substantial portion of his account of the religion of protestants to an attack on Walzer illustrates at least that the question is still a live one.[19] Was there a radicalism inherent in puritan thought all along, deeply dormant perhaps in the pacific generations before Charles and Laud, but ready to surface in times of stress? A look beyond Collinson's terminal date, 1625, suggests that this idea may not be devoid of merit. If it is correct, was this element, as Walzer, Hill, and others assume, the intellectual offspring of Calvinistic protestantism? Was social reformism a puritan distinctive? Puritan advocacy of the 'culture of discipline' is undeniable, and even conceding the cooperation of some bishops with the godly in reforming community manners seems still to connect Calvinist protestantism with the genesis of reformist ideology.

The time has come to ask whether the body of social thought which we associate with advanced English protestants could have sprung fully formed from purely Calvinist heads. To grant that puritans were concerned with social ethics is one thing; to transmute their concern into the creation of a new ethical system is quite another. To the extent that historians have described and provided evidence for puritan social theory as activist, progressive, practical and reformist in its methods and aims, they have made a positive

---

perfectly adequate ideology of social reform: they labored to institute the culture of discipline.'   [18] Hunt, pp. 146, 195–6.

[19] *Religion of Protestants*, pp. 150–88. In 'The Elizabethan Church and the New Religion,' in *The Reign of Elizabeth I*, pp. 169–94, Collinson describes the Elizabethan chapter of the English Reformation as tending toward 'a Protestant nation containing deep tension and potential confusion with an outward shell of consensus' (p. 176). He simply argues that the tension was not clearly manifest in the period before 1625, the terminal point of *The Religion of Protestants*. But its rapid development from the mid-1620s and its explosion in the 1640s surely demands further exploration of the intellectual genesis of the undeniable puritan radicalism of the Civil War and Interregnum.

contribution to our understanding of puritanism. To the extent that some have failed to recognize the appeal of puritanism to its numerous well-born patrons and identified it with a hypothetical middle class, they have been guilty of anachronism and distortion, but have stimulated useful discussion. But to the extent that they have ignored the ubiquity of reformism in sixteenth-century England, and indeed Europe, and failed to consider puritans as only one component, if a vocal one, of an important tradition of social activism and progressivism which had existed among Catholics as well as protestants since the beginning of the century, they have committed a serious error of omission.[20] They have wrenched puritans not only from the social, political, and ecclesiological mainstream, but from their intellectual moorings as well.

Historians of puritan ideas, even to the present day, have been like intellectual historians and literary scholars of an earlier generation: they have clung tenaciously to a 'great tradition', seeking to establish a single and direct channel of influence on puritan thought. Yet the best recent work in the field of intellectual history has demonstrated tellingly the complexity of the intellectual context in which a writer and thinker operates, and the foolishness of attempting to understand the intricate web of his thought by trying to unravel a single strand. The methodological object lessons provided by J. G. A. Pocock and Quentin Skinner[21] in the history of political theory have been too little appreciated by other scholars, and among the consequences are the monolithic appearance of puritanism and the inflated claims made for protestantism in the historiography of early modern ideas. Applying contextualism to detailed case studies in the history of political thought has borne out the contentions of Pocock and Skinner that only thus does the intellectual historian begin to do justice to his sources. Applying this methodology to puritan social thought will begin the long-overdue shifting of the historiography of puritan ideas onto the path which has been so well laid by modern intellectual historians and in the process reveal

[20] Peter Burke, *Popular Culture in Early Modern Europe* (London, 1978), notes that throughout western Europe, in Catholic as well as protestant countries, traditional popular culture was under pressure from the influence of a 'major shift in religious mentality' in the period 1500–1800 (p. 212).

[21] J. G. A. Pocock, 'Working on Ideas in Time,' *The Historian's Workshop*, ed. L. P. Curtis (New York, 1970); *Politics, Language, and Time* (1972); and *The Machiavellian Moment* (Princeton, 1975). Quentin Skinner, 'Meaning and Understanding in the History of Ideas,' *History and Theory*, 8 (1969), 3–53; 'Motives, Intentions, and the Interpretation of Texts,' *New Literary History*, 3 (1971), 393–408; 'Some Problems in the Analysis of Political Thought and Action', *Political Theory*, 2 (1974), 277–303, 283ff; and *Foundations of modern political thought*, 2 vols (Cambridge, 1978).

puritans as people of their own times, rather than as the mythical creatures of modern academics.[22] It will also offer a parallel in intellectual history to recent developments in the ecclesiastical, social, and political history of puritans.

It is imperative that we begin to adopt this more historical approach to puritan social thought, to examine puritanism within the context of broader, European intellectual developments in the early modern period. We must cease being unduly influenced by categories of analysis which we have invented for our own convenience and begin to take the wider view. Having said that, of course, brings us back to the question of how to define what some now call an inconvenient historians' invention, 'puritan'. However tiresome the debate, it is necessary at the start to have a clear understanding of whose ideas we are seeking to identify and examine in this study of social thought. And however skewed the old categories, the evidence will not allow us to dispense altogether with the term 'puritan' even if it is regarded as nothing more than 'an admirable refuge from clarity of thought.'[23] The people who called themselves the 'godly', 'professors', and even 'saints', and were called 'puritans' by their foes, were a sufficiently self-conscious and popularly identifiable group in their own day to deserve a name, and the traditional 'puritan' seems as good as any. The historian who talks about the likes of Laurence Humphrey and John Rainolds as 'advanced protestants' need not disturb us.[24] We know what he means by the term because we know of whom he speaks: a puritan by any other name is still a puritan. And in the midst of semantic confusion, historians reveal a remarkable convergence in their identification of particular individuals as puritans (or advanced protestants). Historians who quibble over definitions in theory have less trouble than might be expected when confronted with the need for flexible, working categories to apply to particular historical situations. If we allow room for the theological controversies of the 1620s and 1630s and the ecclesiological confusion of the Civil War and Interregnum in our definition, it is really not so

[22] Locating English protestant thought within the mainstream of early modern intellectual development also necessitates a repudiation of the geographically insular approach of many earlier historians: English protestants were part of a larger, European intellectual community, one that extended beyond the Geneva–London axis. The myth of the isolated, self-sufficient Englishman is just as misleading as the myth of Calvinist innovation in social theory. To find the sole continental influence on puritanism in the Geneva Bible and the *Institutes* is to look at history through peculiarly English spectacles.
[23] Hill, *Society and Puritanism*, p. 13. This statement is followed by 500 pages of analysis of 'puritan' social theory.   [24] Dent, *Protestant Reformers, passim.*

difficult to group together Rainolds, Cartwright, Perkins, Preston and Cromwell, while excluding Brownists, Barrowists and Laudian bishops from a useful and comprehensible category.

Basil Hall arrived nearly two decades ago at a limited but not inflexible definition of puritanism which more nearly conforms to modern historiographic practice than did earlier attempts.[25] A version of his definition, modified in light of recent work on 'moderate puritanism', has guided the work at hand. Hall, drawing extensively from contemporary use of the term, acknowledged that theological distinctions within English protestantism – Calvinism and Arminianism – only emerged in the 1620s.[26] Accordingly, his definition applies to the entire period from 1564 to 1640 by not making predestinarian theology a defining characteristic: he labels as puritan all those 'restlessly critical and occasionally rebellious members of the Church of England who desired some modifications in church government and worship, but not . . . those who deliberately removed themselves from that Church.' His puritans 'ranged from the tolerably conformable to the downright obstreperous, and to those who sought to

---

[25] Hall, 'Puritanism: The Problem of Definition,' *Studies in Church History*, 2 (1965), 283–96. Earlier contributors to the debate made 'puritan' practically synonymous with 'presbyterian.' A. S. P. Woodhouse identified Perry Miller and W. K. Jordan in this group and then went to the opposite extreme, encompassing by the term presbyterians, independents, separatists, baptists, radical millenarians and ranters: *Puritanism and Liberty* (1938), p. 36. William Haller, in his *Rise of Puritanism*, pp. 82–5, adopted Woodhouse's definition with the added proviso of predestinarian theology. Charles and Katherine George, focusing on that proviso and noting the shared Calvinism of non-conformists and pre-Laudian Anglicans, were the first to deny the term 'puritan' any meaning at all before the Civil War; *Protestant Mind*, pp. 6–8, 399–407, and 'Social Interpretations,' pp. 327–42. In the same year that Hall's essay was published, Christopher Hill offered a similar definition of puritans as 'radical Protestants who wanted to reform the Church but (before 1640 at least) did not want to separate from it,' but he somehow managed to identify all such people with the 'industrious sort' who in his view composed an expanding bourgeoisie in early modern England: *Intellectual Origins*, p. 26, and *Society and Puritanism*, pp. 13–29, 124–44.

[26] Nicholas Tyacke has traced the emergence of Arminianism in 'Puritanism, Arminianism and Counter-Revolution,' in *The Origins of the English Civil War*, ed. Conrad Russell (London, 1973), pp. 119–43; and 'Arminianism in England, in Religion and Politics, 1604–1640' (unpublished D.Phil. thesis, University of Oxford, 1968). He defines puritanism in terms of presbyterianism or non-conformity, but after the rise of anti-predestinarian theology in the 1620s he adds the theological criterion of doctrinal Calvinism, by that time a point of contention between dissenting and some conformist clergy. Whether that contention was actually between Calvinism and Arminianism or whether it was in fact simply a dispute about varieties of doctrinal Calvinism within the context of diplomatic and political troubles during the 1620s is duscussed by Peter White, 'The Rise of Arminianism Reconsidered,' *P&P*, 101 (1983), 34–54. The contention clearly existed, however, and even if we were to accept White's thesis that the rise of Arminianism was mythical, puritans did see themselves as defenders of predestinarian orthodoxy in the face of Anglican indifference, if not heterodoxy.

presbyterianise that Church from within.' Separatists are excluded from the definition on the basis of contemporary opinion.[27] Indeed, membership in the Church of England as part of the definition of puritan seems to imply for Hall, as it did for contemporaries, that the puritan attitude toward and approach to reforming the church were qualitatively different from those of separatists. The latter were not, strictly speaking, reformists at all; rejecting the established church as a hopeless case, they opted to seek the true church elsewhere.

The breadth of Hall's definition allows inclusion of the category 'moderate puritanism' illumined by the work of Peter Lake. Lake defines puritanism as 'committed evangelical protestantism' facing a 'tension between protestant principle and the brute facts of the partially reformed nature of the English church' and characterized by 'an intense vision of the reality and mutuality of the community of the godly and of the way in which that community could and should be called together through the word, particularly the word preached.'[28] While this definition includes the whole of Hall's range from the conformable to the obstreperous, Lake focuses on the hitherto neglected conformable, those moderate puritans who can be found in Elizabethan Cambridge in the circle of Laurence Chaderton, and in early Stuart Cambridge in that of Samuel Ward. Moderate puritans did not refuse to conform, but they bowed to the demands of the hierarchy under protest, and only when failure to conform would jeopardize their preaching ministry.[29] And they continued their campaign for the simplification of ceremonies and their denunciation of the hierarchy's insistence on conformity at the expense of a sufficient preaching ministry. It is clear from Collinson's look at Jacobean episcopal preaching that devotion to the preached word *per se* in the absence of demands for further reform is not a sure sign of puritanism.[30] The combination of criteria in Lake's definition is useful, because it excludes those who drifted uncomplainingly in that vast protestant mainstream so well described by Collinson, where the prevailing current of antipopery effectively engulfed whatever eddies of discontent with the Elizabethan Settlement

[27] Hall, pp. 290, 294; on separatists, pp. 290–2. Both Tyacke ('Puritanism, Arminianism and Counter-Revolution,' p. 120) and Hall make special reference to presbyterians, recognizing the conviction of Elizabethan presbyterians that godly authorities could impose the classis system on the established church in time; however, presbyterian polity is not a defining characteristic of puritanism for either.   [28] Lake, 'Matthew Hutton,' p. 182, and *Moderate puritans*, p. 3.
[29] Lake, *Moderate puritans, passim*; Margo Todd, ' "An Act of Discretion": Evangelical Conformity and the Puritan Dons,' *Albion*, 17 (1986), 581–99.
[30] Collinson, *Religion of Protestants*, pp. 48–52, focusing on Tobie Matthew.

diverted the more reform-minded from willing conformity. Hall's definition, so far as it goes, does so as well; but it falls short in two other aspects, the one chronological, the other related to the mentality which Lake so well describes in terms of zeal, intensity and self-consciousness.

Hall declines to apply his definition to the period after 1640, preferring to the general label of puritan the 'party names ... Presbyterian, Independent, and Baptist' used by Richard Baxter when discussing the war years.[31] He thus avoids the difficulty of fitting his definition of puritan to the likes of Cromwell and Milton; however, he thus implies that puritanism ceased to exist during the war – a position to which few historians adhere in practice. If the ecclesiological confusion of the Church of England during this period is acknowledged,[32] then the definition of puritans as zealous reformers within the established church can apply during the 1640s and 1650s as well to independents and presbyterians as to those who maintained a predilection (however muted) for godly episcopacy. The drastic changes which occurred in the nature and government of the church during the Civil War and Interregnum simply confronted reformers with a different established church and a wider range of options for church government than their predecessors had known. While the radical sectaries should continue to remain outside the puritan pale during this period for the same reasons that the followers of Henry Barrow were excluded earlier, it is surely legitimate to include the independents in light of their combination of religious zeal, ecclesiastical reformism and opposition to separatism *per se*, however tolerant of it they became in practice. Cromwell and Ireton were convinced, after all, that heaven would in time grant their cause, that their perception of godly church order, ruled neither by old priest nor by new presbyter, would in fact be incorporated into the reformation of the established English church.

The other change which would help Hall's definition is one of emphasis. Here, too, Lake's work offers a valuable corrective, as does Hunt's study of Essex puritanism. Hunt defines puritanism as 'a body of opinion within English protestantism characterized by intense hostility to the Church of Rome as the incarnation of Antichrist; an emphasis on preaching and Bible study rather than ritual as the means of salvation; and a desire to impose a strict moral

---

[31] Hall, p. 289; *cf. The Autobiography of Richard Baxter*, ed. J. Lloyd Thomas (London, 1931), pp. 35–6.

[32] Claire Cross, 'The Church in England 1646–1660,' in *The Interregnum*, ed. G. E. Aylmer (1972), pp. 99–120; John Morrill, 'The Church in England 1642–9,' *Reactions*, pp. 89–109.

code, which I term the culture of discipline, upon society as a whole.'
But he attaches an important rider to his definition: 'These
attitudes,' he says, 'were not necessarily peculiar to the people I consider puritans, but puritans were distinguished by the intensity with
which they held them.' Anglicans he describes as 'more complacent
Protestants' who 'placed a high value on ceremonial splendor and
uniformity'; in comparison with puritans they were 'irenic', less fac-
tious, relatively unconcerned with the 'trauma of regeneration'
which obsessed puritans.[33]

Puritans were similarly distinguished from other protestants by
their contemporaries, who observed not only puritan desire that the
English Reformation proceed beyond the Elizabethan Settlement
and its Jacobean and especially Caroline interpretations, but also,
and perhaps pre-eminently, the 'singularity in zeal and piety'[34] with
which puritans sought the further reform of the church, of the
individual believer and of the larger society as well. Puritans were the
'hotter sort' of protestants, remarkable, in the words of one contemporary, for the substance of their 'strict life, and precise opinion . . .
their more religious and conscionable conversation',[35] but even
more for the degree to which these differed from the manners and
religiosity of their conformist neighbors. It was this difference of
degree which allowed puritans to perceive themselves as forming a
distinct cultural community, to claim the capacity 'of being able to
recognise one another in the midst of a corrupt and unregenerate
world' and to call themselves 'saints'.[36] The young Richard Baxter
certainly had no trouble at all distinguishing puritans from the rest
of the mainstream. Puritans were distinguishable from conformists
not in that the latter approved of blasphemy and profanation of the
Sabbath – certainly did not – but in the intensity and zeal with which
puritans denounced and prosecuted these evils, and in the narrow
precision with which they defined them.[37] Most Anglicans approved

---

[33] Hunt, pp. xxi, 119.
[34] [Henry Parker], *A Discourse Concerning Puritans* (n.p., 1641), p. 9.
[35] *Ibid.*, pp. 9, 53.   [36] Lake, *Moderate Puritans*, p. 282; Hunt, p. xi, chs. 5–6.
[37] It is inconceivable, as Hunt points out, that an Anglican would make the claim that
Richard Rogers put forward in 1623, that 'those who love preachers . . . can be
assured against committing the sin against the Holy Ghost' (*The Practice of Christianity*, p. 44, quoted by Hunt, p. 114). On the other hand, Parker, 'Thomas
Rogers,' offers a persuasive challenge to older interpretations of sabbatarianism as
a characteristically puritan phenomenon (Collinson, 'The Beginnings of English
Sabbatarianism,' *Studies in Church History*, 1 (1964), 207–21; Greaves, 'The Origins
of English Sabbatarian Thought,' *SCJ*, 12 (1981), 19–34; Keith Sprunger, 'English
and Dutch Sabbatarianism and the Development of Puritan Social Thought,
1600–1660,' *CH*, 51 (1982), 24–38) by presenting evidence from visitation articles,
sermons, and church court registers of episcopal commitment to and enforcement
of strict sabbath observance. I am grateful to Dr Parker for allowing me to read an
early draft of this article.

of preaching itself (although there were exceptions like William Osboldston, whose infrequent sermons were noted for their preaching against frequent preaching), but the propagation of the gospel in the 'dark corners' of Wales and North was a puritan enterprise.[38] Puritans were zealously Protestant – always eager for a sermon, ever anxious about their own spiritual states, constantly driven by the need to expel from the English church the popish accretions which the bishops continued to tolerate – and this intensity, however subjective a criterion, ought to be incorporated into our understanding of puritanism. They were, as Collinson has said, 'the more enthusiastic and committed of Elizabethan Protestants', believing 'what other protestants believed, but more intensely.'[39]

As a working definition, then, 'puritans' were a self-conscious community of protestant zealots committed to purging the Church of England from within of its remaining Romish 'superstitions', ceremonies, vestments and liturgy, and to establishing a biblical discipline on the larger society, primarily through the preached word. They are distinguished not by adherence to a particular form of church government or to predestinarian theology, but by intensity of evangelical concern and vocal commitment to further religious reform within the state church. They can be further classified as 'moderate' or 'radical' based on whether in order to further the preaching of the protestant gospel they chose to conform to the ceremonies which they found objectionable, or whether they refused conformity in the conviction that compromise would undermine the gospel.

As for the rest of the protestant mainstream, despite its nineteenth-century accretions 'Anglican' continues to be used most effectively to describe that portion of the Church of England in the sixteenth and seventeenth centuries whose commitments were protestant yet ceremonial, whose devotion was to the unity and the traditional

---

[38] Christopher Hill, 'Puritans and "the Dark Corners of the Land",' *TRHS*, 5th ser., 8 (1963), 77–102; *Society and Puritanism*, pp. 30–123. Osboldston is mentioned by David Cressy in *Literacy and the Social Order* (Cambridge, 1980), p. 82, but contrast Collinson's account of Matthew, *Religion of Protestants*, pp. 48–52.

[39] Collinson, 'Elizabethan Church,' p. 180, and 'The Jacobean Religious Settlement: The Hampton Court Conference,' in *Before the English Civil War: Essays on Early Stuart Politics and Government*, ed. Howard Tomlinson (New York, 1984), 27–52, p. 29. In 'The Early Dissenting Tradition,' Collinson talks about puritanism as 'an evolved but still... primitive and fresh Protestantism' with its 'free, popular and expansive impulse' (p. 535). *cf.* Christianson, *Reformers and Babylon*, who sees puritanism as the most vigorous and successful of religious tendencies contained within Anglicanism, and Greaves, *Society and Religion*, ch. 1, who talks about puritans in terms of relative spiritual intensity or 'warmth.'

liturgical practices of the English church, and who were 'less sure than some that they could identify the godly' within the church.[40] Derek Hirst finds 'Anglicans' so defined diverging from puritans in temperament if not in intellectual conviction even in the sixteenth century. For all their apparent lack of zeal in the pre-war period, John Morrill has found an 'Anglican party' prepared to suffer persecution in defense of the Prayer Book in the 1640s.[41] Interestingly, these Anglicans are not identified with the Arminian theology and high church formalism that had set the Laudian bishops decidedly apart from the mainstream in the 1630s.[42]

---

[40] Derek Hirst, *Authority and Conflict* (Cambridge, Mass., 1986), 68–9. Lake, 'Puritan Identities,' p. 119, and Collinson, 'A Comment,' p. 485, dismiss 'Anglican' as anachronistic for this period. Lake, however, finds it necessary to substitute terms like 'mere conformist' (e.g., in 'Matthew Hutton,' p. 182). In the present study, 'Anglican' will sometimes be modified or replaced by 'conformist' as a reminder that it is not being construed more broadly as membership in the Church of England. While Hirst's (and Morrill's) definition may seem etymologically arbitrary, it is both useful and historiographically accepted usage.

[41] Morrill, 'The Church in England 1642–9.'

[42] The departure of Laudianism from both Anglican and puritan tradition is considered at length in chapter 7. Few of the published writers considered in the following chapters were difficult to identify as puritan or Anglican. Where the definition was put to the test was in designating the religious persuasion, if any, of the authors of the anonymous commonplace books and notebooks discussed especially in chapter 3. It was very tempting to label 'puritan' any notebook overwhelmingly concerned with religious issues and guidelines for individual godliness. These indices of religious zeal were not, however, adopted as sufficient criteria for the puritanism of a writer; if they had been, John Donne would have qualified for admission to the spiritual brotherhood. A document which combined these criteria with remarks disparaging ceremonies, however, was tentatively accepted as a puritan production, and additional comments praising acknowledged puritan leaders and objecting to enforced conformity were regarded as definitive (e.g., St John's, Cambridge, MS S.20). By contrast, Queens', Cambridge, MS Horne 41, despite its being 'overcharged with passions and sorrows over sin' and obsessed with other 'signs of true contrition,' is not regarded as necessarily puritan, given the absence of other criteria. Particularly intense biblicism and sabbatarianism, combined with opposition to popish ceremonies and high regard for puritan preachers (e.g., St John's, Cambridge, MS S.44), were also seen as indicating probable puritan authorship. Arminianism was not considered a disqualification for puritanism, particularly in the case of documents written during the 1640s, but by the same token, opposition to Arminianism was not necessarily associated with puritanism: St John's, Cambridge, MS S.20, for example, an obviously puritan document by the above criteria, also argues that God's grace is ineffectual without the consent of the human will (p. 159, my pagination). CUL, MS Gg. 1.29, on the other hand, contains a negative definition of puritanism (fol. 84v, *cf.* pp. 1–9), together with arguments against Arminianism (fols. 85, 104v–105v) written during the 1620s. A notebook defending episcopacy was not labeled Anglican without further evidence. Subordination of the authority of the Scriptures to that of bishops, however, eliminated the possibility of a 'puritan episcopalian' label for such a document, however pious, and in combination with such sentiments as 'A Puritan is called the Pest of the Church' (e.g., Balliol, MS 337, n.f.), Anglican authorship was assumed.

Having identified whose social ideology we shall be exploring in the study that follows, let us turn now to the intellectual context in which they found themselves. If puritans were a self-conscious community of zealous religious reformers, they were also possessed of a clear and characteristic vision of godly social reform, a vision which we associate not incorrectly with the 'culture of discipline' and the 'spiritualized household' and the 'reformation of manners'. However, they were not the inventors of this reformist vision. They did not see themselves as intellectual innovators, nor did their contemporaries, nor should we. The notion that they were truly innovative in their social thought is as fallacious as the assumption that they represented an early form of capitalist class consciousness, or that they comprised a bitterly alienated oppositionist group in Elizabethan England. Puritans as social theorists were instead a vitally important group of popularizers and practitioners of earlier ideas – more properly associated with Renaissance than with Reformation.

It is because scholars have failed to see puritans as the heirs of a complex intellectual legacy – classical, medieval, and Renaissance humanist as well as Reformed – that the historiography of puritan social thought has plodded along first in one direction, then in another, through a muddle of contradictions and seemingly inexplicable inconsistencies. Were puritans genuinely charitable or maliciously repressive of the poor?[43] Were they patriarchalists or did they lean toward egalitarianism in their attitudes toward women?[44] Were they revolutionary or conservative in their political values?[45] If as historians we cannot make up our minds, it is doubtless because puritan minds were simply not so neatly divided into logical categories as we, and perhaps they, would wish. The intellectual development of sixteenth-century protestants was no more monochromatic than ours, and they were no better at drawing lines and making distinctions than most people, contemporary or modern. So we find their social and political treatises citing Xenophon and St Paul in the same breath, Erasmus and Zanchius in the same marginal note. Heretofore, our solution to this apparent paradox has been simply to ignore half of their sources and insist that the other half was exclusively formative – of a single, consistent, protestant social ideology.

[43] The opinions of Jordan and Hill, respectively.
[44] cf. Hill, *Society and Puritanism*, pp. 450–8, with William and Malleville Haller's 'The Puritan Art of Love,' *HLQ*, 5 (1942), 235–72; Wright, p. 227; Keith Thomas, 'Double Standard,' *JHI*. 20 (1959), 195–216.
[45] cf. Walzer with his many critics: e.g. Lawrence Stone, 'The Century of Crisis,' *NYRB* (3 March 1966), p. 13, and J. F. H. New in *William and Mary Quarterly*, 24 (1967), 478–9.

The time has surely arrived to discard this traditional approach and to look at the other half of the puritan mind. We must recognize that the Bible and Calvinist theology are not in themselves sufficient sources for the development of a social ideology. Protestant theology offers distinct alternatives for one's approach to society and politics. One may conclude from God's sovereignty and man's subjection that human action is powerless to affect the course of earthly events or the conduct of human affairs; on the other hand, the Calvinist view of the elect as God's instruments to implement his will in the world necessitates an activist stance on the part of the believer. Likewise, the Bible provides a text for every occasion: it may be variously interpreted to imply that this world is not our home, or to demand Christian involvement in mundane affairs. The Scriptures, like the theological systems which derive from them, are ambiguous, apparently contradictory, and particularly vague when it comes to specifying the details of social regulation and relationship in the Kingdom of Christ. It is, therefore, necessary to analyze in some depth those ideas which conditioned the way puritans approached Scripture and theology, those presuppositions which led them to ask certain questions of the Bible and to derive certain conclusions from texts which could be interpreted in a variety of ways.

The thesis of this study is that that conditioning influence, in the sixteenth and early seventeenth centuries, was Christian humanism, and that one of the defining characteristics of puritan social thought in the seventeenth century was its maintenance of Erasmian ideals and methods in the face of growing conservatism and authoritarianism on the part of its enemies. The importance of puritans as social thinkers lies in the fact that they contributed heavily to the propagation of a belief in social reform, which they, along with contemporaries both protestant and Catholic, had derived from the Renaissance and its classical sources. Puritans were educated *à la mode*, subject to assumptions and perspectives characteristic not so much of protestantism narrowly conceived as of the northern European Renaissance. They were products of the same printed books, tutors, and university curricula as other Englishmen; their world view was spawned no more from Calvin's *Institutes*, which they generally read as adults, than from Erasmus' *Enchiridion* and Cicero's *De Officiis*, which they read as youths.[46] Puritans were imbued with

<hr />

[46] See chapter 3, below. Leonard J. Trinterud, *Elizabethan Puritanism* (Oxford, 1971), has suggested the importance of Erasmus to puritan piety and religious reformism by including John Gough's prologue to Erasmus' *Enchiridion* in his collection of excerpts from puritan documents; he is not interested in puritan social ideology, however.

the presuppositions of early modern England, and those were, in the
final analysis, heavily Erasmian.

It is quite true, to use Geoffrey Elton's caricature, that 'People did
not read Erasmus ... and say, with a sudden inspiration: indeed,
indeed, this is what we will do.'[47] But the generations of Englishmen
brought up on the *Colloquies* and *Adages*, the *Praise of Folly* and the
Enchiridion, were people whose assumptions about the social order
and its prospects were subtly shaped by the presuppositions that
underlay all of Erasmus' works – that all is not well with the world,
and that change for the better is possible. The ideal of social reform
germinating in the generation of Colet and Vives and More would
not come to full fruition until the decades of Civil War and
Interregnum. But the landscape of the intervening generations was
enlivened by an increasingly lush growth of the practical divinity and
reformist ideology that characterized Christian humanism. Its color
was heightened by blossoming schemes for the abolition of poverty,
the reformation of manners, the expansion of educational opportunity. No social revolutionary, Erasmus would hardly have expected
quick results from his proposals; the inclusion of his works in the
ordinary curricula of grammar schools and universities and, in translation, in the libraries of increasingly literate tradesmen and
merchants, yeomen and artisans, meant that Tudor and early Stuart
Englishmen approached social problems from a different perspective from that of their medieval counterparts, with reformist
assumptions unknown to the Middle Ages, but now shared by
Catholic and Calvinist alike. While internal contradictions are to be
expected from an intellectual milieu which in England combined
humanist optimism with the Calvinist doctrine of human depravity,
it was the activism and the reformist ethic of Christian humanism
which proved most formative for protestant social theory. It was
Christian humanism which determined how protestants would apply
their biblicism and their theological grounding in their day-to-day
conduct in the family, in the market-place, in Parliament.

This is not to suggest that puritan theology proper was in any
significant sense Erasmian. The famous exchange of 1524 between
Erasmus and Luther on free will best represents the radical theological
differences which would prevent puritans, however enamoured of
Erasmus' social criticism, from relying very heavily on his theological
perspective. They may well have borrowed certain elements of his

[47] Elton's criticism of J. K. McConica's *English Humanists and Reformation Politics* in *HJ*,
10 (1967), 137–8.

religious thought: the adiaphorism of the moderate puritans recently studied by Lake, Collinson and Dent, for instance, might be seen as partly Erasmian in origin. Historians have also explored possible connections between Lutheran ecclesiology and Christian humanist thought in Germany which may have implications for England.[48] Certainly the impact of Erasmian humanism on English protestant theology is a promising field for further investigation. But the scope of this study is limited to the continuity of humanism in puritan social thought; the question of theological interaction between humanism and puritanism must be left to other investigators.

An additional caveat should be offered. No attempt to trace the intellectual roots of a reform movement can presume to be exhaustive. It is not the intention of this study to rule out the possibility of other pre-Reformation influences on puritan thought besides Christian humanism and its classical sources. The approach taken here obviously presupposes the interaction of a multiplicity of traditions in any intellectual development, but of the pre-Reformation roads to puritan thought, the reformist ideology of Christian humanism, itself an intellectual composite, stands out as the high road to protestant social thought. It is an avenue badly in need of exploration by those who seek to understand puritanism not by mythologizing it, but by locating it in all the complexity of its historical context.

A second problem in intellectual history is addressed in this study, and a second thesis about early modern social theory arises as that problem is confronted. Ways of thinking (in this case, about the nature of the social order) develop in history, but they also collapse over time in the face of other historical change. Puritan social thought, important in and of itself because of its impact on early modern society and politics, also offers to intellectual historians a proving ground for new methods of tracing the sources of idea systems. In addition, it provides an opportunity for explaining in contextualist terms how accepted ideas fall into disfavor.

Puritans emerge from an attempt to place them within the context of their own intellectual milieu as part of a consensus in the sixteenth century about possibilities for social reformation. Protestants of all sorts adopted the hope of Catholic humanists like Erasmus for a godly social order established through education and discipline.

---

[48] See for example Wilhelm Maurer, *Das Verhältnis des Staates zur Kirche nach humanistischer Anschauung, vornehmlich bei Erasmus* (Giessen, 1930); W. Hentze, *Kirche und kirchliche Einheit bei Desiderius Erasmus von Rotterdam* (Paderborn, 1974); and on broader theological issues than just ecclesiology, Ernst-Wilhelm Köhls, *Die theologische Lebensaufgabe des Erasmus und die oberrheinischen Reformatoren* (Stuttgart, 1969); *cf.* Köhls, *Die Theologie des Erasmus*, 2 vols (Basel, 1966).

Puritans and Anglicans joined in the religion of protestants were similarly joined in the social thought of Catholic humanism. In order fully to understand the social reformism of puritanism, it has proven necessary to examine not only the nature and development of that consensus among protestants and between protestants and Catholics, but also the decline of that consensus into conflict, first between protestantism and Tridentine Catholicism, then between puritanism and Anglicanism. It is only after the disintegration of the Renaissance consensus that it becomes possible to speak first of a 'protestant' and then of a 'puritan' social ethic. To attempt to distinguish puritan from other contemporary approaches to the family, to education or to poor relief before that time is to separate them from their historical context. It is also to ignore the fact that just as ideas influence history, history in turn affects ideas.

It was Pope Paul IV who sounded the retreat of Roman Catholic thought from the arena of social reform to the immediate safety of eccelsiastical authoritarianism and centralized control when, in 1559, he declared all of Erasmus' works anathema. A similar re-action against social change and progressive ideology occurred in seventeenth-century Anglicanism, particularly under the leadership of Archbishop William Laud during the 1630s. Again, the hierarchy's rejection of the reformist consensus can be understood as a preference for enforced conformity as the safest means of insuring social order in the face of increasing discontent with the establish-ment in church and state. In Laudian sermons, as in Tridentine con-ciliar and papal declarations, passive obedience to constituted authority replaced the conscientious individual activism upheld by Erasmian humanists as the proper response to the needs of the commonwealth. Repression replaced innovation as the projected cure for social ills. A genuine opposition was bound to emerge.

The intellectual pedigree of those English protestants who resorted to arms in the 1640s helps to explain both the irenic nature of church and society in the Elizabethan and Jacobean periods and the conflict of Charles' ill-fated reign. The thesis that Erasmian assump-tions about the social order were part of the protestant mainstream in the pre-Laudian period renders comprehensible the consensus of puritans and Anglicans before the 1620s on social issues; it also illumines the radicalization of puritanism when those in authority began to reject humanist reformism. As long as the mainstream of English protestantism operated within the reformist assumptions of Christian humanism, puritans and conformists could cooperate in building the New Jerusalem in England. It was only when Laud and

Charles, in their drive for control and conformity, attempted to divert the mainstream into an apparently absolutist channel, that puritans found themselves in opposition. They were alienated not by the religion of protestants, but by Laudian innovation and Caroline enforcement. When this happened, when those in authority rejected humanist reform, puritans and parliamentarians had a radical social ideology at hand with which to legitimate their revolutionary actions: the logical implications of humanist anticlericalism and opposition to hereditary aristocracy and monarchy were released. The reformist consensus that had held in check the hidden potential of Erasmian social thought was destroyed by the authoritarianism of the Caroline establishment.

By the beginning of the Civil War, then, the Erasmian social consensus no longer existed. Only puritans were left holding the banner of reformism. Christian humanist social theory had survived, and it was to dictate the actions of its puritan advocates during the Civil War and Interregnum to such an extent that later historians would come to label it 'puritan' social theory. But let us follow the preachers' example and give credit where it is due. When we do so, we will have to acknowledge puritan social theorists as Christian humanists of the hotter sort.

2

Christian humanism as social ideology

The humanist social ethic which puritans would find so attractive was biblical in its apologetic, eclectic in its sources, mundane in its concerns but religious in its goals, practical in its methodology, and activist in its approach. It was a distinctively *Christian* humanism, aimed at formulating a model for godly behavior which would apply equally to prince and commoner, clergy and laity. The moral reconstruction of the social order was its ultimate objective– and its supreme attraction for protestant reformers.

For humanists, both Italian and transalpine, a disdain for ecclesiastical corruption had combined with a veneration of ancient literature and the society which had produced it to bring forth a new conception of human potential, social as well as individual. Christendom, they agreed, had a bad track record as compared with the intellectual, political and social achievements of ancient civilization. In the Renaissance view, both Roman Stoics and primitive Christians evinced more purity of life and a more godly social and political ethic than the despised medieval church had been able to achieve. Humanists accordingly divided their time between satirizing their own immediate social and intellectual milieu and reviving a true knowledge of the Greco-Roman and patristic Golden Age. The centuries between St Augustine and their own day were, in Renaissance minds, uniformly dark, barbaric and intellectually stagnant. The brilliance of the medieval schoolmen was among the casualties of this not altogether enlightened perspective; however, we must remember that the scholasticism of Erasmus' Paris was in fact a far cry from that of St Thomas. The Renaissance reformer sought to rescue humanity from the shadow of the waning Middle Ages both by condemning the darkness of 'tradition' and by rekindling the light of ancient civilization. For northern humanists, rooted as they were in the lay spirituality of the late fifteenth-century *devotio moderna*, the avowed aim of this endeavour was to achieve a reformation of Christendom. They aspired to redesign individual, social, and political behavior along the lines defined by what were regarded as the most instructive of ancient texts – the Bible, and the works of the Church Fathers and of Greek and Roman moralists. It was this intentionally pious reformism which distinguished northern from southern European humanism in the sixteenth century.

Ideally, the Bible was to be the pre-eminent guiding force behind this transformation of society. Northern or Christian humanists' love of ancient literature was conditioned neither by abstract aesthetic commitments nor by secularized philosophical inclinations, but rather by their devotion to a biblical reformation of Christendom. The Renaissance demand for a return to the sources became for Christian humanists an imperative to apply the critical assumptions and the exegetical techniques of the Italian humanists to the Christian's most authoritative text, and to render the Scriptures thus properly understood the chief guide to right living. Their perceived motivation for scholarship and action was biblical; their ultimate goals were also, at least in intent, biblical. An overriding biblicism may be regarded, in fact, as a defining characteristic of Christian humanists. It was their regard for the Scriptures which guided their extra-biblical intellectual pursuits: their perception of a biblical concern for individual morality attracted them to the Roman Stoics; the need to understand the Bible contextually drew them to the study of ancient history; the need for a purified text of the Scriptures impelled them to pursue knowledge of Greek and Hebrew and of classical grammar and rhetoric; and the Church Fathers were revered, given their proximity to the first century, for the light they shed on the Scriptures.[1] The text of the Bible itself was, of course, paramount among Christian humanist concerns.

It is essential to recognize that for the Christian humanist there need be no conflict between the teachings of the Bible and a belief in great human potential for achievement. However serious the prob-

---

[1] On Erasmian patristic studies, see Denys Gorce, 'La Patristique dans la réforme d'Érasme,' *Festgabe Joseph Lortz*, 2 vols (Baden-Baden, 1958), vol. I, pp. 233–76; Robert Peters, 'Erasmus and the Fathers: Their Practical Value,' *CH*, 36 (1967), 254–61; John C. Olin, *Six Essays on Erasmus* (New York, 1979), pp. 33–47; and Olin, 'Erasmus and his Edition of St. Hilary', *Erasmus in English*, 9 (1978), 8–11. Characteristic Christian humanist patristic editions include Erasmus' *Hieronymi opera*, 9 vols (Basel, 1516) and Vives' commentaries on *De Civitate Dei* (Basel, 1522). Erasmus' *Hieronymi Stridonensis vita* is in *Erasmi opuscula*, ed. Wallace K. Ferguson (The Hague, 1933), pp. 178–80.

lem of human sinfulness, it did not preclude individual understanding of the law of Christ within the context of a truly Christian commonwealth; but for the *philosophia Christi* to be realized in the commonwealth, a true understanding of the gospel must be made available to every individual, at every social level. The dissemination of biblical knowledge accordingly became a primary goal for northern humanists, just as it would later become the obsession of zealous English protestants. Humanist critics charged that true understanding of the Bible was not being mediated to the people by late medieval churchmen; rather, the church had for centuries kept both itself and its charges in unconscionable ignorance of the truth. It had maintained a monopoly of the Scriptures themselves by prohibiting vernacular translations; moreover, it had neglected even to take advantage of its own intellectual dominance to study the biblical texts in its care. Erasmus' *Praise of Folly* places scholastic theologians in the vanguard of Folly's disciples, notable for

their happiness in their self-love ... [being] fortified with an army of schoolmen's definitions, conclusions and corollaries, and propositions both explicit and implicit. . . Such is the erudition and complexity they all display that I [Folly] fancy the apostles themselves would need the help of another holy spirit if they were obliged to join issue ... with our new breed of theologian.

These 'argumentative Scotists and pigheaded Ockhamists and undefeated Albertists' are in fact so preoccupied with their 'tomfooleries' that 'they haven't even a spare moment in which to read even once through the gospel or the letters of Paul.'[2] Monks, who are described by Folly as most nearly approaching theologians in happiness, are unable to read the Scriptures even if they can find the time, for 'they believe it's the highest form of piety to be so uneducated that they can't even read.'[3] The *Enchiridion Militis Christiani*, having established a knowledge of Holy Writ as an essential weapon of the Christian soldier, warns him against modern clerics who fail to read the Scriptures but are entranced with the writings of Duns Scotus instead: 'Duns Scotus gave them such confidence that they considered themselves master theologians without even reading the sacred texts. But even if they do speak very cleverly, let other men judge whether they have said anything worthy of the Holy Spirit.' Erasmus was careful to explain to his readers, 'I say this not because I reject the moderns, but because I prefer what is more useful and conducive

---

[2] Erasmus, *Praise of Folly*, tr. Betty Radice (New York, 1971), pp. 153, 156, 160–1.
[3] *Ibid.*, p. 164.

to achieving your purpose . . . My intention was to outline a way of life for you, not a course of study.' The ultimate objective of the reading assigned in the *Enchiridion* was to 'make your character better equipped for that kind of satisfactory living with others which the ancients call "ethical".'[4]

Given the church's failure to provide the knowledge of Scripture which is requisite for the imitation of Christ and the biblical reformation of society, the Christian humanists demanded that the Bible be made available in accurate vernacular translations of the best Greek and Hebrew texts to every Christian. They rejected the principle of priestly mediation of the Bible, opting to campaign for sufficient popular literacy and availability of the Scriptures that the farmer might 'sing some portion of them at the plow, the weaver hum some parts of them to the movement of his shuttle, the traveler lighten the weariness of the journey with stories of this kind.'[5] Every Christian, whatever his social status, would thus be made responsible both for his own spiritual status and for the godly transformation of the social order.

The need for a more accurate text than the Vulgate and for a proper use of the text for instruction in practical piety drove northern European scholars to apply the New Learning to the Bible and to theology. A return to the sources, read in their original languages, contextually, and in their entirety, was to replace what Erasmus saw as the flippant proof-texting of the scholastics and so 'call back theology, sunk too far in sophistical subtleties, to the sources and to ancient simplicity.'[6] Only thus could the purity of the primitive church be restored to Christian society. Accordingly, Erasmus devoted his most intense scholarly effort to the production of an accurate edition of the Greek New Testament (the *Novum Instrumentum*, published by Froben in 1516) with a Latin translation and simple paraphrases for ordinary readers, and editions of the works of those Church Fathers who best illuminated the sense of Scripture. But he hastened to

[4] Erasmus, *Enchiridion Militis Christiani*, tr. and ed. Raymond Himelick, *The Enchiridion of Erasmus* (Bloomington, Indiana, 1963), pp. 53, 55. The 1534 English translation has been edited for the Early English Text Society by Anne M. O'Donnell (Oxford, 1981). While Erasmus had theological quarrels with Duns Scotus, his objections here are to the substitution of commentators for the Scriptures themselves, and to the irrelevance of scholastic theology to practical concerns of daily Christian living.

[5] Erasmus, *Paraclesis* (1516), in *Christian Humanism and the Reformation*, ed. John C. Olin (Gloucester, Mass., 1973), p. 97.

[6] Erasmus to John Gacy, *ca.* 17 October 1527, *Opus Epistolarum Des. Erasmi Roterodami*, ed. P. S. Allen, H. M. Allen and H. W. Garrod, 20 vols (Oxford, 1906–1958), vol. VII, ep. 1891, p. 208 (*Theologiam nimium ad sophisticas argutias delapsam, ad fontes ac priscam simplicitatem revocare conatus sum*).

remind his readers of the ultimate purpose for which this labor was undertaken: to restore a theology 'far more conducive to Christian learning and a pious life than that which is now treated far and wide in the schools.'[7]

It was the hope of establishing the *philosophia Christi* in the daily existence of individual and society which lay behind Erasmus' scholarly endeavors. It was a hope fostered by the Scriptures and implemented by studying the Scriptures, and a hope which would later be eagerly adopted by protestants, in part because they shared the biblicism of the Christian humanists. But it could not be achieved by a narrowly biblical focus alone, as Erasmus well knew and as his intellectual progeny would quickly discover. In good humanist fashion, Erasmus recognized that just as an understanding of the biblical text could be enhanced by examining the Church Fathers and ancient history, so the effective application of Christ's teachings could be aided by a study of other ancient moralists. The truths discovered by the pagan philosophers of antiquity – those of their doctrines not incompatible with the Scriptures – were not only a permissible area of study for the Christian; they were essential for the believer anxious to apply ancient wisdom to contemporary problems.[8] The Bible provided the outlines of Christian morality and social ethics; for the details, the would-be reformer was directed to the best ancient writers, those enlightened by the Holy Spirit only slightly less than was St Paul.

It is in its regard for the pagan classics, of course, that Christian humanism reveals its roots in the Italian Renaissance. Northern humanists had learned from their southern mentors to look to the ancients for exemplary Latin style and elegance of expression; they followed the lead of the Italians in producing purified editions of ancient texts, Greek and Latin, pagan and Christian. But for Christian humanists, the pursuit of stylistic excellence was a secondary consideration in the reading of ancient literature. Of primary importance to them was the content of that literature, and especially those classical ideas which could be applied to the practical problems of

---

[7] From the preface to his edition of St Jerome, tr. and quoted by Olin in *Six Essays*, p. 34. Erasmus produced editions of the complete works of Jerome (1516, 1524–6), Cyprian (1520), Hilary of Poitiers (1523), Augustine (1529), Ambrose (1529), John Chrysostom (1530), Basil (1532) and Origen (1532), and select works of Irenaeus (1529) and Gregory Nazianzen (1531).

[8] The thesis of Erasmus' *Antibarbari*, tr. Margaret Mann Phillips in *CWE* 23 (Toronto, 1978), 16–122.

godly living.[9] Thus, while Erasmus wrote manuals of style and lauded eloquence, he also satirized the idolatry of Cicero to which his Italian colleagues were so prone, on Quintilian's premise that style is but the 'dress of thoughts.'[10] What should be imitated in Cicero is 'not his words or what is on the surface of a speech', but his understanding of the truth.[11] John Colet similarly combined an Italian concern for style with a northern focus on moral improvement: his final statutes for St Paul's School read, 'I would that they were taught always in good literature both Latin and Greek, and good authors such as have the very Roman eloquence joined with wisdom ... for my intent is by this school specially to increase knowledge and worshiping of God and Our Lord Christ Jesu and good Christian life and manners in the children.'[12] For Christian humanists the pagan classics were servants of Christianity.

Their highest regard, therefore, was reserved for those ancient writers who likewise put scholarship to the service of individual and social reformation – the Roman Stoics.[13] It was Erasmus' insistence on an activist social ideology and his focus on the civic involvement as well as the spiritual condition of the lay person which motivated him to edit and publish Plutarch's works, Cicero's *De Officiis* (which he called in the dedication of the first edition (1501) 'books of gold', an 'enchiridion' to be 'learnt by heart'), and the complete works of Seneca, 'whose writings are wonderfully stimulating and excite one to enthusiasm for a life of moral integrity.' 'Nothing can excel the

---

[9] It is partly for this reason that the Neo-platonism of the Italian Renaissance never dominated the northern movement. Erasmian humanists rejected the intellectualism of the Neo-platonists and stressed action over contemplation. See for example Sears Jayne, *John Colet and Marsile Ficino* (Oxford, 1963), pp. 52–7, 75. This is not to suggest, however, that there were no moral reformers among Italian humanists, or that the humanists of northern Europe were all as socially aware and reform-minded as the author of the *Praise of Folly*. Erasmus is representative of the best of Christian humanist activism, but his following was significant and (as it is hoped that this study will show) effective in spreading reformist assumptions for generations after his death.

[10] *Ciceronianus*, tr. Izora Scott (New York, 1908), and the colloquy *Echo* (*Coll.*, p. 376) are both jibes at Ciceronians; *De copia* quotes Quintilian's maxim (*CWE* 24, p. 306); cf. Quintilian's *Institutio Oratoria* 8, preface 20).

[11] *Ciceronianus*, p. 129.

[12] Quoted in Craig R. Thompson's introduction to *CWE* 23, pp. xxx–xxxi. On the influence of Colet on Erasmus, see P. Duhamel, 'The Oxford Lectures of John Colet,' *JHI*, 14 (1953), 493–510.

[13] On the practical focus of Seneca's writings and his opposition to 'quibbling about words' while making 'no progress toward real living,' see his *Epistles to Lucilius*, tr. Richard M. Gummere (Cambridge, Mass., 1953), nos. 45, 48, 71, 88 and 111 (vol. I, pp. 293, 321; vol. II, pp. 77, 373; vol. III, p. 277).

holiness of Seneca's teachings,' exclaims Erasmus' preface to his first edition of this Stoic's works (1515). 'He alone lifts up our hearts to heaven, inspires us with contempt for what is vulgar, instills in us a loathing for what is base, and kindles in us the love for what is good.'[14]

Part of Seneca's appeal to Erasmus, and later to protestants, lay in the fact that Stoics, like Erasmians, were syncretistic in many of their assumptions and objectives. They struggled, as their Renaissance and Reformation followers would, to combine a sense of the gravity of sin with their reformist optimism. They acknowledged the individual's call to wage an internal spiritual war against evil, but they also saw man as a political animal, called to live for the common good. Philosophically no more consistent than their sixteenth-century readers, the Stoics provided an ideal source for Christians intent on fleshing out the ethical skeleton of the Bible in light of the problem of sin.[15]

Accordingly, humanist editions of Cicero and Seneca formed the most popular textbooks of sixteenth-century social speculation, and it was primarily from those classical moralists that humanist theoreticians drew their new vocabulary of virtue– terms descriptive neither of the chivalric nobleman nor of the religious contemplative, but rather of the godly layman, active in forum and marketplace. Words like prudence, temperance, gravity and fortitude form the key descriptive terms of both Stoic and Christian humanist manuals of behavior. Cicero's belief that man's rational soul, following the law of nature, bids him subdue his selfish passions and act for

---

[14] *CWE 2, The Correspondence of Erasmus*, tr. R. A. B. Mynors and D. F. S. Thomson (Toronto, 1975), no. 152, p. 30; preface to first edition of Seneca's works, tr. and quoted by F. L. Battles and A. M. Hugo in *John Calvin's Commentary on Seneca's De Clementia* (Leiden, 1969), p. 588. *cf. CWE 2*, nos. 264 (Erasmus to Peter Gilles, 1512), 281 (Erasmus to Ammonio, 1513) and 284 (Erasmus to Wolsey, 1514); *Erasmus and Cambridge*, tr. and ed. D. F. S. Thomson and H. C. Porter (Toronto, 1963), nos. 205–11 (letters from Erasmus to Robert Aldrich, 1525–7); and Albert Hyma, *The Life of Desiderius Erasmus* (Assen, The Netherlands, 1972), p. 53. Among Erasmus' proverbial collections is a *Flores Senecae*. In his *Institutio Principis Christiani*, he cited Cicero, Quintilian and Seneca, '*qui non solum absunt ab obscenitate verum etiam saluberrimis praeceptis vitam instituunt*' – quoted in W. H. Woodward, *Desiderius Erasmus concerning the Aim and Method of Education* (New York, 1964, first publication, 1904), p. 112, n. 1.

[15] Margo Todd, 'Seneca and the Protestant Mind: The Influence of Stoicism on Puritan Ethics,' *Archiv für Reformationsgeschichte*, 74 (1983), 182–99, and William Bouwsma, 'The Two Faces of Humanism: Stoicism and Augustinianism in Renaissance Thought,' in *Itinerarium Italicum*, ed. Heiko A. Oberman and Thomas A. Brady, Jr. (Leiden, 1975), p. 9 *et passim*.

the common good, was echoed by Christian humanists.[16] Acknowledging with their classical mentors the power of sin, Erasmians held tightly to the hope that the sort of guidance offered by Seneca, Cicero, Sallust, Plutarch and others could liberate the rational soul within the individual and allow it to respond to the call of nature/God to act for the common weal.

Christian humanists were not exclusively dependent on Stoic writers, of course. They were sufficiently eclectic and non-systematic to combine elements of Aristotelian philosophy with Socratic ethical theory and Roman moralism to achieve their reformist ends. Humanist social theorists drew heavily on both Aristotle and Plato, for instance, largely ignoring the differences among these and other ancient Greek philosophers.[17] Thomas Lupset's *Exhortation to yonge men* (1534) provided a reading list headed by the Bible, but including Plato's *Republic*, Aristotle's *Politics*, Xenophon's *Oeconomica*, Cicero's *De Officiis*, Seneca's works, and Erasmus' *Enchiridion*.[18] But perhaps because their syncretism was as great as that of the Roman moralists, and certainly because their concerns were as practical as those of Seneca and Cicero, the Christian humanists' dependence on the Roman Stoics was second only to their deference to the Bible.

The active reforming enthusiasm of the *philosophia Christi* was to be implemented, then, by the study of a variety of authors, though always guided by Scripture. Erasmus, having defined the philosophy of Christ as 'a rebirth . . . the restoration of human nature originally well formed', went on to argue that

although no one has taught this more perfectly and more effectively than Christ, nevertheless one may find in the books of the pagans very much which does agree with His teaching . . . The Stoics understood that no one was wise unless he was good . . . What shall we say of this, that many –

[16] Jerrold E. Seigel, *Rhetoric and Philosophy in Renaissance Humanism* (Princeton, 1968), ch. 1 *et passim*. Notes 5 and 6 of my 'Seneca and the Protestant Mind' give publication figures for Seneca's works in the sixteenth and early seventeenth centuries.

[17] Bouwsma, pp. 4–7. Contrasting Aristotle and Plato was, according to Bouwsma, 'not a major or a regular concern of humanism; hence it can hardly be expected to illuminate its central concerns' (p. 5). The contradictions inherent in humanism itself were in fact 'scarcely recognized by the humanists themselves, more frequently latent than overt for even the most acutely self-conscious among them' (p. 4).

[18] Lupset, *Works*, ed. J. A. Gee (New Haven, 1928), pp. 245–6, 250–1. Lupset translated Xenophon's *Oeconomica* into English (from Greek). Aristotle's *Politics* vii and viii were recommended in the 1544 edition of his *Exhortation* (sig. Cii) on the rearing of children.

notably Socrates, Diogenes, and Epictetus – have presented a good portion of His teaching? .. , Christ both taught and presented the same doctrine.

The new, rational, humane social order which was to be created was thus both Christian and humanist. [19]

The new biblicism, conditioned by revived classical moralism, defined a new social type: a pious, self-controlled, industrious lay person, active in civic and ecclesiastical affairs, seeking always the common good. This combination of good citizen and Christian soldier was to be the essential building block of the new society. The formulation of the ideal had resulted from humanist textual studies; the inculcation of the ideal became the goal of another humanist literary genre (one whose popularity would continue in protestant guise for the next two centuries) – the *enchiridion*, or handbook of moral instruction.

The self-improvement manuals of Erasmus and his followers were characterized by a deep concern with sin and by a Stoic conviction that self-understanding and self-control were essential to overcome evil. Erasmus' view of sin was derived from the Bible and the Fathers, but it was at the same time conditioned by the humanism of the ancient pagan moralists: the depredations of sin need not be merely absolved or tolerated, but could be held in check and even reversed by means of right instruction. He reminded the Duke of Cleves in 1529 that during children's earliest years,

their behavior is guided by instinct more than by reason, they are inclined equally to good and evil – more to the latter, perhaps – and it is always easier to forget good habits than to unlearn bad ones. This truth was already known to pagan philosophers and caused them great perplexity, but their speculations were unable to penetrate to the real cause, and it was left to Christian theology to teach the truth that since Adam, the first man of the human race, a disposition to evil has been deeply engrained in us. While this is indisputably man's condition, however, we cannot deny that the greater portion of this evil stems from corrupting relationships and a misguided education.

Nevertheless, he said, God's human creation has been gifted with reason, which, properly guided, can govern sinful human passion. 'A

[19] Erasmus, *Paraclesis*, pp. 100–1. On the less pietistic concerns of Italian humanism, see Wallace K. Ferguson, *Renaissance Studies* (New York, 1970); or Walter Ullmann, *Medieval Foundations of Renaissance Humanism* (Ithaca, 1977), which ignores northern humanism altogether in its exclusive stress on secularization. Craig Thompson's definition of Christian humanism as 'the interaction between classical culture and Christianity in the thought and work of Erasmus and like-minded men' is broad but useful (Woodward, p. xiii).

proper and conscientious instruction,' he concluded, 'is the well-spring of all moral goodness.' The individual directed from early childhood by reason rightly informed 'takes on the best possible character.' The parent who properly educates his child 'will fashion, if I may use such a bold term, a god-like creature.'[20] The social order can be reformed, but the initial appeal must be made to individual reason, enlightened by the Scriptures and directed toward godly behavior in all areas of daily living.

The humanist literary guides which were to offer this direction are best exemplified by Erasmus' *Enchiridion*. Using the Pauline military imagery which would be enthusiastically adopted by protestants later in the century, Erasmus here portrayed life in this world as a war against sin in which every Christian must be constantly urged to do his duty. It is noteworthy that his duty is neither retirement from the conflict to the cloister, nor simple obedience to hierarchical superiors in the world of conflict, but rather positive individual action in righteous response to specific moral dilemmas.[21] Practical moral instruction is no less visible, however, in Erasmus' other works, even in such popular school texts as the *Colloquies* and *Adages*. In these works as in the *Enchiridion* Erasmus consistently prescribed a discipline at least as 'puritanical' as that of the followers of Calvin or Perkins, including a demand for daily self-examination. His godly youth in the colloquy *Confabulatio pia* (1522) practices an extreme form of religious self-discipline, and his comments on the adage *Quo transgressus* recommend Pythagoras' advice to his disciples to correct their lives by examining themselves each time they return home with the questions, 'Where have I gone wrong? What have I done that I should not have done? What have I left undone which I ought to have done?' Erasmus urged that this discipline be followed since, as his translator Richard Taverner rendered it, 'there be no affections so wild, so unruly, but discipline and awe may tame them.'[22]

---

[20] *De pueris statim ac liberaliter instituendis declamatio, CWE* 26, ed. J. K. Sowards (Toronto, 1985), pp. 301, 305, 321. Erasmian divergence from the theology of the *via moderna* is most obvious here. It underlay the disagreement between Erasmus and Luther, and would continue to be a problem for protestants who were attracted to Erasmian reformism but convinced of the depravity of fallen humanity. But Luther's break with Erasmus simply reveals that he was a more intellectually consistent protestant than most. Puritans intent on social reform would either ignore the contradiction between the doctrine of total depravity and the appeal to reason or add it to the other theological paradoxes with which they lived. On the similarity between their uneasy eclecticism and Seneca's on this and other issues, see my 'Seneca and the Protestant Mind.'   [21] Erasmus, *Enchiridion*, ed. Himelick, pp. 37–46 *et passim.*
[22] *Coll.*, pp. 30–41; *The 'Adages' of Erasmus*, tr. Margaret Mann Phillips (Cambridge, 1964), pp. 33–4; *Proverbs or adagies with newe addicions gathered out of the Chiliades of Erasmus by Richard Taverner* (1539), fol. xxxiii (*Exercitatio potest omnia*).

The list of those wild, unruly affections to be tamed is a traditional one for the most part – drunkenness, lechery, gluttony, gambling, blasphemy, avarice, pride.[23] But the fact that a considerable amount of space devoted to moralizing on these vices is to be found in nearly all of Erasmus' writings, whatever the subject, illustrates his overriding concern with behavior in daily life. He condemned not only lechery, but also the telling of 'silly, bawdy stories' and the singing of 'dirty songs'. He condemned debauchery, but went to great lengths to include in his censure the various forms of self-indulgence which would lead to it – dancing, lute-playing, pipes, and jesters.[24] Moreover, his obsession with idleness as the root of most other evils, individual and social, foreshadowed an overarching concern of later sixteenth-century moralizers.

Erasmus was not alone among the Christian humanists in his demand for discipline. The behavior of More's Utopians won Erasmus' wholehearted approval, and it has been aptly paralleled to the godly discipline demanded by Calvin and his followers; in fact, 'so many things that a good many people want are banned in Utopia that Calvin's Geneva looks a bit frivolous by comparison.'[25] Utopia boasts no wine shops, no alehouses, no dicing, no hunting, no 'opportunity for corruption . . . On the contrary, being under the eyes of all, people are bound either to be performing the usual labor or to be enjoying their leisure in a fashion not without decency.'[26] A Utopian is, in short, of precisely that industrious, temperate, disciplined social type idealized by Erasmus.

In the same tradition, Erasmus' protegé Thomas Lupset exhorted his readers to flee idleness and to practice self-control and frugality; and Thomas Starkey condemned 'hunting, hawking, dicing, carding, and all other idle pastimes and vain', extravagance, drunkenness,

---

[23] For example, *Proverbes*, fol. xxxi; *A sermon of the Chylde Jesus . . . to be pronounced and preached of a chylde unto chyldren* (n.d.), sig. Bviii; *Apophthegmes*, tr. Nicholas Udall (London, 1542), fols. 8–9; *Enchiridion*, ed. Himelick, *passim*, and esp. pp. 177–200; *Folly*, pp. 89–90, 124–5, 143, 176 *et passim; Coll.*, pp. 195–8, 380–1; *Adages* (1964), pp. 185, 210–12, 217, 268; *CWE* 31 (*Adages* Iil to Iv100, tr. Margaret Mann Phillips, Toronto, 1982), p. 230.

[24] *Convivium religiosum* (1522), *Coll.*, pp. 56, 76; *cf. Auris batava, Adages* (1964), p. 210; *Liber de Sarcienda Ecclesiae Concordia, The Essential Erasmus*, ed. and tr. John P. Dolan (New York, 1964), p. 335.

[25] J. H. Hexter, *The Vision of Politics on the Eve of the Reformation* (New York, 1973), pp. 52–3, 125, 107–17; Hexter, *More's 'Utopia': The Biography of an Idea* (Princeton, 1952), p. 47; *cf.* D. B. Fenlon, 'England and Europe: *Utopia* and its aftermath', *TRHS*, 5th ser. 25 (1975), p. 120, which sees *Utopia* enacted in More's household.

[26] *The Complete Works of St. Thomas More*, vol. 4, *Utopia*, ed. Edward Surtz and J. H. Hexter (New Haven, 1965), pp. 129, 147, 171.

and gluttony, 'of the which things the officers [overseers of community morals] should have as much regard as of robbing and
adultery.' From the Bible and the 'wisdom of antiquity' Starkey concluded that mankind is not born to idleness and pleasure, but to
labor, and to labor not in 'making and procuring things for the vain
pastime and pleasure of other' but rather in the production of
necessities for the commonwealth, in the education of youth, and in
the good government of the realm.[27] A like concern with the reformation of manners is found in such humanists as More's friend
Richard Whitforde, Sir William Forrest, and Sir Thomas Elyot. The
latter, for instance, condemned idleness as a vice and parent of all
other vices and commended instead (with Cicero) the active life, 'in
business well occupied.'[28]

The individual reformation of manners to which Christian humanists
devoted so much of their writing was aimed ultimately at the creation
of a godly society, and it is to the larger, social objectives of
Erasmianism that our attention must now turn. With Cicero,
humanists argued that the good man is a good citizen; he must subdue his inclinations toward self-indulgence in order to live and act
for the common good. This is the *vocatus*, the natural/divine calling
to which the truly pious individual must respond. Christian
humanism was a call to social action. It was not so much idealistic as
ideological, pious not in the narrowly devotional sense of the word
but with overtones of a zealously active godliness. Christian
humanists saw social ills rooted in individual sin; however, their response did not stop at the sort of moralizing which had characterized
medieval social criticism. Rather, they extended their critique from
the individual to the larger society and demanded that the reformed
individual reform the corruptions of his society. They paralleled
individual sin to social evil; in fact, on occasion they sought the
causes of individual failure in the social structure itself.[29]

---

[27] Lupset, pp. 245–6 *et passim*; Thomas Starkey, *A Dialogue between Reginald Pole and Thomas Lupset*, ed. K. M. Burton (London, 1948), pp. 79, 80–2, 123–5, 157.
[28] Richard Whitforde, *The werke for housholders* (n.p., 1537), sigs. Avii, Dv–viii, Ei–ii, Fiii; Sir William Forrest, *Pleasaunt Poesye of Princelie Practise* (London, 1548) in *England in the Reign of King Henry the Eighth*, ed. S. J. Herrtage (London, 1878), p. xvi; Sir Thomas Elyot, *The Boke Named the Governor*, ed. S. E. Lehmberg (London, 1962), vol. 1, pp. 42, 48, 105, 175, 270.
[29] For example, Starkey, *Dialogue*, p. 146, said of the problems of division and social disharmony, 'this disease riseth chiefly from lack of common justice and equity.' *cf.* Richard Morison, *A Remedy for Sedition* (London, 1536), ed. E. M. Cox (London, 1933), pp. 35–6; and *TED*, vol. 3, p. 112 (*A treatise concerninge the Staple*). On the transition from medieval to Renaissance social analysis, see Arthur Ferguson, *The Articulate Citizen and the English Renaissance* (Durham, NC, 1965).

Their stance was not simply neo-Stoic; nor is it accurate to identify it simply with the civic humanism of Italy. Biblicism, patristic influences, Stoicism and civic humanism were all tightly interwoven in Erasmianism to produce a thoroughly distinctive movement, religious and civic, Christian and humanist. With Seneca and Christ, humanists called for individual self-control; with Cicero, they called for good government; with the Old Testament prophets, they called for social justice. The search for practical solutions to real problems in this world came to be seen by them as the believer's true calling. This amalgam of pious yet practical social activism should be seen as another hallmark of Erasmian humanism.

The *vita activa* is the prescribed model of behavior which emerges from Erasmian writings. The reformed layman is called to act in the context of an institutional framework itself subject to reformation. The truly good life is not reserved for the next life; rather, it is to be lived in the present world, in the here and now. Humanists clearly rejected the contemplative ideal of the Middle Ages in favor of action in a civic milieu. Christ at his judgment seat, said Erasmus, will prefer common sailors and waggoners – men who live in the world and are not 'segregated from civil life' – over the useless lives of monks.[30] Juan Luis Vives likewise urged the superiority of workshop to cloister, as did More, who scoffed at those who think it godly to 'squat with the monks' believing that 'to reside forever in the same spot like a clam or sponge, to cling eternally to the same rock is the last word in sanctity.'[31]

It was no accident that John Colet chose to turn over the manage-

---

[30] *Folly*, p. 167; *Convivium religiosum, Coll.*, p. 59. *cf.* the medieval viewpoint of Langland, *Piers the Ploughman*, ed. J. F. Goodridge (Baltimore, 1959), pp. x, 300–1, 120–1; and Arthur O. Lovejoy, *The Great Chain of Being* (Cambridge, Mass., 1936), pp. 24–44, 84–6. A possible objection to the thesis of humanist activism is evidence of the contemplative ideal in Erasmus' *De contemptu mundi*. This is, however, a very early work (1490), and the chapter added in 1521 condemning monasticism should be taken as much more representative of Erasmus' mature thought. This chapter was apparently added when Erasmus' friends insisted on publication of the little treatise despite the author's desire to dissociate himself from it. See R. Bultot, 'Érasme, Épicure et le "De Contemptu Mundi",' *Scrinium Erasmianum*, 2, edited by J. J. Coppens (Leiden, 1969), 205–19. Note also the progressively more anti-monastic editions of the *Antibarbari* between 1492 and 1520 (Hyma, pp. 22–8, 31). Erasmus explained in his *Compendium Vitae* (1524; included in Olin, *Christian Humanism*, pp. 25–7) that he was himself forced into a monastery by his evil guardian, who wanted only to be rid of his responsibility. *cf.* Beatus Rhenanus' *Life of Erasmus* (1540) in Olin, p. 33.

[31] On Vives' rejection of Plato's 'blind prejudice' in praising contemplation at the expense of practical application, see R. Hooykaas, *Religion and the Rise of Modern Science* (Grand Rapids, 1972), pp. 88–90, and the same author's *Humanisme, science et réforme* (Leiden, 1958), pp. 28–31, 105–6; *The Correspondence of Sir Thomas More*, ed. E. F. Rogers (Princeton, 1947), p. 201.

ment of St Paul's School to laymen (members of the Mercers' Company). The reformed Christianity of the northern humanists was in fact centered on lay piety – the contemplative life had no intrinsic value whatsoever in the modern, activist scheme of the sixteenth-century reformer. Erasmus went so far as to charge that the religious are all too often found to be fleeing the world because they are 'proud with a false conviction of their holiness . . . lacking in human kindness, and incapable of doing anything' at all useful in the world. Monasteries he saw as 'schools of impiety', conducive to a life of depravity rather than one in which godliness is developed in response to the challenges of everyday life:

And so those that verily need to live honestly in the world [and] should have cause to use frugality, to have been diligent and industrious: in monasteries they give themselves to sloth and luxury. And those that were in the world very poor, and of low degree, under the profession of poverty they follow the pomp, the sumptuousness, and stately array of princes and great lords . . . So that by feigned profession of poverty, they flee poverty, by feigned profession of chastity, they provide for their carnal lust; and by feigned profession of obedience, they find the means that they will be constrained to obey no man.

Erasmus recommended as an alternative to this misguided notion of the 'good life' a doctrine of calling which required the individual to 'fulfill his proper duties' in *this* world; whether pope, magistrate, tradesman or artisan, his calling is to 'carry on his business in good faith.'[32]

It was this positive, aggressive view of the Christian life in this world which resulted in the practical questions with which humanist (and later protestant) social theorists would concern themselves. Because men are called to act out the Christian life in the marketplace, they must be instructed in the application of virtue to the most mundane areas of life. Erasmus saw his own vocation as that of an instructor in the principles of the reformed social order, and he proceeded to publish seminal comments on all aspects of social conduct.

Other humanists followed suit, both in exhorting the laity to action and in directing that action. The author of the *Discourse of the Common Weal* urged men of all degrees to participate in the discussion of public affairs and to offer solutions for social problems, and the participation of such laymen as the London merchant Clement Armstrong (who experimented with and offered to Thomas Cromwell

[32] *Liber de Sarcienda*, Dolan, pp. 355, 378; *De contemptu mundi*, fols. 86–7.

a plan for setting the poor on work) in practical civic involvement reveals that this goal was not altogether unrealistic.[33] Starkey's *Dialogue between Reginald Pole and Thomas Lupset* (1533) also preached the *vita activa*, since 'to this all men are born and of nature brought forth: to commune such gifts as be to them given, each one to the profit of others, in perfect civility, and not to live to their own pleasure and profit, without regard of the weal of their country, forgetting all justice and equity.' He decried the fact that

many men of great wisdom and virtue fly from it [wealth and worldly involvement], setting themselves in religious houses, there quietly to serve God and keep their minds upright with less jeopardy. Which thing surely is not amiss done of them which perceive their own imbecility and weakness, prone and ready to be oppressed and overthrown with these common and quiet pleasures of the world, by whom they see the most part of mankind drowned and overcome. Howbeit, meseemeth they do like to fearful shipmen; which for dread of storms and troublous seas keep themselves in the haven.

More praiseworthy is the mariner who braves the tempest and brings his ship to port.[34]

The humanist model for social conduct, then, was characterized by activism, laicism, and immediate concerns which were mundane and practical. When Starkey listed his qualifications for service to the prince in a letter to Cromwell, he included his education in 'natural knowledge' and the Scriptures, but he took care to point out his opinion that 'all other secret knowledge not *applied to some use and profit* or other' is 'but as a vanity . . . In diverse kinds of studies I have occupied myself, ever having in mind this end and purpose at the last in this commonality where I am brought forth and born to *employ them to some use*.'[35] The same judgment was expressed in the context of practical treatises and correspondence by Elyot, Vives and many other humanists.[36] Their learning was to be an applied learning; its usefulness to society was to be its justification.

[33] *A Discourse of the Common Weal of this Realm of England*, sometimes attributed to Sir Thomas Smith and probably written in 1549, was first published in 1581. A modern edition by Mary Dewar has been published for the Folger Shakespeare Library (Charlottesville, 1969). On some implications of the *Discourse*, see Arthur B. Ferguson, 'The Tudor Commonweal and the Sense of Change,' *JBS*, 3 (1963), 11–35. On Armstrong, see Ferguson's *Articulate Citizen*, pp. 153–4.

[34] Starkey, pp. 22, 53. Starkey, Pole's secretary when the *Dialogue* was written, served the government as chaplain to Henry VIII from 1535 to 1538.

[35] Quoted in Mark Curtis, *Oxford and Cambridge in Transition, 1558–1642* (Oxford, 1959), pp. 74–5 (emphasis mine).

[36] For example, Elyot, *Governour, passim*; a statement of the Erasmian educational and political program, according to James McConica, *English Humanists and Reformation Politics* (Oxford, 1965), pp. 121–2. On Vives, see Carlos G. Noreña, *Juan Luis Vives* (The Hague, 1970); Simon, chapter 3; and Vives' *On Education* (*De tradendis disciplinis*, 1531), tr. Foster Watson (Cambridge, 1913).

An additional characteristic of the humanist model was the conviction that institutional as well as individual reform is mandatory and possible for the reformation of the social order. The social structure itself was as much a concern of Erasmians as was the problem of sinful behavior by the individual. Social institutions were regarded as legitimate objects of analysis, criticism, and reform. Partly because of their perception of a biblical mandate to create a just society, and partly because of the temporal perspective arising from their study of ancient history and literature, humanists did not see society or its institutions as changeless, either in theory or in fact.[37] They saw both Golden and Dark Ages in the past; it did not seem unreasonable to them that with sufficient enlightenment and reforming zeal, a 'Golden Age' would arise very soon in the future.[38] Accordingly, they addressed themselves to those institutional defects of society which they held responsible for many social ills, and their writings consistently embodied concrete recommendations for structural changes to remedy those ills.

More's *Utopia*, for example, should be read as just such a practical reformist document. More clearly believed that the goodness of a commonwealth depends upon the structure and quality of its fundamental institutions. A properly structured social and political order will encourage the development of godly citizens. More, like other Christian humanists, agreed with the Stoic ideal of social virtue based on rationalized social, rather than personal, ties.[39] Accordingly, he established in Utopia the political equality of citizens, the universal requirement of labor, and the communality of property as consistent structural and institutional alternatives to the inequitable and thoroughly corrupt social system of sixteenth-century England.[40]

This is not to say that More did not attribute much social evil to moral failure; however, in his ideal scheme he established social

---

[37] The 'new historical consciousness' of sixteenth-century humanists is the subject of a study by Arthur B. Ferguson, *Clio Unbound: Perception of the Social and Cultural Past in Renaissance England* (Durham, NC, 1979). The implications of the new awareness of the 'process of time' for theories of social order and hierarchy are discussed more fully in chapter 6, below.

[38] Erasmus to Wolfgang Capito, 26 February 1517, *CWE* 4, pp. 261–8.

[39] *Utopia*, p. 245; Hexter, *Vision of Politics*, p. 117, notes More's use of the terms *fundamentum, forma, vitae institutum*, construes them together as 'social order' and plausibly argues that the transformation that More desired was nothing less than 'social revolution.' On the Stoic conception of social virtue, see Bouwsma, pp. 24–6. Fenlon, p. 119, stresses the influence of Plato, St Augustine and the Church Fathers (especially in regard to *meum et tuum*), as well as pagan natural law tradition, on More.

[40] The nature and seriousness of his communitarianism has been treated by Hexter in *Vision of Politics*, pp. 121–5, and *Biography of an Idea*, pp. 35–43; *cf. Utopia*, pp. 103–7, 239–43. On labor, *Utopia*, pp. 127–31, 147.

institutions to deal with individual weakness. A sound educational
system was to be provided by the state, for instance, for the production of righteous citizens, and censors of morals were set up as
overseers, guides, and disciplinary agents.[41] Acknowledging the per-
vasiveness of sin, the Utopians 'brace weak conscience with strong
legal sanctions.'[42] More's humanism thus evinced its biblical assumptions while rejecting the medieval conclusion that since social ills are
a divine punishment for sin, no human remedy for them is
conceivable.

Erasmus, too, bequeathed to Renaissance Englishmen the hope
that an intelligent re-structuring of society could curb the detrimental
effects of sin. Like More, he advocated creation of the office of
censor of public morals, and he commended the strict sumptuary
laws of the ancients not as reinforcers of social hierarchy, but as
restraints on extravagance.[43] He traced social disorder and sedition
to such institutional defects as immoderate taxation and suggested
practical remedies: taxes should be kept low (by abolishing idle
ministries, avoiding wars, and suppressing graft among office-
holders), and a graduated taxation system should be instituted.[44] His
typically humanist theory of crime saw the criminal as a victim of
man-made circumstances which could be changed for the better.
Erasmus told the Christian prince that the poor were being driven to
the gallows through 'unrestrained despoilation of their goods' by the
idle aristocracy, suggesting that crime would decrease if this
exploitative situation were eliminated. Even if crime cannot be
eliminated, however, in the Erasmian scheme the criminal is not
inevitably destined to remain in his state of rebellion: through
exhortation, education, or in the last resort, punishment, he can be
reformed.[45] Education is, of course, the most desirable of these
options. Erasmus instructed the Christian ruler faced with the problem of crime to try first education, then threat of punishment, then
mild punishment. It is only at the last extreme that 'the incorrigible
must be sacrificed by the law (just as a hopelessly incurable limb
must be amputated) so that the sound part is not affected.' Erasmus

[41] *Utopia*, pp. 159, 227–9. Hexter parallels these censors to the Geneva consistory in *Vision of Politics*, pp. 110–11. [42] Hexter, *Vision of Politics*, p. 124.
[43] Erasmus, *The Education of a Christian Prince* (*Institutio Principis Christiani*), ed. and tr. L. K. Born (New York, 1936), p. 227; cf. *Adages* (1964), p. 215.
[44] *Institutio*, pp. 158–9, 215–17; *Adages* (*CWE* 31), p. 235.
[45] *Institutio*, pp. 184, 162. cf., for example, Émile Chénon's conclusion that the cruel punishments employed in medieval France sought not to reform the criminal, but above all to prevent those who might be tempted to imitate him. *Histoire Générale du droit français public et privé* (Paris, 1926), vol. 1, p. 687.

repeatedly stressed that the good prince must have 'the attitude of a friendly doctor, who amputates or cauterises the limb which he despairs of healing' for the good of the social whole.[46]

The punitive system recommended by Erasmus operated on the premise that the end of punishment is the instillation of virtue in the criminal. Accordingly, it should be characterized by mercy, and not by harshness. A good prince 'should strike fear into the hearts of none but evil doers and criminals; and yet even to them he should hold out a hope of leniency, if only they reform.'[47] None the less, when the good of society is threatened, Erasmus did not hesitate to recommend punishment, either as a deterrent or, in the extreme case, as a means of eliminating the criminal: 'If the really worthless, who are not restrained by reason or shame, find that the law has a big stick ready for them,' they may 'mend their ways.'[48] In a case in which the ultimate punishment is imposed, 'the example is before everyone', and in addition, society is protected from further wrong from the felon. Another discussion of the death penalty Erasmus concluded with the remarkable understatement, 'it is morally right to inconvenience a few for the sake of the public good.'[49] Nevertheless, his primary concern was always with eliminating the causes of crime and other social evil – ignorance (and the resultant lack of virtue) and exploitation of the weak by the powerful.

More and Erasmus were typical of Christian humanist social theorists – More in his structural approach to social problems, and Erasmus in his common sense solutions. They were also sufficiently influential on subsequent generations of English social theorists for Renaissance England to have been aptly described as a common-wealth in which the articulate citizen, recognizing the operation of social mechanisms, functioned as an effective social critic.[50] A literature of public discussion, diagnosis, and prescription arose in the sixteenth century to address classical questions: how should the commonwealth be ordered? What is the nature of the social organism? To what extent can rational analysis shape public policy?

[46] *Institutio*, p. 224; *Aut regem aut fatuum nasci oportere, Adages (CWE* 31), p. 231. The colloquy *Adolescentis et scorti* (1523) shows a harlot reformed by persuasion (*Coll.*, pp. 153–8).   [47] *Institutio*, p. 158; *cf.* pp. 162, 224; *Adages (CWE* 31), p. 229.
[48] *Festina lente, Adages* (1964), p. 184.
[49] *Dulce bellum inexpertis, Adages* (1964), p. 340; *Coniugium impar, Coll.*, p. 411. *cf. Dicta sapientū . . . Very necessary and profitable for children to lerne . . .* [1527], sig. Biii.
[50] Ferguson, *Articulate Citizen, passim*. Ferguson's definition of humanism is useful in this connection: it is 'the conscious reinterpretation of the literature and history of Greece and Rome, of *literae humaniores* . . . made within the specific historical context of a society in the process of transition from a medieval to a modern form' (p. 162).

Government came to be perceived as a constructive agency; the concept of positive change dominated a literature devoted to adapting classical precept and example to the demands of Christian ethics and active citizenship.[51]

The tradition of More and Erasmus, in other words, was continued in the generation of the commonwealth men (and beyond) by the ideal social type of the Christian humanists – the lay intellectual, educated in the classics with the aim of ordering the commonwealth, exercising his virtue in practical social perception and action. And the analysis offered by these humanists continued to focus on institutional as well as individual corruption. Richard Morison's location of the causes of sedition in the dearth of practical job training for those who must be skilled in crafts to get their living is typical. Rebels, beggars and thieves are the brood of a society unwilling to provide education for its children, according to Morison, and he echoed here the opinions not only of More and Erasmus, but also of the Spanish humanist brought to prominence in England as a member of Catherine of Aragon's circle, Juan Luis Vives.[52] Vives' works on education had consistently argued that society can be improved to a significant degree by laws and teaching which repress man's evil impulses and foster his good ones; but he had also argued that the commonwealth must provide both mechanical training in the crafts and a sufficiently well-ordered economic system for jobs to be available for those so trained. What is significant is that the emphasis in both Morison's and Vives' works is on institutional solutions to what had hitherto been interpreted as purely individual moral failure.

Thomas Starkey, Sir William Forrest and the author of the *Discourse of the Common Weal* similarly focused their analyses on the structural defects of English society. Starkey, for instance, devoted much of his *Dialogue* to the dearth and poor distribution of population, high rents and prices, the flourishing luxury trade, unemployment, and enclosure as causes of social disorder.[53] His

---

[51] *Ibid.*, pp. 42–69, compares with the humanist stance the typically medieval approach of social critics like John Gower and William Langland: most medieval commentary was negative, political issues were not put within the context of constructive policy, and the analysis of cause focused on the moral responsibilities of individuals functioning socially according to their places in a static hierarchy. *cf.* Robert P. Adams, 'Designs by More and Erasmus for a New Social Order,' *Studies in Philology*, 42 (1945), 131–46, esp. p. 135.

[52] Richard Morison, *A Remedy for Sedition* (London, 1536), pp. 35ff; Vives, *De subventione pauperum* (1526) in *Some Early Tracts on Poor Relief*, ed. F. Salter (London, 1926), pp. 4–31.

[53] In the *Discourse*, see especially the Second Dialogue (pp. 38ff in the Dewar edition); Starkey, pp. 75–82, 93–4, 138–45.

criminology was obviously Erasmian: having traced crime to its social as well as its moral causes, he pleaded for the rehabilitation, rather than the hanging, of criminals, observing, 'better it were to find some way how the man might be brought to better order and frame.' The proliferation of beggars he attributed to 'ill policy' as well as idleness, and he prescribed a drastic economic re-ordering, the redistribution of land, stricter laws, public works projects, the implementation of Vives' system of poor relief (devised for the Flemish city of Ypres), and an expanded and explicitly Erasmian public education system to deal with this problem. Only God, he concluded, can create a perfect man and a perfect society, but God none the less requires human effort to remedy imperfection.[54] Forrest agreed: in his *Pleasaunt Poesye of Princelie Practice* he recommended compulsory education (free to the poor and overseen by an appointed official), rent control and the enforcement of higher wage scales as solutions to the problem of social disorder.[55]

This literature of analysis, criticism, and prescription, indebted to the Scriptures and the classics, characterized by a dual focus on moral reform and institutional restructuring, comprised both a model for behavior and a call to action. It embodied a clear challenge to the contemplative ideal of scholasticism; its highest good was identified with the *vita activa*. It looked forward to the establishment of the *regnum Christi* in this world, by pious, educated, self-disciplined, industrious laymen. Its call to action did not go unanswered. Christian humanists were more than theorists. They participated actively in government, in church reform, and (perhaps most importantly for their puritan successors) in education.

More's activity in law and government is well known, as is Colet's in educational reform and the establishment of new educational institutions. Their circle of influence included city merchants, corporations and publishers. (It is significant that the first English translations of the *Praise of Folly* and *Utopia* were made by two citizens of London – a mercer and a goldsmith – at the request of London entrepreneurs.)[56] Vives had similar connections, giving rise to his

[54] Starkey, pp. 113–15, 89, 140–5, 160, 177, 185–6. The best educational system, he said, is that outlined by 'the most famous divine, Erasmus, whose counsel I would in our studies we might follow' (p. 187).
[55] Forrest, pp. lxxxi, xcii–xcix. This work was written during the reign of Edward VI; Forrest later became chaplain to Queen Mary.
[56] McConica, pp. 258–9; J. A. Guy, *The Public Career of Sir Thomas More* (Brighton, 1980), *passim*; Richard Marius, *Thomas More* (New York, 1984), *passim* and esp. chs. 3–4, 13–14; Erasmus noted More's active 'commitments to the affairs of state' in *De pueris* (*CWE* 26), p. 322.

development of practicable schemes for the reform of municipal poor relief and education.[57] Even Erasmus, usually pictured as a 'pure' scholar, was seen by his contemporaries as an activist. More contrasted Erasmus with lazy, sedentary monks who contributed nothing to the common good, boasting that Erasmus 'defies stormy seas and savage skies and the scourges of land travel, provided it further the common cause' of educating people to live as Christians. He bears 'seasickness, the tortures of tossing waves, the threat of deadly storms' and plods 'through dense forest and wild woodland, over rugged hilltops and steep mountains, along roads beset with bandits' – hardly the ivory tower scholar![58] His treatises on political and social questions were more than speculative. The *Querela pacis* (1517), for instance, was composed at the express request of Jean le Sauvage, Chancellor of Burgundy and a member of the court of Prince Charles of the Netherlands. Erasmus himself had become a councilor to Prince Charles in 1515, so that his pacifist doctrine was conceived and developed as relevant advice, practical instruction for a specific ruler in a very real ethical dilemma.[59]

In this and the next generation, the humanists Lupset, Pace, Elyot and Clerk (all patronized by Wolsey) found jobs at court, and Coverdale, Cheke and Ascham (members of Catherine Parr's circle) participated directly in church and educational reform. Thomas Cromwell's recruitment of Starkey, Morison, Taverner, Cox, Paynell, Berthelet, Vaughan and Marshall, among others, as propagandists for Henry's divorce, had mobilized considerable humanist influence at court during a period crucial for reformist interests.[60] As a patron both of second generation humanists seeking government service and of published translations of Erasmian and classical treatises, Cromwell created the necessary conditions for a humanist reformation of church and state. This humanist influence was evident from the Erasmian attacks on clerical privilege in the reform

[57] Noreña, *passim*; Hooykaas, *Humanisme*, pp. 27–9.
[58] More, *Correspondence*, pp. 201–3.
[59] Olin, *Six Essays*, pp. 25–7; James D. Tracy, *The Politics of Erasmus: A Pacifist Intellectual and his Political Milieu* (Toronto, 1978).
[60] On these groups, see McConica, pp. 7, 58, 127–41, 206–13; cf. Elton, *Reform and Renewal*, pp. 26, 38ff. Taverner's translation of Erasmus' *Encomium Matrimonii* [1531] was dedicated to Cromwell just before Taverner began writing to him to request patronage (SP 1/73 [1532], fols. 143–5). Among the preferments that Cromwell obtained for Vaughan were an absentee clerkship in Chancery and the position of under-treasurer of the mint. Starkey was appointed the king's chaplain in 1535 and was immediately commissioned by Henry to seek Pole's support for the new order. Morison was a member of Cromwell's official household from 1534 to 1540, working as a professional propaganda writer (Elton, pp. 46–58).

proposals of 1529–30 and the Six Articles, to the official sponsorship
of a vernacular Bible and the adiaphoristic awareness in the Ten
Articles and the Injunctions of 1536 and 1538.[61] In the meantime,
translations of Erasmus' and Vives' writings continued to be
officially sponsored; new works by Morison, Taverner (who became
Clerk of the Privy Seal) and other humanists were commissioned;
and social reformers like Starkey corresponded directly with the
king on such matters as his choice of councilors, the leasing of
monastic lands by copyhold, and involvement in European wars. By
Cromwell's death in 1540, England could be described with some
justification as 'an Erasmian polity.'[62]

Christian humanist influence continued during the reign of
Edward VI. It is visible in the King's 1547 Injunctions authorizing
Erasmus' *Paraphrases* of the Gospels and Acts to be chained in all
parish churches and requiring all clerks under the degree of B.D. to
own the *Paraphrases* of the Epistles and 'diligently study the same'. It
is visible, too, in the Erasmian social theorists who continued to be
added to the humanists at court: Sir Thomas Smith, for instance,
served as Principal Secretary to Edward and to Elizabeth, and he
both wrote and spoke volubly on everything from education to
sumptuary legislation.[63] Long after protestants had parted ways with
Catholic humanists on issues like free will and the authority of
ecclesiastical tradition, they retained an Erasmian hope in the corrective power of education and of godly social institutions.

If a single area of reform can be isolated as that in which Christian
humanists had their greatest effect on sixteenth-century English
society, that area would be education. In their authorship of new
pedagogical theory and in their participation in concrete reforms,
they acted upon their conviction that a good education is the best
means to combat social evil. Sin, they argued, springs at least partly

---

[61] Lutheranism obviously functioned to mediate humanist influence here. Erasmian
influence on Lutheran theology and ecclesiology is described by Wilhelm Maurer,
Das Verhältnis des Staates zur Kirche nach humanistischer Anschauung, vornehmlich bei Erasmus
(Giessen, 1930).

[62] McConica, pp. 108–10, 159–99. Zeeveld's *Foundations of Tudor Policy* (Cambridge,
Mass., 1948) also argues for a considerable humanist impact on political theory
during this period. Starkey's letters are included in *England in the Reign of King Henry
the Eighth*, ed. S. J. Herrtage (EETS, 1878), pp. liv–lxiii.

[63] McConica, pp. 237–41; M. Dewar, *Sir Thomas Smith: A Tudor Intellectual in Office*
(1964), *passim*; Dewar, 'The Authorship of the "Discourse of the Commonweal",'
Economic History Review, 2nd ser., 19 (1966), 388–400. The Erasmian protestant
Martin Bucer joined the theology faculty at Cambridge during this period, by royal
invitation.

from false opinions; therefore, education is requisite for the instillation of virtue, whether individual or social.[64] So convinced were they of human potential for the achievement of virtue through learning that they came close to the notion of the young child's mind being a blank slate upon which the educator could write what he pleased. Erasmus advised parents to provide that 'thine infant and young babe be forthwith instructed in good learning, while his wit is yet void from cares and vices, while his age is tender and tractable, and his mind flexible and ready to follow everything.'[65] He multiplied metaphors in *De pueris*: 'Press wax while it is softest; model clay while it is still moist; pour precious liquids only into a jar that has never been used before; and only dye wool that has just arrived spotlessly white from the fuller.' He continued in his favorite mode with a classical anecdote:

Antisthenes once made a witty allusion to this truth when he was asked by the father of one of his pupils what he needed: 'a new book, a new pen, and a fresh writing-tablet,' was his answer, meaning, of course, that he was looking for a mind that was still raw and unoccupied. You cannot preserve this quality of rawness and freshness forever; if you do not mould your child's soul to become fully human, it will of itself degenerate to a monstrous bestiality.[66]

He instructed the educator of an infant prince to 'instil into this childish mind, as yet blank and malleable, opinions worthy of a prince.'[67]

---

[64] Paul A. Fideler, 'Christian humanism and poor law reform in early Tudor England,' *Societas*, 4 (1974), 169–86, p. 274, has located a source for the humanist correlation of knowledge and social concord in Cicero's *De Officiis*: 'the knowledge of things human and divine, which is concerned . . . with the bonds of union between gods and men and relations of man to man'; *cf.* Fritz Caspari, 'Erasmus on the Social Functions of Humanism,' *JHI*, 8 (1947), 78–106, pp. 81, 84, on the classical notion that education based on *literae* will produce *virtus, morum integritas*. Caspari mentions in passing the implication which Erasmus derived from this, that degree of knowledge at least indirectly determines one's position in relation to God. See too Bouwsma, pp. 10–11, on the Stoics' identification of reason with a divine spark within mankind and their conclusion that virtue can be attained through rational control: to know the good is to do it. The inconsistency of Stoic belief in the power of inborn sin over human action with this optimistic view parallels that of Christian humanist thought.

[65] Erasmus, *That chyldren oughte to be taught* . . . in Richard Sherry's *A Treatise of Schemes and Tropes* (1550; Scholars' Facsimiles, Gainsville, Florida, 1961), sig. Gi; *cf. A ryght frutefull Epystle. . . in laude and prayse of matrymony*, tr. Richard Taverner, [1531], sig. Diii. On the uneasy acceptance of both humanist optimism concerning reason and the protestant doctrine of human depravity by early Lutheran pedagogues, see Gerald Strauss, *Luther's House of Learning* (Baltimore, 1978), pp. 1–107.

[66] *De pueris*, (*CWE* 26), pp. 305–6.

[67] *Aut regem aut fatuum, Adages* (*CWE* 31), p. 233; *cf. Institutio*, p. 140. Erasmus did not quite deny the effects of original sin, of course: 'Since the natures of so many men

Education of the future ruler, of course, was regarded as of special importance for the well-being of the commonwealth; none the less, the establishment of a system of public education was viewed as essential if a truly well-regulated, virtuous society was to be created. According to Erasmus,

A prince who is about to assume control of the state must be advised at once that the main hope of a state lies in the proper education of its youth ... [Take care that] children may be placed under the best and most trustworthy instructors and may learn the teachings of Christ and that good literature which is beneficial to the state. As a result of this scheme of things, there will be no need for many laws or punishments, for the people will of their own free will follow the course of right.[68]

His concern for virtuous behavior in the individual was thus a reflection of Erasmus' hope of creating a truly good society.

Herein lay the reason for the Utopians' stress on the education of citizens. As More's friend Vives argued (quoting Xenophon), for children to become good, it is 'only necessary that they should be placed in a well-directed state' where a sound educational system is provided to instruct citizens in virtuous behavior.[69] Later, Ascham's *Toxophilus*, a treatise on the state of the realm, would promote education as a means of national regeneration, and Starkey would call the 'good education of youth in virtuous exercise ... the ground of remedying of all other diseases in this our politic body.' Cromwell, well-versed in these humanist assumptions, accordingly sponsored educational improvement 'to the great advancement of the common weal.'[70] He was well aware of Erasmus' warning that parents who neglect their children's education do no less wrong to their country than to their children by giving it dissolute citizens. Erasmus had insisted that it 'ought to be a public responsibility entrusted to the secular magistrates and the ecclesiastical authorities' to provide fit teachers for a nation's youth.[71]

Christian humanists addressed themselves not only to the ultimate aims of education, but also to the best techniques by which

---

are inclined towards the ways of evil, there is no nature so happily born that it cannot be corrupted by wrong training' (*Institutio*, p. 143).
[68] *Institutio*, pp. 212–13. This system is to be supported by public funds, since it is to benefit the commonwealth. *cf. Festina lente, Adages* (1964), p. 184.
[69] *Utopia*, pp. 129, 159–61; Vives, *On Education*, Watson, pp. 266–67.
[70] Starkey, p. 144; McConica, p. 191. *Toxophilus* was published in 1545.
[71] *De pueris*, (*CWE* 26), pp. 306, 333. He continued (p. 333): 'Appropriate training is provided for those who are to serve in the army or sing in church choirs; the same should be provided by the authorities for those who are to give the young people of the nation a sound education based on humane ideals.'

those aims could be accomplished. Humanists were preoccupied both with educational theories and with the production of textbooks which would simultaneously inculcate good grammar and virtuous behavior into the student of letters. While Erasmus' *Adages*, for example, was obviously a vehicle intended to convey classical moralizing to early modern minds, its stated intention was to 'smooth the path to a knowledge of the classics for the *mediocriter literati*,' Erasmus produced 'Epitomes' of the *Adages* since they would be accessible to students of limited means and therefore would instruct a broader spectrum of the population in virtuous behavior.[72] Likewise, the *Colloquies* were originally compiled as a combination of social satire and advice and a pleasant means of learning Latin: 'if the ancient teachers of children are commended who allured them with wafers, that they might be willing to learn their first rudiments, I think it ought not to be charged as a fault upon me, that by the like regard I allure youths *either to the elegance of the Latin tongue or to piety*.'[73] Education must be pleasant, Erasmus argued in the *Institutio*, since the child should not be 'cut by the severity of its training and learn to hate worthiness [the goal of education] before it knows it.'[74]

The moral instruction thus pleasantly (and therefore firmly) implanted in the student was intended by Christian humanists above all to be practical and concrete; it was to be *applied* learning. The most significant curricular changes in sixteenth-century grammar schools and universities are attributable to this emphasis.[75] It was the drive to educate for living which motivated humanist reformers to elevate moral philosophy over theology and metaphysics, and rhetoric over logic. 'Let young men declaim, before their teachers,

---

[72] Noted by Phillips in her Introduction to *Adages* (1964), p. 5.
[73] *Coll.*, Epistle to the Reader, p. 625 (emphasis mine). It is significant that Thomas Cromwell's son was raised on the *Colloquies*, 'the most popular schoolbook of the time,' and that by the following century, English puritans had made it required reading in New England grammar schools: Simon, p. 72; Elton, p. 31; Samuel Eliot Morison, *The Intellectual Life of Colonial New England* (Cornell, 1936), p. 106. Erasmus' other educational productions include *De ratione studii, De copia verborum* (both in *CWE* 24, ed. C. R. Thompson), *De conscribendis epistolis* and *Conficiendarum epistolarum formula* (on writing good Latin letters), *De recta latini graecique sermonis pronuntiatione dialogus* (on correct speaking of Latin and Greek), *De civilitate morum puerilium* (on good manners), *De pueris* (the last five in *CWE* 25 and 26, ed. J. Kelley Sowards), and the voluminous collections of ancient wisdom explained for students, the *Adages,* the *Parabolae* (in *CWE* 23), and the *Apophthegmata*.
[74] *Institutio*, p. 142; cf. *De pueris*, (*CWE* 26), pp. 334–40.
[75] The implementation of this concept at Deventer, St Paul's and the Collège de Guyenne is noted by R. R. Bolgar, 'Education and Learning,' *The New Cambridge Modern History*, vol. 3, ed. R. B. Wernham (Cambridge, Mass., 1968), p. 430. See also F. L. Schoell, *Études sur l'humanisme continental en Angleterre à la fin de la Renaissance* (Paris, 1926), pp. 43–61 *et passim*.

on those matters which may afterwards be useful in life,' Vives demanded of schoolmasters, 'and not, as was the habit of the ancients in the philosophical schools, on matters which never occurred in real life . . . let all eloquence stand in full battle array for goodness and piety, against crime and wickedness.'[76] While dialectic remained part of the curriculum, a recent study of specific logic textbooks shows a corresponding change in emphasis, away from the peculiar requirements of academic exercises, and toward a more practical study of discourse. Peter of Spain's *Summulae Logicales* (the favorite medieval text) was, for instance, replaced in most universities in the 1520s with the texts of Cicero, Quintilian and later humanist dialecticians who favored 'persuasive types of argument as crucial tools in "ordinary language" or oratorical discourse.'[77] The focus in rhetoric, too, shifted to stress the precise nature of the discussion, the audience, the type of situation, and the extent of the evidence – in short, the 'art of discourse' for practical ends.[78]

The demand for practical moral and ethical instruction in both grammar schools and universities gave rise to a 'textbook revolution' consisting in a revived use of ancient moralists and an enthusiastic adoption of new humanist textbooks. The most admired classical writers were used both as pedagogical guides and as instructors in virtuous behavior. Plutarch's treatise on the upbringing of children (first translated from Greek by Guarino in 1411), Quintilian's *Education of the Orator* (first published in full by Poggio in 1417), and Cicero's *De Oratore* (rediscovered in 1422) were among the most popular of such dual-purpose manuals. Also widely used in England were the works of Xenophon, Terence, and Isocrates on education. Sixteenth-century grammar schools saw the replacement of such medieval favorites as the *Doctrinale* of Alexandre de Villedieu with these and other works of Cicero (especially the *Epistolae, De Officiis, De Amicitia* and *De Senectute*), Livy, Seneca, Quintilian, Virgil, Horace and Ovid. Higher forms used such Greek authors as Isocrates, Demosthenes, Plutarch, Lucian, Thucydides, Plato, the New Testament writers and

[76] Vives, *On Education*, pp. 180, 185–6. His complaint against the ancient 'philosophical schools' is the standard humanist/Stoic critique of the Sophists.
[77] Lisa Jardine, 'The Place of Dialectic Teaching in Sixteenth Century Cambridge,' *Studies in the Renaissance*, 21 (1974), 31–62, esp. p. 39. This move was presumably a rejection both of the stilted formality of medieval methods of argumentation and of Peter of Spain's corrupt Latin, although Jardine stresses the former. See below, p. 77, for the implications of this change for the Elizabethan curriculum.
[78] Paul O. Kristeller, 'The Aristotelian Tradition,' in *Renaissance Thought* (New York, 1961), pp. 24–47, points out (p. 40) that while Aristotle's *Rhetoric* had been treated as part of moral philosophy in the Middle Ages, it became important in rhetorical training in the sixteenth century because of this practical emphasis.

the Church Fathers.[79] It is significant, moreover, that the works of these authors were being read contextually (frequently in their entirety) and in their original languages, with the explicit intent of applying the wisdom of the ancients to modern living.

The other major aspect of the textbook revolution was the production by Christian humanists of numerous new textbooks, many of which have been discussed above. These emphasized not only principles of grammar and style, but also the importance of classical wisdom in learning to deal with the affairs of this world. When John Colet 'set out to place learning at the service of living, to present it as a means of preparing the individual to live well himself, and to do good in society' at St Paul's School, he deliberately chose as the first Master William Lily, a layman and author of both a humanist *Grammar* and of the *Carmen de Moribus*, a book of instruction in good manners and virtuous behavior for schoolboys. From Erasmus he commissioned the *De copia verborum ac rerum*, which was intended to reform both language and behavior, and the school also made use of the *Colloquies* and the *Adages*.[80] Later examples of humanist textbooks of piety and of grammar include Elyot's *Dictionary* (1538), and his *Banquette of sapience* and *Castel of helth* (1539).

On the university scene, the most significant changes in favor of the 'new learning' began upon Colet's return from Italy to Oxford in 1497. Colet's lectures on the Pauline epistles (1497–99), approaching the Bible as a book to be read within its historical context and designed to effect reform and a revival of godly living, had an inestimable influence on both curriculum and pedagogy at the universities. They provided a trend-setting example of humanist educational assumptions in action. They were so marked a contrast to the biblical exegesis dependent upon scholastic 'glosses' which had characterized the previous centuries that they drew from Erasmus the comment (in a 1499 letter to Robert Fisher), 'it is marvellous how general and abundant is the harvest of ancient learning in this country.'[81] They caused the lines between humanist innovators and the scholastic old guard to be drawn with great clarity. And, due to the immediate popularity of humanist methods, those lines of division

---

[79] Of 195 printed editions of the *Doctrinale*, only nine postdated 1525. Bolgar, pp. 433–5.
[80] Simon, p. 80; *De copia* was published in 1512. See M. M. Phillips, 'Erasmus and the Art of Writing,' *Scrinium Erasmianum*, I, 335–350. Phillips remarks that the dual title, *De copia verborum ac rerum*, embodies Erasmus' assumption that the classics are not merely a matter of style; they are also expressions of opinion (p. 342).
[81] Erasmus to Fisher, 1499, (*CWE* 1), pp. 235–6.

were sharpened in the ensuing decades. Erasmus wrote to Colet in 1511, 'Sometimes I have to do battle here on your behalf against the Thomists and Scotists,' the 'most successfully complacent class of men there is,' and in Colet's own view a 'swarm of flies.'[82] To More in 1513 he exulted, 'Lupset thinks that with my help he has been reborn and has fully returned from the underworld. But the Masters are trying every trick to drag the youth back to their treadmill; for at once on the same day he has sold his books of [scholastic] sophistry and bought Greek ones instead!'[83] Despite the impact of Christian humanists upon Oxbridge curricula during the first decades of the sixteenth century, More still found it necessary in 1518 to defend secular learning, Greek studies, the hope of evangelical reform and Erasmus himself against the attacks of the Oxford Trojans.[84]

The accomplishments of Christian humanist reformers at both universities during this period were, none the less, significant and lasting. This was, of course, particularly true in such new foundations as Christ's and St John's Colleges, Cambridge, and Brasenose and Corpus Christi Colleges, Oxford.[85] The 1516 statutes of St John's (based on the Christ's statutes of 1505) established Greek and Hebrew as parts of the curriculum; fourteen years later, Arabic and Chaldaic were added. At Corpus Christi, Foxe's public lecturer in Greek was to read to the university three days each week from Lucian, Philostratus or the orations of Isocrates; a humanities reader was to give instruction in Valla's *Elegantiae*, Aulus Gellius (both favorites of Erasmus) and Politian; and the reader in theology was specifically instructed to exclude the Schoolmen in favor of the Church Fathers.[86] Between 1515 and 1520, both universities established public lectureships in Greek. Furthermore, book inventories at a variety of colleges show that scholars were investing in humanist editions and treatises for their private libraries, indicating that these works were forming part of the unofficial curriculum even in the less

[82] Erasmus to Colet, 1511 (*CWE*, 2), no. 227, p. 170, and no. 278, p. 183. Colet's reply is *CWE* II, no. 230.   [83] *CWE* 2, no. 271, p. 249.
[84] More, *Correspondence*, pp. 111–20, *cf*. p. 60.
[85] Lady Margaret founded Christ's and John Fisher St John's primarily as means of reforming the secular clergy and establishing a vernacular preaching ministry; Brasenose was founded by Bishop Smith and Sir Richard Sutton (steward of the monastery of Syon) and Corpus Christi by Foxe (1517) explicitly as centers for humanist learning. C. E. Mallet, *A History of the University of Oxford* (1924–7), vol. 2, pp. 22–3; J. B. Mullinger, *The University of Cambridge from the Earliest Times ...* (Cambridge, 1873–1911), pp. 423–552. On Renaissance foundations at Oxford, see James McConica, 'Scholars and Commoners in Renaissance Oxford,' in *The University in Society*, ed. Lawrence Stone (Princeton, 1974), vol. 1, pp. 151–81.
[86] T. Fowler, *History of Corpus Christi College* (Oxford, 1893); *Statutes of the Colleges of Oxford* (Oxford, 1853), vol. 2, p. 10.

progressive colleges. The Oxford bookseller John Dorne recorded selling more of Erasmus' works than of Aristotle's in 1520.[87]

The direct involvement of Christian humanists in the formation and reformation of colleges is noteworthy, both as an explanation for their relative success and as an illustration of their activism. Aside from the founding fathers who have been mentioned, Erasmus himself lectured in Greek at Queens', Cambridge, from 1511 to 1513; More's adopted son John Clement served as the first Greek reader at Corpus Christi, Oxford; both Lupset and Vives lectured in humanities at Corpus; and Wolsey's Cardinal College (later Christ Church) was established as a humanist addition to Oxford in 1525. It is hardly any wonder that the *literae humaniores*, with all of their implications for social theory, became the dominant aspect of university curriculum and that the scholastic approach to biblical and patristic texts was widely rejected in favor of a genuinely humanist biblicism. By 1514, Erasmus was able to write to Servatius Rogerus that in England 'are colleges in which there is so much religion and so marked a sobriety in living that you would despise every form of religious regime in comparison, if you saw it.'[88] Two years later he recounted the history of this new regime:

About thirty years ago nothing was taught in the university at Cambridge except Alexander, what they call the *Parva logicalia*, and the traditional doctrines of Aristotle with Scotistic *quaestiones*. As time went on the humanities were added; then mathematics; then a new, or at least a new-fangled Aristotle; then the knowledge of Greek; then all those authors whose very names were unknown in the old days even to the brahmins of philosophy Iarcas-like enthroned. And what, pray, was the effect of this on your university? Why, it flourished to such a tune that it can challenge the first universities of the age, and there are men there compared with whom those earlier scholars are mere shadows of theologians, not the reality.[89]

In 1517 he was able to respond with equanimity to the criticism of the New Learning coming from the University of Paris by contrasting the situation at Cambridge: 'The extraordinary language they are using in Paris causes me no anxiety. You will see a great part of this pedantry sent packing. Cambridge is a changed place. The university

---

[87] McConica, pp. 88–92. Erasmus' works similarly dominated the inventory of Cambridge bookbinder Nicholas Pilgrim (1545): the 382 titles listed include twenty-two works of Erasmus. G. J. Gray and W. M. Palmer, *Abstracts from the Wills and Testamentary Documents of Printers, Binders, and Stationers of Cambridge, from 1504 to 1669* (London, 1915), pp. 10–26.

[88] *CWE* 2, *The Correspondence of Erasmus*, tr. R. A. B. Mynors and D. F. S. Thomson, p. 299 (8 July 1514).

[89] *CWE* 4, p. 52 (Erasmus to Henry Bullock of Queens', Cambridge, 22? August 1516).

there has no use for this frigid hairsplitting, which is more conducive to wrangling than religion.'⁹⁰

The pace of change increased under Cromwell's guidance during the 1530s and under the influence of Edward VI's Royal Commissioners.⁹¹ Cromwell was responsible for the reforming injunctions at both universities which proscribed late medieval scholasticism from Peter Lombard and Duns Scotus on, instructed the more prosperous colleges to establish two daily public lectures in Greek and Latin, and required that all students be allowed to study the Scriptures for themselves. With the Reformation, canon law study was abolished, and biblical readings were substituted for previously required theological texts, to the delight of humanist reformers. Masters of colleges in 1535 received royal injunctions to guard their students 'from the darkness worse than chimaera, from the frivolous "*quaestiuncula*" and from the blind and obscure glosses of Scotus, Burleius, Anthony Trombeta, Thomas Bricot, Brussels and others of that pack.'⁹² The alternative, certainly evident in the newly endowed royal colleges of Trinity, Cambridge and Christ Church, Oxford, was a fresh, humanistic emphasis on moral reformation through education and on the training of laymen for their civic responsibilities.

To the extent that this alternative was implemented in the universities, an important Christian humanist goal for social reconstruction was realized. Education – in classical morality and Christian piety, in the Scriptures uncontaminated by scholastic glosses, in the civic consciousness and social responsibility of the ancients – was, after all, the Christian humanists' first step to both individual and social reform. Having involved themselves deeply in educational improvement, and having injected elements of social criticism and moral exhortation into the curriculum, they fully expected to see the results of their efforts in meaningful social change.

Christian humanist social theory was in essence, then, a framework for the reformation of the commonwealth. Its implementation in the early Tudor period was perhaps spotty, but the availability of printed editions of classical and humanist works, the reformed pedagogy and curriculum of the humanist-infiltrated universities, and the nature and practicability of the humanist reform program itself would guarantee that the Erasmian vision would not die with

⁹⁰ *CWE* 5, p. 225 (Erasmus to Ludwig Baer, 6 December 1517); a similar description is found in Erasmus to Capito, also 6 December 1517, *CWE* V, p. 227.
⁹¹ The latter established a new curriculum based on the classics: see Simon, chapter 10.
⁹² Curtis, pp. 6–29; Elton, pp. 33–5; William J. Costello, *The Scholastic Curriculum at Early Seventeenth-Century Cambridge* (Cambridge, Mass., 1958), p. 9.

its authors. In bookstores, in colleges and in the intellectual receptivity of the earliest protestant reformers lay the mechanisms by
which the goals of the humanists would be transmitted to and eventually in some measure practiced by subsequent generations of
Englishmen. It is time now to look more closely at the actual
transmission of humanist ideas to Elizabethan and early Stuart
Englishmen in general, and to puritans in particular.

3

◁ ═══ ▷

The transmission of Christian humanist ideas

The impact of Christian humanist reforms on university curriculum and pedagogy during the Henrician and Edwardian periods has been described at some length because of the importance of the university experience of later puritan divines for the formation of puritan social thought. The sermon was, after all, the primary vehicle by which ideas were propagated in early modern England, especially among fervent protestants. An increasingly literate populace read printed sermons (frequently aloud, to less educated auditors), and sermon and lecture attendance was a popular form of entertainment among the hotter sort of protestants. The sources of ideas being transmitted to the puritan laity must, therefore, be traced to the intellectual background of the preachers. Now while this can be accomplished in some measure by looking at the marginal notes of printed sermons, the puritans' predilection for Scriptural authority often precluded a methodical listing of extra-biblical sources in their notes. It is necessary, then, to discover the writings which conditioned the way puritans used Scripture by looking at their library catalogues, their commonplace books and correspondence, and (most importantly) the curriculum to which they devoted their university years.[1] It will be seen that for at least the century and a half following Erasmus' death, puritan readers were entirely typical of their less zealous contemporaries in imbibing large quantities of

---

[1] On the importance of the university experience for puritan preachers, see Patrick Collinson, *The Elizabethan Puritan Movement* (Berkeley, 1967), p. 127, and *The Religion of Protestants* (Oxford, 1982), ch. 3; Mark H. Curtis, *Oxford and Cambridge in Transition, 1558–1642* (Oxford, 1959), pp. 195–206; William Haller, *The Rise of Puritanism* (New York, 1938), pp. 52–3; and John Morgan, *Godly Learning: Puritan Attitudes towards Reason, Learning, and Education, 1540–1640* (Cambridge, 1986), chs. 6–7. The majority of puritan clergy, even in the north-western diocese of Chester, for instance, attended Oxford or Cambridge: R. C. Richardson, *Puritanism in the North-West of England* (Manchester, 1972), pp. 56–63.

humanist literature, and that their taste for it had been developed in part by their educational experiences.

The similarity of puritan, early Anglican, and Christian humanist social theory is explained in large part by the nature of university curriculum, for the literature – both classical and contemporary – that formed the basis of the humanist social program also formed a major portion of the Oxbridge arts course throughout the period with which we are concerned. There is scant evidence that changes of consequence were made in the curriculum after the humanist reforms of the Henrician and Edwardian periods; those which have been suggested by historians were at most expansions of the essentially classical curriculum advocated and made possible by humanist publications. And while this curriculum was superimposed on a scholastic framework and methodology[2] and was never as thoroughly reformed as its sponsors had desired, it still provided a continuous, characteristically humanist emphasis on the development of practical morality and true piety as the aim of education throughout the sixteenth and early seventeenth centuries.

Unfortunately, while few historians would deny the significant humanist impact on curriculum and pedagogy at the early Tudor universities, the continuance of that influence during the following century has been denied in favor of a 'discontinuity pattern' for early modern university studies. The inexorable drive of historians to periodize and classify has produced a pattern which delineates 'scholasticism in the first generation of the sixteenth century, humanism in the second, Ramism in the third . . . [and], in the last decade of the century . . . a revival of scholasticism.' This version by Hugh Kearney, following the lead of Mark Curtis and William Costello, has Neo-scholasticism dominating the scene through the 1640s, giving way to 'Baconianism' in the later 1640s and 1650s.[3]

---

[2] Demonstrated by William J. Costello in *The Scholastic Curriculum at Early Seventeenth Century Cambridge* (Cambridge, Mass., 1958); *cf.* Curtis, pp. 86–92.

[3] Hugh Kearney, *Scholars and Gentlemen: Universities and Society in Pre-Industrial Britain, 1500–1700* (London, 1970), pp. 77, 98–100. It should be noted that 'generation' is rather loosely defined to allow the second to continue to 1590 in Humphrey's influence in Magdalen College, Oxford, apparently in the midst of an already triumphant Ramism. Kearney's thesis rests partly on assumptions made by Costello and Curtis; however, Costello's study focuses on scholastic methodology, and Curtis' primary concern is not with curriculum, but with institutional reforms and the social composition of the colleges. Christopher Hill, in *The Intellectual Origins of the English Revolution* (Oxford, 1965), pp. 301–14, perceives a continuous influence of scholasticism throughout the seventeenth century. The most important recent illumination of early modern Oxbridge curricula is Mordechai Feingold's *The Mathematicians' Apprenticeship* (Cambridge, 1984), which corrects earlier historians' devaluation of mathematics and astronomy in both undergraduate and graduate studies before the Civil War.

Even the humanist phase itself has been subdivided chronologically:
a 'court' stage represented by Sir Thomas Elyot's *The Boke Named the
Governour* (ca. 1531), with its emphasis on service to the king by an
educated gentry, allegedly gave way to a 'country' stage heralded by
Lawrence Humphrey's *The Nobles* (1563) and characterized by
reformism and social criticism. The artificiality of this distinction
has been successfully argued by (among others) Lawrence Stone and
James McConica.[4] But while this and other aspects of Kearney's
work on the social history of the universities have been criticized,
the accuracy of the discontinuity pattern itself has hardly been questioned. The received version has humanism disappearing from
university curriculum by the 1580s, and (until McConica's recent
suggestion that the Aristotelians John Case and John Rainolds maintained a humanist tradition in Elizabethan Oxford) historians have
been content to accept Ramism and Neo-scholasticism as the dominant trends in university teaching during the Elizabethan and early
Stuart periods respectively.[5]

McConica's work has provided a valuable first step for a reevaluation
of Elizabethan curriculum; however, in order fully to address the
problems posed by Kearney's thesis, it is necessary to take another

[4] Kearney, pp. 34–45. Lawrence Stone in 'The Ninnyversity?' *NYRB* (28 January
1971), p. 23, argues that the two 'merely represent different stages in the
acclimatization of an Italian prototype rather than distinctive intellectual
positions.' More incisively, McConica points out that John Case and John Rainolds
(the latter, according to Kearney, Oxford's leading Ramist) are typical of
humanists who combined elements of both 'court' and 'country' humanism:
'Humanism and Aristotelianism in Tudor Oxford,' *EHR*, 94 (1979), 291–317, p.
310, n. 3. Certainly the authors that Kearney (pp. 42–3) associates with court
humanism (Homer, Horace, Lucian, Ovid, Virgil [*Aeneid*], Catullus and Martial)
and country humanism (Seneca, Terence, Virgil [*Georgics*], Josephus and Calvin)
were read by humanists difficult to identify with court or country, as well as by
people whom Kearney would not call humanists at all, throughout the sixteenth
and early seventeenth centuries (see below, pp. 62–5, 82–94, and my 'Seneca and
the Protestant Mind: The Influence of Stoicism on Puritan Ethics', *Archiv für
Reformationsgeschichte*, 74 (1983), 182–99). Moreover, if social criticism is characteristic of country humanism, what do we do with Vives, Ascham, and Sir Thomas
Smith? Curtis (p. 57) incidentally sees Elyot as an exception to the humanist rule
on pedagogical issues. Were Kearney aware of Lawrence Humphrey's letter to
Elizabeth commending his *Nobles* as supportive of the authority of Crown and
Court (BL, Harl. 7933, fols. 351v–353v), he might question his own categories.
[5] R. R. Bolgar, in *The Classical Heritage and its Beneficiaries* (Cambridge, 1958), sees a
continuation of humanist classicism after 1600 'partly as a survival, and partly as a
necessary adjunct to the education of the time' (p. 379). This, however, forms part
of the rather tentative conclusion of his book, which concentrates on the period
before 1550. For criticisms of other aspects of Kearney's book, see Stone's
'Ninnyversity?'; four articles by McConica – his review of *Scholars and Gentlemen* in
EHR, 87 (1972), 121–5, his 'The Prosopography of the Tudor University,' *Journal of
Interdisciplinary History*, 3 (1973), 543–55, his 'Social Relations of Tudor Oxford,'
TRHS, 5th ser., 27 (1977), 115–34, his 'Humanism and Aristotelianism'; and
Elizabeth Russell, 'The Influx of Commoners into the University of Oxford before
1581: An Optical Illusion?' *EHR*, 92 (1977), 721–45.

look at those under-used sources upon which it allegedly rests – the numerous, lengthy, and usually tedious student notebooks of sixteenth- and early seventeenth-century Oxford and Cambridge. The notebooks must be used with care; one must guard against concluding too much from the relatively small number of volumes which are extant. But in combination with the data provided by university and college statutes, tutorial directives, library inventories, correspondence and other sources, they can contribute substantially to answering some of the most obvious questions arising from earlier treatments of university studies: What was the relationship of protestantism to humanist educational reforms? How did humanist objectives and methods for education affect the way and the extent to which classical sources were used in the curriculum? Is Ramism an alternative to humanism? How and for what purpose were the Schoolmen used by early seventeenth-century protestant scholars? To what degree were students aware of the conflict between humanism and scholasticism in the seventeenth century? Finally, does the weight of the evidence support the idea that humanism indeed disappeared from the universities in the mid-Elizabethan period, or has our search for change blinded us to continuity in early modern university studies – a continuity based on the use of humanist and classical literature?

The attraction which Christian humanism had for early protestant reformers provides a good starting place for tackling these questions: it supplies us both with an indication of the close relationship which could develop and would continue to exist between humanism and protestantism, and with the identity of an important conduit between early Tudor humanism and Elizabethan puritanism. Many of the early Reformers, both continental and English, were explicitly Erasmian. Zwingli and Calvin, whose works wielded great authority in protestant England, were humanists by education and inclination: Calvin called Erasmus the 'glory and the darling of literature' and was clearly familiar not only with his edition of the New Testament, but also with his *Apophthegmata* and *Adagia*. Viret and Beza illustrate the ongoing influence of humanism on continental Calvinism.[6] Illustrative

[6] Calvin's *Commentary on Seneca's De Clementia*, tr. F. L. Battles and A. M. Hugo (Leiden, 1969), pp. 37* (On Calvin's humanistic education), 108*, and 6/7. On parallels between Erasmus' *Adages* and Calvin's *Institutes*, see Battles' *New Light on Calvin's Institutes* (London, 1966). On the influence of Christian humanism on Calvin, Viret, and Beza, see Robert D. Linder, 'Calvinism and Humanism: The First Generation,' *CH*, 44 (1975), 167–81. On Zwingli's Erasmianism, see G. W. Locher, 'Zwingli und Erasmus,' in *Scrinium Erasmianum*, ed. J. J. Coppens (Leiden, 1969), vol. 2, pp. 325–50. Erasmus' influence on the Reformers of the upper Rhineland is the subject of E.-W. Köhls, *Die theologische Lebensaufgabe des Erasmus und die oberrheinischen Reformatoren* (Stuttgart, 1969).

of the direct personal as well as literary influence of humanist protestants in England is Martin Bucer, Regius Professor of Divinity at
Cambridge from 1549 until his death in 1552. Bucer was a close
acquaintance of Erasmus' biographer, Beatus Rhenanus, and of the
humanist protestants Wolfgang Capito and Peter Martyr (the latter
also brought to England by the Edwardian Reformers). He began a
long correspondence with Erasmus himself in 1517, and a catalogue
of his library compiled in 1518 shows that he possessed nearly all of
Erasmus' then published works. He wrote in 1520, 'It gives me great
joy that the world is daily enriched with new writings of Erasmus; I
have managed several secret economies so that I might be able to
procure them all, if possible.'[7] After the Heidelberg disputation of
1518, Bucer described himself as 'Erasmianer und Martinianer.'[8] His
humanist vision of social reform, *De Regno Christi*, was written during
his tenure at Cambridge and must have inspired his auditors there as
it later would its readers, for he boasted that at Cambridge, 'I am permitted to set forth the Kingdom of Christ with the most entire
freedom, in my lectures, disputations, and Latin sermons.'[9] Certainly the impact of this seminal work of humanist social theory on
subsequent generations of protestants was significant and illustrates
the importance of first generation protestants for the transmission
of humanist social ideas: we know that Edmund Grindal as Bishop of
London collected this and other materials written by Bucer in
England for Conrad Hubert's edition of the *Scripta Anglicana* (Basle,
1577), and a resume of *De Regno Christi* by the puritan Thomas
Sampson was sent to Lord Burleigh in 1577. The work was later

---

[7] Nicole Peremans, *Érasme et Bucer d'après leur correspondance* (Paris, 1970), pp. 9, 27–
30; Henri Strohl, *Bucer, humaniste chrétien* (Paris, 1939), and E.-W. Köhls, 'Erasmian
Studies in Germany,' *Erasmus in English*, 3 (1971), 28–9. On the influence of Erasmus
on Bucer's theology, see F. Kruger, *Bucer und Erasmus* (Wiesbaden, 1970). Calvin
spent the years 1538–41 in Strasbourg with Bucer.

[8] Köhls, 'Erasmian Studies,' p. 29.

[9] *Original Letters Relative to the English Reformation*, ed. H. Robinson (Cambridge,
1846–7), vol. 1, p. 19. *De Regno Christi* has been translated by Wilhelm Pauck and
Paul Larkin in the *Library of Christian Classics*, (Philadelphia, 1969), vol. 19. A copy
of the 1557 Basel edition was donated to the St John's College library in
Cambridge in 1632 (St John's, Cambridge, MS U.5; the volume is still there,
catalogue no. F.10.13). This was the first edition; a German translation was
published in Strasbourg and a French translation in Geneva the following year.
We know that John Cheke and Peter Martyr read this work in manuscript and
agreed with it: John Strype, *Life of Cheke* (Oxford, 1821), pp. 55f. It echoed Erasmus'
opinions on such diverse topics as marriage and divorce (*cf.* Erasmus' *In laude and
prayse of matrymony*, tr. Richard Taverner [1531] and his *Censure and judgment . . .
Whyther dyvorsement betwene man and wyfe stondeth with the lawe of God*, tr. Nycolas Lesse
[1550?]), education, wealth, and poverty (parallels detailed in chapter 5, below),
and the nature of true nobility. On the latter, *cf. De Regno Christi*, pp. 176–7, 267–8,
with Erasmus' *Institutio principis Christiani*, tr. L. K. Born (New York, 1936), p. 140,
and BL, Royal MS 17.A.xliv, fols. 2–2v.

quoted by such diverse protestants as John Whitgift and Thomas Cartwright, its recommendations for poor relief were published in 1557, and the long section on divorce was translated and published by John Milton in 1644.[10]

It has been convincingly argued that 'the Reformation in Cambridge began with love of letters, among a company devoted to the New Learning and whose excitement at the new text [of the New Testament] established by Erasmus was the ferment of the new reform.'[11] The Cambridge of Fisher and Erasmus was also that of Cranmer (A. B. Jesus, 1512) and Latimer (a fellow of Clare by 1510), and the future Marian exile Edmund Allen (of Corpus) was one of the translators under Udall of Erasmus' *Paraphrases*. Thomas Bilney of Trinity Hall and the Corpus Reformer William Warner were first known as despisers of scholastic subtleties 'and such fooleries'; Erasmus and Latimer alike advocated advancing the Gospel by decrying the Schoolmen.[12] Also among the earliest Cambridge Reformers were such prominent classical scholars as Robert Barnes, who doubtless knew Erasmus when both were at Louvain (1517–21), and who later numbered among his enthusiastic Cambridge students of Terence and Cicero one Miles Coverdale.[13] In both universities, English Reformers from Thomas Cranmer and Alexander Nowell to John Jewel and John Rainolds helped to build solid and long-lasting bridges between humanism and protestantism.[14]

A more detailed examination of the humanism of these Reformers

---

[10] Wilhelm Pauck and Paul Larkin, Introduction to *De Regno Christi*, pp. 172–3; Scott Pearson, *Thomas Cartwright* (Cambridge, 1925), pp. 226, 409f; Martin Bucer, *A Treatise How by the Worde of God, Christian mens Almose ought to Be distributed* [1557]; *The Judgment of Martin Bucer concerning Divorce* tr. John Milton (London, 1644). On Bucer's influence see also August Lang, *Puritanismus und Pietismus* (Neukirchen, 1941), and Patrick Collinson, 'The Reformer and the Archbishop: Martin Bucer and An English Bucerian,' *Godly People* (London, 1983), ch. 2. Collinson notes (p. 29) that a copy of the *Scripta Anglicana* was owned successively by John Field and Thomas Coleman, but his focus is on episcopal Bucerians.

[11] E. G. Rupp, *Studies in the Making of the English Protestant Tradition* (Cambridge, 1949), p. 196. The more complete argument, however, is H. C. Porter's in *Reformation and Reaction in Tudor Cambridge* (Cambridge, 1958).

[12] Porter, pp. 41–4, 80; Joan Simon, *Education and Society in Tudor England* (Cambridge, 1966), p. 87; cf. Hugh Latimer, *Sermons*, ed. G. E. Corrie (Cambridge, 1844), vol. 1, pp. 67, 334–5, and 46 (directly identifying himself with Erasmus) and Erasmus' *An Exhortation to the diligent studye of scripture* (n.p., 1529), p. 12.

[13] Rupp, pp. 17–19, 23, 31–2.

[14] McConica, 'Humanism and Aristotelianism,' and *English Humanists and Reformation Politics under Henry VIII and Edward VI* (Oxford, 1965), pp. 280–1. G. R. Elton, *Reform and Renewal: Thomas Cromwell and the Common Weal* (Cambridge, 1973), opposes McConica's view of the near-ubiquity of Erasmianism in the early protestant Reformation, but see also J. P. Cooper's review of Elton's book in *EHR*, 92 (1977), 373–7.

is unfortunately beyond the scope of this study; however, it is clear from extant manuscript notebooks that the Reformers continued to exercise great influence on subsequent generations of university students, and that they provided one avenue by which the appeal of the humanist reform ethic was passed on to later protestants. Peter Martyr, for example, was read by arts as well as divinity students at both universities through the mid-seventeenth century. The notebooks of such puritans as Arthur Hildersham, John Rogers, the Carnsew brothers, Alexander Cooke and Oliver St John reveal, furthermore, that his works were read not only for their insights into the Scriptures, but also for their humanistic commentary on Aristotle.[15] Zwingli's and Bullinger's treatises on education and family government, based explicitly on classical, biblical and humanist precepts, were translated into English and read both by students and by lay people.[16] The role of Bucer's *De Regno Christi* in disseminating humanist social theory has already been mentioned, and the ideas thereby transmitted will be analyzed in later chapters; however, it should also be noted that his biblical commentaries, based on Erasmian exegetical principles and aimed at inculcating practical piety rather than scholastic subtlety, were also read by both arts and divinity students through the early Stuart period.[17] It would be an exercise in tedium to list all of the notebook citations of Calvin, Beza, Bullinger, Musculus, Oecolampadius, Jewel, Humphrey and Rainolds; suffice it to say that they are legion.[18]

---

[15] PRO, SP 46/15; BL, Harl. 3230, fol. 17v; Bodl., Rawl. D. 273, pp. 250–1; BL, Harl, 5247, fols. 53v, 103, 104; BL, Add. MS 25,285, *passim; cf.* CUL, Add. MS 6867. For the seventeenth century, see CUL, MS Dd. 12.57 (Thomas Brathwaite), fol. 38; Pembroke, Cambridge, MS LC II.16 (n.p.); CUL, MS Gg. 1.29 Emmanuel, 1583–1628), p. 51 (also citing Bucer and Musculus). Peter Martyr's works were also among those given to St John's College in 1623 (St John's, Cambridge, MS U.5).

[16] Ulrich Zwingli, *Of the Upbringing and Education of Youth in Good Manners and Christian Discipline* (1523), in *Library of Christian Classics* tr. G. W. Bromiley (Philadelphia, 1942) vol. 24; Heinrich Bullinger, *The Christen state of matrymonye,* tr. Miles Coverdale (London, 1541). The impact of these will be discussed further in chapter 4, below.

[17] For example, BL, Harl. 3230, fols. 19, 52v; CUL, MS Gg. 1.29, pp. 51, 103; CUL, MS Dd. 3.85(5), a sermon of Overall's at Emmanuel in 1600, quotes Peter Martyr, Beza, Oecolampadius and Musculus as well as Bucer on the interpretation of Scripture (n.p.). The Cambridge bookbinder Bennet Waulker's 1588 inventory included works of Bucer and other Reformers: G. W. Gray and W. M. Palmer, *Abstracts from the Wills and Testamentary Documents of Printers, Binders, and Stationers of Cambridge, from 1504 to 1699* (London, 1915), p. 72.

[18] It is important to note, however, that the influence of these first and second generation protestants continued to make itself felt in the Stuart universities: see Balliol, MS 438; Pembroke, Cambridge, MS LC II.16; and St John's, Cambridge, MS S.20, pp. 14–15, 52, 132, and 409. The latter is a puritan notebook which also

Of more significance than numbers of citations are the reasons for which the Reformers' works were read, and the contexts in which citations of them are found. Of course, they were being read primarily for their theology and biblical commentary, not for their social theory, but their biblical scholarship was the product of the New Learning, and as such it was concerned both with exegetical sophistication and with the application of learning to behavior. As a result, the Reformers' names are frequently found among those of Christian humanists and ancients in student notes on social questions and on techniques of biblical interpretation. John Stone, an Elizabethan puritan student at Christ Church, Oxford, for example, kept a theological commonplace book which combined the authority of Italian and northern humanists, ancient authors, and protestants (Peter Martyr, Oecolampadius, Jewel and Rainolds in particular). The issues discussed in the notebook are very frequently just the sort of practical problems with which Stone's humanist authorities (Erasmus, Petrarch and Ascham) were most concerned – the education of children in piety, for example, and the necessity to advance learning throughout society in order to achieve reform. His notes on a 1580 sermon of Humphrey's indicate the approval given by his protestant mentors to humanist authority: Humphrey argued for the expansion of educational opportunity by quoting Erasmus' colloquy *Abbatis et eruditae*.[19] The notebook of the puritan Alexander Cooke of University College, Oxford, is very similar both in concerns and in authors quoted: Petrarch, Sir Thomas More and Erasmus figure among the humanists; Seneca, Cicero, Juvenal and Lucian among the ancients; and Rainolds, Peter Martyr and Thomas Becon among the protestants. From these, Cooke derived such typically humanist sentiments as 'ignorance makes men strangers from the life of God.' The conclusion of his discussion of fasting, in which Erasmus is frequently quoted, identifies the anti-humanist Bellarmine as 'the wrangling Sophister' in the tradition of the despised Schoolmen.[20] Humanist methods of textual analysis – a major aspect

quotes Erasmus' *Paraphrases* and Cicero, Seneca, Pythagoras and Plato on the godly life: e.g., pp. 52, 54. CUL, Add. MS 6314 contains an encomium of Calvin in the midst of commentary on a text of Demosthenes; see also Sidney Sussex College, Cambridge, Ward MSS A–C, F, G, and I. The Ward manuscripts are classified and described in my 'Samuel Ward Papers at Sidney Sussex College, Cambridge,' *Transactions of the Cambridge Bibliographical Society*, 8 (1985), 582–92.
[19] Bodl., Rawl. D.273, pp. 31, 51, 78, 111, 149, 152, 180, 208, 232, 276, 342–345. He quoted Erasmus on pp. 118–135, 343; Petrarch on p. 345; Ascham on pp. 185, 264, and 276. Humphrey's sermon is on pp. 265–6. *cf. Coll.*, p. 221.
[20] BL, Harl. 5247, fols. 109, 76v–80; *cf.* fols. 2–3, 37, 46v–51, 53v, 103, 104, 136v–137v.

of the appeal of Erasmianism to early protestants – are likewise evident in Stone's notebook and in that of his puritan colleague at Christ Church, Anthony Parker. Both students were admirers of Rainolds' approach to Scripture, which was in turn that of Vives. As, in Parker's words, Christ 'freed the law from the false interpretations and glosses of the scribes and Pharisees,' so Erasmus, Vives and their protestant progeny freed the Bible from the Thomists and Scotists.[21]

Herein lay the core of the humanist reformation of Oxford and Cambridge, and the point of greatest affinity between Erasmians and protestants. The Bible, among other ancient texts, had been abused and its meaning obscured by late medieval scholastic commentary and glosses. But after the humanist reforms, academicians would no longer be satisfied with snippets of Aristotle or the New Testament in Latin interspersed in voluminous, esoteric commentary. Commentary was not thought to be unnecessary or irrelevant; however, it was to be subordinated to the text itself. Now all classical literature, from Aristotle to the Scriptures and the Church Fathers, was to be restored to its proper glory and clarity by applying humanist principles of interpretation: the text must be read contextually, in its original language, with an understanding of its historical and literary milieu, and with an eye toward practical application. In urging these principles, university educators showed unflagging zeal in carrying what was in essence a humanist banner throughout the Elizabethan and, as will be seen, the early Stuart period. Moreover, they and their students were well aware of the techniques which they were using and of the goals which they wished to achieve.

Looking first at the Elizabethan period, it is difficult to avoid the conclusion that the reading of ancient texts in their original languages formed the basis both of the arts course and of theological studies. The latter were, of course, to be based primarily upon the Greek and Hebrew Scriptures, and only secondarily on past theologians. Lawrence Chaderton's lectures at Emmanuel exemplify the use of such humanist techniques (including use of Greek, Hebrew and Arabic texts of the Psalms) and the goal of practical application. Similarly, Anthony Parker rejected all commentators in

[21] BL, Harl. 4048, pp. 37–93, and especially pp. 83, 88; *cf.* Rainolds' annotated working copy of Aristotle's *De arte dicendi libri tres* (Paris, 1562), Bodl., Auct. S.2.29, and his MS lectures, Queen's, Oxford, MS 354, fol. 5; McConica, 'Humanism and Aristotelianism,' pp. 303–9. Kearney asserts that Parker had 'no interest in classical literature' (p. 44); if so, it was not due to the curriculum at Christ Church. But it does not seem unlikely that Parker divided his notes on theology from his classical commonplace book, and that the latter may have been lost: note Simonds D'Ewes' division of his notebooks by authors as well as topics (below, pp. 88–9).

his theological notebook, relying solely on Scripture.[22] As for the arts course, the medieval structure of trivium (grammar, rhetoric and dialectic), quadrivium (arithmetic, geometry, astronomy and music), and the three philosophies (moral, natural and metaphysical) was maintained by the statutes, as were medieval pedagogical methods (lecture, disputation and declamation). But the way in which such integral parts of the medieval curriculum as the Aristotelian texts were presented to undergraduates had changed drastically. The reformed statutes themselves embody some of the changes, for they were written by men who saw the inculcation of virtue, rather than of logical subtlety, as the proper end of education.[23] Thus, students at Elizabethan Oxford were to hear two terms of grammar lectures on the humanist Linacre's *Rudiments*, with extensive readings from such ancient moralists as Cicero, Horace and Virgil. Aristotle or Cicero were to be read in connection with four terms of rhetoric, and Aristotle or Porphyry were to be the sources for five terms of dialectic.[24] The Elizabethan statutes for Cambridge established first year lectures on rhetoric from texts of Quintilian, Hermogenes or Cicero; second and third year studies devoted to Aristotelian dialectic and Cicero's *Topics*; and fourth year philosophy lectures treating Aristotle's *Ethics* or *Politics*, Pliny or Plato. A lecturer in Greek, to read Homer, Isocrates, Demosthenes and Euripides, among others, was also to broaden the older course of study.[25]

But the crucial step forward was in how these classical texts were to be taught. The statutes for both universities emphasized the necessity of Greek (Hebrew and Arabic would be added in the next century). Thus, Aristotelian texts, beloved but (from a Renaissance perspective) abused by the Schoolmen, were now read in Greek, in their entirety, and in connection with other Greek literature and history. The presbyterian Thomas Cartwright, in a letter to Hildersham on the study of divinity, emphasized not only knowledge of languages, but also the humanist requirement of knowing 'the

---

[22] Pembroke, Cambridge, MS LC II.164; fols. 78–148v; fols. 26–26v and 36v apply biblical injunctions to marriage and to visitation of the sick and disabled. In Parker's notebook (BL, Harl. 4048), see pp. 37–93 *et passim*.

[23] J. B. Mullinger, *The University of Cambridge from the Earliest Times to the Decline of the Platonist Movement* (Cambridge, 1873–1911), vol. 2, pp. 109–12; C. E. Mallet, *A History of the University of Oxford* (1924–7), vol. 2, pp. 83–6; Curtis, pp. 70–92.

[24] *Statuta Antiqua Universitatis Oxoniensis*, ed. Strickland Gibson (Oxford, 1931), p. 320. Contrast the medieval grammar course based on Priscian and Donatus, with their dialectical glosses.

[25] George Dyer, *The Privileges of the University of Cambridge* (1824), vol. 1, pp. 161–5.

stories of the times wherein the writers lived.'[26] Elizabethan logic notebooks like those of Richard Morton of Queens', Cambridge, Robert Batti of Brasenose and University College, and John Day of Oriel all rely on the complete Greek text of Aristotle.[27]

The notebooks reveal, moreover, the Erasmian aims of dialectic teaching. The most frequently used dialectic handbooks of the sixteenth and seventeenth centuries were humanist productions – Agricola's *De inventione dialectica* (1515), Melanchthon's *Dialectices* (1527), Seton's *Dialectica* (1572 edition) and Ramus' *Dialecticae institutiones* (1543). All of these challenged medieval pedagogy and insisted that dialectic instruction ought to be concerned with practical ways to communicate knowledge to others. Agricola's work, which was required by the Cambridge statutes of 1535, was modeled on Cicero and Quintilian, de-emphasizing the use of syllogistic logic and focusing rather on the selection and classification of material on given subjects to be used in discussion (hence the importance of the commonplace book in early modern education). Melanchthon, Seton and Ramus all identified their works explicitly with that of Agricola, while espousing a purified Aristotle. The development of late sixteenth-century dialectics is thus accurately interpreted as 'a direct response to a humanist view of learning . . . the art of reasonable discourse,' and the core of a continuing program of reading classical literature.[28]

The statutes provided only a bare outline for student reading; tutors were expected to assign considerable additional readings from the *literae humaniores*. The bulk of the actual curriculum, then, went beyond the statutory requirements, and its content, methods and goals can only be determined from student notebooks and tutorial directives.[29] These sources reveal that for the period under consideration, in tutorial as in statutory studies, both humanist and classical authors were consistently read and regarded as authoritative – and they were authoritative no less on social and theological

---

[26] *Cartwrightiana*, ed. Albert Peel and L. H. Carson (London, 1951), p. 113.

[27] Queens', Cambridge, MS Horne 43 (*ca.* 1600); Bodl., Rawl. D.985 (1581–4); Bodl., Rawl. D.274, fols. 3–125.

[28] Lisa Jardine, 'The Place of Dialectic Teaching in Sixteenth Century Cambridge,' *Studies in the Renaissance*, 21 (1974), 50–62. The notion that Aristotelian logic is inherently a scholastic enterprise (e.g., Costello, p. 8) is absurd: Erasmus himself had approved the study of logic, stipulating that one should 'learn his dialectic from Aristotle and not from that prolix breed, the sophists.' See his *De ratione studii ac legendi interpretandique auctores,* (*CWE* 24), tr. Brian McGregor, ed. Craig R. Thompson (Toronto, 1978), p. 670.

[29] The importance of tutorial as opposed to statutory education has been very properly emphasized by both Curtis and Kearney.

questions than on matters of style and interpretation. It will be seen
that students read the classics as Christian humanists: that is, not
merely for the rhetorical or grammatical principles they might convey, not even solely for their linguistic purity, but for instruction in
virtuous and godly living, for answers to practical ethical questions,
and for political precepts and directions on civic involvement. They
collected commonplaces, as Erasmus had urged in his *De duplici copia
verborum ac rerum commentarii duo*,[30] not merely as an academic exercise, but as a means of filing away the wisdom of the ages (under useful, frequently very mundane headings) for future reference in
debate or as handy guidelines for action. This is not to say that it was
the avowed intent of every tutor to preach an Erasmian message to
his students; some tutors were surely more interested in pure Latin
style than in Ciceronian political theory, and others doubtless
assigned classical texts simply because those texts had become a
traditional part of the curriculum by their day. However it is clear
that there was a tradition of classical studies at both universities, and
that the net effect of the sources themselves and the humanistic
methods prescribed to study them was the exposure of generations
of English students to Erasmian ideas.

Virtually all of the extant Elizabethan notebooks quote ancient
authors, so that it would be an exercise in futility to attempt an
exhaustive list of the references. Among the most popular were
Cicero (notably the *De Officiis*), Seneca, Isocrates, Xenophon, Plato,
Aristotle, Pythagoras, Plutarch, Euripides and Sophocles. The pro-
priety of making pagan authors so central to the curriculum and
therefore such important sources for the preachers produced by the
universities was occasionally questioned, but the answer given by
puritans as well as conformists was the humanist one. The
Cambridge Vice-Chancellor's Court registers for 1596, for instance,
record the agreement of puritan as well as conformist heads of
colleges on the utility of classical pagan writers to modern
preachers: when John Rudd of Christ's suggested in a sermon at
Great St Mary's that the works of pagan authors might not be
appropriate sources for reforming preachers to use, he was ordered
by the court to affirm that the works of Plato, Aristotle, Plutarch,
Seneca, and the 'poeta' could be 'used to good and profitable ends
for the belief of the auditory.'[31]

It is worthwhile to analyze how these authors were being used and

[30] Translated by Betty I. Knott in *CWE* 24 (Toronto, 1978).
[31] CUL, MS CUR 6.1, fols. 25–7.

made useful and on what issues they were regarded as authoritative. Of particular interest to this study, of course, is the use of ancient authors as sources for social theory, and in fact all of the 'favorites' were important authorities for the social ideas which would come to characterize puritan sermons. John Stone's notebook is typical, for instance, in relying on Isocrates and Cicero for a discussion of the education of children. Hildersham's notebook quotes Plutarch on the same issue, as does Lucas Challoner's, kept in the far-off Elizabethan foundation of Trinity College, Dublin.[32] It is interesting to note that Hildersham's notebook also shows a broad interest in pagan theology as relevant and instructive to Christians, and so great was his admiration for Cicero that he could not bring himself to argue with Erasmus' inclination 'to think that Cicero was saved.'[33] Robert Batti praised Cicero's elegance of language, but in good Erasmian fashion commended him more for his concern with the realities of daily living in the political world.[34] John English of St John's, Oxford, quoted extensively from Greek and Roman Stoics in his discussions of such varied topics as frugality, the veneration of age and the usefulness of education to governors. His conclusion on the last topic is a civic humanist's apology for education: 'Learning is necessarily requisite to state government; for the experience of one man's life cannot produce examples or precedents enough for the events of one man's life.'[35] A student at King's likewise depended heavily in his 1597 notebook on Seneca's *Epistles* and *De Clementia* and Cicero's *Republic* for insight into social and political regulation: from Cicero he derived a humanist definition of political leadership as care of and service to the commonwealth, and from the Stoics, Pliny, Quintilian, Xenophon and Pythagoras he took advice on everything from the discipline of children to the control of such social evils as blasphemy and poverty.[36] The problem of how to prevent and relieve poverty was obviously an important one to Elizabethan students, and their veneration for the opinions of Cicero and Seneca on this subject is reflected not only in their commonplace books, but also in the poor laws which they would eventually see through Parliament.[37]

[32] Bodl., Rawl. D.273, p. 149; BL, Harl. 3230, fol. 48v; TCD MS 357 (1595–*ca.* 1612), fols. 85v, 139.
[33] BL, Harl. 3230, *passim*, and esp. fol. 114, citing Erasmus in the margin.
[34] Bodl., Rawl. D.985, fols. 69–79.   [35] Bodl., Rawl. D.1423.
[36] Bodl., Rawl. D.318(6), fols. 1, 4, 6, 14, 17, 25, 28, 36, 39–40. Kearney identifies this student as a typical Ramist.
[37] St John's, Cambridge, MS S.31, fol. 43 (Christ Church, *ca.* 1600); BL, Add. MS 25,285 (Oliver St John); see chapter 5 below.

Elizabethan students were well aware of the way they were using the classics. They stood squarely in the tradition of Erasmus; accordingly, their opposition to the Schoolmen was scarcely less vehement than that of their humanist predecessors. Gabriel Harvey of Pembroke Hall, Cambridge, rejoiced that 'scholars in our age are rather now Aristippus than Diogenes: and rather active than contemplative philosophers'; he dated the happy transformation from when Duns Scotus and St Thomas 'with the whole rabblement of schoolmen were abandoned our schools and expelled the University.' He was exultant that Aristotle's *Organon* was as little read as Duns Scotus' works, while his *Oeconomica* and *Policraticus*, of which humanist social theorists thoroughly approved, 'every one hath by rote.'[38] Robert Batti's notebook contains a diatribe against Duns Scotus, St Thomas, and such latter-day 'barbaros' as the Neo-scholastic Joseph Scaliger. He concluded that true wisdom is quite a different thing from what passes for philosophy, and that Aristotle, even correctly interpreted, conveys only a small portion of the truth.[39] John Day's notebook, which pits the ancients (especially Cicero, Quintilian, Plutarch and a purified Aristotle) against Aquinas and such modern scholastics as Zabarella, gives similar warnings against being 'taken in by philosophy': the only true philosophy is 'sound knowledge attained by natural . . . reason.'[40] A late sixteenth-century Emmanuel student, enamored of ancient authors and clearly familiar with both medieval and contemporary scholastics, likewise condemned the subtle distinctions of the Thomists and declared his preference for the methods of the 'new writers', especially the 'reformed': Luther, Melanchthon, Zwingli, Musculus, Oecolampadius, Calvin, Bucer, and – Erasmus![41]

Student use of classical literature was thus conditioned by humanist assumptions regarding the methodology and purpose of a literary education. And it should not be assumed that these humanist assumptions were mediated to students solely by their tutors and lecturers. The notebooks demonstrate that the influence was much more direct: it is unusual to find a notebook in which Erasmus is not cited, and references to Vives, More, Petrarch, Agricola and other humanists are far from rare. The authority attributed to Erasmus, More and Petrarch by John Stone and

[38] *The Letter-Book of Gabriel Harvey, 1573–1580*, ed. E. J. L. Scott (London, 1884), pp. 78–9.
[39] Bodl., Rawl. D.985, fols. 9, 66v–67v.   [40] Bodl., Rawl. D.274, fol. 126 *et passim.*
[41] CUL, MS Gg. 1.29 (1583–1628), fols. 17–17v. This student incidentally regarded Erasmus' Greek and Latin *Proverbs* as a useful source for correctly understanding angels (fol. 44).

Alexander Cooke has already been documented; in addition, John English, Gabriel Harvey and John Walker all quoted Erasmus; Walker further cited the opinions of the humanists Johannes Sturm, Conrad Pellican and Rudolph Agricola; Harvey cited Ascham, Sturm and Castiglione; and John Day of Oriel deferred to Beatus Rhenanus on the position of women in a godly social order.[42] Even in a pre-dominantly theological notebook like that of Arthur Hildersham, deference to Erasmus is evident on a variety of issues, exegetical, theological and social.[43] The correspondence of university dons bears out the same theme: when John Rainolds of Corpus Christi, Oxford, wrote to Dr Thornton concerning the inappropriateness of women players on the stage, he cited Vives' treatise on Christian womanhood.[44] Perhaps the most remarkable indicators of the Erasmianism of Elizabethan curriculum, however, are some statistics derived from the extant book inventories of members of Oxford and Cambridge colleges in the respective University Archives: of the eighty-one Oxford lists dating from 1558 to 1603, sixty-eight (eighty-four percent) contain at least one work of Erasmus.[45] Of the eighty-five surviving Cambridge inventories from the same period, fifty-six (sixty-six percent) contain at least one Erasmus work. Erasmus appears in the Cambridge lists more often than any other single author; the next most frequently cited is Cicero, whose works appear in forty-eight lists. By contrast, works of St Thomas appear in only eight lists, and Ramus appears in only fourteen of the lists.[46]

In the light of these data, it is impossible to conclude that Elizabethan Oxbridge saw the replacement of humanism with Ramism. But it is a curious understanding of Ramism which would demand such an interpretation in any case. Pierre de la Ramée, or Petrus Ramus (1515–72), was hardly (as Kearney implies) an opponent

[42] Bodl., Rawl. D.1423 (John English), fol. 41; *Letter-Book of Gabriel Harvey*, pp. 66, 134, 167; CUL, Add. MS 6867, fol. 17 *et passim*; Bodl., Rawl. D.274 (John Day), fol. 234.   [43] BL, Harl. 3230, e.g., fols. 11, 24, 114.

[44] Bodl., MS Tanner 77, fol. 43v (1592). He also cited Plutarch and Xenophon in the letter.

[45] Booklists from Wills and Inventories in Chancellor's Court Registers, Oxford University Archives. Nine of these contain between five and thirteen Erasmus titles; forty-one contain two or more different works. Eight include works of Vives, four of More.

[46] Cambridge University Archives, Booklists from Wills and Inventories in Vice-Chancellor's Court Registers. I am grateful to Elizabeth Leedham-Green for invaluable assistance in locating, deciphering and evaluating the Cambridge inventories; her forthcoming edition of them will be an enormous boon to scholars of early modern university curricula. Lucas Challoner's booklist at Trinity College, Dublin, also includes nearly all of the published works of Erasmus, in addition to those of predominantly Calvinist theologians and of the ancients. Very few Neo-scholastic works are listed: TCD, MS 357, fols. 2–15v.

of ancient literature or humanist exegesis. He was in fact a
thoroughgoing humanist, in his opposition to the Aristotle of the
Sorbonne, in his drive to apply dialectical principles to practical
problems, in his dislike of superfluous commentary and glosses on
classical texts, and in his de-emphasis of metaphysics.[47] Ramist logic,
like that of Vives, Agricola, and Ramus' mentor at Paris (1529–37)
Johannes Sturm, was both humanist and empiricist; in fact, the
Ramist concept of the essential unity of rhetoric and logic has been
described as the link between the literary humanism of the fifteenth
and sixteenth centuries and the scientific empiricism of the seventeenth and eighteenth. Ramus' Aristotle, like Vives', was not that of
the medieval sophists, but the 'true' or 'purified' Aristotle understood
from a careful and complete reading of the original sources in
Greek. His attitude toward Aristotle was ambivalent: having undermined the absoluteness of the philosopher's authority as a scholastic
invention, Ramus none the less joined other humanists in citing
Aristotle's authority whenever he agreed with him. He charged the
Sorbonnists with ignorantly condemning him for following the true
Aristotle, rather than for refuting him.[48]

Ramus' Socrates was that of Xenophon, rather than of Plato,
which at least partly explains his very humanistic emphasis on the
practical. The ancients are there to be used, said Ramus, not to be
worshipped; the liberal arts should therefore be reformed to render
them practical. The sophistical subtleties of Paris should give way to

[47] cf. Kearney, pp. 46–70. Note that whereas such puritan Ramists as William
Perkins are used by Kearney (p. 53) to illustrate Ramus' anti-Aristotelian bias,
Perkins, like the puritan Ramist William Gouge of King's, actually drew freely and
approvingly from Aristotle for his social theory (see, for example, the Aristotelian
derivation of their concepts of the nature of the family and of parental duties in the
following chapter). cf. Curtis, p. 118. Curtis' overall assessment of Ramus is much
more accurate:

In a very real sense Ramus was a humanist reconstructing logic in line with the insights
humanistic linguistical studies had brought to the learned world of his time. He stands in a line
of intellectual descent collateral to that which for England runs from Valla through Colet to
Erasmus and then to English humanists of the second and third generations of the
sixteenth century (p. 254).

[48] R. Hooykaas, Humanisme, science et réforme: Pierre de la Ramée (Leiden, 1958), pp. 1, 5–
16, 27–9. Ramus criticized the University of Paris for forbidding the reading and
discussion of 'impious' passages of philosophy, even that of Aristotle. He
espoused the necessity of reading texts in their entirety and gleaning what is true
and useful from them (Hooykaas, p. 8). Richard Bauckham puts William Fulke of
St John's, Cambridge, in the same category as Ramus: he was 'characterized by . . .
attempts to return to a purer Aristotelianism than was to be found in the scholastic
commentaries' and was not slavishly bound to Aristotle. Fulke's works of natural
philosophy, according to Bauckham, 'sprang naturally out of his broad humanist
interests.' Richard Bauckham, 'The Career and Thought of Dr. William Fulke,'
(unpublished Ph.D. thesis, University of Cambridge, 1972), pp. 8, 28.

the simple explanation of principles and their practical application.[49] Theology should likewise be studied in good Christian
humanist fashion as '*doctrina bene vivendi. . . Finis doctrinae non est notitia
rerum ipsi subjectarum, sed usus et exercitatio.*'[50]

Such humanist sentiments were as characteristic of Ramists as of
Ramus. A classic example is provided by John Rainolds, the puritan
reader in Greek at Corpus Christi College, Oxford from 1572 to
1578, who has been portrayed as the leading Ramist of Elizabethan
Oxford. While Rainolds was actually far from indiscriminate in his
praise of Ramus, he did defend the Frenchman by correctly pointing
out that he had attacked not Aristotle, but the Sorbonne's Aristotle;
Ramus' position was comparable to the earlier criticism of the
Ciceronians by Erasmus and Budé. Rainolds himself was best known
for his lectures on the Greek text of Aristotle's *Rhetoric*, in which he,
like Ramus and other humanists, expounded the 'true Aristotle.'
McConica has demonstrated clearly that 'Vives, not Ramus, was his
true master in the teaching of Aristotle.'[51] The two commentators
who dominated his lectures were Vives and Cicero: he echoed Vives'
opinion that the finest Greek is that of Aristotle and Isocrates, and
he followed his explanation of the practical benefits of rhetoric in
the attainment of the good life.[52] Ramus, of course, also espoused
explicitly Vivesian views on the study of classical literature. But it is
significant that Rainolds spoke from a direct knowledge of the
Spanish humanist's writings, and not from a Ramist mediation.
Rainolds, like Ramus, was a thoroughgoing humanist.

But one need not be a Ramist to be a humanist in Elizabethan
Oxbridge. John Case, whose treatises and commentary on Aristotle
served as the 'unofficial textbooks of the Elizabethan faculty of
Arts,' was both a humanist critic of sophistical subtlety and an
explicitly anti-Ramist Aristotelian.[53] Case's combination of

---

[49] Hooykaas, pp. 2, 23–5, 59–61, 105. Later puritan reliance on Xenophon as a
source for social theory is noteworthy. *cf.* Vives' *De tradendis disciplinis*, in *Opera*
(Basel, 1555), vol. 1, p. 439; W. S. Howell, *Logic and Rhetoric in England, 1500–1700*
(Princeton, 1956), chapter 4. That such goals were communicated not only to
students, but also to the ordinary auditors of sermons by university-trained
divines, is implied by the charge of one Aristotelian that 'because of Ramus, every
cobbler can cog a syllogism, every carter crack of propositions. Hereby is logic
prophaned,' in A. Fraunce, *The Lawiers Logicke* (1588), quoted in Hill, *Intellectual
Origins*, p. 32. One is reminded of Erasmus' desire for a knowledge of the Scriptures
to descend to weavers and plowmen – *Paraclesis*, p. 97, in *Christian Humanism and the
Reformation*, ed. John C. Olin (Gloucester, Mass., 1973).

[50] Ramus, *Commentariorum de religione Christiana* (Frankfurt, 1576), p. 6. *cf.* Bucer's
definition of the end of a theological education: to learn '*bene beateque vivere*' (*De
Regno Christi*, p. 166).   [51] McConica, 'Humanism and Aristotelianism,' p. 309.

[52] *Ibid.*, pp. 305–6.   [53] *Ibid.*, pp. 299–302.

Aristotelianism and the humanist traditions of Elizabethan Oxford, the subject of a recent study by Charles Schmitt, provides perhaps the best illustration of the need to modify old historiographical categories to take into account the eclecticism of Renaissance thinkers. Case's Aristotelianism was such that he is often labelled 'scholastic.' Yet in analyzing his intellectual milieu, Schmitt notes the importance of peripatetic works in the thought of humanists from Bruni on and portrays Erasmus accurately as an enemy not of Aristotle, but of the 'subtle Scotist metaphysics' and modernist logic of the late Middle Ages. Case's Aristotelianism he locates in line with this humanist criticism, vigorously opposed to those aspects of late medieval scholasticism that had in any case largely disappeared from the curriculum by the mid-sixteenth century.[54] Elizabethan education, he says, 'represents humanism run rampant,' and one of the products of its philological renaissance was 'an eclectic brand of Aristotelianism.'[55] The 'reinvigorated logic' of Case's generation was closer to the reformed humanistic dialectic of Agricola and Melanchthon than to the terminist logic of the later Middle Ages; not only was it based on a 'purified' Aristotle, but its emphasis was on the logic of moral discourse rooted in rhetoric.[56] And it is clear from Schmitt's work that Case used and taught his understanding of Aristotle as a humanist, that is, as an illuminator of contemporary events, politics, society and morality. He retained the scholastic organizational unit, the *quaestio*, but frequently related discussions to current problems. Like other humanists of his generation, Case had come to accept the value of Aristotelian logic, but had translated it into humanistic terms, with the focus on practical application of classical principles.[57] Schmitt concludes that there were many tendencies within the peripatetic tradition in the sixteenth century,

---

[54] Charles B. Schmitt, *John Case and Aristotelianism in the Renaissance* (Montreal, 1983), pp. 5, 15, 17–19, 33. He notes that Costello and Kearney seem to have forgotten that post-Reformation 'scholasticism' in England was radically different from that of the earlier period, and nothing like continental protestant scholasticism emerged in England until the end of the sixteenth century (p. 20). A caustic criticism of Scotus, Schmitt notes (p. 153), characterized all of Case's work.

[55] Schmitt, p. 20, n. 24 and p. 28.   [56] Schmitt, pp. 38, 141.

[57] Schmitt, p. 147. On the mundane issues addressed in disputations set by Case and his colleagues, see pp. 135–6, 142, 144–5, 180. Schmitt himself is equivocal about Case's humanism: at one point he emphatically denies that Case should be seen as a 'humanistic interpreter of Aristotle' but immediately qualifies this with an acknowledgement of Case's 'awareness of humanistic critical method' (p. 178). And much of his work deals with Case's rhetorical intent and practical focus – both hallmarks of the humanist approach to any classical text. McConica's more straightforward admission of Case as humanist does not seem seriously threatened by anything in Schmitt's study.

ranging from slavish dependency on medieval interpretations of a limited range of Latin texts to a philologically sophisticated and highly selective use of that in Aristotle which could be construed as useful in the contemporary situation.[58] The stereotypic 'scholastic' does not fit the latter end of the spectrum, which produced Aristotelianisms opposed to many of Ramus' conclusions but none the less recognizably both Aristotelian and humanistic.

The example of Case illustrates not only that one need not be a Ramist to be a humanistic Aristotelian in Elizabethan Oxbridge, but also that Ramism may not have held as prominent a position in the Elizabethan universities as has been assumed. Case's reputation alone would have guaranteed that Ramus was taken with a grain of salt by Oxford students of his day; indeed, student notebooks reveal that many who cited Ramus' opinions were not in wholehearted agreement with them. Robert Batti, having castigated the Schoolmen, questioned whether the interpretation of Aristotle offered by Ramus had any more valid claim to being seen as eternal truth. Of course, even Rainolds himself vigorously condemned Ramus' immoderate criticism of Aristotle.[59] Moreover, while humanist and ancient authors are ubiquitous in Elizabethan notebooks, citations of Ramus' works are frequently absent – even from notebooks which have been identified as characteristically Ramist.[60] Where Ramus is found in the notebooks, his works are cited among those of Christian humanists and the humanists' favorite classical authors. Hildersham outlined Ramus' dialectic, but quoted Erasmus just as often on theological questions; and Batti was much more a Ciceronian than a Ramist. Accordingly, Cambridge bookbinders like John Denys stocked many of Ramus' works, but many more of Cicero, Seneca, Isocrates, Plutarch and Aristotle; Denys' 1578 inventory also includes nine different Erasmus titles, More's *Utopia*, and the works of Valla and Vives.[61] Ramus certainly functioned to some extent as a conduit for Christian humanism in the universities, but the fact is that he found his way into a prominent place in relatively few Elizabethan notebooks. If number, length, and weight attached to citations are to be the criteria, the direct authority of Erasmus and Vives, Cicero and Seneca, and Aristotle far outweighed that of Ramus in the sixteenth century. If anything, his popularity may have been somewhat

[58] Schmitt, pp. 218–19. [59] Bodl., MS Rawl. 9.85, fols. 66v–67; McConica, p. 307.
[60] Bodl., MS Rawl. D.318(6), a classical commonplace book by a student at King's, Cambridge, dated 1597; *cf*. Kearney, p. 63.
[61] BL, MS Harl. 3230, fols. 2–4, 11, 24, etc.; Bodl., MS Rawl. D.985, fols. 66v–67, *cf* 14–15v, 69–79; Gray and Palmer, *Abstracts*, pp. 35–60; note also Thomas Thomas' 1588 inventory, pp. 64–71.

greater in the Stuart universities.[62] But by this time, we are told, the universities had become irretrievably enmeshed in the web of Neo-scholasticism, a vastly more pernicious enemy of humanism than even Kearney's version of Ramism.[63] Let us turn now to the curriculum of the seventeenth century and pursue the fate of humanism in this new, more hostile environment.

There is no doubt that after 1600, Oxbridge students were increasingly being exposed to the writings of Jesuit and other Neo-scholastic theologians and dialecticians. References to both contemporary and medieval scholastics abound in early seventeenth-century notebooks. In Cambridge, for instance, Robert Boothe of Trinity was obviously acquainted with Zabarella as well as St Thomas; Alexander Bolde of Pembroke knew Bellarmine, St Thomas and Peter Lombard; and Nicholas Felton of Pembroke cited Vasquez, Cajetan, Molina and Durandus, along with Duns Scotus.[64] The phenomenon was characteristic of distinctively puritan colleges as well: William Sancroft of Emmanuel noted his purchase of works of Suarez in one notebook and in another cited Molina repeatedly on Aristotelian logic, and another Emmanuel student recorded having read Cajetan, the Dominican de Soto, St Thomas and Peter Lombard. As Master of Sidney Sussex Samuel Ward noted his purchase of Medina's and Bellarmine's books (at Blackwell's) and in his theological and logic notebooks frequently cited Bellarmine, Becanus, Molina, Mendoza, Canisius, Bañez, Zabarella, Cajetan, Suarez and other 'Scholastici,' both medieval and contemporary.[65] Oxonians like Thomas Brathwaite of Queen's likewise knew the opinions of Bellarmine, Medina, Zabarella and Albertus Magnus, and the examples could easily be multiplied from anonymous notebooks from both universities.[66]

[62] Sidney, Ward MS A; BL, MSS Harl. 5356 (1605), Harl. 190 (1618), Landsdowne 797 (mid-seventeenth-century); Bodl., MS Sancroft 87 (1630–40), pp. 1–66.
[63] Kearney, pp. 77–90; Costello, passim; Curtis, pp. 1–2, cf. R. R. Bolgar, 'Education and Learning,' in The New Cambridge Modern History (Cambridge, 1968), vol. 3, p. 441.
[64] BL, MS Harl. 5356, e.g., fols. 2–5v; St John's, Cambridge, MS S.34; Pembroke, Cambridge, MS LC. II.5. On the new Thomists, see Quentin Skinner, The Foundations of Modern Political Thought (Cambridge, 1978), vol. 2, pp. 135–73.
[65] Bodl., MSS Tanner 467, fol. 39, and Sancroft 87, pp. 67–91; CUL, MS Gg. 1.29; Ward MSS A, B, C, D, G (fols. 14v–15), I, J, L.3–5, L.15, M.1–4, P, S. See also Holdsworth's instructions for students, Emmanuel College, MS I.2.27(1), published as an appendix to H. F. Fletcher's The Intellectual Development of John Milton (Urbana, 1961), vol. 2, pp. 623–55.
[66] CUL, MS Dd.12.57, fols. 9v–10, 14, 38, 67, 73; Queen's, Oxford, MS 196 (notes on Crackenthorpe's Logic) cites Zabarella, St Thomas and Scotus (fols. 3, 54, 116–17, et passim); BL, MS Harl. 977 (Exeter) cites Bellarmine and 'Scholastics' (e.g., fols. 1, 26, 37v); BL, MS Landsdowne 797 cites Cajetan, Tolletus, and Zabarella, along

Of more significance than the fact that scholastic authors were being read, however, is the issue of why and how they were being used in the curriculum. Scholars have concluded from the reading habits of the students and from the continuation of a medieval pattern of education (dialectical, Aristotelian, and organized around lecture, disputation and declamation) that seventeenth-century Cambridge 'held with, and understood, the scholastics.'[67] 'Understood,' yes, but 'held with?' It has been argued above that a dialectical education can be humanistic, rather than scholastic, and that the Aristotelianism of Ramus, Rainolds, Case and others was rather Vivesian than Thomistic. Why, then, must the reading of Jesuit and Dominican authors and the use of their opinions in declamations and disputations automatically imply agreement with their ideas and techniques? On the contrary, there is considerable evidence that students and their tutors viewed the reading of Neo-scholastics as a necessary evil – and many students even questioned how necessary it was. The revival of Thomism in the sixteenth century was, after all, the response of papist enemies to the protestant doctrines of *sola scriptura* and the priesthood of all believers: it was the philosophical counter to the perceived anti-authoritarianism of the Lutherans. The reason for protestant students to read these authors was their need to know the enemy. 'Read also the Adversaries,' Thomas Cartwright had recommended to Elizabethan divinity students.[68] His hope, and that of his successors, was not that divinity students would internalize scholastic assumptions about theology or logic, but that they would come to understand those assumptions in order to refute them. They were to study scholastic argumentation to equip themselves to participate in debate; but their position in the debate was squarely opposed to that of Bellarmine or Cajetan or Suarez, and their opposition was based both on their protestant convictions and on their humanist intellectual foundations.

Many of the theological notebooks which have been used to demonstrate the scholasticism of seventeenth-century Oxbridge are thus in fact substantially devoted to refutations of scholastic

with the medieval Schoolmen; Overall noted opinions of Suarez and Cajetan, CUL, MS Dd.3.85(5); one Trinity, Cambridge student cited Cajetan (St John's, Cambridge, MS S.18, p. 57), and another (Trin. MS R.16.19) cited Zabarella, Suarez, St Thomas and Albertus Magnus.

[67] Costello, p. 121; *cf.* Kearney, pp. 77–90; Hill, *Intellectual Origins*, pp. 301–14.

[68] *Cartwrightiana*, p. 114. On theological reasons for the revival of Thomism, see Skinner, vol. 2, pp. 138–48. Humanists confronted with the perceived anti-authoritarianism of Lutherans were forced to take sides at the Council of Trent: see Dermot Fenlon, *Heresy and Obedience in Tridentine Italy* (Cambridge, 1972), and chapter 7 below.

theology.[69] These arguments are generally couched in good Thomistic style and cite the sort of evidence not unlikely to convince the popish opponent – the authority of medieval and contemporary scholastic theologians, the Church Fathers, and councils. The object was, after all, to liberate minds enslaved by Romish superstition and error as efficiently as possible. Occasionally the guidelines for discussion were broadened: Thomas Brathwaite of Queen's, for example, added to his conservatively styled argument against Bellarmine's doctrine of the efficacy of the sacraments a demand for greater fidelity to the Greek text and context of Scripture.[70] But even where the grounds for disagreement were not so explicitly humanistic, both the content and the context of such arguments belie the contention that their proponents were wedded to scholasticism. Their positions are protestant, however pragmatically Catholic their logic. Arts and divinity students were well aware that 'most of these books of logic we use were written by popish authors' and must, therefore, be used with great care; their tutors had warned them that only 'when you are of ripe understanding, to read them with some judgment' would the Schoolmen (from Lombard to Cajetan) be useful. But there was no doubt as to their usefulness as illustrations of how to handle theological controversies. The tutor who penned this advice certainly had no intention of converting his students to scholasticism. He was careful to have them also read such 'practical lively English authors' as Perkins, Bolton, Preston, Rogers, Sibbes, Dod and Gataker; furthermore, he regarded as essential parts of the curriculum the writings of Vives, Erasmus and the ancients.[71]

As a matter of fact, the seventeenth-century Oxbridge logic, theology and commonplace books which cite Neo-scholastics never do so apart from citations of Christian humanist and/or classical authors,[72] and this humanistic context must not be disregarded

---

[69] BL, MS Harl. 977, fols. 26, 37v, etc. (with an outline of scholastic definitions and methods on the unfoliated flyleaf); BL, MS Harl. 3230, fols. 10v, 15v, 21, 49, 64, 73v, etc. (fol. 110 is a brief summary of scholastic methodology); Ward, MSS F, I, L.15, M.3 and 4, J, K, S; see also, e.g., St John's, Cambridge, MS S.34 and CUL, MS Dd.12.57, fols. 9v–10, 14, 38, *et passim*.   [70] CUL, MS Dd.12.57, fols. 9v–10 (1642).
[71] A *'Library for Younger Schollers' Compiled by an English Scholar–Priest about 1655*, ed. Alma Dejordy and H. F. Fletcher (Urbana, 1961), pp. 1–2, 49; *cf*. pp. 43–4, 10, 18, 23, 32–3, 66. The editors of this selection from St John's, Cambridge, MS K.38 suggest that the document was written by Thomas Barlow, librarian of the Bodleian from 1642 to 1660.
[72] Notebooks combining Christian humanist and Neo-scholastic sources include BL, MS Lansdowne 797; Bodl., MSS Sancroft 87 and Tanner 462; Sidney Sussex, Ward MS G; St John's, Cambridge, MS S.34; and CUL, MSS Gg. 1.29 and Dd. 12.57. Notebooks combining ancient and Neo-scholastic sources include BL, MSS Harl. 5356 and Add. 25,285; Sidney Sussex, Ward MS F; Queen's, Oxford, MS 196; St John's, Cambridge, MSS S.18 and S.34; and Trin. MS R.16.19.

when gauging the effect of scholasticism on students. It was in part the continuity of humanist influence on the curriculum which conditioned the way students would approach the new Thomists. This is perhaps most apparent in the Erasmian critique which many students leveled at the methods and content of Neo-scholasticism. William Bright of Emmanuel, for instance, criticized 'contentious learning, as that of the school men . . . fantastical, full of imposture.'[73] He expressed very humanistic objections to the proof-texting often required of students, in a poetic introduction to his 1644 notebook:

> Here's many an author torn in many pieces;
> Instead of abstracts, these are ragged fleeces;
> Nothing but linsey-woolsey; ropes of sand:
> In methodical notes. I'd best disband
> This ragged regiment: at least confess
> To every author a debt more or less.

It should come as no surprise that Bright acknowledged his greatest debts to Sir Thomas More, Erasmus, and the usual array of classical authors.[74] Nor was he alone among seventeenth-century Cantabrigians in despising the scholastic aspects of the curriculum. Bacon's description of scholasticism as the 'cobwebs of learning, admirable for the fineness of the thread and work but of no substance or profit,' and Milton's Vivesian criticism of scholasticism, are doubtless too well known to need discussion.[75] Less known, however, is that of Samuel Ward. In a notebook kept during his years as a fellow of Emmanuel, Ward copied a lengthy letter of humanistic advice which said of the Schoolmen,

One had need to beware of these writers that do give their resolutions so like magistrates with a *respondeo dicendum*, as if they were arbitrators; and rather to read them which deliver their opinion with reservation and in matters not decided do not play the pedants over others . . . If you will read the controversies that do at this present time exercise the world, you shall do well to bear in mind that the writers do all of them exceed in affection to their own side, and do accommodate matter to their own taste, and in the ancient writers do see not that which is there, but that which they desire.

---

[73] CUL, Add. MS 6160, p. 142.

[74] *Ibid.*, unfoliated flyleaf; pp. 21, 96, 166 (More); fols. 153v–154v (Erasmus). Bright also indicated admiration for Richard Pace (p. 110), Pico della Mirandola (p. 176), and a host of ancient, mostly Greek authors. (This MS is partly foliated, partly paginated; much of it is blank.)

[75] Francis Bacon, 'The Advancement of Learning,' in *Works*, ed. J. Spedding, R. Ellis and D. Heath, 15 vols (Boston, 1863), vol. 6, p. 122; John Milton, *Of Education* (1644); see also comments by Charles Webster, *The Great Instauration* (New York, 1975), p. 190. Milton is also known for his criticism of humanism; however, it was that branch of the humanist movement which inspired a mere imitation of the ancients in style (an aspect despised by Erasmus himself) which drew his fire.

The author explained Jesuit reliance on St Thomas 'as a writer very easy, and who doth not entangle the mind of the reader with doubts, but resolves him indeed too much.' The letter concludes in the same sardonic manner with 'a general and infallible rule' which goes far toward explaining the function of scholasticism in the seventeenth-century curriculum: 'for all the difficulties that may occur in the process of your studies, I take it to be the best to consult with the Jesuits, to resolve the clean contrary to that which they say.'[76]

When students failed to see the error in the popish authors assigned them, their masters made it very clear that those who 'held with' the enemy had no place in the reformed universities of England. John Pocklington of Pembroke Hall, Cambridge, was permitted in 1616 to 'articulate before divers young gentlemen and young students of Pembroke Hall with great earnestness of words and countenance to argue for pontifical doctrines' – until his master and colleagues noticed that he never drew 'to any contrary conclusion whereby to inform them otherwise.' Then he was charged with error by the heads of colleges assembled in consistory. The court acknowledged that for the pedagogical technique of disputation to work, the arguments of Neo-scholastic theorists of papal supremacy must be understood thoroughly and even expressed clearly, but they made it very clear that the outcome of such a disputation must not be a defense of their views.[77] John Normanton of Caius was similarly hauled before the Vice-Chancellor's court in 1635 for 'commending of Bellarmine his books of controversies and disparaging the protestant writers who have refuted him and charged him with contradictions, whom he compared to mice nibbling at him, but were not able to hurt him.' The court forced his recantation – the pedagogical principle, 'know the enemy,' had clearly backfired in this case.[78] But very few such cases came to the Vice-Chancellor's court; for the most part it seems to have been made very clear to students that they were to read the works of Bellarmine and the rest critically, with an eye to the defense of the true faith.

Criticism of Neo-scholasticism was not limited to Cambridge. Thomas Newnan of Exeter, an avid reader of Isocrates, recorded his reaction when his tutor read Duns Scotus and Keckerman's com-

---

[76] Sidney Sussex, Ward MS I (1608?).
[77] CUL, MS VC Ct I.8 (1616), fols. 255–8, quote from fol. 257v. Pocklington was ordered to recant.
[78] CUL, MS Com Ct I.18, fol. 130.

mentary on Aristotelian logic: 'such divisions, subdivisions, and a crew of terms and words, such as I never knew! Yea, I remained in that amazed plight . . . ashamed to find myself still mute and other little disputants disputing that . . . could by heart, like parrots, in the schools stand prattling, though some . . . were pretty foolish.' Henry Vaughn of Oriel denounced the 'Schoolmaster, or untrusser' who 'though otherwise he hath but little skill in logic, is well read in Aristotle's *Posteriors*, [and whose] rod is the syllogistical trident, which ever concludes in the angry mood of *fecio*, under the figure of human nakedness.' His notes on Aristotelian logic are punctuated by lengthy passages on ancient history and quotes from Seneca, Cato, Demosthenes and Isocrates.[79] Other Oxonians condemned the useless logical subtleties of the new Thomists in terse marginal notes indicating their preference for the 'evident and plain words' of the text rather than the 'scholastic distinction-making' which they associated with the Council of Trent.[80] Some students, however, broadcast their dissatisfaction beyond the privacy of their own notebooks – and suffered the consequences for doing so. A Corpus Christi student named Ganning was kept from his graces in 1631 'for railing in his Clerum against school divinity, whereas King James and King Charles commanded young students here in divinity to begin with Lombard and Thomas.' Ganning was reinstated after moderating his criticism, professing that 'he had no ill meaning against school divinity, but against too much of it in sermons' and claiming that in any case he had never heard of the royal orders. The Cambridge student Thomas Randolph reaped more positive consequences from his 'Catch against the Schoolmen': the volume which included it, *Aristippus or the Jovial Philosopher* (1631) proved immensely popular among seventeenth-century students and so profitable for its author.[81]

Certainly someone was pushing a scholastic curriculum in the seventeenth century, and Ganning's case would tend to support Kearney's contention that it was the court.[82] The exalted status accorded to the authority of Aristotle by the Laudian statutes was certainly an attempt to foster conservative interpretations of

---

[79] Bodl., Top. Oxon. fol. 39 (Newnan, 1624), fols. 19–19v; St John's, Cambridge, MS K.38 (Vaughn, 1634–9), p. 140 *et passim*.
[80] For example, BL, Sloane MS 1981; St John's, Cambridge, MS S.34 (Oxford, 1635–6), pp. 71, 78–81 (my pagination).
[81] PRO, SP 16/193/91 (14 June 1631); Randolph's work was published in London.
[82] Kearney, pp. 78–9.

hierarchy and obedience.[83] Unconvincing, however, are Kearney's
further arguments that scholasticism was revived with any great deal
of success, that it was an effective support for the authority of central government, or that it was intended as a weapon against
puritanism. Neo-scholastics were used in puritan as in non-puritan
colleges for instruction in theological debating techniques, and it is
impossible to identify all of their critics as puritans. Furthermore, if
it was indeed 'in its emphasis on religious and social authority that
the great power of scholasticism lay,'[84] then the absence of a consensus on the locus of religious and social authority and the political
upheaval of Caroline England would certainly indicate that the new
interest in scholasticism was at best a partial, tenuous, ineffective
and short-lived phenomenon.

It would seem, then, that if any aspect of the scholastic revival
demands explanation, it is its abortive nature. And while theological
objections to Thomism presented major barriers to its acceptance in
the universities, these were surely buttressed by the continued pre-
dominance of Christian humanism and its classical sources in the
university curriculum during the period. Early Stuart scholars were
not less avid readers of Erasmus, Vives, More and the ancients than
their predecessors had been; moreover, they evince the same
humanist assumptions about the nature and aims of education which
the Christian humanists had preached a hundred years earlier.

Just as humanist presuppositions and methodology had created a
distinctively Vivesian Aristotelianism in Tudor Oxbridge, so they
would determine the way students in the next century would
approach Aristotle and other ancient authors. The Aristotelianism
of humanist commentators did not necessarily imply a 'conservative
view of government and society,' as Kearney has asserted; it was no
more indiscriminate in its application of Aristotelian ideas than in its
analysis of the text. And there is no evidence that the Aristotelianism

[83] cf. the Thomist Aristotelianism of Richard Hooker's *Of the Laws of Ecclesiastical
Polity* (Folger Library edition, Cambridge, Mass., 1977–81). Hooker lectured on
Aristotelian logic at Corpus Christi College and has been appropriately called 'the
precursor of the movement towards scholasticism' (Kearney, p. 81; cf. Schmitt, p.
65) in his defense of authority. Laud was Chancellor of Oxford from 1629, and certainly made it his mission to increase the control of central authority over the
universities: Kevin Sharpe, 'Archbishop Laud and the University of Oxford,' in
History and Imagination, ed. Hugh Lloyd-Jones, Valerie Pearl and Blair Worden
(New York, 1982), pp. 146–64. See also ch. 7, below.
[84] Kearney, pp. 81–2. Kearney asserts (p. 90) that puritans generally seem to have
been anti-scholastic. This is quite true of Milton, the early Ward and others. But I
have not been able to identify Ganning, Randolph, Vaughn, or Bright as puritans,
although there is no evidence to the contrary other than their silence on usual
puritan issues.

of the Stuart universities was any more scholastic than that of
Rainolds and Case. In fact, the commentaries of these Elizabethan
humanists continued to be used by seventeenth-century tutors
along with the more recent works of Keckerman, Crackenthorpe,
Brierwood and Sanderson.[85] The works of these seventeenth-
century commentators, while occasionally criticized by their
students as dry and overly subtle,[86] none the less evinced considerably more humanistic assumptions than did the Jesuit commentaries. Keckerman, for instance, argued that the works of Aristotle
must not be judged 'from the interpretations of commentators,
scholastics or Sorbonnists, but from the intention of the author, the
collation of texts and the agreement and harmony of the whole of
peripatetic philosophy.'[87]

A comparison of the notes of Oxbridge logic students with those
of contemporary members of Catholic universities reveals some-
thing of the extent to which this humanist presupposition permeated the teaching of Aristotelian dialectic in England. Extant
notebooks of English Catholic students at Cagliari, Rome and
Salamanca consist either of unadulterated Thomistic commentary
on the Latin text of Aristotle, or of the combined comments of the
medieval Schoolmen and such contemporary figures as Cajetan,
Tolleta, de Soto, Medina, Molina, Suarez, Becanus and Vasquez.[88]
References to the Aristotelian text are only rarely direct; most are
mediated by commentators. The Salamanca notebook which survives in the Cambridge University Library is unusual in that it goes
beyond straight commentary on the text and whenever possible
attempts to demonstrate Aristotelian support for Tridentine or
papal rulings on theological issues; however, it is remarkable among

---

[85] The German Bartholomew Keckerman's *Gymnasium logicum* (1606) and *Systema ethica* (1607) were both very popular in the seventeenth century. Richard Crac-kenthorpe, a fellow of Queen's College, Oxford, wrote *Introductio in metaphysicam* (Oxford, 1619) and *Logicae libri quinque* (London, 1622). Edward Brierwood (or Brerewood), first Gresham professor of astronomy, published his *Elementa logicae* in 1614 in London. The *Logicae artis compendium* of Robert Sanderson, logic reader in Lincoln College from 1608, appeared in 1618. Ranking with these works in popularity was another sixteenth-century Catholic humanist commentary, the *Dialectica* of John Seton (1545).

[86] CUL, MS Dd. 6.30, fol. 1; Randolph, *Aristippus*, p. 21.

[87] Keckerman, *Systema Systematum*, ed. J. H. Alsted (Hanover, 1613), p. 23. *cf* Ward's belief that it is 'best to read those histories which rely on contemporary sources... [and] in reading to bear a neutral affection' (MS I, 1608).

[88] Balliol, MS 332 (Cagliari, a Jesuit seminary in Sardinia); St John's, Cambridge, MS I.37 (Rome, 1623) does contain a handful of references to Seneca; CUL, Add. MS 4359 (Salamanca, 1652) also has a few references to Plato, Pythagoras and Seneca (p. 70); the real authorities in all three, however, are clearly the scholastic and Neo-scholastic philosophers.

English notebooks in that even when theology is discussed, the Scriptures are never cited.[89] Contrast the heavy reliance of protestant theological notebooks on the Bible and of Oxbridge logic notebooks on the Greek text of Aristotle read contextually and in light of other ancient literature and history.[90] James Duport's advice to his students at Trinity, Cambridge, might have been written by Erasmus: 'Greek and Hebrew,' he said, 'are two eyes for seeing God's word . . . Read an author in his own language . . . You cannot be a scholar without Greek.'[91] Humanist veneration of the ancient texts in their original languages had clearly permeated the English universities.

Having attempted to determine Aristotle's intentions, Cambridge and Oxford students were also discriminating in their acceptance of his conclusions. Again, Duport's advice is typical of the conditional respect accorded the philosopher in seventeenth-century Cambridge: having told his students to quote Aristotle always in his own words and in Greek, he added, 'reject not lightly the authority of Aristotle *if his words will permit of a favourable and a sure interpretation.*' The goal, in other words, is first of all a correct textual analysis, and secondly an acceptance of only those ideas which are in accord with Christian truth.[92] Aristotle continued to be used as he had been by Case and Rainolds to prepare students to argue the truth; logic was to be stripped of late medieval technicalities and suited for use in public debate. But, as one Oxford student asserted, ''tis not Aristotle but truth that should be the rule of our opinions.'[93]

English students were aware, furthermore, of the differences be-

---

[89] CUL, Add. MS 4359, pp. 17, 93–5, 118, 190 and 226 comment on orthodox Catholic doctrines of transubstantiation, faith and free will. This notebook is also unusual in containing several folios of complaints in English about the length and pace of the lessons and the faults of the master, written covertly in the form of appendages of two to ten words at the end of each paragraph of Latin commentary on Aristotle. Thus, for example, 'I have seldom felt a more piercing cold at any . . . time than I felt when I writ this lesson . . . I believe our Master . . . was a little more than half weary with dictating . . . In the . . . precedent leaf you may behold the true . . . shape of a very handsome blot' (pp. 77–9). One wonders whether this student has some prescience of a twentieth-century scholar in need of relief from the tedium of reading scholastic logic notebooks.

[90] The Aristotelian notebooks of Robert Boothe (BL, Harl. 5356, 1605), John Robinson (Queen's, Oxford, MS 200, 1625), Richard Seymes (Queen's, Oxford, MS 438, 1622), Edmund Sheapheard (Queen's, Oxford, MS 437, 1617), Simonds D'Ewes (BL, Harl. MS 191, 1619), and Daniel Foote (BL, Sloane MS 586, 1646), among others whose authors are less easily identified, all rely on the Greek text.

[91] James Duport, *Rules for Students* (1660), Trin. MSO.10A.33, pp. 3, 12.

[92] *Ibid.*, p. 11 (emphasis mine); *cf.* p. 14.

[93] McConica, 'Humanism and Aristotelianism,' pp. 313–14; Wilkins, *Discovery of a World in the Moone* (1683), pp. 30–32.

tween Aristotle and his master, frequently noting Plato's divergent opinions (again, usually from the Greek text) in their marginal notes.[94] Robert Boothe's notes on Aristotle's logic, physics, rhetoric and ethics include not only analysis of the Greek texts and comparisons with the opinions of Plato, Euripides, Plutarch, Pythagoras, and a variety of Roman rhetoricians and moralists, but also commentary and attempts at application by such various authors as Scaliger, Zabarella, Ramus and Perkins. The notebook is very appropriately entitled *Synopsis totius philosophiae*, and it is not at all atypical of the sort of humanist analysis which Cambridge students of the seventeenth century were applying to Aristotle.[95] The logic notebook of Richard Seymes of Wadham is similarly filled with the opinions of Plato, Socrates, Plutarch, Cicero, Seneca and Quintilian. And Aristotle is by no means the sole authority in John Cole's *Logical Exercises*: in addition to contrasting the opinions of ancient Greek and Roman authors, he quoted medieval and contemporary scholastics; English commentators like Brierwood and Sanderson; and (perhaps most significantly) the textual analyses of the humanists Valla, Agricola, Sturm, Melanchthon, Piscator and Ramus.[96] Seventeenth-century English students were using the exegetical techniques developed by those Renaissance humanists to understand Aristotle – examining his historical and literary context, using the Greek text critically, rejecting the distorted Aristotle of the Thomists, and accepting as authoritative only those conclusions both genuinely Aristotelian and consonant with Christian doctrine and morality. The Aristotelianism of seventeenth-century Oxbridge was clearly of the Christian humanist variety.

Aristotle, therefore, was no more the reigning authority for budding social and political theorists at the universities than were the Neo-scholastics. By 1654, as a matter of fact, Seth Ward observed that while Aristotle was respected at Oxford, the university did not insist that his works be studied. Thomas Barlow in 1655 opined that 'Aristotle's *Metaphysics* is the most impertinent book (*sit venia*) in all his works; indeed, a rhapsody of logical scraps.'[97] The sources most widely used by students for advice on behavior in forum, marketplace and household were instead the Erasmian favorites – Isocrates,

[94] Sheapheard of Queen's cited Plato, Xenocrates and Cicero in conflict with Aristotle (Queen's, Oxford, MS 437); Queen's, Oxford, MS 196 (notes on Crackenthorpe's *Logic*) cites Plato and Socrates; CUL, MS Dd. 5.47 cites Plato, Socrates and Virgil.   [95] BL, Harl. 5356.
[96] Queen's, Oxford, MS 438 (Seymes, 1622); BL, Lansdowne 797.
[97] *Vindiciae Academiarum*, pp. 32, 58–60; *Library for Younger Schollers*, p. 4.

Xenophon, Plutarch, Cicero, Seneca and Quintilian. As in the preceding century, students were referred directly to the ancients for practical instruction on mundane matters, and the notebooks devoted to such a use of classical authors are more characteristic of seventeenth-century college curricula than the handful of strict logic notebooks which have misled previous historians.

Of particular interest in this context is the proliferation of classical commonplace books by early Stuart university students. While the recording of favorite quotes on particular subjects in more or less organized books was not a seventeenth-century innovation, the number of extant commonplace books by Cambridge and Oxford students of this period points to a contemporary consensus among educators on the importance of such an activity as part of one's university training. Tutors like Thomas Barlow and Richard Holdsworth went into some detail on methods of commonplace-keeping: Barlow emphasized the need to keep two separate commonplace books, one to list references, the other to record notes on the authors. Holdsworth told his students to

Get some handsome paper books of a portable size in octavo, and rule them so with ink or black lead that there may be space left on the side for a margin and at the top for a title. Into them collect all the remarkable things which you meet with in your historians, orators, and poets . . . These collections you shall render so ready and familiar to you by frequent reading them over on evenings, or times set apart for that purpose, that they will offer themselves to your memory on any occasion.

The keeping of a commonplace book was intended partly to inform the tutor of a student's progress in reading assigned works,[98] but more importantly to provide an organizational technique which would render the opinions of the authors read more readily available for later disputation or other discourse. A glance at puritan sermons of the Elizabethan and early Stuart period reveals one of the uses to which commonplace books were eventually put. Marginal notes on virtually every subject include a vast number and variety of authors—more than the most literary of preachers would be likely to read in the usual course of sermon preparation. Commonplace books kept during a divinity student's college days thus provided an efficient means of filling out later sermons and incidentally highlight for the historian the sorts of authorities that shaped a preacher's interpretation of Scripture and theology on a variety of issues.

The dependence of seventeenth-century tutors on the Greek and

---

[98] *Library for Younger Schollers*, p. 50; Emmanuel, MS I.2.27(1), pp. 50–1.

Latin classics and the writings of Christian humanists as guides for
behavior in virtually every area of life – from marriage to the
accumulation of wealth to the punishment of criminals to the rearing of children – is perhaps most strikingly illustrated by a remarkable collection of commonplace books in the library of Trinity
College, Cambridge.[99] The fourteen immense volumes (the longest
contains 725 closely-written folios) would seem by their similarity to
each other and their distinctive size and organization as compared
with other student commonplace books to have been written by
several students of the same tutor. Only three indicate authorship
on the flyleaf, two being signed 'Edward Palmer,' the third showing
the monograph 'W. Ga.'[100] Two others[101] are written in a hand
similar enough to Palmer's to have been his as well, a hypothesis supported by the fact that each of these four contains a different set of
authors or works. But it is impossible to conclude too much about
the number of students responsible for the extant collection. What
is certain is that the putative common tutor of Palmer and his
colleagues instructed his pupils above all to make their collections
incredibly large and their topical organization strictly alphabetical.
Thus, all fourteen volumes proceed with their Latin or Greek topical
headings in strict alphabetical order (amicitia ... dives ...
matrimonio ... rex, or ἀγών ... ἀπαρχαί ... γάμος ... θεός),
with as many as eighty folios devoted to a single topic. Each page is
divided into a narrow and a wide column, the former containing not
marginal comments on the contents of the latter, but simply further
commonplaces on the topic at hand. Roughly the same topical divisions are common to all fourteen books, and all rely heavily on the
same collection of authors, the vast majority classical and patristic.
Not all are as dominated by Seneca as the two explicitly attributed to
Palmer; all but Palmer's and three others show extensive reliance on
Erasmus' *Adages*; some are more consistent than others in quoting
Greek authors and the New Testament in Greek; a few attempt to
translate Greek authors into Latin and Latin into Greek (a favorite
humanist pedagogical device). But these variations are not as
obvious as the common characteristics of the notebooks.[102] And
the most apparent of these is the fact that all of these students
devoted the bulk of their study time to the reading of classical
authors for instruction in practical as well as theoretical matters.

[99] Trin. MSS R.16.6–19.   [100] Trin. MSS R.16.6–19.
[101] Trin. MSS R.16.12 and R.16.13.
[102] Trin. MSS R.16.6, 11–13, 16, 18 and 19. The most heavily Erasmian is R.16.7;
     R.16.18 is dominated by Vives and the ancients.

In addition to the headings listed above, the students responsible for the Trinity commonplace books were without exception concerned with such topics as love, adultery, luxury, poverty, family, nobility, education, ignorance, work, charity, justice: the notebooks are effectively highly organized compendia of ideas on all aspects of social theory. And the authors used most frequently and consistently by all of the students – Seneca, Cicero, Quintilian, Ovid, Virgil, Plutarch, Pythagoras, and Isocrates – guarantee that most of the conclusions drawn about the social order are in line with Christian humanist thought, even in those notebooks where humanists are not cited. Seneca, for instance, is almost inevitably the source of most of the commonplaces related to wealth and poverty; his requirement that charity be given with discrimination as to the character of the recipient (an assumption introduced to sixteenth-century England by humanist admirers of Seneca) was recorded in more than one book.[103] Quintilian is the most common authority on education, Plutarch on motherhood; Cicero on government.[104] Trinity students were certainly using the ancients as Erasmus had prescribed.

The majority of the Trinity commonplace books, furthermore, provide irrefutable evidence that an integral part of the seventeenth-century Cambridge curriculum was composed of a direct reading of Christian humanists for the purpose of drawing conclusions in the area of social theory. Erasmus and/or Vives predominated among the modern authors cited in eight of the volumes (three of the remaining six volumes cite no contemporary authors at all).[105] Students obviously attached a great deal of importance to their opinions on wealth and poverty, work and idleness, war and peace, education, marriage, parental responsibilities, the government of servants, friendship, justice and political authority. Under the heading *Educatio*, they copied Vives' humanistic advice that education aim at learning to live simply and righteously, rather than at mastering endless dogmatic subtleties and logical curiosities; under many other headings, they acted upon this advice.[106]

---

[103] For example, Trin. R.16.6, fols. 89–129v; R.16.9 (fol. 152v on charity); R.16.17, fol. 72v.

[104] For example, Trin. R.16.6, fol. 535v; R.16.9, fol. 336v; R.16.18, fols. 378v–382; R.16.17, fol. 126v.

[105] Trin. R.16.6, R.16.12 and R.16.13 restrict citations to classical and patristic sources; Casaubon is the only modern writer quoted in R.16.16; Lipsius and Brisson are occasionally cited in R.16.11.

[106] Trin. R.16.9, fols. 129–129v. This volume, incidentally, also quotes Valla, Machiavelli and Montaigne, the latter in English.

While the Trinity commonplace books do include theological sections, theology would seem to have been a subordinate concern;
where it is the subject, the Bible, ancient moralists, Church Fathers
and humanists still outnumber the contemporary theologians cited.
The section headed *Trinitas* in one notebook, for instance, supplements Scriptural citations with quotations from the Church Fathers,
Virgil, Pythagoras and other ancient monotheists; *Evangelica* is
almost exclusively biblical in content; *Conscientia* quotes Chrysostom,
Gregory Nazianus, Juvenal, Cato, Plutarch, Seneca, Ovid, Plato,
Aristotle, and only three modern authors – Erasmus, Luther and
Montaigne.[107] In only one commonplace book do scholastics
appear at all, and even in this clearly philosophical commonplace
book, ancient Greek authors (cited consistently in Greek) predominate.[108] The Trinity students doubtless maintained separate
logic, philosophy, and theology notebooks which, had they survived, might have given evidence for their familiarity with Neo-
scholasticism; however, to assume that the focus of early Stuart
curriculum was Neo-scholastic rather than humanistic is to disregard thousands of folios of evidence in the Trinity College library
alone. It is inconceivable that the time devoted by the Trinity students in question to scholastic philosophy and syllogistic logic could
have been greater than that devoted to the reading and recording of
commonplaces from the works of Christian humanists and ancients
during the period when these notebooks were being kept. (The
internal consistency of the notebooks suggests that this period was a
relatively short one – perhaps a year or two of undergraduate work.)
It seems clear that at least one seventeenth-century tutor had not yet
gotten wind of scholastic revival having displaced the classical
curriculum of the sixteenth-century.

Other tutors and other commonplace books show that this Trinity
tutor was not alone in his ignorance. Richard Holdsworth, Master of
Emmanuel College from 1637 to 1649, may have assigned medieval
and Neo-scholastic authors to his charges, but he was careful to construct for them a list of fundamental readings drawn from Erasmus
(the *Colloquies, Adages, De lingua* and *Moriae Encomium* are specifically
mentioned), Cicero (portions of whose works were to be committed
to memory), Quintilian, Seneca, Ovid, ancient history, and the
Bible. Curtis has aptly described Holdsworth on the basis of his

[107] Trin. R.16.9, fols. 210ff, 318ff, 193–194v.
[108] Trin. R.16.19 is the only vaguely 'Aristotelian' notebook in the group (R.16.10–
19) which Costello (p. 155) describes as especially Aristotelian. In all of the others,
as in R.16.6–9, Aristotle takes at best second place to the Roman Stoics.

tutorial directive as 'a humanist who wholeheartedly accepted the principle of Quintilian that . . . the man proficient in rhetoric needs learning and character as well as facility in expressing himself.'[109]

Joseph Mead of Christ's College, Cambridge, likewise required his students to read the works of Erasmus (*Adages, Apophthegmata, Colloquies, De conscribendis epistolis, De lingua, Institutio principis christiani* and *Moriae Encomium*), Ascham, Vives and the ancients, in addition to contemporary theologians and logicians.[110] Thomas Barlow followed suit at the other university, including Erasmus, Vives and the ancients among the Neo-scholastics and puritans in his 'Library for Younger Schollers.'[111] James Duport of Trinity, Cambridge, provided a short list of the 'best authors' for his students to read – Demosthenes and Cicero for oratory, Homer and Virgil for poetry, Aristotle, Seneca and Plutarch for logic and ethical instruction – and specified that at least one entire book of each of these writers was to be read, in the original language.[112]

These are thoroughly humanistic instructions, and they were given for humanistic reasons: the concern of seventeenth-century tutors was that their students should learn to live virtuously. Duport, for example, echoed Erasmus when he told his charges not only to read the ancients, but also to follow their advice for living godly lives: 'Call yourself to an account at night, what you have done the day past, and wherein you have failed, *according to the Greek rule of Pythagoras.*'[113] Sir Simonds D'Ewes, who had read the ancients and Erasmus under Holdsworth's guidance during his own undergraduate years at St John's, sent his brother Richard to 'a very religious tutor, called Mr John Knowles, of Catherine Hall, Cambridge,' in 1632 because it was his 'chief care to have him religiously and virtuously educated.'[114] Milton likewise defined 'the end of learning' to 'repair the ruins of our first parents'; he read Bacon and More not to 'sequester

---

[109] Emmanuel, MS I.2.27(1), pp. 7–13, 23, 24, 27, 41, 43; Curtis, pp. 112–13. Holdsworth's directive for students also recommends the protestant theologians Hall, Sibbes, Preston, Bolton, Davenant and Perkins (p. 28); Crackenthorpe, Keckerman, Molina, Sanderson and Burgerdicius for logic (pp. 20–21); and Valla as well as Erasmus for grammar (p. 30). 'Short memorial notes in Greek' are to be gathered from Aristotle (p. 33), and the student is repeatedly instructed to 'collect some idiotisms [sic]' from Cicero for his paper book and to memorize portions of Cicero's works (p. 39). More's *Utopia* was also commended (p. 44).

[110] H. F. Fletcher, *Milton*, Appendix I, 'Book Purchases in Mead's Accounts, 1614–1637,' pp. 562–3, 588, 620–1. Case's *Logic* was also recommended by Mead (p. 597).   [111] *Library for Younger Schollers*, pp. 10, 18, 32, 44, 66.

[112] Trin. MS O.10A.33, pp. 9, 13.

[113] *Ibid.*, p. 3 (emphasis mine); *cf.* Erasmus' *Confabulatio pia (Coll.*, pp. 30–41), and *Quo transgressus* in *Adages* (1964), pp. 33–4.

[114] D'Ewes, *Autobiography and Correspondence*, ed. J. O. Halliwell (1845), vol. 1, pp. 121–40; vol. 2, pp. 69–71.

out of the world into Atlantic and Utopian polities,' but to achieve insight into social and political reform.[115] His undergraduate education at Christ's College had been as Erasmian as any: he reported in 1628 that 'we are all familiar with that sprightly encomium of Folly, composed by an author of no small repute.'[116]

If the goals of many tutors were as humanistic in the seventeenth century as they had been in the preceding era, so were the accomplishments of their students. Milton and the student authors of the Trinity College commonplace books were not at all atypical of their contemporaries in applying humanist learning to everyday life. An anonymous student at Pembroke, Cambridge, not only read, but also painstakingly copied into his notebook, long passages from Erasmus' *Enchiridion militis christiani* on the practical value of ancient literature. Other portions of the notebook discuss the harvest of philosophical truth to be gleaned from Erasmus and his editions of ancient proverbs, and list commonplaces on a variety of subjects by a very catholic group of authors – ancient pagans, Reformers, Neo-scholastics and Christian humanists.[117] Another Pembroke student applied his extensive reading of Greek authors to such mundane problems as parental education of children and the necessity for maternal nursing of infants.[118] Alexander Bolde, also of Pembroke, quoted Sir Thomas More on respect for parents, Erasmus on the practice of piety, Seneca on poor relief, Cicero on dealing with misfortune, and Xenophon, Pythagoras, Epictetus, Democritus, Diogenes, Virgil, Cato and Ovid on other practical and theoretical issues.[119] The classical commonplace book of an early seventeenth-century St John's student quotes Cicero, Cato, Pliny and Aristotle, but is most heavily reliant on Seneca for opinions on the virtue of frugality, the use of reason and the nature of providence.[120] Seneca's

[115] John Milton, *Complete Prose Works*, ed. D. M. Wolfe (New Haven, 1953), vol. 1, p. 934; vol. 2, pp. 366–7, 527; *cf.* vol. 1, p. 296 and Webster, *Instauration*, p. 100, comparing Milton's view of education with Vives' and Ascham's. Note the motivations of Camden and Lord Brooke for the establishment of chairs in history at Oxford and Cambridge, respectively – for 'observations . . . useful and profitable for the younger students of the university' (Curtis, pp. 116–17).

[116] Milton, 'Prolusion VI,' in *Complete Prose Works*, vol. 1, pp. 273–4. Erasmus' *Colloquies* was also a textbook at St Paul's when Milton was there.

[117] Pembroke, Cambridge, MS LC II.16 (n.p.).

[118] Pembroke, Cambridge, MS LC II.12, pp. 38–46.

[119] St John's, Cambridge, MS S.34, fols. 2–4, 10, 12–12v, 18 *et passim*. All Greek authors are carefully quoted in Greek.

[120] St John's, Cambridge, MS I.34, e.g., pp. 61–2, 160, 348; Bellarmine was known to this student (e.g., p. 240, but the ancients predominate in the notebook. Presumably for this reason, Costello calls this volume 'a curious philosophical medley.' It is actually much more typical than the straight logic notebooks which he apparently finds less 'curious.'

comments on wealth and poverty, Quintilian's on ambition and
Erasmus' on religious self-discipline are among the commonplaces
of William Sancroft of Emmanuel, and another of Sancroft's
notebooks commends Erasmus' *Colloquies* and Cicero's *De Officiis* for
instruction in daily living. [121] William Bright of Emmanuel cited
More's *Utopia* on government, education, clothing and war; Xenophon,
Diogenes and Plato on gambling; Pythagoras on self-examination;
and Erasmus and Richard Pace on the education of children. Samuel
Ward, during his sojourn at Emmanuel, cited Quintilian on family
government and Seneca in criticism of those who 'live otherwise
than they teach'; one should study philosophy, he insisted in good
humanist fashion, 'as a handy work, to make advantage of it.' In a
1606 notebook he recommended the reading of Demosthenes,
Isocrates, Plato, Cicero, and Cato as a means of learning '*vel bene
vivendi praecepta.*' [122]

The extant notebooks of Simonds D'Ewes reveal that he, too,
followed his tutor's directions and spent a great deal of time gleaning
practical advice from the ancients. This group of five school and five
college notebooks in the British Library is of interest, too, as an illustration of the error of concluding from a given scholastic logic
notebook that a student is non-humanistic in his interests or that the
curriculum of his college is exclusively scholastic. D'Ewes' is the
most nearly complete set of notebooks surviving for a single college
student in this period. If only one had remained to us – say the 1619
logic notebook – historians might easily surmise that the education
of a St John's student in the early seventeenth century consisted
exclusively in scholastic treatments of Aristotelian logic, physics
and metaphysics, and that Costello, Kearney, Hill and others are
correct in stressing the importance of a Neo-scholastic revival in the
early seventeenth-century university curriculum. [123] If another [124] had
been the sole survivor of D'Ewes' notebooks, one might wonder at
the tenacity of Ramism in Stuart Cambridge. But taken together
with the other notebooks kept by D'Ewes during his student years, a
rather different impression is formed of the breadth of curriculum
available to early seventeenth-century scholars. D'Ewes clearly had a
firm grasp on Christian humanist and classical writings before he
matriculated at St John's, and Erasmian assumptions about the ends

---

[121] Bodl., Sancroft 87, pp. 92ff, 189–201; Bodl., Sancroft 25, pp. 122–3.
[122] CUL, Add. MS 6160, pp. 21, 76–7, 110, 131, 142; fols. 153v–154v; Ward MS F, fols.
9v–10.
[123] BL, Harl. 191; the school notebooks are Harl. 118–21, 185; notes taken at St
John's are Harl. 182, 190–2.   [124] BL, Harl. 190.

of learning had become a deeply rooted part of his expectations. He had spent much of the period from 1615 to 1617 translating Ovid, Virgil and Cicero (into both English and Greek), and Isocrates, and writing essays on virtue, education, discipline, respect for parents, temperance, friendship, work, ambition, wealth, and other aspects of social behavior which quoted these and other classical authorities (Seneca, Xenophon, Pythagoras, Pliny, Cato). Erasmus was clearly one of his chief guides in learning *bene vivere*; thirty-six folios of one notebook are devoted to discussing the social implications of Erasmian *Adages*.[125] The concerns of his Cambridge notebooks are not for the most part noticeably different: he evinced a growing interest in ancient and medieval English history and in logic, but all of the university notebooks are replete with obviously respectful citations of classical authorities on practical issues.[126]

The same humanist curriculum is visible in notebooks from the other university. Seymes of Wadham regarded Cicero as the pre-eminent authority on education and noted Seneca's disparagement of idleness among his other classical commonplaces.[127] Thomas Brathwaite of Queen's quoted Plutarch on fortune, Quintilian on fame, Sophocles on government, Seneca (and William Perkins) on conscience, and Vives on reason, truth, friendship, sleep and death.[128]

Numerous other examples could be given;[129] the notebooks supply a superabundance of evidence for the continuity of the humanist curriculum into the seventeenth century. It is clear, moreover, from the nature as well as the number of citations that Erasmus and Vives were not quoted lightly, but that they were regarded as genuinely authoritative teachers of doctrine and of virtuous behavior. For

---

[125] BL, Harl. 118, 119, 120, 121, 185; Erasmian advice is found (e.g.) in Harl. 120, fols. 18, 27, 30; Harl. 121, fols. 31–67v; Isocrates' advice on child-rearing, temperance in the execution of disciplinary action, and the virtue of hard work is translated in Harl. 185 (1615), fols. 12–27.

[126] Historical notes are found in BL, Harl. 192 (with morals continually drawn from Roman examples), Harl. 182, and the post-collegiate commonplace book, Harl. 186. Notes on logic are restricted to Harl. 190 (citing mainly Cicero, Plutarch, Quintilian, and occasionally Ramus, Zabarella, Keckerman, Molina and Aristotle) and Harl. 191 (Aristotelian). The most apparently respected ancient writers are Cicero, Plutarch, Quintilian and Pythagoras. Harl. 182, e.g., cites Plutarch on poor relief, drunkenness, social hierarchy, crime, and punishment (fols. 25 ff).

[127] Queen's, Oxford, MS 438, fols. 67, 110–110v, *et passim.*

[128] Queen's, Oxford, MS 423 (n.p.); cf. CUL, MS Dd. 12.57 (also Brathwaite) citing Erasmus, Seneca and Plutarch.

[129] Bodl., Rawl. D.947; St John's, Cambridge, MS S.44 (Oxford, 1635–6); Queens', Cambridge, MS Horne 41; BL, Sloane MS 586 (Daniel Foote); BL, Sloane MS 1981. Ward MS B (1600) moralizes about ignorance, drunkenness, and blasphemy, citing Xenophon and Plutarch.

both the puritan Ward and his conformist enemy Wren, Erasmus had the last word on questions of authorship or textual authenticity.[130] For Thomas Laurence of Balliol, Erasmus' authority was a sufficient reason to study ancient wisdom, and the *Adages* were portrayed as the best textbook of ancient thought.[131] Sancroft called Erasmus a doctrinal luminary, stimulating to study and understanding, and worthy of honor as a great scholar. Vives he described as the author of many great books and as '*vir doctissimus.*'[132]

As Ward and Wren illustrate, humanist assumptions were restricted neither to Arminian Anglicans, as Morgan asserts, nor to puritans, as Webster believes.[133] Students at such non-puritan colleges as Caius listed Erasmus' *Colloquies* and *Adages* among their books and cited a variety of classical authors in their notes. But the record of book loans kept by the young puritan Samuel Ward at Christ's College includes Seneca's *Tragedies*, Cicero's *De Officiis*, Plutarch, Quintilian and other ancient writers, along with Perkins and other Reformed theologians and the scientific works of Copernicus, Tycho Brahe and Erastus.[134] An Arminian puritan student at St John's, Cambridge, read Erasmus and the ancients as avidly as he read protestant theologians; in fact, he noted in a discussion of female fashion that Erasmus and William Perkins could be found 'of the same mind.'[135] And the notebooks of seventeenth-century Emmanuel students leave no doubt about the humanist emphasis of the tutorial curriculum at that puritan college: '*legimus Seneca et antiquissimi graecorum sapientes*', one Emmanuel student wrote (in admittedly inelegant Latin), and when he forgot to bring his books on a holiday trip home, he requested his chamberfellow to send his volumes of Horace, Juvenal and Sir Thomas Smith's *Commonwealth of England*.[136]

[130] Ward MSS M.3, G (fol. 26); Pembroke, Cambridge, MS LC. II.134.
[131] Balliol, MS 438 (1615), pp. 15, 47, 86. Petrarch's authority is also highly regarded (p. 65).   [132] Bodl., Sancroft MS 25, p. 124.
[133] Irvonwy Morgan, *Prince Charles's Puritan Chaplain* (London, 1957), p. 39; Webster, *Instauration*, pp. 1, 100. On the other hand, Webster (p. 106) also mistakenly thinks that classical authors and their Renaissance commentators faded from the university scene during the 1640s.
[134] BL, Sloane MS 3308 (F. Glisson, Caius, 1638); Sidney Sussex, MS Ward A.
[135] St John's, Cambridge, MS S.20, pp. 51–3. The Arminianism of this student is deduced from his statements on free will and reprobation (pp. 159–61), his puritanism from his strong condemnation of blasphemy, drunkenness, and 'ceremonies' (pp. 14–15, 131–2, 175ff). *cf.* BL, Harl. 1779 (Balliol, 1637), a non-puritan notebook which Kearney describes as 'scholastic' (p. 82) but which in fact relies most heavily on the Greek texts of Plato, Pythagoras, Hesiod, Homer and the Bible.
[136] Bodl., Tanner 462 (Sancroft), fols. 11–12v, 19; he quoted Seneca, Cicero, Quintilian and Plutarch in his letters (e.g., fols. 1–3, 21, 23, 32–3); *cf.* Bodl., Sancroft 25, which lists Sancroft's studies at Emmanuel as Latin, Greek, Hebrew, history, mathematics and physics and contains *no* references to scholastics or Neoscholastics. *cf.* also CUL, MS Gg. 1.29 (Emmanuel).

Humanism was, in short, pervasive in collegiate curricula at puritan and non-puritan colleges of both universities; furthermore, it continued to be the defining characteristic of English university studies throughout the Civil War and Interregnum.[137] The library listings, like the notebooks, of Anglican as well as puritan students of the 1640s and 1650s bear witness to the continuity of humanism in the midst of very catholic curricula. John Patricke of Peterhouse, Cambridge, later a bishop, compiled a book inventory which included both puritan and anti-puritan theology, medieval School-men and a few Neo-scholastics, Erasmus' *Colloquies* and Greek New Testament, and the Greek and Roman classics.[138] At Royalist Oxford, Robert Barrell of Magdalen, Thomas Cole of University College and John Hutton of New College all listed works of Vives or Erasmus and the ancients among their meager possessions.[139] The instructions of Cambridge tutors of the period insured that students in the Parliament-occupied university were reading the same works.[140] Oxford Visitors commissioned by the Saints Parliament of 1653 encouraged the humanist combination of 'godliness and learn-ing' and criticized monkish aloofness from the public concerns of the commonwealth; however, they found no reason to interfere with the curriculum.[141] Those who proposed to reform the universities of the Commonwealth focused their criticism on the same kinds of abuses to which Erasmus had objected: scholastic techniques, the narrowness of traditional academic exercises, and an overemphasis on metaphysics.[142] To the extent that the more radical of the would-be reformers wished to subordinate the study of humane letters to a mechanical education they were unsuccessful; both grammar schools and colleges remained faithful to the Erasmian tradition of classical studies throughout this period.[143]

Graduates of the arts and divinity courses of Cambridge and Oxford were thus well prepared to disseminate the humanist evangel in Elizabethan and early Stuart England. Whether self-consciously

[137] See the Civil War notebooks of Brathwaite (Queen's, Oxford, MS 1423; CUL MS Dd. 12.57), Bright (CUL, Add. MS 6160), and Daniel Foote (BL, Sloane MS 586); the notebook kept from 1650 to 1657 by a University College, Oxford, student (St John's, Cambridge, MS O.64), citing especially Greek authors and Erasmus' *Adages* (e.g., pp. 1–37, 65, 70–2); and such undated mid-seventeenth-century notebooks as Queens', Cambridge, MS Horne 41 (kept by a puritan student); Pembroke, Cambridge, MSS LC II.11, 12, and 16; and BL, Sloane MS 1981.
[138] CUL, Add. MS 84; *cf.* Sidney Sussex, MSS Ward B, F, G.
[139] Oxford University Archives, Inventories dated 1651, 1652, and 1653, respectively.
[140] Trin. MS O.10A.33; Emmanuel MS I.2.27(1).
[141] Charles Webster, *Instauration*, pp. 197–8.
[142] John Webster, *Academiarum Examen* (London, 1654), *passim.*
[143] Charles Webster, *Instauration*, pp. 205–9.

Erasmian or not, they had been exposed to the key documents of Christian humanist ideology, and the reform-minded among them did not come away unaffected. How influential were they in turn on the adoption of humanistic values, and more particularly Erasmian social thought, by their less educated lay audiences?

The evidence of sermons (which will be considered in detail in the following three chapters) and of commonplace books certainly indicates that university-trained divines retained the assumptions of their humanist education and preached accordingly long after their university careers had ended. William Rawley, Francis Bacon's chaplain and spiritual advisor to Bacon's household, provides one example. After his graduation from Corpus Christi College, Cambridge, a brief stint as rector of Bowthorpe, and several years' service to Bacon, Rawley began a commonplace book which clearly indicates his continued respect for Erasmus, his disdain for Aristotelianism, and his acquaintance with the opinions of other ancient writers on social theory. His admiration for his patron's reformist ideas and his devotion to seeing Bacon's works into print after the latter's death in 1626 are surely explained in part by Rawley's humanist training.[144]

University-educated preachers transmitted classical and Christian humanist ideas through both the spoken and the written word. William Gouge, trained at St Paul's School, Eton and King's College, Cambridge, preached and published sermons on practical topics liberally sprinkled with ancient and humanist authorities. These were frequently purchased by puritan heads of families concerned with the instruction of children in godly behavior: Nehemiah Wallington, for instance, recorded,

This year 1622, my family increasing and now having a wife, a child, a man servant, and a maid servant, and thus having the charge of so many souls, I then bought Mr. Gouge's Book of Domestical Duties that so every one of us may learn and know our duties and honor God every one in his place where God had set them . . .[145]

Sir Robert Harley and Sir Simonds D'Ewes purchased the same volume when their children began to arrive on the scene.[146]

---

[144] Lambeth Palace, MS 2086, pp. 3, 16, 40 (Plutarch on wealth and women), 42, 68; on p. 30 he remarks, 'Will you tell any man's mind, before you have conferred with him? So doth Aristotle, in raising his axioms, upon Nature's mind.' On Rawley's career, see the *DNB*.

[145] Wallington, Folger Shakespeare Library MS V.a.436, pp. 13–14 (I am grateful to Derek Hirst for this reference); Gouge, *Of Domesticall Duties* (London, 1622). Gouge's academic career is recounted in the *DNB*.

[146] Andrew G. Watson, *The Library of Sir Simonds D'Ewes* (1966), p. 168; Harley's library catalogue is BL Loan 29/202 (from the Duke of Portland), 1637 (mistakenly

But these university-educated lay puritans also exposed their children first hand to Christian humanist and ancient literature. Harley, a graduate of Oriel College and a parishioner of John Stoughton (the Emmanuel-educated curate of St Mary Alderman-bury), possessed not only a large collection of puritan literature, but also writings of Cicero and the complete works of Seneca. D'Ewes' library, much of which was acquired explicitly for the edification of his family, included much classical literature and such humanist works as Erasmus' *Adages* and *Colloquies*, More's *Utopia*, Ascham's *Epistles* and *The Scholemaster*, the grammars of Lily and Colet, and Sir Thomas Smith's *De Republica Anglorum*; moreover, the commonplace book which he kept from 1622 to 1646 reveals his dependence on these authors for advice on parental duties and on various aspects of social ethics.[147] The humanist education of both preachers and laymen at Cambridge and Oxford was thus disseminated to their congregations, to their readers, and to their children and servants.

While the universities were a signally important transmitter of humanist social theory, a direct exposure to humanism and to classical literature did not require a university education. The English publishing history for Erasmus' works reveals that their market was far larger than the university educated portion of the English population. Looking only at some of the most popular works: seven editions of the *Adages* were printed on English presses between 1539 and 1622, six editions of the *Apophthegmata* between 1540 and 1564, and ten editions of the *Enchiridion militis christiani* between 1533 and 1576. Partial or complete editions of the *Colloquies* appearing between 1540 and 1639 number fourteen; twenty more were published between 1643 and 1699, seventeen in English translation. Of course, these figures account only for those editions published in England; many English readers purchased continental editions.[148] This data would seem to lend some credibility to McConica's argument for a deliberate resolve on the part of Tudor government to bring Erasmian reformism before the general public. Whether or not such a policy existed, however, it is clear that Englishmen – and women – from the royal household down were reading Erasmus, and reading him for very Erasmian reasons: Catherine Parr directed the Princess Mary to

listed under July, 1627). I am indebted to Jacqueline Levy for the latter reference.
[147] BL, MS Loan 29/202; Andrew Watson, pp. 101, 117, 139, 177, 180, 190, 196, 309, *et passim*; *cf.* BL, MS Harl. 186, *passim*.
[148] *STC*; D'Ewes' two copies of the *Adages* were published in Venice (1508, acquired by D'Ewes in 1624) and Florence (1575), and his copy of the *Colloquies* was the 1621 Amsterdam edition. He also had a 1536 Leyden edition of *De ratione conscribendi epistolas* (Andrew Watson, pp. 101, 117, 139, 190.)

read Erasmian editions of the ancients no less for the usefulness of his advice than for the accuracy of his textual rendition.[149]

Vives' works were also remarkably popular: his *Ad sapientiam introductio* went through twelve editions between 1539 and 1623 (eleven in translation), and nine English printings of Richard Hyrde's translation of his *Instructiō of a christen womā* were produced between 1529 and 1592. More's *Utopia*, to list one more representative humanist publication, appeared in seven English (as well as countless continental) editions from 1551 to 1639.[150]

If space allowed, even more striking figures could be provided for the publication of classical texts in the sixteenth and seventeenth centuries. These were available in both Latin and Greek for scholars and in English translations for the less erudite. 'Scholars,' furthermore, need not be restricted to the university educated: such well-instructed women as Lady Mary Fitzalan not only collected commonplaces from Greek and Roman authors, but also took extensive notes on Roman history and produced volumes of translations from Greek authors on ethical issues – in this case, Euripides, Demosthenes, Pythagoras, Xenophon, Democritus, Plato, Plutarch, Isocrates and Sophocles, on such subjects as temperance, gratitude, luxury and prodigality.[151] Noteworthy, too, are the numerous sixteenth- and seventeenth-century collections of excerpts from ancient writers – works patterned after Erasmus' *Adages* and *Apophthegmata*. Because of the ready availability of such publications, a direct familiarity with Christian humanist ideas was possible even for the relatively uneducated populace. The puritan Brilliana Conway did not know Greek or Latin, but her commonplace book is replete with excerpts from Seneca's *Epistles*, as well as from protestant theologians and the Bible, on most aspects of everyday behavior.[152]

The impact of humanist writings and editions of classical works on early modern social theory cannot be ignored. It must no longer be regarded as an adequate explanation of sixteenth-century innovations in social regulation and seventeenth-century political activism to point to the protestant response to a perceived Scriptural mandate. Protestants, and particularly puritans, were certainly strongly motivated by their faith to reform the social order and

[149] BL, Vespasian F.III. no. 35; McConica, *English Humanists*, pp. 68–9.
[150] *STC*; the first edition of *Utopia* was printed at Louvain in 1516.
[151] BL, Royal 12A.1–4; *DNB* under Mary Fitzalan (b. 1541).
[152] Nottingham University, Conway MSS, Box 166 (inconsistently foliated). See, e.g., the sections headed 'Of the duty of children to their parents,' 'Of conscience,' 'Of good works.' I am grateful to Jacqueline Levy for drawing my attention to this manuscript.

establish a godly commonwealth, but for specific instructions on how to accomplish this feat, they turned to the Christian humanist authors who populated their libraries. There they discovered the same regard for the Scriptures and for the hypothetical Golden Age in which they were written, the same compulsion to criticize the degenerate *status quo*, the same drive for godly reformation of the social and political order which lay at the roots of the protestant Reformation itself, and to which they as protestants laid claim. Accordingly, they seized the Christian humanist banner of their Catholic mentors and marched with it against the forces of Catholic reaction. They might not have consciously identified themselves as Christian humanists; they were certainly aware of their theological divergence from Erasmus and More. But in at least one area – social thought – they were deeply and often explicitly indebted to the biblical and classical interpretations of the humanists. If, as a result, they cannot be credited with innovation, they nevertheless deserve recognition as humanist activists in the realm of social reform. And when so recognized as products of a definable intellectual milieu, they begin to lose the proportions of protestant giants and to acquire instead the human dimensions of rather ordinary, if morally earnest, sixteenth-century people.

4

The spiritualized household

Among the innovative social ideas with which puritans have been credited is the doctrine of the family, rather than the parish, as the fundamental spiritual unit of society. To protestantism, and particularly to protestantism of the hotter sort, are attributed the exaltation of marriage over virginity, the requirement for parents to occupy a religiously didactic and disciplinary role, and a slight tendency toward sexual egalitarianism in light of the spiritual role of women within the household. We are told, for example, that 'the Reformation, by reducing the authority of the priest in society, simultaneously elevated the authority of lay heads of households,' and that the stress on household religious instruction and discipline 'was part of the protestant inheritance.'[1] We are told that since the Reformation, the family has become the basic and most essential unit of church government, and that the head of the protestant, and especially of the *puritan* household is expected to oversee the spiritual welfare of his family and to conduct daily worship in the home.[2] Furthermore, it is asserted that 'until Puritan ideals came to have some influence, the average characterization represented women as at best a "necessary evil" for the propagation of the race,' and that it was puritanism which heralded the shift from the

---

[1] Christopher Hill, *Society and Puritanism* (New York, 1964), pp. 445–6.
[2] Keith Thomas, 'Women and the Civil War Sects', *Past and Present*, 13 (1958), 42–62, p. 42. More recently, Richard Greaves (*Society and Religion in Elizabethan England* (Minneapolis, 1981), Parts II and III, esp. ch. 7, has maintained the spiritualized household as a puritan distinctive. Levin L. Schücking, *The Puritan Family*, tr. B. Battershaw (New York, 1970), argues that before the Reformation marriage was seen as a 'necessary evil' (p. 21).

patriarchal to the conjugal family.[3] Both Catholics and conforming Anglicans can be found who minimized the religious responsibilities of householders – *ergo*, the spiritualization of the household was a puritan accomplishment.[4]

This thesis is temptingly neat, but the foregoing discussion of Christian humanist social thought in protestant England should suggest the danger of attributing these ideas exclusively to puritanism. A close examination of Christian humanist conceptions of the family and recommendations for domestic conduct in those areas dearest to puritan hearts will reveal the extent of the danger. In regard to the family, the biblicism of Erasmus led to many of the same conclusions which protestant biblicism would derive, and the common classical sources of humanists and protestants produced common assumptions and ideals. In the marginal notes of domestic conduct manuals by Bartholomew Batty, William Gouge and Heinrich Bullinger (whose *Christen State of Matrimonye*, translated by Miles Coverdale, was the source book for much of puritan domestic theory), references to Erasmus and the ancients are frequently found among the admittedly more numerous citations of the puritans' ultimate authority – Scripture.[5] As a result, the writings of Christian humanists, puritans and many Anglican conformists are found to be in substantial agreement regarding the superiority of the married state over virginity, the religious duties of householders, the necessity for parents to catechize their children and the spiritual equality and didactic responsibilities of women in the family. Not

---

[3] Chilton Powell, *English Domestic Relations, 1487–1653* (New York, 1917), p. 147; Louis B. Wright, *Middle-Class Culture in Elizabethan England* (Ithaca, NY, 1935), p. 203; Schücking, p. 40; Michael Walzer, *The Revolution of the Saints* (New York, 1972), p. 188. Walzer here opposes Hill's emphasis on puritan patriarchy. Greaves, p. 739, asserts that 'much more than Anglicans, the Puritans developed marriage as a partnership.'

[4] Hill, chapter 13.

[5] Bartholomew Batty, *The Christian mans Closet*, tr. William Lowth (London, 1581), *passim*; e.g., he quoted Vives and 'Erasmus, that worthy man' (fol. 41) on the godly education of children (fols. 17v, 18v, 33v–34v, 41, 74v, 89v, 98v); Aristotle's *Oeconomica*, Plato's *Laws* and Cicero's *De Officiis* in arguing that fathers should instruct their children for the good of the commonwealth; and Seneca, Plutarch, Pliny, Epictetus, Xenophon and other ancients throughout the treatise on these and other aspects of child-rearing. Gouge's *Of Domesticall Duties* (London, 1622) cites Erasmus, as does Bullinger's *The Christen State of Matrimonye*, tr. Miles Coverdale (London 1541), fol. 89v. Bullinger also quoted from the ancients. *cf.* citations in Vives' *Instruction of a Christian Woman*, tr. Richard Hyrde (1540) in Foster Watson, *Vives and the Renascence Education of Women* (New York, 1912), pp. 29–136; or the humanist Thomas Lupset's *Exhortation to Yonge Men* (1544), which attributes to Aristotle (*Politics,* vii and viii) the last word on child-rearing (sig. Cii). The use of classical authors by puritans and humanists is precisely parallel.

only is puritan domestic conduct theory indistinguishable from that of the protestant mainstream, but the spiritualized household of protestant England proves to be flowing in precisely the same direction as Catholic humanist thought about the family in the sixteenth century.

The influence of classical domestic theory on both humanists and puritans explains the most basic of those common assumptions underlying their doctrines of the family.[6] Aristotle, in the *Oeconomica* (I, 3) stated that the association of man and wife is based on reason and that its purpose is not merely existence, but the good life. The humanists combined this idea with elements of Stoic egalitarianism and with the biblical doctrines that marriage was created by God and that woman, redeemed by Christ as man is, is also possessed of a reasonable soul and of religious responsibility.[7] The result which emerged in humanist writings was a concept of marriage as a state of intellectual and spiritual companionship. Reacting partly against monastic abuses, the humanists exalted the married state over unnatural (in the Aristotelian sense) and unbiblical celibacy. Thus, Erasmus, in a treatise translated into English by Richard Taverner and dedicated to Cromwell, called religious bachelorhood 'a form of living both barren and unnatural,' and he commended marriage on the biblical basis of Christ's presence at the wedding at Cana. Even the Virgin Mary, the Apostles, and St Paul were married, he said (contrary to medieval Catholic orthodoxy), and matrimony was advised by Scripture and practiced by the ancients, animals and trees, precious stones (according to Pliny), Indians, Italians, Persians, Britons and Jews.[8] 'Dame nature herself hath enacted marriage,' according to Erasmus, and he even went so far as to equate celibacy with infanticide: 'for there is small diversity betwixt him that murdereth that which begin[s] to be borne, and him which procureth that nothing can be born.'[9] In the Erasmian tradition,

---

[6] Blair Worden, 'Classical Republicanism and the Puritan Revolution,' *History and Imagination*, ed. H. Lloyd-Jones, V. Pearl and B. Worden (New York, 1981), 182–200, notes in passing the 'classicism of the household' (p. 188).

[7] Noted by Paul Siegel in 'Milton and the Humanist Attitude toward Women,' *JHI* 11 (1950), 42–53, p. 45.

[8] Erasmus, *A ryght frutefull Epystle . . . in laude and prayse of matrymony*, tr. Richard Taverner (n.d.), sigs. Aiii–Av, Bi–Bvi. In *An Exhortation to the diligent studye of scripture* (1529), he suggested that St Paul was a widower (sigs. Diii ff).

[9] Erasmus, *Prayse of matrymony*, sigs. Aiiii, cv. He went on to say, 'This that in your body either dryeth up, or with a great danger of your health putrifieth and corrupteth, which in your sleep falleth away, had been a man if ye were a man yourself.'

Juan Luis Vives, tutor to the Princess Mary, devoted the second book of his *Instruction of a Christian Woman* (1523) to the theme of the superiority of the married state, particularly commending his parents' happy union.[10] Thus, Bartholomew Batty was saying nothing distinctively protestant when he asserted that 'marriage is the most excellent state and condition of life . . . which all the godly both by preaching and example have commended unto us, and placed the same in the top of all good works.'[11]

Marriage was seen by all of its sixteenth-century commentators as having three primary goals: companionship, procreation and avoidance of fornication. In both Prayer Books of Edward VI, the last two purposes were placed before companionship. It has been argued that, during the course of the seventeenth century, puritans gradually rearranged this order to place mutual help or companionship first.[12] This argument is suspect in view of the order given in the new homily on matrimony which was authorized in 1562 by Elizabeth: matrimony was 'instituted of God, to the intent that man and woman should live lawfully in a perpetual friendship, to bring forth fruit, and to avoid fornication.'[13] But even the notion that protestantism is at the root of the stress on companionship is wide of the mark. Here, too, the humanist contribution has been ignored. Vives, in his treatise on the duties of husbands, told the husband that he should regard his wife 'as a most faithful secretary of thy cares and thoughts, and in doubtful matters a wise and a hearty counsellor. This is the true society and fellowship of man . . .'[14] Erasmus, in his encomium of matrimony, called it 'an especial sweetness to have one with whom ye may communicate the secret affections of your mind, with whom ye may speak even as it were with your own self.' So vital was companionship as an end of marriage in Sir Thomas More's vision of the ideal commonwealth that his Utopians allowed divorce by mutual consent for 'intolerable offensiveness of disposition' or 'when a married couple agree insufficiently in their dis-

[10] Vives, *Instruction of a Christian Woman*, in Watson, pp. 116–19. Hyrde's translation of this work ran into eight editions by 1592.
[11] Batty, fol. 4v.
[12] James T. Johnson, 'Ends of Marriage,' *CH*, 38 (1969), 429–36; William and Malleville Haller, 'The Puritan Art of Love,' *Huntington Library Quarterly*, 5 (1942), 235–72, pp. 265–6, 270.
[13] *Sermons and Homilies Appointed to be Read in the Churches in the Time of Queen Elizabeth* (1840), p. 506. In any case, H. C. Porter has drawn my attention to the fact that the Prayer Book ordering of 1549 remained unchanged down to 1662.
[14] Vives, *The office and duties of an husband*, tr. Thomas Paynell (1550), in Watson, p. 209.

positions.'[15] Sir Thomas Elyot, citing Aristotle's *Oeconomica*, wrote
that 'the company most according to nature, is that which is
ordained of man and wife, which was constituted, not to the intent
only to bring forth their semblable, but for love especially, and
mutual assistance.'[16] It would seem, then, that the puritan Robert
Cleaver was merely restating a humanist ideal when he said, 'There
can be no greater society or company, than is between a man and his
wife.'[17] In the sixteenth century, the assertion that companionship is
pre-eminent among the ends of marriage was an innovation of Christian humanism, rather than of puritanism.

But procreation as an end of marriage was not much diminished in
importance because of its subordination to companionship. The
exalted ideal of the family which was held by most puritans rather
expanded this goal into the production of good commonwealthmen
and citizens of the Kingdom of God. The family was raised to the
level of a church and commonwealth in microcosm. Batty taught
that 'Marriage is the origin and fountain of all private and public
government . . . [It is] for the procreation and virtuous education of
children, to the preservation of his Church and common wealth.'[18]
Daniel Rogers believed marriage to be 'the seminary of the
commonwealth, seed-plot of the church, pillar (under God) of the
world . . . supporter of laws, states, orders, offices, gifts and services
. . . the foundation of countries, cities, universities, succession of
families, crowns, and kingdoms.'[19] Gouge's parallel statement that
'families are the seminaries to Church and Commonwealth' rested
on the argument that since families 'were before other polities, so
they are somewhat the more necessary: and good members of a
family are like to make good members of Church and commonwealth.' The origins of this supposedly puritan idea should be

---

[15] Erasmus, *Prayse of matrymony*, sigs. Cvi–Cvii; *The Complete Works of St. Thomas More*,
ed. Edward Surtz and J. H. Hexter (New Haven, 1965), vol. 4 (*Utopia*), pp. 189–91.
cf. Erasmus' *Whythe dyvorsemente betwene man and wyfe stondeth with the lawe of God*, tr.
Nycolas Lesse, London [1550], sigs. D–Dii.

[16] Elyot, *Defence of Good Women* (*ca.* 1531–8), in Watson, p. 225.

[17] Robert Cleaver, *A Godly Form of housholde government* (1598), p. 151.

[18] Batty, fol. 3v; see also Cleaver, p. 1, and Thomas Cartwright *Cartwrightiana*, ed.
Albert Peel and Leland H. Carson (1951), p. 159; *cf.* p. 59.

[19] Daniel Rogers, *Matrimoniall Honour* (1642), p. 7; Samuel Ward traced all 'scandals
and enormities' in the commonwealth to parental neglect of religious education
and discipline of children and servants (Sidney Sussex, MS Ward O.8.a, early
hand, n.f.). *cf.* William Jones, *A Briefe Exhortation to all men to set their houses in order*
(1612), p. 3; Richard Baxter, *Christian Directory* (1673), p. 514; 'most of the mis-
chiefs that now infest or seize upon mankind throughout the earth consist in, or
are caused by, the disorders and ill-governedness of families.'

obvious from Gouge's premise: they lie not in protestant theology, but in the Aristotelian notion that the household is the primary essential human association, out of which the highest form of human society, the state, grows (*Politics*, I, 2). Perkins, who clearly saw family government as part of the natural order, actually cited Aristotle as his source when he used the image of the family as the 'seminary of all other societies' and concluded,

It followeth that the holy and righteous government thereof, is a direct means for the good ordering both of Church and Commonwealth; yea that the laws thereof being rightly informed, and religiously observed, are available to prepare and dispose men to the keeping of order in other governments. For this first society is as it were the school, wherein are taught and learned the principles of authority and subjection.[20]

These are classical ideas, transmitted to the puritans by humanist authors and editors, and not drawn from protestant theology.[21] Christian humanism is responsible for the combination of Roman civic-mindedness and Greek notions of the family as the natural basic unit of society – the seminary of the Kingdoms of God and man. Vives identified the household as a commonwealth writ small and a training-ground for church and state. And Erasmus described one of the purposes of marriage in the words of a young man to his love:

We will get subjects for the king and servants for Christ, and where will the unchastity of this matrimony be? . . . I will be your king, and you shall be my queen, and we will govern the family according to our pleasure . . . We will do our endeavour to be good ourselves, and then take care to instruct our children in religion and piety from the very cradle.

In another colloquy, a would-be nun is advised to find 'an agreeable husband, and set up a college in your own house, of which he should be the abbot and you the abbess.'[22] Likewise, Elyot saw the early virtuous education of children in noble households as necessary for them to be made 'apt to the governance of a public weal.'[23] Precisely because of these didactic functions of the household, marriage was portrayed by the Elizabethan humanist Edmund Tilney as some-

[20] Gouge, Dedicatory Epistle. Gouge also used Aristotle's beehive analogy for the family (pp. 16–17); William Perkins, *Workes* (Cambridge, 1618), vol. 3, pp. 669, 698; *cf.* Gouge, p. 5.
[21] *cf.* Hill (pp. 458–9), and Walzer (pp. 183–7), who thinks that the idea of the family as the source and principal constituent of the commonwealth derives from Bodin.
[22] Vives, *Duty of Husbands* in Watson, pp. 202–3; *Coll.*, pp. 95–7, 106.
[23] Elyot, *The Boke Named the Governour* (1531), fols. 15v–16.

thing akin to civic duty, a necessity for the preservation of the realm.[24]

Later in the century, this humanist concept of the household as the seminary of church and commonwealth became an important basis for the puritan stress on household education. The puritans saw a purpose of marriage in the procreation of children to be brought up 'in the fear and nurture of the Lord, and praise of God, that they may be meet for his Church and the commonwealth'; only with godly instruction in the household, they warned, will 'your families... be reformed, your town happily governed.'[25] For Gouge, the family was 'a school wherein the first principles and grounds of government are learned.' Nor was this humanist tradition passed on only to puritans. The seventeenth-century Anglican Jeremy Taylor differed from neither puritans nor Catholic humanists when he described the family as 'seminary of the church' and 'nursery of heaven.'[26]

It is significant that a stress in both humanist and puritan writings (and, as will be seen, in Anglican as well) is on education *in* the household, *by* parents. Not only is this education for the benefit of church and commonwealth, but the family is itself church and commonwealth in microcosm. The significance of marriage, the family and the role of parents – king and queen of the little commonwealth – is thereby greatly increased. This emphasis on religious and moral education within the context of the family has been attributed by historians to the Reformation, with its requirement that everyone be able to read the Bible, appreciate his need for faith in Christ, and acquire the means of participating in a direct communication with God, independent of the mediation of the priesthood. The constant urging, by puritan authors of domestic conduct manuals, of parents to catechize their children and to conduct daily prayer and Bible-reading sessions in the home is seen as evidence that, since 'a special caste of priests no longer mediated between God and man, the residuary legatee was (or in the puritan view should be) the father of the family.' The insistence of puritans

[24] Edmund Tilney, *A brief... discourse of duties in Marriage, called the Flower of Friendshippe* (1568), sig. Aviii.

[25] Batty, fol. 4v; Bartimeus Andrewes, *A very short and pithie Catechisme* (1586), Dedicatory Epistle (to the author's congregation at Yarmouth). A puritan student at St John's, Cambridge, in 1635 also called the family a 'little church' (St John's, Cambridge, MS S.44, p. 49), as did Thomas Brathwaite of Queen's, Oxford (Queen's, MS 423, n.p.).

[26] Gouge, p. 18; Taylor, *Works*, ed. R. Heber (1828), V, pp. 252–3.

on the father's religious responsibilities is incidentally seen as increasing the dependence of the wife on the husband.[27] Thus, it is allegedly puritanism – extreme protestantism – which has spiritualized the family and sacerdotalized the role of the father by entrusting him with the responsibility for household religious education.

This interpretation is understandable in view of the prominence of household instruction in puritan theory and practice. The insistence of early protestants like Bullinger, Becon and Latimer on parental responsibility for religious instruction, was followed later by, for instance, Thomas Gataker, who called parents 'instructors under him [God], for the framing and molding of our minds and souls,' and by Robert Cleaver, who required that the governor of a household 'set an order in his house for the service of God, to wit, that morning and evening, before meals and after meals, prayers and thanks may be made unto God.' He was to be responsible for

the private instruction [of his family], and dealing with them in matters of religion, for the building of them up in true faith and for the inuring and bringing of them to a conscience toward God, that they may not only know and profess religion, but also feel and show the power of religion in their lives ... So it is not enough to bring thy children to be catechised at the church, but thou must labor with them at home after a more plain and easier manner of instruction, that so they may the better profit by the public teaching.

Scripture was to be read daily by the assembled household, according to Cleaver, and the father was to prepare his children to receive the sacraments with short lectures followed by examinations of what they had learned from this instruction.[28] William Perkins also discussed the frequency and composition of household worship: the master of the family was to call the house together at the beginning and end of each day and before and after meals for prayer and 'a conference upon the word of God, for the edification of all the members, to eternal life,' and he should designate periodic fast days, particularly during family crises.[29] William Jones, Perkins and

[27] Hill, pp. 466, 457.
[28] Bullinger, fols. 81v–82v; Thomas Becon, *Catechism* (Cambridge, 1844), pp. 348, 519; Hugh Latimer, *Sermons*, ed. G. E. Corrie (Cambridge, 1844), p. 107; Gataker, *Certaine sermons* (1637), p. 4; Cleaver, pp. 35, 38–40.
[29] Perkins, p. 670; *cf.* John Dod, *Bathshebaes Instructions to her Sonne Lemuel* (1614), pp. 1–2, 61, 64; William Jones, *Briefe Exhortation*, pp. 7, 14, 18–19, 20–24, and *A pithie & short treaties whereby a godly christian is directed how to make his last will* (1612), sig. Aiii. Laurence Chaderton, in a 1590 sermon at Emmanuel College, Cambridge, said that godly parents who train their children in the principles of religion and right behavior are not responsible for their subsequent profanity (Pembroke, Cambridge, MS LC II.164, n.f.).

104   CHRISTIAN HUMANISM AND THE PURITAN SOCIAL ORDER

Dorothy Leigh instructed householders to pray for as well as with their children and servants several times each day.[30] Finally, when the dislocations of the 1640s allowed puritans to establish a presbyterian system of discipline, their exhortations were embodied in the resolutions of church governing bodies. The provincial synod meeting in London in November of 1648 ordered ministers to exhort parents and masters to catechize their children and servants at home, and a meeting of presbyterians and independents at Manchester in 1659 resolved that in order to be admitted to communion, householders must be 'such as maintain the exercises of Christianity, viz., pray in and instruct their families, reading the word . . .'[31]

Ardent protestants of the sixteenth and seventeenth centuries were diligent in carrying out these instructions. Sir Anthony Cooke taught his own five daughters as well as the young Edward VI, and it was said that his goal for his family was 'to embue their infancy with a knowing, serious, and sober religion, which went with them to their graves.'[32] The seventeenth-century puritans Simonds D'Ewes, Ralph Josselin and Richard Baxter all received much of their religious education from their parents and in turn catechized their own children at home.[33] When Bulstrode Whitelocke's family began to increase, he 'began to think indeed, that every man ought to be a priest in his own house, and he formed a resolution of reading prayers daily to his wife and servants – a custom that he never after neglected to observe.'[34] In London, the godly Nehemiah Wallington took to heart his minister's exhortation to 'governors of families to imitate God, to be to those of our family as God is unto us . . . [for] those that you entertain into your family you take not only a charge of their bodies but also of their souls too.' He prayed with his family

[30] Perkins, p. 698; Dorothy Leigh, *The Mother's Blessing* (1621), p. 62; Jones, *Briefe Exhortation*, pp. 20–4.
[31] *Minutes of the Manchester Presbyterian Classis*, ed. W. Shaw (Chetham Society, 1890), pp. 117, n. 1; 400.
[32] Quoted in D. M. Meads' introduction to *The Diary of Lady Margaret Hoby* (1930), p. 13. That his goal was amply realized is evident from the godly households ruled in turn by his most prominent daughters, Mildred Cecil, Lady Burghley, and Lady Anne Bacon. See Pearl Hogrefe, *Women of Action in Tudor England* (Ames, Iowa, 1977), pp. 3–56.
[33] Sir Simonds D'Ewes, *Autobiography and Correspondence*, ed. J. O. Halliwell (1845), vol. 1, pp. 104, 177; cf. D'Ewes' commonplace book, BL, Harl. MS 227, fol. 14v; Alan Macfarlane, *The Family Life of Ralph Josselin* (Cambridge, 1970), pp. 109, 122, 124. Baxter, *Autobiography* (1931), pp. 4–5.
[34] R. H. Whitelocke, *Memoires of Bulstrode Whitelocke* (1860), p. 67. He did so despite the fact that he maintained a household chaplain (p. 83).

and servants daily, reading to them from the Scriptures and instructing them in points of doctrine.[35] The more moderate puritan Simonds D'Ewes is also noteworthy for his devotion to praying and fasting with his young wife, and later in the century, Baxter's work with the congregation at Kidderminster was aimed at training householders to teach their own children. His instructions to pastors exhort them to

> have a special eye upon families, to see that they are well ordered, and the duties of each relation performed ... if you could but get the rulers of families to do their duty, to take up the work where you left it, and help it on, what abundance of good might be done! ... Go occasionally among them ... and ask the master of the family whether he prays with them, and reads the Scripture, or what he doth? Labour to convince such as neglect this, of their sin ... Persuade the master of every family to cause his children and servants to repeat the Catechism to him, every Sabbath evening, and to give him some account of what they have heard at church during the day.[36]

The notion that women were repressed by the religious significance of the father's role, however, is difficult to support given the didactic responsibilities bestowed on mothers or on parents as joint governors of the household by puritans. Wives were given the responsibility by Cleaver for early education of children, for 'a child wisely trained up by the mother in the young years will be the easilier brought to goodness, by the Father's godly care.' Dod, Jones and Batty gave mothers the responsibility for older as well as younger children. Mothers were to oversee the development of a religious vocabulary in young children: the child's first word should be 'God,' 'from whence as from a most lucky lot, all the whole web of speech should begin. For this motherly care and discipline shall be very profitable to all children of young and tender years, and shall make them more apt and ready for the attaining of greater studies.' The mother's duty to older children was 'to teach them the true knowledge and worship of the Almighty ... the duty they owe to their country, the reverend love they should bear toward their parents and kinfolk'; further-

---

[35] BL, Add. MS 4088, fols. 121 v–122; *cf.* fols. 14, 21 v, 78 v, 84, 104 v, 105 v, 127, 128 v, 129 v–130 v, 136 v, 138 v. He purchased a copy of Gouge's *Domesticall Duties* in 1622 to aid him in this task: Folger Shakespeare Library MS V.a.436, p. 13. I am indebted to Derek Hirst for this reference; it is also noted by Paul Seaver, *Wallington's World* (Stanford, 1985), p. 79.

[36] D'Ewes, *Autobiography*, vol. 1, pp. 363, 375, 409, 429–30, 435; Baxter, *The Reformed Pastor* (1656), ch. 2, section i, 4; *The Catechising of Families* (1683), *passim*.

more, mothers were to teach both sons and daughters.[37] Gouge addressed husband and wife jointly as 'parents' and 'masters' when informing them of their religious duties, and he gave both of them responsibility for the instruction of children and servants.[38] So exalted was the spiritual role of the mother in Brilliana Conway's estimation, that she called godly mothers 'living images of God' for their families.[39]

Puritan women took their religious responsibilities as seriously in practice as in theory. Cleaver's work on household government was dedicated to three puritan gentlemen *and their wives*, in view of the 'holy exercises daily used and exercised in all your houses,' and in such puritan households as that of Lady Margaret Hoby, the role of the mistress in maintaining the daily regimen of family prayer and Bible study is apparent. Despite the fact that the Hoby household seems to have maintained a chaplain, Lady Margaret frequently took it upon herself to supervise the catechizing of her servants, hear their repetitions of Sunday sermons, or read to them from the works of puritan divines. She was responsible for the religious education of Hoby's heir, John Sydenham, and of her young relation, Jane Lutton, and herein she followed the godly pattern of the puritan Countess of Huntingdon, who had been entrusted with Margaret's own upbringing.[40] Similarly, Mildred Cecil supervised the religious education of her son and stepson, and her sister Lady Anne Bacon's spiritual overseeing of her own two sons even after they had attained adulthood is well known.[41] In the next century, Simonds D'Ewes' mother and grandmother, Ralph Josselin's wife, Samuel Clarke's wife and Mrs Ratcliffe of Chester provide other examples of puritan women who occupied a didactic role in the household.[42] Grace Wallington's

---

[37] Cleaver, pp. 40–1; Batty, fol. 55; *cf.* Dod, *Bathshebaes Instructions*, p. 3, and Jones, *Briefe Exhortation*, pp. 10–11. D'Ewes pointed out that the mother was 'ordinarily the chief bringer up of children in their tender years' (BL, Harl. MS 227, fol. 14v); this was a commonplace frequently drawn from Plutarch (e.g., by the author of Pembroke, Cambridge, MS LC II.12, p. 41). Thomas Brathwaite noted the importance of mothers catechizing daughters as well as sons in his commonplace book, Queen's, Oxford, MS 423, n.p.

[38] Gouge, Dedicatory Epistle, pp. 253–66, 497–505, 518–83, 646–93.

[39] Nottingham University MSS, Box 166 (Conway), fol. 53v, my translation of her '*Meres sont les images des dieu . . . les vives images de dieu*' [sic].

[40] Cleaver, Dedicatory Epistle, p. 13; Hoby, *Diary, passim*, p. 238, n. 12; *cf.* Claire Cross, *The Puritan Earl* (1966), pp. 24–7, 57.

[41] Hogrefe, pp. 7, 35, 46–9.

[42] D'Ewes, vol. 1, pp. 104, 112–13, 117; BL, Harl. 227, fol. 14v, Harl. 118 (fol. 26v is D'Ewes' note of thanks for his mother's letter of 'grave counsel'), BL, Harl. 373; Macfarlane, pp. 109, 122; R. C. Richardson, *Puritanism in North-west England* (Manchester, 1972), pp. 105, 107–9, 134, 179.

religiously didactic role extended to instruction of her husband in accepting as providential the disasters that befell the family.[43]

But a glance at the domestic activities of Catholics and Anglicans of both sexes will once again reveal that the puritans were not unique in their theories of household religious education. Lettice, Lady Falkland, surely no puritan, was as devoted to public prayers and lectures as Lady Margaret Hoby, and she usually spent an hour with her maids each morning, praying with them and catechizing them. The Anglican Lady Danvers, 'with her whole family ... did, every Sabbath, shut up the day at night with a general, with a cheerful singing of Psalms,' and the Laudian John Cosin's eulogy of Dorothy Holmes recorded that 'as of herself, so she was sedulous and very affectionate in the education of her children, that they might serve God and the commonwealth.'[44] The predominantly female household of Nicholas Ferrar at Little Gidding was certainly characterized by pious domestic activities.[45]

Clearly, a consensus on parental responsibility for catechism existed among protestants of all stripes, from the author of the sermons on marriage in the Elizabethan *Book of Homilies*, to the puritans, to such inveterate opponents of puritanism as Cosin.[46] But the basis of the consensus is not to be found exclusively in protestant doctrine. Once again, protestants are indebted to Christian humanism for their household teaching. It was the humanist promotion of religious and classical education, at least as much as protestant biblicism, which established the strong trend of household instruction that characterized religious families of early modern England. Erasmus, in his commentary on the Ten Commandments, directed children to honor their parents, 'by whom he [God] hath instructed and taught us unto the knowledge of God'; and in a sermon on the wedding at Cana, he informed parents that 'to have brought up or taught their child well is the office more properly belonging to the father and mother than to have begotten it or to have born it.'[47] The

[43] Seaver, pp. 86–9.
[44] H. C. White, *English Devotional Literature, 1600–1640* (Madison, 1931), pp. 60, 63; John Donne, *A Sermon of Commemoration of the Lady Danvers* (1627), p. 133; John Cosin, *Works* (Oxford, 1863), I, p. 27. John Donne, *Sermons*, ed. G. R. Potter and E. M. Simpson (Berkeley, 1955), vol. 2, pp. 223ff, also lauded household prayer and religious instruction.
[45] A. M. Williams, *Conversations at Little Gidding* (Cambridge, 1970), Introduction.
[46] *Book of Homilies*, p. 507; cf. also the official catechism of Alexander Nowell, tr. Thomas Norton (1570), fols 9v–10, 73; Cosin, *Works*, I, p. 184.
[47] Erasmus, *A playne and godly exposytion or declaratiō of the comune Crede and of the x. comaundementes* (1533), fol. 162v; cf. *Prayse of Matrymony*, sig. Diii, and *Sermon... in the second chaptyre of the Gospell of saynt Johan* (n.p., n.d.), fols. 12–13v.

Erasmian Richard Whitforde, in his *Werke for housholders* (1537), urged parents to begin religious instruction of their children 'as soon as they can speak,' adding that for householders, 'a very good sure pastime upon the holy day, is to read . . . and gather thereunto as many persons as you can.'[48] The educational responsibilities of mothers as well as fathers were set forth by the Christian humanists: Erasmus and Whitforde addressed their instructions to 'parents,' not just to 'fathers,' and Hyrde, Elyot and Tilney commended Christian women who taught their children.[49] Vives specifically told Christian women to teach their children. Men, he said, should choose their wives carefully, for 'a woman well brought up is fruitful and profitable unto her husband, for so shall his house be wisely governed, his children virtuously instructed, the affections less ensued and followed, so that they live in tranquility and virtue.' A century later, the puritan Brilliana Conway echoed this humanist advice, stressing the spiritual benefits that would accrue to the husband himself from his wife's wise counsel and religious guidance: a man, she said, should choose a wife who can 'further him in religion and serving God purely.'[50]

The Catholic humanist, Nicholas Harpsfield, in his biography of Sir Thomas More, has provided a picture of a truly ideal religious household, one that (theological contents aside) would surely have been admired by Gouge, Cleaver and Perkins as much as by devout Anglicans and Catholics. More had one son and three daughters, 'which children from their youth he brought up in virtue, and knowledge both in the Latin and the Greek tongues, whom he would often exhort to take virtue and learning for their meat and play for their sauce.' The family gathered daily to say psalms and litanies, and before bedtime, More again gathered them – children, wards and servants included – to say psalms and collects with them. His renowned daughter Margaret was to her own children a 'double mother':

as one not content to bring them forth only into the world, but instructing them also her self in virtue and learning. At what time her husband was upon a certain displeasure taken against him in King Henry's days sent to the Tower, certain sent from the king to search her house, upon a sudden run-

---

[48] Richard Whitforde, *The werke for housholders* (1537), sigs. Biii, Eii.
[49] Hyrde in Watson, p. 50; Elyot, *Defence*, p. 233; Tilney, sigs. Ciii, Cv, Cviii.
[50] Vives, *Duty of Husbands* in Watson, pp. 202–3, 209; *Instruction of a Christian Woman*, Watson, p. 128; Conway MS, fol. 176. Vives had also recommended that fathers teach their children (*Duty of Husbands*, p. 201).

ning upon her, found her, not puling and lamenting, but full busily teaching her children.[51]

She followed the example of her father, lauded by Erasmus because 'despite his commitments to the affairs of state [he] did not hesitate to serve as tutor to his wife, son, and daughters, beginning with their religious education and then advancing to their Greek and Latin studies.'[52] Vives' advice and Margaret More's example were later followed by the protestant humanist Catherine Parr, who was chided by the king for her didactic role in the 'royal nursery.'[53]

Both Catholics and puritans argued that religious education should begin as soon as possible, and that it should be made a pleasant experience for the child. Erasmus urged that Christians 'be instructed with the doctrine of Christ, being yet tender infants in our parents' arms and wanton children at our nurse's teat, for it is imprinted most deep and cleaveth most surely which the rude and unformed shelf of our soul doth first receive and learn.' His sermon on Jesus' childhood was written 'to be pronounced and preached of a child unto children,' since 'no age is unripe to learn holiness, nay rather none other age is more timely and meet to learn Christ than that which knoweth not yet the world.'[54] Richard Whitforde likewise recommended that 'as soon as they can speak, we must also teach our children to serve God,' and Elyot argued that the formation of a future governor must begin at birth.[55]

So convinced were they that 'no age is unripe to learn holiness' that they even directed their attention to the catechetical potential of the nursing period. Despite a recent historian's attribution of the sixteenth-century concern with maternal nursing to puritanism, it was Erasmus and Vives who first demanded an end to the common practice of wealthy mothers of sending their infants out to wet nurses

[51] Nicholas Harpsfield, *The life and death of Sir Thomas More . . . written in the tyme of Queene Marie*, ed. E. V. Hitchcock (1932), pp. 19. 75, 79; cf. pp. 83, 92; More's 1521 letter to Margaret (Watson, p. 185), reveals that he considered the education and discipline of his family more important than any other duty:

I pray thee, Meg, see that I understand by you, what your studies are. For rather than I would suffer you, my children, to live idly, I would myself look unto you, with the loss of my temporal estate, bidding all other cares and businesses farewell, amongst which there is nothing more sweet unto me than thyself, my dearest daughter.

[52] Erasmus, *De pueris statim ac liberaliter instituendis declamatio, CWE* 26, ed. J. K. Sowards (Toronto, 1985), pp. 322–3.
[53] J. K. McConica, *English Humanists and Reformation Politics* (Oxford, 1965), ch. 7.
[54] *Studye of scripture* (n.p.); *A Sermon of the chylde Jesus* (n.d.), title page, sig. Bviii; *cf. De pueris, CWE* 26, *passim*.
[55] Whitforde, sigs. Biiii–Bv; Elyot, *Governour*, citing Quintilian, Plutarch and Erasmus.

during their earliest formative years. Erasmus' Magister, in his commentary on the Ten Commandments, answering the student's question regarding the woman who 'refuses the irksomeness of giving
her children suck, and . . . doth [not] teach and nurture them to good
manners,' replies that the less diligently parents perform their duty
to their children, the less honor is due to them.[56] The juxtaposition
of nursing and education here is noteworthy. Vives, in his *Instruction
of a Christian Woman* (1523), used Quintilian and Plutarch as his
authorities when he advised that children 'have all one both for their
mother, their nurse, and their teacher.' And Richard Hyrde, in his
introduction to Margaret More's translation of Erasmus' *Precatio
dominica in septem portiones* (1524), dedicated to Frances, daughter of
Charles Brandon, Duke of Suffolk, concluded from the fact that
Frances had been nursed by her mother that she would probably
turn out well.[57]

Zealous protestants accepted all of these humanist precepts
wholeheartedly. Batty explicitly cited Erasmus and the ancients
when he urged an early start on domestic religious instruction and
insisted that education must not be a negative experience, and
Perkins echoed the motivation of Erasmus' *Colloquies* and the
explicit instruction of his pedagogical treatise, *De pueris statim ac
liberaliter instituendis declamatio*, when he taught that 'the first instruction of children in learning and religion must be so ordered, that
they may take it with delight.'[58] Perkins, Batty, Gouge and Elizabeth
Clinton (the puritan Countess of Lincoln) likewise drew on the
humanist tradition in recommending that mothers nurse their own
children because of the effects of this early experience on the child's
spiritual development. Batty was certain that 'odious errors' would
be sucked in with the milk of 'lewd Nurses,' and he repeated Vives'
exhortation to nurses not to sing silly songs and rhymes to their
charges, lest 'they be nouseled in folly, and fraught with corrupt conditions.'[59] Thus, in the very crucial area of household religious teach-

---

[56] R. V. Schnucker, 'The English Puritans and Pregnancy, Delivery, and Breast Feeding,' *History of Childhood Quarterly*, 1, 4 (1974), 637–58; Erasmus *Playne and godly
exposytion*, fols. 163v–164; *cf. De pueris, CWE* 26, p. 315.

[57] Vives, *Instruction of a Christian Woman*, Watson, pp. 39–40, 123; Hyrde in
Watson, p. 172.

[58] Batty, fols. 10–13v; Perkins, p. 694; Leigh, pp. 46–7; *cf.* Erasmus, *Colloquies*, Preface, and *De pueris, passim* and esp. pp. 339ff.

[59] Perkins, p. 693; Batty, fol. 54 (*cf.* Vives, *Instruction of a Christian Woman*, Watson, p.
125); Gouge, pp. 513, 515; Clinton, *Countess of Lincolns Nurserie* (1622), *passim; cf.*
Erasmus, *De pueris*, 315. An apparently puritan student at mid-seventeenth-
century Pembroke College, Cambridge, devoted several pages of his theological
notebook to this subject, citing the authority of Plutarch in favor of maternal

ing, puritan doctrine varied little, if at all, from that of Catholic humanists.

In addition to their stress on the didactic responsibilities of parents, the puritan emphasis on the householder's disciplinary duties has been interpreted as spiritualizing the family and sacerdotalizing the role of the father. To 'the preachers' is attributed the idea of the father as governor of a little state and priest of a little church; accordingly, protestantism is credited with the logical implication of this idea – a spiritually authoritarian household.[60] Undeniably, puritan domestic conduct books without exception urged children to show deference to their parents and parents to exercise strict control over their charges; furthermore, it is clear that discipline was seen as a religious responsibility: the child was to be corrected 'in zeal of God's glory.'[61] The parent, rather than the priest, was made responsible for the child's spiritual state, so that Batty could call parents God's vicars on earth, while Perkins equated masters of families with bishops.[62] But the acknowledged Augustinian sources for this 'puritan' doctrine had been utilized both by protestants and by Catholics, and especially by Christian humanists, so that once again the originality of puritan domestic conduct theory must be denied. More's deference to his father is well known, and the submission required of children by the Erasmian Whitforde was neither less extreme nor less religious than that demanded of puritan children. Whitforde recommended that children kneel before their parents each evening and request their benediction, and he provided formulae both for the request by the children and for the parents'

---

nursing (Pembroke MS LC II.12, pp. 42–45; *cf.* Trin. MS R.16.9, fols. 336–336v, also citing Plutarch.) The preachers' exhortations were heeded by such puritan wives as Mrs Josselin, who nursed all of her children (Macfarlane, p. 83), and D'Ewes' mother (*Autobiography*, vol. 1, pp. 24, 26). It is interesting to note that the Anglican bishop Jeremy Taylor followed the humanist/puritan tradition on this point: in a discussion of early education by parents, he judged the nursing of children to be 'the first, and most natural and necessary instance of piety which mothers can show to their babes' (*Works*, vol. 4, p. 157).

[60] Hill, pp. 458–62.

[61] Becon, *Catechism*, pp. 353–5; Baxter, *Christian Directory*, p. 543; Dod and Cleaver, *A Godly Forme of Householde Government* (1598), p. 279; Cleaver, p. 43; Batty, fol. 22.

[62] Batty, fols. 15, 57v, 65v; Perkins, p. 699. Both cited Augustine: *Quilibet pater familias, quia superintendit domui, episcopus dice [sic] potest* (fol. 15 in Batty). Brilliana Conway drew the more extreme analogy, '*Peres et meres sont les Images des dieu. Nous sont diue domestique* [sic] . . .' (fol. 53v). Batty came to the not very protestant conclusion that parents who acted diligently on his advice would thereby save their own souls, even if their children rebelled against their authority (fols. 22, 58).

response which clearly placed mothers and fathers in a quasi-priestly role.[63]

Humanists and puritans further agreed on the nature of correction, both showing a decided preference for reasoning with the wayward child or servant, rather than executing corporal punishment, and both emphasizing the need for justice, understanding and mercy to be shown. Elyot's discussion of early education urged the use of kindness, rather than stripes, and Vives told mothers to balance correction of disobedience with affectionate rewarding of good behavior.[64] Whitforde's statement that

Whosoever do the correction, whether it be in lashes or in words, let it be done with the charity of our Lord and with a mild and soft spirit, that ever it be done for the reformation of the person, rather than for the revenging of the fault; and therefore should you never do any manner of correction while you be vexed, chafed, troubled, wroth, or angry . . .

was later echoed by the protestant Batty: 'Teach not by means of threatenings and blows, but by persuasion . . . It is the part of wise parents, to rebuke their children without contumely, cheek, or taunt, and to praise them without flattery or adulation . . . that their children reverence them for their gravity of life, and love them for the pleasantness of their manners.'[65] Puritans agreed that above all, parents should never correct a child in anger. Perkins ordered that disobedient children 'be restrained by the bridle of discipline. First, by reproof in word, and when that will not help, by the rod of correction. Yet in this point two extremes are carefully to be avoided: that the parents be not either too severe, or too indulgent to the child.' Cleaver urged that discipline be consistent, just and merciful. Ignorance of the law should be taken into account, as should the offending child's motive, age and general habits.[66] Gataker urged gentle discipline to 'entice and allure' children to good behavior, since 'the name of *children* is a most sweet name, savouring strongly of love,' without which 'there is little hope of learning.'[67]

[63] Schücking, p. 6; cf. St John's College, Cambridge, MS S.34 (1620), p. 10; Whitforde, sigs. Eiii–Eiiii.
[64] Elyot, *Governour*, fol. 32; Vives, *Instruction*, Watson, pp. 126–7, 129–32.
[65] Whitforde, sig. Dvi; Batty, fols. 7–8, 24–27. cf. Erasmus' long diatribe against the corporal punishment of children which comprises much of *De pueris*, CWE 26.
[66] Perkins, p. 694; Cleaver, pp. 43, 46–7.
[67] Gataker, pp. 4–5; cf. Dod, *Bathshebaes Instructions*, p. 6. It is noteworthy, given recent literature on the supposed absence of affection in the early modern family, that both humanists and puritans found it necessary to caution parents against the opposite extreme: Batty, fol. 55; Perkins, p. 694; D'Ewes, vol. 1, pp. 30, 36, 63–4; BL, Harl. 227, fol. 14v; cf. Lawrence Stone, *The Family, Sex and Marriage in England* (New York, 1977), chs. 3 and 5. Lucy Hutchinson noted her mother-in-law's 'indulgent tenderness to her infants' in her *Memoires of the Life of Colonel Hutchinson*, ed. Julius Hutchinson (1822), vol. 1, p. 63.

Both likewise held the mother's role in family discipline to be as important as the father's. Whitforde, for instance, made mothers the primary domestic disciplinarians, and Harpsfield recorded approvingly that More married his second wife 'for the ruling and governing of his children, house, and family.'[68] Gouge, therefore, did little more than echo humanist sentiments when he wrote to his parishioners at Blackfriars that the husband ought to make his wife 'a joint governor of the family with himself, and refer the ordering of many things to her discretion, and with all honourable and kind respect to carry himself toward her.' Perkins similarly called the wife 'the associate, not only in office and authority, but also in advice, and counsel' of her husband, and one of the ways in which she was to govern the household was 'by ordering her children and servants in wisdom, partly by instruction, partly by admonition, when there is need.'[69]

The importance of women which has been noted in puritan theories of domestic conduct, as well as the exaltation of marriage and the household – the woman's primary sphere of influence – obviously belies the thesis that protestantism reduced the significance of women when it banned veneration of the Virgin and the saints (many of whom were female) and gave the father a semi-priestly role upon which the wife was dependent.[70] In fact, puritans vehemently renounced the notion that the wife's salvation depended on her husband's priestly intervention. The puritan woman was as responsible for her degree of sanctification as was her husband for his, since 'most true it is, that women are as men are, reasonable creatures, and have flexible wits, both to good and evil.'[71] Men and women were seen by puritans as spiritually equal, and this equality was to be manifest in the marriage relationship. More than one puritan sermon argued that

The husband is also to understand, that as God created the woman, not of the head, and so equal in authority with her husband, so also he created her not of Adam's foot that she should be trodden down and despised, but he took her out of the rib, that she might walk jointly with him, under the conduct and government of her head.[72]

[68] Whitforde, fol. Dvi; Harpsfield, p. 93.
[69] Gouge, p. 5; Perkins, pp. 700ff; *cf.* Cleaver, pp. 85ff; Batty, fol. 3v. Mrs. Josselin certainly functioned as a joint governor: Macfarlane, p. 96.
[70] Hill, pp. 450, 457.   [71] Gouge, p. 35; Batty, fol. 3v; Cleaver, p. 157.
[72] Cleaver, p. 201; Perkins, p. 691; Griffith, *Bethel* (1633), p. 289; *cf.* the very different conclusion of the Anglican John Donne that Eve was taken from Adam's side, 'where she weakens him enough, and therefore should do all she can to be a helper,' in *Sermons*, ed. G. R. Potter and E. M. Simpson (Berkeley, 1955), vol. 2, p. 346 (*cf.* pp. 337, 344–5).

Daniel Rogers taught that woman was created 'of man, equal to him in dignity ... Hence, marriage is called a match.'[73] The idea of spiritual equality which the puritans held militated against popular notions of female inferiority:

Such statements as 'It is better to bury a wife, than to marry one' or 'if we could be without women, we should be without great troubles': These and such like sayings, tending to the dispraise of women, some maliciously, and indiscreetly, do vomit out, contrary to the mind of the Holy Ghost, who saith that she was ordained as a helper, and not a hinderer.[74]

Historians have naturally adopted the position that the necessity of education for women and the allowance of freedom of conscience for women resulted from this theological stance.[75] It explains the fact that Bale not only lauded Anne Askew for her knowledge of Scripture, but he also excused her desertion of her husband since he persecuted her for her true faith.[76]

The principle of obedience to God before husband has been regarded by historians of puritanism as 'the camel's head of liberty within the tent of masculine supremacy.'[77] It has even been very plausibly suggested that the women petitioners of the Civil War period used sexual equality before God as their legitimation for political action by women, arguing that women and men have an equal interest in the affairs of the church, since they have been equally redeemed by Christ.[78] In most circumstances, however, public activity by women was not considered at all proper. Puritans agreed with the majority opinion of their day that a woman's place is in the home.[79] Nevertheless, the fact that the home had been raised to the level of church/commonwealth in microcosm and that the mother's duties within that home in the areas of discipline and instruction were so strongly emphasized by puritans indicates a relatively high position for women in their social scheme. Gouge elevated the mother's status within the household to that of a public servant: a calling to be joint governor of a family must be as significant (and as time-consuming) as a public calling, he said; otherwise

---

[73] Rogers, p. 60; cf. pp. 61–71.   [74] Batty, fol. 156.
[75] For example, Powell, pp. 147ff; Hallers, *passim* and especially p. 249; cf. Becon, *Catechism*, pp. 376–7; Batty, fol. 75v.
[76] John Bale, *Examinations of Anne Askewe* (1547) in *Select Works* (Cambridge, 1849), pp. 155–6, 198–9.   [77] Hallers, p. 252.
[78] Patricia Higgins, 'The Reactions of Women, with Special Reference to Women Petitioners,' in *Politics, Religion, and the English Civil War*, ed. Brian Manning (1973), p. 215.
[79] For example, H. Smith, *Preparative to Marriage* (1591), p. 46; Cleaver, p. 19.

'what comfort in spending their time should most women have, who are not admitted to any public function in Church or commonwealth? Indeed, in that proper fulfilment of household duties benefits both church and commonwealth, the mother's role 'may be accounted a public work.'[80] A note of caution should be injected here, however. It must not be concluded that the puritan marriage relationship was in actuality egalitarian, or that puritan women were completely 'liberated' from the control of their spouses. Obedience to husbands was strongly enjoined and surely expected under most circumstances, and the authority of the woman in the household, however exalted, was still even in the most liberal theory a slight degree less than that of her husband. Cleaver taught that the charge of household government lay unequally on husband and wife, the husband being the 'chief governor' and the wife a 'fellow helper,' exercising maximum authority in her husband's absence; however, Gouge pointed out the 'smallness of the disparity' between spouses in light of spiritual equality of the sexes and of the significance of female domestic responsibilities.[81]

It would seem logical to conclude that puritans, by teaching sexual equality before God and a wife's duty to obey God before her husband, by encouraging female education on the basis of equal rationality and spiritual responsibility of men and women, and by elevating the marriage relationship and the woman's spiritual role as educator and governor within the household, can be considered responsible for the first tentative steps toward a modern vision of sexual equality. However the thesis that it was protestantism, and especially protestantism of the hotter sort, which raised the position of women to a level only slightly inferior to that of men, fails to account for all of the data. If protestant theology is the source of the idea of spiritual equality of the sexes in puritan thought, then one would expect Catholics writing about domestic conduct to be teaching spiritual inequality and female inferiority. In fact, this is not the case; there is no evidence that protestants in the sixteenth century were saying anything about women and their role in the household

---

[80] Gouge, p. 18.
[81] Gouge, p. 273; Cleaver, p. 9. Kathleen Davies, 'The Sacred Condition of Equality—How Original Were Puritan Doctrines of Marriage?', *Social History*, 5 (1977), 563–78, argues that puritan marriages were altogether traditional in their patriarchy; however, Edmund Leites, 'The Duty to Desire: Love, Friendship, and Sexuality in Some Puritan Theories of Marriage,' *Journal of Social History*, 15 (1982), 384–408, has presented evidence to the contrary in puritan practice, as has Richardson, pp. 107–9. One must conclude that the ambivalence toward egalitarianism in theory was reflected in uncertain and various practice.

which Catholic humanists had not already said. Erasmus posited long before the puritans that wives should obey God's command over that of an ungodly husband; Hyrde urged women's education since 'they are the one half of all mankind'; and Vives, in words directly copied (but not attributed to Vives) by Cleaver, said that 'the woman, even as man, is a reasonable creature and hath a flexible wit both to good and evil.'[82] Not only do women share rationality with men, according to Vives, they are also spiritually men's equals: 'The Lord doth admit women to the mystery of his religion . . . and he doth declare that they were created to know high matters, and to come as well as men unto the beatitude, and therefore they ought and should be instructed and taught, as we men be.'[83] Furthermore, the opinion that marriage was seen by Catholics as a necessary evil and by protestants as a positive good, and that 'this difference of attitude toward marriage accounts to a large extent for the difference in the way woman was regarded, the Puritan conception being much the higher,' is nonsense if the very positive humanist views of marriage and housewifery are taken into account.[84]

Thus, rational and spiritual equality of the sexes, as well as the elevation of marriage and the household as spiritual entities, are humanist, rather than puritan, propositions. To say this is not to diminish the importance of either the propositions themselves or of puritanism as a means by which they were transmitted to generations of English protestants. The impact of these ideas on the lives of the godly and of their neighbors was significant, perhaps even transformative.[85] The fact that puritans devoted so much sermon time to humanist ideas about the family helped to create a vital area of consensus in Tudor and early Stuart England, one intimately related to the larger puritan goal of establishing a truly godly commonwealth. But puritans did not invent these ideas; they were

[82] Erasmus, *Studye of scripture*, sig. Fii; Hyrde, in Watson, p. 30; Vives, *Duty of Husbands*, Watson, pp. 198, 201; *cf.* Cleaver, p. 157. Similar sentiments were expressed by Elyot and More (Watson, pp. 228, 179).
[83] In Watson, p. 201.   [84] Powell, p. 121.
[85] To say this, on the other hand, is not to suggest that humanism was the only transformative influence on the puritan household. Peter Lake, 'Puritan Identities,' *JEH*, 35 (1984), 112–23, p. 117, is correct to observe that in many of its activities the puritan household was 'a center not of Christian humanism but of an aggressive style of puritan piety, actively concerned to confront and face down the "superstitions" of the surrounding populace.' Puritans added their own peculiar accretions to the humanist intellectual tradition of which they were a part. Lake's example of family acts of iconoclasm directed by the patriarch is obviously irrelevant to the humanist assumptions that underlay the more pacific aspects of John Bruen's family religion.

simply carrying the Erasmian tradition of the family as church and commonwealth in microcosm into the next century. In similar fashion, they would transmit humanist ideas about reforming the larger society to ensuing generations, ultimately becoming so identified with that body of reformist social thought that it would come to be labeled 'puritan.'

5

Work, wealth and welfare

The assumption that puritan concern with discipline led to a stereotypically bourgeois disdain for the idle as social parasites and the poor as justly condemned of God has become an historiographical commonplace. The material prosperity which in at least some cases accompanied the puritans' single-minded devotion to labor in a calling has brought against them charges of greed, uncharitable attitudes and exploitative business practices, from both contemporary opponents and modern historians. Richard Bancroft accused puritan preachers of complacent unconcern with gentry oppression of the poor and failure to exhort their congregations to charity. And in a 1636 sermon preached in Great St Mary's, Cambridge, John Normanton of Caius charged that the love of money would 'make the puritan leave ruling of the rest amongst his sisters and singing of preserve us, lord, from Turk and pope, and turn bishop and put on a rochet. This is that which makes the rich city cormorant, he that pays the poor water man by the statute of Harry the eighth . . . to devour the widow and the orphan.'[1]

The assertions of the enemy ought to be viewed with some suspicion; nevertheless, historians since Weber and Tawney have followed the lead of the anti-puritans and attributed to the hotter sort the doctrines that wealth is a sign of God's favor and poverty an

---

[1] Richard Bancroft, *Tracts*, ed. Albert Peel (Cambridge, 1953), p. 72. Normanton's sermon is recorded in Sidney Sussex, Ward MS F, fol. 28v; Ward and the other heads reviewed the sermon in consistory court on 14 March 1636 because of its popish leanings on a number of points. There is no evidence, however, that Normanton was censured for this judgment against the precisians, or that he failed to satisfy the heads as to his orthodoxy at this time. He was finally deprived of his fellowship in 1639 and subsequently joined the Roman church. See Normanton entry in John Venn, *Alumni Cantabrigienses* (Cambridge, 1922), Part I, vol. 3, and Venn's *Biographical History of Gonville and Caius College, 1349–1897* (Cambridge, 1897), p. 248.

indication of divine disapproval. They have concluded that puritans were indeed proponents of a ruthlessly capitalist ethic. Louis B. Wright traced the growth of bourgeois culture in England in part to the 'gospel of work as outlined by Perkins . . . [which] became a fundamental dogma in the religion of the Puritan middle class of the seventeenth century.'[2] Christopher Hill has elaborated the theme, arguing that it is since the Reformation that 'the sordid sin of avarice has been transmuted into the religious and patriotic duty of thrift'; labor, formerly a curse, is now a religious duty; and poverty is no longer a holy state, but presumptive evidence of wickedness.[3] Puritan employers, carrying the preachers' innovations to the extreme, are said to have set the poor on work in order to expand industrial production and enrich their own rising class: 'there is the very closest connection between the protestant ideology of hard work and the economic needs of English society,' according to Hill.[4] While Catholics maintained the merit of indiscriminate generosity, a systematic repression of the poor, its roots 'deep in protestant theology,' is laid at the feet of puritans.[5]

Of course, this thesis has not been without its critics. It has been modified by historians who find puritans and Anglicans in broad agreement on economic issues, and significantly undermined by those who question whether Elizabethan and early Stuart theorists (whatever their religious orientation) were in any sense capitalistic or even very business-like in their economic theory. C. H. and Katherine George admit the development of an 'acquisitive rationale' and a 'work ethic' (the corollary of the doctrine of calling, they tell us) in the sixteenth century, but they insist that the intellectual precursors of the full-blown capitalist society of the later seventeenth century were not exclusively puritans. Timothy Breen agrees that a consensus on proper attitudes toward work and wealth existed between puritans and Anglicans; moreover, he argues that the capitalistic spirit of the pre-Civil War period was as non-existent as

[2] Louis B. Wright, *Middle-Class Culture in Elizabethan England* (Ithaca, 1935), p. 185. On the Weber thesis, its modifications and its critics, see *Protestantism and Capitalism*, ed. Robert W. Green (Boston, 1959); for a recent defense of it, see Gordon Marshall, *Presbyteries and Profits* (Oxford, 1980).
[3] Hill, *Puritanism and Revolution* (New York, 1958), p. 218; *cf.* Richard Greaves, *Society and Religion in Elizabethan England* (Minneapolis, 1981), p. 751.
[4] *Ibid.*, p. 221, and *Society and Puritanism* (New York, 1964), p. 276. Perkins, according to Hill, 'inherited, and developed, a tradition of *Protestant* thought on the subject' of poverty (p. 219 of *Puritanism and Revolution*, emphasis mine).
[5] Hill, *Society and Puritanism*, p. 271. Margaret James, *Social Problems and Policy during the Puritan Revolution* (1930), pp. 249–51, charges that puritan severity toward the poor produced a drastic decline in poor relief during the 1640s and 1650s.

was the puritan/Anglican economic controversy. C. John Sommerville has recently gone further and produced evidence for a work
ethic only after 1660, and then with stronger Anglican than dissenter
support.[6] Other historians have followed suit, describing Elizabethan
and early Stuart attitudes as monastic, anti-entrepreneurial and
traditionalist.[7] One recent contribution to the argument assumes
puritan economic conservatism and suggests that the London sponsors of many puritan sermons were struggling artisans, rather than
those wealthy merchants whose economic ethics were clearly in conflict with the instructions they received from the pulpit.[8]

Undeniably, some light has been shed on puritan attitudes in the
course of this scholarly conflict. However the intellectual origins of
puritan ideas have been rather obscured by the smoke of battle than
illuminated by the occasional flashes of historiographical insight. It
seems reasonable to expect that an investigation of the puritans'
sources would reveal a great deal about the nature and context of
their economic ethics, about the puritan/conformist economic consensus, and ultimately about the relationship between protestantism and capitalism. Accordingly, let us examine what those Christian
humanists who informed puritan household theory had to say about
work and idleness, getting and spending, poverty and poor relief,
and evaluate the extent to which puritan thought in these areas of
social theory was derived from Erasmian humanism.

We have seen that while humanist domestic conduct theory was in
most of its aspects a radical departure from medieval values, it still
maintained a degree of traditional patriarchalism. In similar fashion,
Christian humanists can be seen continuing a medieval campaign
against idleness and avarice, but with a distinctively Renaissance

---

[6] C. H. George, 'The Making of the English Bourgeoisie, 1500–1700,' *Science and
Society*, 35 (1971), 385–412, and C. H. and Katherine George, *The Protestant Mind of
the English Reformation* (Princeton, 1961), pp. 120–73. The Georges argue for the
growth of a spirit of work, frugality and rationality before 1640, but reserve for the
post-war period the 'spirit of capitalism.' *cf.* Timothy Breen, 'The Non-Existent
Controversy: Puritan and Anglican Attitudes on Work and Wealth, 1600–1640,'
CH, 35 (1966), 273–87. C. John Sommerville, 'The Anti-Puritan Work Ethic,' *JBS*,
20 (1981), 70–81.

[7] Irvonwy Morgan, *The Godly Preachers of the Elizabethan Church* (1965), pp. 138–52; *cf.*
Bernard Bailyn, *The New England Merchants in the Seventeenth Century* (Cambridge,
Mass., 1955), who also describes puritan social theory as 'medieval' (p. 39 in the
1964 Torchbook edition). Laura Stevenson O'Connell, 'Anti-Entrepreneurial
Attitudes in Elizabethan Sermons and Popular Literature,' *JBS*, 15 (1976), 1–20; C.
John Sommerville, 'Religious Typologies and Popular Religion in Restoration
England,' *CH*, 45 (1976), 32–41.

[8] Paul Seaver, 'The Puritan Work Ethic Revisited,' *JBS*, 19 (1980), 35–53.

focus on calling, discipline and the proper use of wealth, and with a new campaign to abolish poverty altogether.

A brief look at *Piers Plowman* will serve to illustrate the attitudes of medieval English moralists toward work and idleness, wealth and poverty. Piers roundly condemned the traditional vice of sloth. His vision gave short shrift not only to 'wolfish wastrels' and sturdy beggars pretending illness or injury to get alms, but also to hermits 'that loth were to work.'[9] On the other hand, the medieval moralist did not exalt work *per se*. For Langland, work was simply the requisite means to stave off hunger, and Henry Parker followed suit a century later when he assured readers of *Dives et Pauper* that in heaven there will be no work. Neither writer disapproved of mendicity: Parker included begging friars among the deserving poor, and Piers gave alms willingly to hermits, anchorites, and friars, however idle, as well as to the sick and disabled poor.[10] As for healthy idlers and wastrels, the only solution provided by Langland was put in the mouth of Repentance; when desperate, even the dissolute received Piers' alms.[11]

The medieval English approach to poor relief seen in *Piers Plowman* was dictated by two assumptions – first, that alms-giving paves the way to heaven whether discriminate or not, and second, that poverty is an intrinsically holy state, neither possible nor appropriate to target for elimination.[12] It is a difficult condition, in Langland's words a 'hateful blessing'; none the less, 'it is the gift of God; it is mother of health; it is a road of peace . . . and it is happiness without care.'[13] The opposite state, wealth, was practically synonymous with greed, and was remedied only by renunciation. That Langland's view was not atypical for his day is apparent in the countless medieval hagiographies that praised the wealthy man who gave up riches for sanctity, and in the sermons of popular preachers from at least the twelfth century recounting the merits of spiritual poverty. The men-

[9] William Langland, *The Vision of Piers Plowman*, ed. Arthur Burrell (1949), pp. 5, 112–13; cf. pp .90–1, 109–11.

[10] *Piers Plowman*, pp. 112–17; Henry Parker, *Dives et Pauper* (1493; Scholars' Facsimiles, Delmar, New York, 1973), sig. H1.

[11] *Piers Plowman*, p. 120; cf. pp. 90–1. *Dives et Pauper* also approved almsgiving to those whose poverty could be traced to their own sin (sig. H1).

[12] *Ibid.*, pp. 20–1, 95, 100, 105, 115. Only God knows the true poor, according to Langland (p. 124). Alexander Gieysztor has presented the twelfth- and thirteenth-century apologia for poverty and asceticism as responses to the harsh realities of life, positing the inability of medieval thinkers to envisage a world without poverty, let alone to develop programs to eliminate it, as a factor underlying their veneration of it. 'La Légende de Saint Alexis en Occident: un idéal de pauvreté,' in *Études sur l'histoire de la pauvreté*, ed. Michel Mollat (Paris, 1974), vol. 1, pp. 125–39, and especially pp. 133–4.   [13] Langland, p. 145.

dicant orders found in deliberate poverty and asceticism the road to salvation, and they joined the secular clergy and such moralists as Langland, Gower and Parker in assuring the destitute that theirs was the better part.[14] Canon lawyers and church doctors agreed with popular preachers and moralists that voluntary poverty was a form of asceticism good in itself, and they made it clear that those who were born poor and willingly endured their hardship for the love of God would share with monks and friars the spiritual rewards of voluntary poverty.[15] And if alternative views of profit became available as such theorists as St Thomas, Peter the Chanter and (ironically) some mendicant preachers began to respond to the commercial Renaissance of continental European towns from the thirteenth century,[16] very little of this sophisticated economic theory is apparent in popular English sermons and moralizing tracts in the Middle Ages. Moreover, scholastic speculation about the just price seems not to have done much to offset the exaltation of poverty in medieval doctrine.[17] Accordingly, while Langland located the causes of some involuntary poverty in individual moral failure, either on the part of the poor themselves or in the exploitative practices of the rich, he failed to seek solutions in institutional change or new economic policy, as the humanists would. He was concerned not with social structure, but with spiritual goodness, and the merit to be found in poverty, both religious and involuntary, placed limits on his social criticism which would not be effectively surpassed until the sixteenth century.[18]

Christian humanists diverged sharply from much, although not all, of this medieval opinion. They continued to condemn sloth as

[14] *Piers Plowman*, pp. 126–7; Gieysztor (Mollat, vol. 1, pp. 125–39); Bernard Metz, 'La Pauvreté religieuse dans le "Liber de diversis ordinibus",' Mollat, vol. 1, pp. 247–54; Jean Longère, 'Pauvreté et richesse chez quelques prédicateurs durant la second moitié du XIIᵉ siècle,' Mollat, vol. 1, pp. 255–72.
[15] *Piers Plowman*, p. 140; Brian Tierney, *Medieval Poor Law: A Sketch of Canonical Theory and its Application in England* (Berkeley, 1959), p. 11; *cf.* St Thomas' *Summa Theologica*, II–II, qu. 25, art. 1; qu. 66, art. 2; and qu. 184, art. 1.
[16] Lester K. Little, *Religious Poverty and the Profit Economy in Medieval Europe* (Ithaca, New York, 1978), and 'Evangelical Poverty, the New Money Economy and Violence,' *Poverty in the Middle Ages*, ed. David Flood (Werl. Westphalia, 1975), pp. 11–26; John Wesley Baldwin, *Masters, Princes and Merchants: The Social Views of Peter the Chanter and his Circle* (Princeton, 1970).
[17] John Wesley Baldwin, *The Medieval Theories of the Just Price: Romanists, Canonists, and Theologians in the Twelfth and Thirteenth Centuries* (Philadelphia, 1959).
[18] See the discussions of Langland and Gower in Arthur Ferguson, *The Articulate Citizen and the English Renaissance* (Durham, NC, 1965), pp. 42–69, and H. C. White, *Social Criticism in Popular Religious Literature of the Sixteenth Century* (New York, 1944), pp. 3–40. Wyclif is the obvious medieval English exception to this rule (White, pp. 15, 24).

conducive to sin. But for Erasmus and his colleagues, labor in a secular vocation was seen as no less holy than a clerical calling, religious vocation was found to be no excuse for mendicity, and discipline was urged on aristocrat and cleric as well as on the traditionally laboring population. The object of these new emphases, moreover, was to insure the common weal. Industry was held to be a value not only as a deterrent to sin at the individual level, but also as a benefit to the larger society. Discipline was required for social reform in both an economic and a moral sense, both for the individual and for the group. As a result, Christian humanists waged a literary campaign against idleness out of a Renaissance concern for the reformation of the commonwealth.

The works of Erasmus and More exemplify this transitional state between medieval and modern attitudes toward work and idleness. As moralists, they followed in the footsteps of medieval preachers against sloth. 'There's no wickedness sloth does not teach,' Erasmus said; among its progeny are gamblers, revellers, gluttons, drunkards, quarrelers, and whore-hunters.[19] As reformers, they continued what had by the sixteenth century developed into a well-established tradition of popular anticlericalism by condemning religious mendicity and its abuses,[20] but as Renaissance advocates of social change, they went further, evaluating the social implications of idleness and offering an alternative model of discipline and industry for emulation by clerics, nobles and commoners alike. They clearly saw idleness as more than an individual failing: it is rather an offense against the commonwealth– in Erasmus' opinion, the source of most evil in the state.[21] Erasmus compared idleness to a contagious disease, which infects the whole society with poverty, exploitation and inequity.[22] What intolerable injustice that great lords should waste

[19] *Confabulatio pia, Coll.*, p. 40; *Apophthegmes*, tr. Nicolas Udall (1542), fol. 11; *Ignavis semper feriae sunt, The 'Adages' of Erasmus*, tr. Margaret Mann Phillips (Cambridge, 1964), pp. 267–8; *cf. Herilia* (1522), *Coll.*, pp. 16–19.
[20] For example, More, *Utopia*, vol. 4 of *The Complete Works of St. Thomas More*, ed. Edward Surtz and J. H. Hexter (New Haven, 1965), p. 131; *cf.* Simon Fish, *The Supplication of Beggars* (1524), identifying the real 'sturdy beggars' – monks and priests. St Francis had, of course, commended manual labor to his followers (*Opuscula Sancti Patris Francisci* (Quaracchi, 1904), p. 79); however, the ideal seems to have been largely discarded by his order by the next century: *cf. Piers Plowman*, pp. 4–5, and Wyclif's opposition to charity for begging friars (White, pp. 15, 24).
[21] *Institutio principis Christiani* (*The Education of a Prince*), tr. L. K. Born (New York, 1936), p. 37, *cf.* pp. 212–13 (on education as a solution), pp. 225–6; *Adages*, pp. 267–8. Colloquies particularly concerned with idleness include Πτωχολγία ('Beggar Talk', 1524), *Confabulatio pia* (1522), *Herilia* (1522), and *Diluculum* (1529). *cf.* Sir William Forrest, *Pleasant Poesye of Princelie Practice* (1548), ed. Sidney J. Herrtage, *England in the Reign of Henry the Eighth* (1878), p. xci.
[22] *Ne bos quidem pereat* (1526), *Adages*, p. 370.

their time in dancing, gaming and revelry while being supported by the labor of the poor! More charged that the idle nobility, living 'like drones on the labors of others,' not only failed to contribute positively to the welfare of the state, they were in fact responsible for driving their tenants to poverty, vagrancy and crime.[23] Lest the idleness of the nobility undermine the common weal, Erasmus warned the Christian prince to 'keep the proportion of idlers down to a minimum among his courtiers and either force them to be busy or else banish them from the country.'[24] Relic-peddling clerics, moneylenders, brokers, procurers, and wardens of large estates catering to frivolous pleasures should also be suppressed. All were considered idlers by Erasmus because their activities were non-productive; all preyed on the social order to support their own sloth and extravagance.[25]

Industry and productivity were to be imposed on all social estates because they were good *per se* in Christian humanist eyes. For this reason Erasmus presaged the protestant Reformers in his condemnation of the Church's proliferation of holy days. These times of enforced idleness were an offense to God, contributing only to the poverty of wage-earners.[26] For this reason, too, humanists made labor a regular feature of their visions of society perfected. While medieval theorists had eliminated toil both from Eden and from Paradise, More extolled the virtue of labor in *Utopia*: Every Utopian was taught a craft and was expected to labor daily in his vocation, idlers were driven from the commonwealth, and free time was devoted to intellectual pursuits. In Utopia, manual labor was not despised, and, as in Erasmus' scheme, no social group was exempted from the ban on idleness.[27]

More and Erasmus were followed and refined by later humanists on this point. Thomas Starkey, expanding on Erasmus' theme of non-production as idleness, offered a closer analysis of the types of sloth which plagued all levels of the English social order. He con-

[23] More, *Utopia*, pp. 63–7.

[24] *Institutio*, p. 225; *Liber de Sarcienda Ecclesiae Concordia*, in *The Essential Erasmus*, tr. John P. Dolan (New York, 1964), p. 378.

[25] *Institutio*, p. 225; *cf*. More's condemnation of goldsmiths, money-changers and merchants as useless to the commonwealth in *Utopia*, pp. 239–41.

[26] Erasmus, *An Epystell . . . concerning the forbedinge of eatynge of fleshe*, [tr. Richard Taverner; *ca*. 1530], n.f.

[27] More, *Utopia*, pp. 113, 125–31; R. Hooykaas, *Religion and the Rise of Modern Science* (Grand Rapids, 1972) attributes the development of modern science partly to the Renaissance demise of a 'scholastic' disdain for manual labor and the mechanical arts.

demned the 'idle rout' maintained by nobles and prelates to wait on
their tables, the 'ill-occupied' who manufactured and procured luxury
goods, singers and composers of 'new songs which tend only to vanity,'
importers of wine, lawyers ('cormorants of the court'), 'idle abbey-
lubbers' and priests who 'patter up their matins' – all because their
activities were non-productive.[28] All estates were subject to the
humanists' insistence on productive, profitable industry, 'profit'
being understood as recognizable benefit, either moral or material,
to the community. Every citizen of Starkey's ideal realm was
required to set his children to letters or to a craft, so that they might
contribute to the common weal, and a person without such a calling
should be banished from the city.[29] Richard Whitforde agreed,
instructing every householder to 'appoint yourself, by a continual
course, unto some certain occupation that may be *profitable*.'[30]

Profit, productivity, industry – 'bourgeois' values in our eyes, but
in Christian humanist opinion they should be the goals of nobles and
priests no less than artisans and merchants. The exaltation of these
values, moreover, made humanists wary of many leisure activities
long condoned or tolerated by the church. Dancing, feasting and
hunting were increasingly held to be suspect as a new critique of
frivolity emerged from the Northern Renaissance. The notion of
pastimes – non-productive activities undertaken solely to while away
the hours – was inimical to the humanist valuation of work. The doctrine of temporal stewardship is visible in humanist diatribes against
non-productive leisure long before it became a staple of protestant
thought: Richard Whitforde warned his readers that they would
have to account on the Day of Judgment for each moment of the
time allotted them to live; therefore, they should 'beware of such
occupations as [have] been called commonly pastimes.'[31] Vives
urged that those who haunt gaming booths and wine shops, even
'youths and sons of rich families,' be forced 'to give an account to the
magistrates, as to their fathers, of the way in which they spend their
time.'[32] Among More's retainers, as in his Utopia, dice, cards, tippling and hunting were conspicuous by their absence, and Starkey
condemned cards and dice not because they are intrinsically evil, but

---

[28] Thomas Starkey, *A Dialogue between Reginald Pole and Thomas Lupset* (1533–6), ed. K.
M. Burton (1948), pp. 79, 82, 92–3, 123–5.   [29] *Ibid.*, p. 142.
[30] Richard Whitforde, *The werke for housholders* (n.p., 1537), sig. Avi, verso (emphasis
mine).   [31] *Ibid.*, sigs. Avi, verso–Avii.
[32] Juan Luis Vives, *De Subventione Pauperum* (Bruges, 1526) in *Some Early Tracts on Poor
Relief*, ed. F. R. Salter (1926), p. 20.

because they are 'unprofitable games and idle exercises.'[33] The hard-working, disciplined life of the godly citizen precluded all pleasures not immediately conducive to health, knowledge, virtue, or the material well-being of the commonwealth – the humanists' usual understanding of 'profit.'

A constantly recurring humanist theme is that the goal of replac-ing idleness with discipline is the good of the commonwealth. Starkey argued that idlers should be banished because they are 'per-sons to the common weal utterly unprofitable.'[34] The humanist author of the scheme of poor relief adopted by the city of Ypres con-demned those who 'nourish idleness . . . to the great undoing of the common wealth', and for the advancement of the public wealth, he encouraged replacement of 'the tickling of pleasure with the exer-cise of sparing.'[35] The English humanist who submitted his treatise on poor relief to Queen Elizabeth around 1580 went a step further and offered a sort of cost analysis of the effects of idleness on the commonwealth: 'A man is not well able to be a good and a profitable member unto the Realm, until he be xxi years of age,' he estimated. Those who 'through the folly and abuse of their parents' are allowed to 'play in the streets til xii or xiii years of age' and are thereby reared with an aversion or inability to work are a drain on the community even beyond their first twenty-one years. Furthermore, these 'old idle beggars breed young thieves,' and the cost to the realm each time such a one is put to death may be estimated at £100 (counting the expense of his bringing-up, non-productive adulthood, crimes, arrest and trial, execution and burial).[36] Accordingly, 'the conquer-ing of idleness is a greater, and a more acceptable conquest to God, yea and more profitable and commodious to the Realm than the win-ning of castles, cities, and forts, yet obtained with less dangers, cares, and troubles.'[37]

Idleness, then, was for Christian humanists more than the individual sin which medieval moralists had condemned. It was an offense against the commonwealth, a drain on the economy, and

[33] D. B. Fenlon, 'England and Europe: *Utopia* and its Aftermath', *TRHS*, 5th ser., 25 (1975), 115–36, p. 120; *Utopia*, pp. 69, 147, 171. Robert P. Adams, 'Designs by More and Erasmus for a New Social Order', *Studies in Philology*, 42 (1945), 131–46, notes that all 'anti-social' pleasures are forbidden in Utopia, but More defined anti-social even more broadly than Adams did. Starkey, p. 148; *cf.* Whitforde, sig. Ei, and Bernard Silvester, *A breve or shorte monyciõ or counseyle of the cure and governaunce of a housholde* (appended to Whitforde's *Werke*), sig. Hiii, also condemning wineshops and alehouses.   [34] Starkey, p. 79.
[35] *Forma Subventionis Pauperum* (ca. 1515), tr. William Marshall as *The Forme and Maner of Subvētion or Helpyng for Pore People devysed and practysed ĩ the Cytie of Hypres in Flanders* (1535), pp. 15, 28.   [36] BL, Lansdowne MS 95, 3, pp. 24–6, 29.   [37] *Ibid.*, p. 122.

poor stewardship of the divine trust of time. It was a denial of the new profile of virtue in which hard work, discipline, and productivity for the common weal were prominent features.

Material gain was the next hurdle confronted by humanist economic ethicists. Prosperity was certainly the most troublesome side-effect of the Erasmian exaltation of work and discipline. The ideal of carefully regulated living which the Middle Ages had known only in monasteries (at least in theory) had now been broadened and secularized. In the already expanding economic setting of the sixteenth century, adherence to this ideal was likely in many cases to produce wealth, and the moral implications of that wealth had to be addressed by Christian humanists. Accordingly, a philosophy of getting and spending was developed in which the medieval idealization of poverty was discarded while traditional condemnation of luxury and greed was maintained.

Christian humanists were not altogether unsympathetic to the medieval notion that poverty is more conducive to holiness than is wealth. They were well aware of the temptations posed by prosperity. Erasmus' paraphrase on 'Blessed are the meek' calls him blessed who 'rather desireth quiet poverty than troublesome riches,' and Starkey noted that worldly prosperity is full of 'manifold perils and dangers.' Christ chose poor men for his disciples, Starkey continued, 'showing us how hard it was to use that [wealth] well and couple thereto his celestial and heavenly doctrine.'[38]

But material prosperity was never condemned as intrinsically evil by the humanists.[39] Starkey qualified his fear of riches: it is to have one's heart fixed in wealth (or pleasure) which is wrong, he said. In fact,

it may not be doubted that the most prosperous state of man standeth in the virtues of the mind coupled with worldly prosperity . . . if we have regard not only of the soul but also of the body, saying with Aristotle that man is the union and conjunction together of them both, and if we have regard also not

---

[38] *The First Tome or Volume of the Paraphrase of Erasmus upon the New Testamente* (1548; Scholars' Facsimiles, Delmar, New York, 1975), fol. xviii; Starkey, pp. 52–3.
[39] They responded to the expanding commercial economy of the sixteenth century as some medieval theologians (notably St Thomas) had to that of the thirteenth century. But the humanists went further, not only justifying limited profit (if used for the common weal), but also denying the hierarchy of callings which in medieval thought made the successful businessman, however just in his dealing, a second-class citizen in the Kingdom of Heaven. As long as the upper echelons of the godly social hierarchy were occupied by propertyless clerics, profit would remain at best suspect.

only of the life to come but also of the life present, then it is true that I say, that felicity in the highest degree is not without worldly prosperity.[40]

Likewise, Erasmus' critique of 'troublesome riches' and of the mercantile classes could not be read as an unqualified condemnation of either as inherently evil. He admitted that 'A man may be rich and not put his confidence in his riches.'[41] Merchants are criticized not because involvement in trade is beyond sanctification, but because, as Folly remarks, they use 'the meanest methods' to achieve financial gain: 'their lies, perjury, thefts, frauds and deceptions are everywhere to be found.'[42] Elsewhere, however, Erasmus drew freely on business terminology and mercantile imagery to press an argument for pacifism, and in the adage *A mortuo tributum exigere* he even remarked that he had nothing in particular against usurers, 'whose skill I can see some reason for defending.' He was not unaware of the facts of sixteenth-century economic life and growth, nor was he ignorant of the benefits which wealth can bring to the community. He was merely calling for an end to the honor given to wealth and to inhumane behavior for the sake of profit. In the same adage, he remarked that

I would sooner approve of an usurer than of this niggardly class of dealers who are on the hunt for profits from every possible source, by trickery, by lies, by fraud, by cheating, buying up here what they sell for more than double there, and robbing the wretched poor with their monopolies – and yet these people, who never do anything else than this in their lives, are the ones we think almost the only people worthy of honour.

Merchants are not the only estate guilty of profiteering; priests

---

[40] Starkey, pp. 53–4; *cf.* the Jesuit Robert Parsons' *The First Booke of the Christian Exercise, appertayning to resolution* (n.p., 1582), pp. 299, 315 (condemning wealth out of hand), and his *Second Part of the Booke of Christian exercise... Or a Christian directorie* (n.p., 1591), pp. 16, 164 (against accumulation). Starkey used Aristotle much as St Thomas had, but the Thomistic approach is as hard to find in English Jesuit thought as in that of Langland, Gower and Parker. For justifications of wealth sixteenth-century English protestants would tend to look neither to medieval nor to post-Tridentine Catholicism, but to classical literature mediated by Renaissance humanism.

[41] *Paraphrases*, fol. xviii; *Proverbes*, fol. xxvii (on *Dives aut iniquus est, aut iniqui haeres*).

[42] Erasmus, *Praise of Folly*, tr. Betty Radice (New York, 1971), p. 142; *Adages*, p. 213. Clarence H. Miller, 'Some Medieval Elements and Structural Unity in Erasmus' *The Praise of Folly*', *Renaissance Quarterly*, 27 (1974), 499–511, has suggested that Erasmus shows a typically medieval bias against the mercentile classes in this satire; however, merchants receive far less negative attention from Folly than do rulers and especially churchmen, and, as Erasmus notes in his preface, 'If every type of man is included [in criticism], it is clear that all the vices are censured, not any individual' (p. 60).

refuse to communicate the Body of Christ or provide a Christian burial except for a profit:

Among Christians it is not permitted to dig a hole in the earth for the dead, unless you have leased a little bit of ground from the priest, and if you pay more (but only then) you can have a larger and grander place. If you have paid a great deal, you may lie and rot in the church near the high altar; if you have given stingily, you can be rained on with the common herd outside.[43]

Profit, here defined in the narrower sense of material gain,[44] was legitimate in humanist eyes if, as Sir Thomas Smith argued, it did not harm the interests of others. 'Harm,' however, was defined very stringently: profit is implicitly harmful if retained by the individual rather than invested in the common weal.[45] Entrepreneurs are condemned when they become, in Starkey's words, 'so blinded with singular [individual] profit and vain pleasure that they never consider this common weal,' when they regard their 'own pleasure and profit, without any respect had of any other.' Otherwise, profit may be condoned. In fact, Starkey noted that individual profit and common benefit may go hand in hand: in what seems to be a calculated appeal to the insistent profiteer, he argued, 'If men knew that when they look to the common profit, that they therewith also regard their own singular and private, surely they would not so negligently look thereunto as it is commonly seen they now do.'[46] When the businessman's yen for personal profit overcomes his responsibility to the commonwealth, his activity is interpreted as greed, and the wealth obtained by it is regarded as illegitimate. But neither business nor possessions were thereby condemned; rather, the process of getting must be regulated by the clear ethical perspective to be derived from a humanist education. And the possession of wealth must likewise be regulated by a concern for social justice, by rational governmental action, and by the instilling of a reasonable standard of possession.

That Christian humanist standard aimed at an equitable economic

---

[43] *Dulce bellum inexpertis, Adages*, pp. 341, 350; *A mortuo tributum exigere, Adages*, pp. 226, 228–9. *cf.* the adages *Sileni Alcibiades* (p. 282) and *Scarabeus aquilam quaerit* (p. 323); the latter notes the benefits of prosperity for a society. It should be said that even the mild defense of usury offered by Erasmus is atypical of humanists and of protestants. *cf.*, for example, Thomas Wilson, *A Discourse upon Usury* (1572), *passim.*

[44] The two definitions of 'profit,' material rewards, or the general well-being – spiritual and material – of the community, seem to vie with each other in the sixteenth century, as one would expect in a rapidly expanding money economy.

[45] *A Discourse of the Commonweal of this Realm of England*, ed. Mary Dewar (Charlottesville, Va., 1969). [46] Starkey, p. 70.

system. If the Erasmians never instructed the rich man to renounce his possessions, neither did they throw poor men the sop of patient indigence as a means of grace. Although they lauded those who were able to live content with few possessions, they were under no illusions about the inherent goodness of material deprivation. Poverty was rather perceived as an evil which must and can be eliminated, not simply by the spiritual mechanism of preaching charity to the rich, but by means of positive, rational action on the part of lay rulers of the Christian commonwealth. Such action is to eliminate the two primary causes of poverty – the ever-present vice of idleness, and extreme social inequities which result in oppression and exploitation of the lower orders. Accordingly, Erasmus recommended the exile of idlers, the enforcement of strict sumptuary laws, and the creation of the office of censor of public morals in part to enforce frugality on the rich. Moreover, he proposed a graduated taxation system so that the burden of public administrative costs should fall on the wealthy, whom it is 'desirable to bring to a simple life.'[47]

This 'simple life' was one in which *mediocritas* was the ideal in regard to possessions.[48] The standard by which Christian humanists measured legitimate gain was neither wealth nor poverty, but a mean between the two. The humanists recognized, with the ancients, that neither wealth nor poverty is conducive to the good life: the former is nearly always accompanied by such vices as avarice, pride and an exploitative attitude toward one's fellows; the latter does not allow leisure for the pursuit of letters or for civic involvement. The mean between luxury and deprivation, on the other hand, would allow the development of individual virtue, provide for the sustenance of life and status, and create a situation in which people of all levels of society can contribute to the good of the community. It is *mediocritas*, agreed the author of the Ypres scheme, which will produce virtue in the commonwealth.[49]

The Christian humanists conceded that the ideal of *mediocritas* would be fully realized in the Christian state only by means of community of property. As Vives opined, 'If charity had any power over us, she herself would be a law for us (although love needs no law) to hold all things in common.'[50] It was More's disgust at the fact that in England the rich 'extort a part of their daily allowance from the poor,' that 'alongside . . . wretched need and poverty you find ill-

[47] *Institutio*, p. 227; *cf. Adages*, pp. 215–17; *Discourse of the Commonweal*, pp. 81–2.
[48] For example, *Summum cape, et medium habebis, Adages*, p. 264; *Philodoxus* (1531), *Coll.*, pp. 478–88; *Apophthegmes*, fol. 39.
[49] *Forma Subventionis Pauperum*, p. 13.   [50] Vives in Salter, p. 10.

timed luxury ... ostentatious sumptuousness of dress and ... excessive indulgence at table' which inspired his vision of community of goods.[51] In Utopia there is 'equality in all respects' because property is not private.[52]

Erasmus' marginal notes to the Basel edition of More's *Utopia* indicate his approval of this theoretical communism. It is because of the equality of goods in Utopia, he said, that all are adequately provided for; he saw More's ideal as a 'holy commonwealth that Christians ought to imitate' and drew the reader's attention with approval to More's description of European commonwealths as 'conspiracies of the rich.'[53] He opened his collection of adages with *Amicorum communia omnia* 'since there is nothing more wholesome' than this principle: 'If only it were so fixed in men's minds as it is frequent on everybody's lips, most of the evils of our lives would promptly be removed.' In his further discussion of the adage, he cited the authority of Plato, Terence and Cicero, but he made the point that Christians should be put to shame by the fact that these pagans were advocating the same economic system to which Christ and the Apostles had given their endorsement:

But it is extraordinary how Christians dislike this common ownership of Plato's, how in fact they cast stones at it, although nothing was ever said by a pagan philosopher which comes closer to the mind of Christ... [Pythagoras] instituted a kind of sharing of life and property in this way, the very thing Christ wants to happen among Christians. For all those who were admitted by Pythagoras into that well-known band who followed his instruction would give to the common fund whatever money and family property they possessed. This is called in Latin, in a word which expresses the facts, *coenobium*, clearly from community of life and fortunes.[54]

The sixteenth-century English translator of this adage, Richard Taverner, selected for his edition of the *Adages* the latter portion of Erasmus' lengthy commentary on it, in which he condemned the two contemporary distortions of this principle, 'monkry' and 'the wicked Anabaptistical sect, which will have no Rulers, no order...'[55] Erasmus held the ideal of community of property in the larger society, not merely in a few other-worldly communities, and he held in contempt

[51] *Utopia*, pp. 241, 69, 131.
[52] *Ibid.*, pp. 103–5, 121. J. H. Hexter has argued persuasively in *More's 'Utopia': The Biography of an Idea* (Princeton, 1952), esp. pp. 35–43, that More's communitarian ideals are genuine, and not to be either dismissed as a mere literary device or reinterpreted as a conservative defense of monasticism or a curiously roundabout bourgeois defense of private property. [53] Hexter, *Biography of an Idea*, pp. 46–7.
[54] *CWE* 31, tr. Margaret Mann Phillips (Toronto, 1982), pp. 29–30.
[55] *Proverbes*, fol. liii.

those communities which combined communism with anarchy and so undermined the public image of that most perfect economic system. He attributed to the Schoolmen the erroneous connection between Aristotle's judgment that 'human felicity cannot be complete without earthly goods – physical or financial' and the conclusion that 'a state cannot flourish where all things are held in common. We try to combine all his [Aristotle's] doctrines with the teaching of Christ, which is like mixing water and fire.'[56] Instead, Aristotle's approval of wealth can be accepted by Christians only in a biblically amended form. Wealth has potential for evil as well as for good; it can be a means to a good life for all if it is used properly and distributed as equitably as it was in Pythagoras' community or the early Christian church. Clearly, for Erasmus, a strictly ordered communism was the ideal economic order.[57]

Nevertheless, the Christian humanists as social critics were not mere visionaries. Erasmus recognized that his contemporaries were no more receptive to communitarianism than they would be to the republican political ideal which he also embraced; consequently, just as he compromised his anti-monarchical stance by writing instructions for princes, so he made only half-way suggestions for the equalization of wealth. He did not want community of property at the expense of order. Because he was aware that past attempts to revive the economic practices of the primitive Christians 'led only to sedition', he concluded that 'concord will be achieved if we agree that property should remain in the hands of its legal owners and its common use be directed, when occasion arises, out of charity.'[58] Only in the New World did humanists have a chance to put their most radical economic theories into practice.[59] But the ideal was by no means completely discarded when the time came for Erasmus to instruct the Christian prince:

---

[56] *Paraphrases*, Acts of the Apostles, fol. xii; *Scarabeus aquilam quaerit, Adages,* p. 331.

[57] It is worth noting that in Erasmus' scheme, as in More's and Plato's, those who have given themselves over to wickedness are excluded from the economic, as well as the other, benefits of the community (e.g., *Amicorum communia omnia,* CWE 31, pp. 29–30); puritan elitism of the godly would follow suit.

[58] *Liber de Sarcienda,* pp. 386–7.

[59] F. Benedict Warren, 'The Idea of the Pueblos of Santa Fe,' in *The Roman Catholic Church in Colonial Latin America*, ed. Richard E. Greenleaf (New York, 1971), pp. 37–46, discusses the application of the socio-economic principles of More's *Utopia* in New Spain by Vasco de Quiroga, the bishop in charge of Michoacán affairs from 1536 to 1565. His *Ordinances* for the pueblo-hospitals of Santa Fe, written *ca.* 1554, outline a six-hour work day for all members of the pueblo, the equitable distribution of goods according to need, the *familia* as the basic political unit, and common tenure of real property. *cf.* Marcel Bataillon, *Erasmo y España,* 2 vols (México,

The prince should try to prevent too great an inequality of wealth. I should not want to see anyone deprived of his goods, but the prince should employ certain measures [in the context, graded taxation, sumptuary laws, etc.] to prevent the wealth of the multitude from being hoarded by a few. Plato did not want his citizens to be too rich, neither did he want them extremely poor, for the pauper is of no use and the rich man will not use his ability for public service.[60]

Responsible stewardship of wealth for the common good thus became an overriding concern for the humanists. They were convinced that if the ideal is not immediately foreseeable, some progress can still be made toward a significant reconstruction of the socio-economic order by the enlightened magistrate in the Christian commonwealth.

That progress would necessitate not only regulation of wealth, but also elimination of poverty. Among the socio-economic theories of the Middle Ages which Erasmus and his followers had rejected was the notion that poverty is inexplicable, insoluble, and (despite its difficulties) sacrosanct. On the contrary, the Christian humanists saw poverty as an intolerable social evil, and they did not hesitate to trace its roots to the most venerable social institutions and to propose sometimes drastic but often very practicable reforms in those institutions in order to alleviate the problem. Their communitarian ideals may have been far-fetched; however, in their capacities as advisers to princes and towns, educators, and occasionally administrators, they attacked the problem of poverty directly and produced a radically new theory of poor relief which was implemented over the following century in towns from Venice and Lyon to the New World, and on a national level in the Netherlands and England.

The humanist plan to eliminate poverty differed sharply from the personal and rather haphazard charity of the Middle Ages.[61] It was

1950), Appendix, 'Erasmo y el Nuevo Mundo,' vol. 2, pp. 435–4; Silvio Zavala, 'Sir Thomas More in New Spain,' *Essential Articles for the Study of Thomas More*, ed. R. S. Sylvester (Hamden, Connecticut, 1977); and Zavala, 'The American Utopia of the Sixteenth Century,' *HLQ*, 10 (1947), 337–47, who summarizes Quiroga's vision of the Golden Age established in the New World thus: 'Once political order and humane relations were established, the roots of all discord, luxury, covetousness, and sloth would be cut out, and peace, justice, and equality would reign' (p. 344). Warren (p. 45) notes that laziness was one of the grounds for expulsion from a pueblo. [60] *Institutio*, p. 217.
[61] Joel T. Rosenthal's possibly overstated thesis in *The Purchase of Paradise: Gift-Giving and the Aristocracy, 1307–1485* (Toronto, 1972) is that medieval philanthropy was purely personal, motivated not by defined hopes for social improvement, but by the desire of noble benefactors to expiate their own sin. He argues partly from the vast sums given to chantries and churches rather than alms for a relative absence of social conscience and sense of social responsibility before the Tudor period.

conditioned by the Erasmian stress on industry, discipline, careful stewardship of time and money, and rationalized solutions to social problems. By contrast, as W. K. Jordan has observed, 'The Middle Ages were acutely sensitive to the spiritual needs of mankind while displaying only scant, or ineffectual concern with the alleviation or cure of the ills that beset the bodies of so large a mass of humanity.' Monastic almsgiving was 'casual and ineffective in its incidence, never seeking to do more than relieve conspicuous and abject suffering.'[62] Medieval charity was indiscriminate, and much of it took the form of ritualized kindness little adapted to real material need. Charitable institutions frequently succored a ritual number of poor (usually twelve), and historians have noted the apparent incapacity of thirteenth-century modes of thought for questioning the structures which fostered injustice and poverty.[63]

The High Middle Ages saw increasing popular criticism of vagrants, healthy beggars, and mendicant friars as drains on the resources of Christian charity.[64] Secular governments concerned about the disruptive effects of an increasingly mobile laboring population and aware of the apparent inability of traditional ecclesiastical charity to address the problem of poverty and mendicity among them, attempted to control vagabondage by prohibiting almsgiving to able-bodied beggars and ruthlessly punishing the wandering poor.[65] Yet churchmen like Henry Parker continued to preach charitable obligations toward not only friars and the impotent poor, but even toward the undeserving poor, those whose poverty could be traced to their own profligacy and gluttony. Monastic rules, too,

---

[62] W. K. Jordan, *Philanthropy in England, 1480–1660* (New York, 1959), p. 17.

[63] Pierre-Andre Sigal, 'Pauvreté et charité aux XIe et XIIe siècles d'après quelques textes hagiographiques,' Mollat, vol. 1, pp. 141–62, and especially pp. 151–2; *cf.* Michel Rouche, 'La Matricule des pauvres,' Mollat, vol. 1, pp. 83–110; Andre Vauchez, 'Charité et pauvreté chez sainte Elisabeth de Thuringe, d'après les actes des procés de canonisation,' Mollat, vol. 1, pp. 163–73.

[64] Jean Batany, 'Les pauvres et la pauvreté dans les revus des "estats du monde",' Mollat, vol. 2, pp. 469–86; Philippe Grand, 'Gérard d'Abbeville et la pauvreté volontaire', Mollat, vol. 1, pp. 389–409.

[65] For example, 36 Edward III, c.8; 7 Richard II, c.5; 12 Richard II, c.3, c.7; 11 Henry VII, c.2. The 1349 Statute of Labourers was the first English law to prohibit almsgiving to 'valiant beggars, who ... as long as they may live of begging, do refuse to labour, giving themselves to Idleness and Vice, and sometimes to Theft and other abominations' (*Statutes of the Realm*, vol. 1, p. 308). 12 Richard II, c.3 (1388), aimed at the fugitive peasant problem which followed the plague, ordered the able-bodied beggar to be placed in the stocks until 'he hath found surety to return to his service, or to serve or labor' (*Statutes of the Realm*, vol. 2, p. 56). See also Tierney, pp. 128–9, on the Statute of Labourers.

continued explicitly to disallow discrimination among paupers – all were to be received as Christ.[66]

The problem did not lie in the church's refusal to recognize the categories of worthy and unworthy poor: St Thomas had made the distinction in his *Summa contra Gentiles*, and the *Decretum* and its glossators recommended charitable discretion on the assumption that the two categories existed.[67] But the discrimination suggested was limited by the overriding medieval veneration of poverty and by the Catholic conviction that almsgiving eased the benefactor's entry into heaven regardless of the nature of the recipient. As we have seen, even popular works of social criticism like *Piers Plowman* defended the sanctity of poverty, and canonists like Rufinus agreed, opposing indiscriminate charity only if the deserving poor were thereby deprived. Humanists would later argue that the impotent poor always suffered thereby, but in any case, the distinctions of the canonists apparently seldom filtered down far enough to influence monastic or private practice.[68]

Historians of poor relief theory have concluded that the medieval heritage incorporated theoretical reverence for voluntary poverty with practical suspicion of the poor.[69] The merger, if it existed at all, was an uneasy one. The former position was clearly held by the church, the latter by secular authorities. Not until the sixteenth century was any attempt made to reconcile the paradox by joining compassion for the poor to practical reformism in a rationalized program of social reconstruction.

In the meantime, the problem of poverty continued to plague English society, for the charitable burden borne by the church in the later Middle Ages was slight as well as inefficiently administered. Even historians whose intent is to refute the charge that medieval poor relief was haphazard and ineffective admit that parochial relief

---

[66] Parker, sig. H1, and D. Willibrord Witters, 'Pauvres et pauvreté dans les coutumiers monastiques du Moyen Age,' Mollat, vol. 1, pp. 177–215. In fifteenth-century France, Howard Solomon has discovered city gates closed to foreign poor, healthy beggars being branded and whipped or set to galley service, and towns refusing to bury the poor in hallowed ground (*Public Welfare, Science, and Propaganda in Seventeenth Century France* (Princeton, 1972), p. 24); however, these actions of secular governments contrast sharply with the theory of poor relief provided by contemporary churchmen in France, as in England.

[67] *Summa contra gentiles*, chs. 133, 141; Tierney, pp. 55–60.   [68] Tierney, p. 60.

[69] Paul Fideler, 'Christian Humanism and Poor Law Reform in Early Tudor England,' *Societas*, 4 (1974), 273–84; *cf.* J. Depauw, 'Pauvres, pauvres mendiants, mendiants valides ou vagabonds? Les hésitations de la législation royale,' *Révue d'histoire moderne et contemporaine*, 21 (1974), 402–7.

mechanisms, which from the twelfth to the fourteenth centuries do seem to have included investigations of recipients, had disintegrated by the fifteenth. The three to five percent of monastic revenues which Brian Tierney estimates were intended for the poor did not amount to a great deal, and his apologetic for monasteries as primarily liturgical rather than eleemosynary institutions is a weak defense of their diversion of revenues intended by the canonists for the poor into spiritual activities in magnificent buildings. Tierney's figures, moreover, may be exaggerated: other estimates for early sixteenth-century England indicate that monastic almsgiving averaged only two and a half percent of their gross annual income.[70] But even if Tierney's more generous figures are correct, medieval assumptions about the 'good life' served to undermine physical social welfare, whatever the church's charitable intent. Furthermore, it has been demonstrated that monasteries, whose charity was less discriminate and effective than parochial relief, frequently appropriated parish revenues for their own use,[71] and if we are to believe contemporary social critics, the already inadequate amount of charity available from the church was being diminished further by monastic and clerical abuses.[72] The consensus of historians is that parish handouts, monastic hospitality, and personal holiday and funeral almsgiving were simply unequal to the task of curbing poverty in the early modern period.[73]

At the beginning of the sixteenth century, a drive finally got underway to reform this state of affairs. Historians have naturally tended to identify the 'great moving impulse' behind this movement with 'the emergence of the Protestant ethic.'[74] As we shall see, the protestant Reformers were certainly active in the restructuring of poor relief; however, their sources of inspiration in this area of their social theory, as in their doctrine of the family, were the Catholic humanists.

---

[70] Tierney, pp. 73, 80–2; cf. pp. 68–80. Tierney admits that his figures are somewhat conjectural. cf. Christopher Haigh, *Reformation and Resistance in Tudor Lancashire* (Cambridge, 1975), p. 120; Joan Thirsk, *Economic Policy and Projects* (Oxford, 1979), p. 123. John Pound, *Poverty and Vagrancy in Tudor England* (1971), finds the average for English monasteries at the beginning of the sixteenth century less than two and a half percent (p. 22).   [71] Tierney, pp. 109–32.

[72] For example, *Mum and the Sothsegger* (*ca.* 1403–6), ed. M. Day and R. Steele (1936), pp. 43, 46–7; *Piers Plowman*, pp. 4–5 *et passim*.

[73] Jordan, p. 59; Solomon, p. 24.

[74] Jordan, p. 151. He sees no clear break from the medieval system until Latimer and his cohorts 'laid forever on the English conscience a sense of the shame of poverty and a moral responsibility for the enlargement of the ambit of opportunity' (p. 156).

The poor relief schemes developed by Christian humanists are characterized by discriminating, rationalized and secular administration; innovative methods of attacking the causes of poverty; the enforcement of discipline and industry on the poor; and faith in the corrective power of education. Renaissance humanists vociferously denounced the disorder implicit in begging as disgraceful, unmethodical and ultimately ineffective. Personal alms doled out on the church steps or at the wedding feast to all and sundry evinced more concern with the merits which would accrue to the giver than with the actual needs of the recipients. Unregulated almsgiving supported what humanists saw as a malevolent institution – begging. Denying the medieval attribution of merit to mendicity (as to poverty), the author of the Ypres scheme argued that begging is in fact a self-perpetuating evil: beggars develop no sense of past or future, no discipline or industry, no understanding of the necessity to save money for harder times to come. Their children are reared in idleness and ignorance and so turn to begging themselves.[75] Where begging is allowed, he lamented, 'such gathered most not that had most need but that had most boldness,' and when the rich saw unworthy beggars (often fraudulently presenting themselves as blind or maimed) spending alms on riot and pleasure while the genuine poor went hungry, many began refusing alms altogether, to the detriment of the truly needy.[76]

Personal doles to beggars were perceived, quite simply, as poor stewardship. Proper use of the wealth with which God has entrusted benefactors must be directed toward the common weal, and the good of the community was hardly served by diverting funds necessary for the life and health of the impotent to that 'right great multitude of strong valiant beggars, vagabonds, and idle persons of both kinds men and women which, though they might well labor for their living if they would,' instead beg alms, to the 'displeasure of almighty god' and 'the hurt of the common wealth.' It should be emphasized that this complaint by an early Tudor humanist is found in the context of a lament for 'impotent persons not able to work, dying of want.'[77] The humanists' concern for discriminate charity was deeply rooted in their compassion for the genuine poor, rather than in an isolated impulse to repress beggars and punish vagrancy. But charity cannot effectively guarantee the *right* of the poor to sus-

---

[75] *Forma Subventionis Pauperum*, pp. 11–12, 17, 19. Prudent accumulation seems to have been regarded highly by this author.　　[76] *Ibid.*, pp. 5–6, 8, 17.

[77] BL, Royal MS 18, C.vi (an anonymous poor relief treatise dated 1531), fols. 1–2.

tenance without guarding the income which is their due from the encroachments of the unworthy. The humanists reasoned that since 'alms should be given to feeble and weak persons, to such as are broken with sickness or foregone in years, and to them that through impotency be not able to get their living . . . those whole and strong persons that take alms [should be regarded] as thieves and robbers' and be banished from the realm.[78] True generosity will firmly reject the pleas of the valiant beggar.

In addition to worthy and undeserving poor, a refined system of sub-categories of poverty was developed by Christian humanist theorists to facilitate discrimination in giving and efficiency in administering relief. The quality and condition of the pauper, his geographic origins, his behavior, the causes of his poverty, and his age and health were all considerations in defining these categories, and appropriate actions were specified for each type. In Vives' plan for Bruges, the foreign poor were sent back to their towns of birth, unless they were from war-stricken areas (a recommendation which was followed in most sixteenth-century relief schemes).[79] The elderly, blind, invalid and dull-witted were to be housed and provided with easy work in municipal institutions, and the more seriously ill (whose sickness or injury required verification by a physician to avoid fraud) were to be hospitalized and treated.[80] The insane were also to be housed in hospitals, where the cause of insanity would be determined and, in Vives' plan, nothing would be done 'to increase insanity or cause it to persist – such as irritating or mocking the sufferer. How inhumane that is!' Vives recommended instead a highly individualized regimen involving a varied diet, gentle treatment, bonds, or education, depending on individual needs. Abandoned children formed the final category of impotent poor to be hospitalized and educated.[81]

The unemployed but able poor comprised a separate set of

---

[78] The canonical judgment was that 'superfluous' wealth, that not needed to maintain life and status, is *owed* to the poor. The canonists had even argued that a man in extreme want who steals to maintain life is not guilty of theft, since he has taken what is rightfully his own (Tierney, pp. 37–8; 147, n. 30). *cf. Forma Subventionis Pauperum*, pp. 23–4, and More, *Utopia*, pp. 61 and 73.   [79] Vives, in Salter, p. 12.

[80] Vives, in Salter, pp. 12–13, 15–16. Fraud was punishable by imprisonment. Erasmus had likewise admonished the Christian prince that those 'broken through old age or sickness and without any relatives to care for them . . . should be cared for in public institutions for the aged and sick,' rather than having to roam the countryside begging or rely on the inconsistent aid of the church or pious individuals (*Institutio*, pp. 225–6). Starkey commended the institutionalization of this plan in Ypres, 'the which I would wish to be put in use with us' (p. 160).

[81] Vives, Salter, pp. 16, 18–19.

categories. One of these consisted of 'persons of good breeding' who had fallen on bad times. Vives suggested that they be treated with special tact and receive relief in secret lest they be humiliated.[82] A second group, non-noble victims of the developing but unstable market economy who were willing to work if work were available, were to be relieved at home and provided with work on public construction or in hospitals so that they could be as self-sufficient as possible. The humanists recognized the problem of unemployment and under-employment and strongly suspected that most of the poor really desired work. 'Yet', as one would remark to Queen Elizabeth, 'no man will set him on work, but say unto him, work, work, when he knoweth not where to have work for his life.'[83] Finally, a hard line was to be taken toward the immoral poor, those 'sturdy beggars' who, as Erasmus said, 'need a job rather than a dole' but, due to their love of idleness and riotous living, must be compelled to accept work. Vives outlined a program aimed at their reformation:

Those who have ruined themselves in disgraceful and base ways, such as gambling, immorality, luxury, greed, must indeed be fed, since no one should die from starvation, but the more disagreeable tasks are to be allotted them bring all these details to the Consuls and Senate in their court. Let those who have endured poverty at home be put on a list with their children, by two Senators in each parish, adding their needs and their means of living hitherto.[89]

The enforcement of morality on the poor was an essential aspect of the humanist program. Vives instructed the Senate of Bruges to appoint two censors annually to 'investigate the life and conduct of the poor,' oversee 'what their children are doing,' and punish those found haunting gaming booths or wine shops. He noted earlier in his treatise that the corrupt opinions and morals of beggars exclude them from church and civic involvement; however, he blamed not the poor themselves for this, but the magistrates who had neglected to instruct, provide for and discipline them. If his plan of censorship

---

[82] *Ibid.*, p. 27.
[83] *Ibid.*, p. 17; BL, Lansdowne 95,3, p. 24. More noted that many tenants deprived by enclosure of their livelihood were driven to poverty, vagrancy, and crime because 'though they most eagerly offer their labor, there is no one to hire them' (*Utopia*, p. 67). Solomon (p. 25) remarks that by the beginning of the sixteenth century, city officers in France, too, had begun to see the poverty problem as one of urban economy as much as public morality, since skilled, dependable city workers were often chronically unemployed but willing to work.
[84] Erasmus, *Convivium religiosum, Coll.*, pp. 70–1; *cf.* p. 254; Vives, in Salter, p. 13. *cf.* Lynn Thorndike, 'The Historical Background,' in *Intelligent Philanthropy* (Chicago, 1930), pp. 27–31, tracing the distinction between employable and derelict poor to the late sixteenth century.

were put into effect, beggars could be integrated into the social order and be of service, rather than harm, to the commonwealth.[85]

Vives' system of categorization and censorship of the poor was all part of his program to rationalize and secularize poor relief in the interests of social reformation: chief responsibility for charity was transferred by all of the Christian humanists from the church to the state in order to render the welfare system more efficient. This transfer is evidence of humanist distrust of the ecclesiastical hierarchy and is reflected, too, in their entrustment of education to the laity (for example, by Colet at St Paul's School); but it is also evidence of their conviction that the governors of the city are the natural caretakers of the poor, sick and insane.[86] In addition, humanists from Erasmus to Sir Thomas Smith recognized that the lay magistrate or the prince is the only possible agent for the reform of many causes of poverty. 'The original cause in everything is to be searched for,' according to the Erasmian reformer, and the locus of 'divers sorts of causes' of poverty – inequitable taxation, enclosure, debasement of coinage, conspicuous consumption, rack-renting, inflation and unemployment – demanded government intervention.[87] Starkey's lay censors, for instance, were to oversee not only the education and discipline of youth, but also municipal craft regulation; import/export policies; and the number, substance and distribution of the nation's population in order to 'conserve the common weal.' He recommended to Henry VIII that the crown lease monastic lands not to a few great lords and gentlemen, whose tenure would not benefit the commonwealth, but rather 'by copyhold, and of a mean rent, to younger brethren living in service unprofitably, and to them which be of lower state and degree' as a preventive means of dealing with the poverty problem.[88]

Humanists also considered secular rulers more appropriate and better equipped to regularize the collection and oversee the fair distribution of alms. Vives outlined the system which was to be more or less adopted by many sixteenth-century towns, both English and continental, and in many of its aspects by the Elizabethan Parliaments which produced England's poor laws:

Wherefore, let two Senators, accompanied by a scribe, visit each of all of these houses [hospitals, asylums, workhouses] and investigate; let them

[85] Vives, in Salter, pp. 19, 9.   [86] Vives, in Salter, p. 10.
[87] *Discourse of the Commonweal*, pp. 96–7; cf. pp. 49–50, 67–77, 81–2, 101–10, 144–5; Erasmus, *Institutio*, p. 227; More, *Utopia*, p. 67; Starkey, pp. 92–3, 95, 140–1.
[88] Starkey, pp. 144, 183; Starkey to Henry VIII in *England in the Reign of Henry VIII*, p. lviii.

make a note of the places of origin, numbers, and names of those who are maintained there, and also of what cause brought each of them there. Let them bring all these details to the Consuls and Senate in their court. Let those who have endured poverty at home be put on a list, with their children, by two Senators in each parish, adding their needs and their means of living hitherto.[89]

The Senators, or overseers, were to check with neighbors of welfare recipients to determine the cause of their poverty, their previous status and present condition, and their moral standards and behavior. Vives was careful, however, to charge them to conduct their investigations 'in a humane and kindly manner,' just as their counterparts in Ypres were to hear the complaints of the poor 'without any sour or grim countenance.'[90]

In addition to determining eligibility to receive aid, the Senators or overseers of the poor were responsible for the collection of alms into a common chest and for fair and honest distribution. No compulsory rate was levied by Vives' plan; his hope was that alternative fund-raising schemes and good administration of established revenues would render even church donation boxes unnecessary. If the able poor themselves were set on work, for instance, their own production should help to pay for both their own sustenance and that of the hospitalized. The city fathers were told to decrease the amount of money spent by the city on public banquets and festivities: instead, they were to spend the revenues thus saved at workshops for the poor, which were to produce statuary, building materials and other commodities useful to the municipality and its wealthier members.[91] Priests should exhort the dying to limit their funeral pomp in favor of charity, and Vives provided them with a set of pragmatic incentives to voluntary almsgiving which they could incorporate into their sermons: he painted the portrait of a city blessed by God, populated by men reclaimed for Christ, and renowned for its peace and concord as a result of its implementation of his plan.[92] God would bless investment in charity by a sort of celestial

---

[89] Vives, in Salter, p. 11.

[90] *Ibid.*, pp. 11, 17; *Forma subventionis pauperum*, p. 32. In Ypres, 'four prefects and overseers of poor folks [were] ordained by the rightwise senate for the common profit,' with four sub-prefects and under-officers in each parish, to visit the homes, shops and cottages of the poor to determine need (*Forma*, pp. 26–8, 31–5). They were to be 'like common parents to the poor of our city and bear toward them such fatherly favor as they should do to their adoptive children' (p. 27).

[91] Vives, in Salter, pp. 14, 21, 23–5.

[92] *Ibid.*, pp. 22, 30–1. In Ypres, it was noted that many of the poor began receiving the sacraments after the implementation of a plan which both succored and enforced discipline upon them (*Forma*, p. 56).

interest on the communal level. Vives reminded the less visionary
that a city uncluttered by beggars not only looks better, it is less
troubled by crime and vices: for this reason, the ancient Athenians,
who lowered rents to the poor and provided jobs as well as doles for
them, 'considered it as good security to part with their money as to
keep it.'[93] In Ypres, where city officials collected 'voluntary' alms
from each household in the town once a week, the subsequent decrease in noise, odors and ugliness at the church gates, in crime and
deception of the citizens by rogues, and in contagious disease, were
all offered as practical incentives to further giving.[94] In similar
fashion, that Elizabethan reformer who estimated the cost to society
of individual idleness in pounds and pence assured the queen that
while the commons were presently charged with at least £1,000,000
per annum in keeping the poor, half that amount would suffice if
idleness were suppressed, and even that £500,000 would return to
the commons by increasing the wealth of the kingdom.[95] The
humanists were also aware that an efficient and honest administrative system would stimulate almsgiving by those concerned that
unscrupulous beggars would waste their dole. For this reason, city
officials were to investigate how goods bequeathed to the church
were used, and overseers of the poor were required to render regular
public accounts of receipts and disbursements.[96] Such a system may
have been less personal than the direct almsgiving of the Middle
Ages, but it was surely of more use to the poor.

The ultimate aim of the system, of course, was to reform the poor
themselves through a program of education and discipline.[97] The
'good education of youth in virtuous exercise is the ground of the
remedying of all other diseases in this our politic body,' Starkey
claimed, and he included poverty and vagrancy among those ills.
Both he and the Ypres reformer traced the problem of theft to idleness and bad example: children of the poor turn to evil ways, 'in their
first and tender years being unhappily brought up in idleness and
sloth and taught evil touches by the fellowship of lewd persons

---

[93] Vives, pp. 7, 30.
[94] *Forma*, pp. 36, 57–60. It is questionable how 'voluntary' a donation was when per-
sonally solicited by the authorities. *cf.* the 1552 English poor law which stipulated
that anyone 'obstinately and frowardly' refusing to give would be sent to the
bishop to be 'persuaded' to reform: 5 and 6 Edward VI, c.2, in J. R. Tanner, *Tudor
Constitutional Documents* (2nd edn., Cambridge, 1948), p. 471. Note also the heavy-
handed 'persuasion' used in sixteenth-century Rouen, where those whose 'voluntary' gifts were too small were threatened with distraint of goods in 1544
(Salter, p. 107).   [95] BL, Lansdowne, MS 95,3, pp. 120–1.
[96] *Forma*, pp. 49–50; Vives, p. 23.
[97] The ideal was expressed by Erasmus in the *Institutio*, pp. 212–13.

among whom they were conversant; they sucked even as of their
nurse most unthrifty manners...'[98] Accordingly, every boy in Ypres
should be sent to school or, 'if their wit will not serve them thereunto,' to learn a craft.[99] Sir William Forrest also called for compulsory education, free to the poor, beginning at age four, as a
solution to poverty, among other social disorders.[100]

The education of children abandoned by poor parents was of especial
concern to Vives. Lest such children perpetuate the problem of
poverty in the next generation, he recommended that at age six both
boys and girls should be moved from their hospitals to public
schools, where they should 'not only learn to read and write, but...
first of all learn Christian piety, and the right way of thinking.' They
would thereby be rescued from a life of undisciplined idleness and
enabled to serve, rather than drain, the commonwealth.[101] These
were the goals of sixteenth-century humanist founders of free
schools in the New World as well as the Old. The Franciscan Bishop
of Mexico, Zumárraga, who possessed a heavily annotated edition of
Utopia and several of Erasmus' works, sponsored public grammar
schools for girls and boys, hospital job training programs, and a
Latin college at Tlatelolco, with these ends in mind.[102]

Vives recognized that there were those for whom an educational
regimen was an inappropriate method of reform. These were to be
subjected to the discipline of work, not only for the material benefit
of the system, but also for their own reformation. Everyone worked
in Vives' scheme. Adults as well as children were to be taught a trade
('that for which they declare themselves most inclined') if at all possible. The untrainable should be given unskilled work, and the elderly
and invalid, light work. Even the blind were to be employed, and
Vives' reasoning here reveals again the high valuation of industry in
humanist thought: 'Some are capable of education, let them study
... others are musical, let them sing ... let some turn lathes or
wheels... or blow bellows in smiths' forges, or make baskets... Let
this be so arranged, in order that the idle thoughts and base desires

[98] Starkey, pp. 144, 177; *Forma*, p. 5; *cf.* Morison, *A remedy for sedition*, condemning the 'evil education' of the poor.   [99] *Forma*, p. 29.
[100] Forrest, *Pleasaunt Poesye*, pp. lxxxi, xcii–xciii.
[101] Vives, in Salter, pp. 18–19. Vives specified that 'if any girl show herself inclined for and capable of learning, she should be allowed to go further with it.' Boys with academic aptitude should pursue teaching or clerical careers; others should enter workshops, 'according to their individual bents' (p. 19).
[102] Richard E. Greenleaf, *Zumárraga and the Mexican Inquisition, 1536–1543* (Washington, DC, 1961), pp. 33–40, and Woodrow Borah, 'Social Welfare and Social Obligation in New Spain: A Tentative Assessment', in *XXXVI Congresso Internacional de Americanistas* (Seville, 1966), vol. 4, pp. 45–57.

that are born of idleness may be checked by occupation and absorp-
tion in work.'[103] It is in this reformist light that the prohibition of
begging and the enforcement of work on vagrants must be
understood. The Ypres law against begging (which was based,
incidentally, on the recommendation of Seneca) was praised as a
device which would 'bring these unthrifties from idleness to labour,
from pleasure to profit, from wasting to sparing.' This list of goals is
of course strikingly reminiscent of Hill's working definition of the
'capitalist spirit,' an 'ethos which, within the framework of a market
economy, emphasizes productive industry, frugality, and accumulation, as ends in themselves.'[104] Work was to the humanists, too,
both morally therapeutic and socially beneficial.

The poor relief plans which have been discussed here were much
more than armchair speculation. The Ypres scheme was implemented
with an apparently high degree of success by the city fathers from the
early 1520s, although the order against begging (only finally passed
in 1529) and the abolition of indiscriminate almsgiving were ordered
to be repealed by the Sorbonne in 1531.[105] Charles V requested a
copy of the plan in 1531 and a month later issued a Pragmatic Decree
forbidding begging throughout the Empire. The Ghent and Brussels
ordinances of 1534 were based on the Ypres scheme, and the
Spanish legislation of 1540 drew elements from it. Starkey was
clearly indebted to it and based the recommendations for England
which he submitted to Henry VIII on it. Its publication in London in
1535 certainly influenced the passage of the 1536 English poor
law.[106] Vives' proposal, not implemented in the city for which it was
written until 1560, likewise formed the basis of poor relief programs
actually implemented elsewhere. From the 1520s to the 1540s, cities
including Nuremburg, Augsburg, Altenburg, Zurich, Lyon, Rouen,

[103] Vives, pp. 13, 15–16; cf. such medieval foundations as the twelfth-century
almshouse of Reading, St Johns House, in which twenty-six people were provided
with shelter, food and clothes with no labor required: *Original Letters, and Other
Documents, relating to the benefactions of William Laud to the County of Berkshire*, ed. John
Bruce (1841), pp. 1–4. Contrast this with BL, Royal MS 18, C.vi, whose humanist
author demonstrates the usefulness to society of setting vagrants on such public
work as highway construction, maintenance of harbors and fortresses, etc. (fols.
3v–4).
[104] *Forma*, pp. 40, 44; Christopher Hill, 'Protestantism and the Rise of Capitalism,' in
*Essays in the Economic and Social History of Tudor and Stuart England in honour of R. H.
Tawney*, ed. F. J. Fisher (Cambridge, 1961), 15–39, p. 16, n. 1.
[105] The University's January, 1531 response to the scheme is printed in Salter, pp. 76–
9; on conservative Catholic interference with humanist poor relief schemes, see
chapter 7 below.
[106] Salter, pp. 33–6; *England in the Reign of Henry VIII*, p. 176. On the benefits reaped by
Ypres from its implementation of the scheme, see the *Forma*, pp. 54–60.

Paris and Venice put into effect poor relief schemes very similar to that of Ypres and to Vives' plan. [107] The French monarchy followed humanist advice and imposed on local secular authorities responsibility for the poor; laws effecting this secularization include the ordinances of Moulins (1566) and Blois (1579). [108]

Most significantly for our purposes, both Vives' tract and an account of the Ypres scheme were translated and published in England in the sixteenth century. These clearly formed a basis for English legislation and for the economic theory of sixteenth- and seventeenth-century English protestants. [109] William Marshall, even before publishing his translation of the Ypres plan, was drafting legislation aimed at eliminating the pernicious evil of mendicity according to the humanist program which he so admired. His 1531 proposal called for the appointment of overseers of the poor for each parish, the apprenticeship of children of the poor, and a program of public works to employ paupers at reasonable wages. [110] The 1536 Beggars Act was apparently modeled on his proposal. It ordered that 'no manner of person . . . shall make . . . any such common or open dole, or shall give any ready money in alms, otherwise

---

[107] On similarities between Vives' tract and French, German and Swiss poor relief, see Salter, pp. 81–2, 88–119. Luther's *Ordinance for a Common Chest* (1522) for the city of Leisneck is very similar to Vives' plan for education of boys and girls, for at-home relief where possible, and for strict financial accountability of guardians of the poor (Salter, pp. 92–3, 95–6). The Rouen legislation (1535) is likewise strikingly similar in its inclusion of charity schools, relief works for the unemployed, at-home relief, and careful categorization of the poor (Salter, pp. 104–19); it may have been directly based on Vives' proposals.

On the humanist-inspired Aumône-Générale of Lyon, see Natalie Davis, *Society and Culture in Early Modern France* (Stanford, 1975), pp. 17–64. Brian Pullan, *Rich and Poor in Renaissance Venice* (Cambridge, Mass., 1971), has treated the influence of Erasmus on Italian poor law reform, 1528–9 (Part II, chapter 2). It should be noted that parallel reforms took place in Florence in the fifteenth century – see Marvin Becker's essay 'Aspects of Lay Piety in Early Renaissance Florence,' in *The Pursuit of Holiness in Late Medieval and Renaissance Religion*, ed. Charles Trinkaus and Heiko A. Obermann (Leiden, 1974), 177–99; however, this is to be expected, since it was the humanist tradition of social criticism and reform which provided the driving force behind all these movements.

[108] Emmanuel Chill, 'Religion and Mendicity in Seventeenth Century France,' *International Review of Social History*, 3 (1962), 400–25, p. 401.

[109] More detailed accounts of the laws discussed in this paragraph and their humanist origins can be found in Fideler, pp. 269–70, 278–84; Jordan, pp. 84–7; and Tierney, pp. 130–2.

[110] BL, Royal MS 18, C. vi. According to this proposal, refusal to work was to result in forced labor or a felony conviction. G. R. Elton (*EcHR*, 2nd ser., 6 (1953), p. 57) has tentatively identified Marshall as the author. A statute passed in the same year, apparently inspired by continental humanist theory and experimentation, was the first English law not only to separate the worthy poor from lusty vagabonds but also to fine persons giving alms to unlicensed beggars. On the 1531 law, see Tierney, pp. 120–4, and Jordan, p. 84.

than to the common boxes and common gatherings.' Instead, parish or municipal overseers were to use donations to the common fund discriminately to maintain the impotent at home if possible, to educate and apprentice poor children, and to compel 'sturdy vagabonds and valiant beggars to be set and kept to continual labour, in such wise as by their said labours they ... may get their own livings with the continual labour of their own hands.'[111] Unfortunately, no public works system was incorporated, with the result that when vagrancy increased in the wake of the bad harvests of 1545 and 1546, the vicious Vagrancy Act of 1547 decreed the enslavement of able-bodied beggars. The extremity of this law brought about its repeal two years later in favor of continued progress toward the more humane ideal of Vives and Erasmus.[112]

Progress was made on both local and national levels. The year 1547 saw the first compulsory poor rate in London, and five years later, citizens of that city presented the Privy Council with a rational, sympathetic argument for publicly-financed employment of the poor: 'It hath been a speech used of all men, to say unto the idle, work! work!', they noted. But the poor, frequently victims of misfortune, cannot comply when opportunities are not made available to them:

we considered also that the greatest number of beggars fallen into misery by lewd and evil service, by wars, by sickness, or other adverse fortune, have so utterly lost their credit, that though they would show themselves willing to labour, yet are they so suspected and feared of all men, that few or none dare, or will receive them to work: wherefore we saw that there could be no means to amend this miserable sort, but by making some generous provision for work, wherewith the *willing* poor may be exercised ...

Their proposed solution was not the punitive institution which Bridewell ultimately became, but a home for 'the poor child, that he might be harboured, clothed, fed, taught, and virtuously trained up,' where, if unapt to learning, he, along with the weak and lame, acquitted prisoners, and the able beggars, could find work appropriate to his abilities.[113] Such relief schemes as this were put into effect at the municipal level long before they were considered by Parliament;

---

[111] Quoted in Salter, pp. 125–6; cf. Fideler, p. 269.
[112] C. S. L. Davies, 'Slavery and Protector Somerset: The Vagrancy Act of 1547,' *EcHR*, 2nd ser., 19 (1966), 533–49.
[113] *Tudor Economic Documents*, ed. R. H. Tawney and Eileen Power (1924), vol. 2, pp. 305, 307–8. Their language would be echoed by the anonymous humanist who proposed to Elizabeth the scheme of national relief discussed above. Bishop Ridley wrote to Cecil in 1552 in support of this suit, arguing the need for 'a place to house Christ' (*TED*, vol. 2, p. 312).

however, national legislation passed in 1551 and 1552 did authorize a census of the poor in each parish and delineate the election process for overseers of the poor throughout the realm.[114]

The rest of the program remained to be realized after the restoration of protestantism to England. After the middle of the century, progressive continental and American relief programs began to languish and finally to change their nature as Catholic conservatives rejected and attacked humanist social values – a phenomenon which will be analyzed in some detail later. But in England (as, apparently, in the Netherlands, some German towns, and certain Huguenot communities), the humanist vision of a disciplined, industrious, productive Christian society unencumbered by mendicants and vagabonds, free of poverty and ignorance, continued to inspire protestant reformers. The Elizabethan poor laws, praised by puritans as 'wholesome laws,' 'being in substance the very law of God,' came closer than any other sixteenth-century legislation to implementing the Vivesian ideal.[115]

The relative success with which the English addressed the poverty problem at the turn of the century was due in large measure to the enthusiastic adoption by protestants of the reform program of Christian humanism and of the humanist philosophy of work and wealth upon which it was based. The sanctification of work, the exaltation of discipline and the drive to repress idleness and frivolity have been properly labeled hallmarks of puritanism. The ideal of *mediocritas* in getting and spending, the doctrine of stewardship, and the demand for discriminate, rationalized, secular poor relief certainly characterize puritanism. All of these principles, however, can be found in the puritans' inheritance from Christian humanism. The inheritance was transmitted in part by earlier English and continental protestants; its authorities were biblical as well as classical; but its form and application were derived from Christian humanism. It was bequeathed, moreover, to protestants of all liturgical and ecclesiological persuasions: humanist economic and social theory formed a common ground for puritans and Anglicans during most of the period that we are considering. Historians have written a great deal about puritan veneration of industry, vocation and discipline,

---

[114] Jordan, p. 86. There was no national compulsory poor rate until 1597, although London established one in 1547, Norwich in 1549.
[115] *Ordinance for the Constant Reliefe and Imployment of the Poore* (17 December 1647) in *Acts and Ordinances of the Interregnum*, ed. C. H. Firth and R. S. Rait (1911), vol. 1, p. 1042; Perkins, *Works*, vol. 1, p. 755.

although only occasionally do they recognize that puritans shared this stance with Anglicans.[116] In fact, protestants of all varieties carried on the denunciation of idleness which can be found in the earliest Reformers.[117] But scant attention has been paid to their common sources, Christian humanist and classical, and it was those sources which defined the nature of puritan analysis of and prescription for the problem of idleness.

The ultimate goal of the work ethic, for protestants as for their Catholic humanist mentors, was the common weal. Both relied on the Roman Stoics, who understood *vocatus* in civic, rather than individual, terms. William Perkins might have been quoting Starkey or Elyot when he defined a legitimate vocation as one 'ordained and imposed on man by God, *for the common good.*' Christians 'may not live idly,' he argued, 'and give ourselves to riot and gaming, but labour to serve God and our country, in some profitable course of life.' The only vacation from work which God allows, according to Perkins, is the sabbath, which itself benefits the commonwealth by allowing time for study and religious exercises.[118] Thomas Cartwright interpreted the eighth commandment to forbid idleness, since one who does not labor to maintain both himself and the poor steals from the commonwealth.[119] Earlier in the century Hugh Latimer had urged Edward VI to set his subjects on work 'that the commonwealth be advanced,' and Martin Bucer called 'slothful and pernicious idleness'

---

[116] Breen, pp. 273–9, cites such Anglicans as George Herbert, Robert Sanderson, Lancelot Andrewes, Nicholas Ferrar, John Donne and Thomas Fuller on the doctrine of particular calling and on the intrinsic goodness of work.

[117] From Luther's railing against begging friars in his 'Address to the Christian Nobility' (*Works*, ed. Jaroslav Pelikan and S. Lehmann (Philadelphia, 1955), vol. 44, pp. 189–90); Zwingli's definition of indolence as 'the mother of all mischief': *Of the Upbringing and Education of Youth* (1523), in *Library of Christian Classics*, vol. 24, ed. G. W. Bromiley (Philadelphia, 1953), p. 117, *cf.* p. 113; and Hugh Latimer's traditional censure of sloth and gluttony (*Sermons*, ed. G. E. Corrie (Cambridge, 1844), pp. 52, 65–7, 117–20); to the more sophisticated plans of Bucer to eliminate idleness, unemployment and luxury in *De Regno Christi* (pp. 171, 182, 335–40, 346, 354). Bucer's sources were frequently classical: he noted (p. 354) Draco the Athenian's opinion that laziness should be punishable by death (Plutarch, *Vita Solonis*, XVII, 1–2). It is significant that the only section of *De Regno Christi* to be translated and published in England in the sixteenth century was that dealing with work, wealth and charity, translated as *A Treatise How by the Worde of God, Christian mens Almose ought to Be distributed* [1557].

[118] Perkins, *A Treatise of the Vocations, or Callings of Man* (1597–1601) in *Workes* (1616), vol. 1, p. 750 (emphasis mine), pp. 774–5; *cf. The Whole Treatise of the Cases of Conscience* in *William Perkins: His Pioneer Works on Casuistry*, ed. Thomas F. Merrill (The Hague, 1966), p. 206; Cicero, *De Officiis*, I, 29; Seneca, *De clementia*, in *Moral Essays*, tr. J. W. Basore (Cambridge, Mass., 1958), vol. 1, pp. 365–9.

[119] *A shorte Catechisme*, in *Cartwrightiana*, ed. Albert Peel and Leland Carson, (1951), p. 165.

a 'pest of the community.' In the next century, Nehemiah Wallington opined that an idle citizenry can bring divine judgment on the whole nation.[120]

For the sake of the commonwealth, then, puritans followed the standard Christian humanist recommendations to instill discipline into the social order: productivity must be encouraged, time discipline imposed and frivolity restrained. Productivity, or profit, was the value which John White hoped to teach in his Dorchester parish, by establishing a school for the poor supported in part by their labor in a municipal brewhouse. His apology for the scheme assumed the principle of 'knowledge causing piety, piety breeding industry, and industry procuring plenty.'[121] While puritans credited God for their material blessings, they were fully convinced of their responsibility both to engage in productive and honest work in order to keep the windows of heaven open, and to use their wealth for the common good, to the glory of God. Wallington, whose diary is replete with thanksgiving to God for 'good trade,' vowed none the less to strive to 'please my loving God that sends me all my customers and gives me freely all that I enjoy' by laboring uprightly in his appointed calling: God's blessings to Job, he noted, came not directly, but 'in blessing his *labor*. So much as you get honestly by your faithful labors and endeavors, so much you may say God hath given you.'[122] Samuel Ward of Ipswich made it clear that legitimate profit was not merely material gain for the seller, but the good of the community, in this case, of both parties in an economic transaction: 'Let the mutual profit of buyer and seller be the rule of buying and selling, and not the gain of one of them alone.'[123]

Far from despising manual arts, puritans agreed with Erasmus and Vives that they were to be highly regarded as profitable to individual and society. The puritan William Bright quoted with approval Morison's observation that the citizens of Nuremberg lived plentifully despite sparse natural resources 'by industry and skill in manual arts.' The notebook which Bright kept during the 1640s graphically illustrates the importance of Morison and other Christian

[120] Latimer, pp. 99–100; Bucer, p. 335, *cf.* p. 216; Wallington, *Diary*, BL, Add. MS 40883, fols. 44, 74.
[121] Quoted in Charles Webster, *The Great Instauration* (New York, 1975), p. 34. The brewhouse also served to police the assize of ale and prevent profiteering. *cf.* Paul Slack, 'Poverty and Politics in Salisbury, 1597–1666,' in *Crisis and Order in English Towns, 1500–1700,* ed. Peter Clark and Paul Slack (Toronto, 1972), pp. 164–203.
[122] BL, Add. MS 40883, fols. 78v, 46v; *cf.* William Ames, *The Marrow of Theology*, tr. and ed. John Eusden (Boston, 1968), p. 323.
[123] Samuel Ward, *A Balme from Gilead to Recover Conscience* (1612), p. 81.

humanists for the puritan doctrine of work: in addition to quoting censures of idleness by Seneca, Cicero and Plutarch, Bright collected numerous Erasmian adages on the subject. His conclusion might have been uttered by Erasmus himself: 'The Angels, beasts and inanimate creatures will not afford one patron or president of idleness. How, then, can it be fancied a privilege and dignity to be one jarring string in this great instrument, and to become the only unprofitable useless part of the creation?'[124]

Occupations which are unprofitable to the commonwealth are not legitimate callings. Perkins, John Dod, Arthur Dent and other puritans accordingly followed the Erasmian lead in condemning monks and friars, dealers in luxuries, profligate aristocrats and their servants no less than rogues and vagabonds for not serving the commonwealth with their time and abilities. Simonds D'Ewes, for instance, called intemperate livers 'vagabonds by their life-leading.'[125] When the House of Commons debated the definition of 'vagabond' for the 1572 legislation against vagrancy, they resolved to include players, bearwards, fencers, minstrels, jugglers and begging scholars as unprofitable to the society, and, therefore, lacking a legitimate calling.[126] But this censure of non-productive occupations was obviously not leveled only by puritans – Anglicans like Robert Sanderson and John Earle joined the attack on 'idle gallants' precisely because they shared with puritans the humanist association of productive work and the common good.[127]

Non-productive recreation was similarly condemned as unprofitable to individual or to commonwealth. Protestants, like their Catholic humanist forebears, quoted Cicero's opinion that 'We have not been so fashioned by nature that we seem to have been made for sport and games, but rather for hardship and for certain more serious and more important pursuits.'[128] Advanced protestants agreed with Erasmus in objecting to holidays because they lure men

[124] CUL, Add. MS 6160, fols. 153v–154v, 157, p. 229.
[125] Perkins, *Works*, vol. 1, pp. 755–6, *cf.* pp. 748, 752, 764, and vol. 2, p. 126; John Dod, *Bathshebaes Instructions to her Sonne Lemuel* (1614), pp. 32–3, 40–6; Arthur Dent, *Plaine mans Pathway to Heaven* (1601), pp. 171–2; BL, Harl. 182 (D'Ewes, 1618), fol. 22; *cf.* Bucer, p. 335.
[126] Simonds D'Ewes, *The Journals of all the Parliaments during the Reign of Queen Elizabeth* (1682), Part I, p. 220 (30 May 1572); *TED*, vol. 2, p. 329 (14 Elizabeth I, c.5). Wallington reported in 1643 his contempt for the Royalist army marching against London, composed as it was of fiddlers, players, ballad singers and rogues (BL, Add. MS 40883, fol. 85).
[127] Robert Sanderson, *Works*, ed. Jacobson (Oxford, 1854), Vol. III, pp. 108–109; Sanderson, *XXXIV Sermons* (1661), pp. 245–246, 248–249; John Earle, *Microcosmographie* (1628), Chapter 19.
[128] Cicero, *De Officiis*, I, 29, quoted by Bucer, p. 346.

from labor to frivolity, from productivity to sloth. While John Gough advocated moderate use of 'lawful, healthy games,' he regarded Christmas as a sure temptation to feasting and card-playing, neither of which could benefit the Kingdom of Christ.[129] It was for this reason that puritans also attempted to regulate or repress alehouses, church ales, dancing, holiday revelling and communal feasting – all forms of popular culture which it was felt were of no profit to the commonwealth and in fact contributed only to idleness, poverty, ungodliness and disorder. The Long Parliament's offensive against 'country disorders' must be understood at least in part as the logical culmination of the Christian humanists' drive to extirpate 'pastimes' and institute instead a hard-working, disciplined social order.[130] This is not to say that the puritans opposed recreation *per se*. Activities 'derived from the musical and gymnastic art' which could contribute to health, grace and piety were condoned as beneficial to church and commonwealth – as long as they were used in moderation and not on the sabbath.[131]

Puritans analyzed both work and recreation carefully because zealous protestants shared with humanists the doctrine of steward-ship of all things, including time. For them, as for Whitforde and More, time was a divine trust for which the trustees would be held responsible on the Day of Judgment. George Webbe charged his auditors to be diligent in their callings, to shun idleness, and to examine their behavior daily for failure to use time well, because

---

[129] Quoted in Patrick Collinson, *The Elizabethan Puritan Movement* (Berkeley, 1967), p. 75. Gough was St Antholin's lecturer and rector of St Stephen's, Cornhill; Perkins, *Works*, vol. 3, pp. 512–13, criticized the papists, who add fifty-two saints' days to fifty-two sabbaths 'and so spend more than a quarter of the year in rest and idleness.'

[130] Keith Wrightson and David Levine, *Poverty and Piety in an English Village: Terling, 1525–1700* (New York, 1979), pp. 133–7, 180–2; William Hunt, *The Puritan Moment* (Cambridge, Mass., 1983), pp. 79–84, 130–55; Wrightson, 'The Puritan Reformation of Manners,' Ph.D. thesis, University of Cambridge, 1973), *passim*. On the 'proscriptive zeal of the Long Parliament and its local manifestations,' see Wrightson, 'Reformation of Manners,' pp. 133–63. It should be noted that much of the social legislation passed during the Civil War and Interregnum was merely a strengthening of early Tudor legislation: for example, in 1657 the Henrician act against gaming was reinforced, and the Elizabethan legislation against vagabond fiddlers and minstrels was repeated; the sabbath laws of 1650 and 1657 were innovative only in their somewhat more stringent penalties (F&R, vol. 2, pp. 383, 1098, 1162, 1249). The increase in regulative activity at local and national levels under puritan rule is an indication of the zeal, rather than the imagination, of the hotter sort.

[131] Some moderate puritans even defended Sunday sports which would aid in prepar-ation for war, as legitimate in God's eyes because profitable to the common-wealth: e.g., Samuel Ward, Bodl., MS Tanner 279, fol. 352. *cf.* Bucer, pp. 347–53; Perkins, *Cases of Conscience*, p. 206.

'you must give account.'[132] Puritans like Richard Rogers took such advice seriously: Rogers kept careful records both of his sins in 'taking too much ease' and 'not rising early' and of his occasional successes in achieving 'freedom from sottish idleness.'[133] Wallington likewise confessed 'backwardness in duty' and 'misspending my precious time' on the one hand, and rejoiced in his disinclination to tipple, bowl, play cards or dice, see plays or read vain books on the other hand.[134]

Time, then, was to be jealously guarded and carefully used, vocation was legitimated by productivity, and diligent labor was enjoined on all. Nevertheless, the focus of all this activity was to be not wealth, but commonwealth. Protestants who followed the preachers' advice were confronted, as humanists had been earlier, with the resultant problem of wealth. They dealt with the problem in good humanist fashion– holding *mediocritas* as the ideal, analyzing motives and defining ethical limits in getting and spending, and prescribing thrifty and discriminate use of material profits for the commonwealth.

It has been suggested by Christopher Hill that puritan preachers articulated a doctrine of 'justification by success' which distinctly appealed to 'a class for whom the accumulation of capital had become an absolute good in itself.'[135] Hill has somehow managed to conclude from William Perkins' sermons that 'the fundamental concepts of puritan thought *are* bourgeois,' and that among them is the notion that accumulation of wealth is appropriate and, indeed, a good sign of election. More recently, Richard Greaves has found puritans 'more receptive than Anglicans to the idea that prosperity could be a reward of godliness.'[136] Certainly, the preachers did argue that work ought to be productive, and they were aware that diligence and thrift were likely to bring material rewards. But in the puritan view, profit was intended for the community of Christ, rather than for the individual; capital was not to be accumulated, but to be used. Accumulating excess wealth was, according to Henry Bedel, not only a temptation to sin; it was a blatant denial of God's providence.[137]

[132] George Webbe, *A short Direction for the dayly exercise of a Christian* in *A Garden of spirituall Flowers* (1610), sig. Fiiii.
[133] Richard Rogers, *Diary*, in *Two Elizabethan Puritan Diaries*, ed. M. M. Knappen (Gloucester, Mass., 1966), pp. 82, 85, 101.
[134] BL, Add. MS 40883, fols. 6v, 44, 69, 112.
[135] Hill, *Puritanism and Revolution*, p. 229; *Society and Puritanism*, p. 292.
[136] Hill, *Puritanism and Revolution*, p. 236; Greaves, *Religion and Society*, p. 751.
[137] Bedel, *A sermon exhortyng to pitie the poore* (1572), sig. Biii, *verso*. He quoted Seneca here on God's providence. *cf.* Hunt, p. 139.

Samuel Ward of Ipswich called wealth a curse, inevitably leading to 'gaming and riotous living.' He called profit, in this context, material rewards for labor, a 'vile chain and easily broken,' held together with 'the sordid cement of avarice.'[138] Those who had labored productively were to retain for themselves only what was needed to maintain life and status – 'necessary riches,' as opposed to abundance.[139] Those whose incomes exceeded their needs were called on to dispense their excess wealth in educating their and the community's children, relieving the poor, and serving church and state, for 'whatsoever is *unserviceable* is of no worth, and that which is of no *use*, is of no estimation.' What may be valued is that which is 'profitable for mankind,' that is, for the community.[140] Money was not condemned. If wealth was not necessarily a sign of divine approval, neither was it intrinsically bad. As Arthur Hildersham pointed out, if this were the case, Abraham could not have been the godly man portrayed by the Scriptures. Riches, said William Ames, are neither good nor evil in themselves; all depends on their use.[141] If properly acquired and well-spent, wealth could in fact be a great boon to the commonwealth.

But an appetite for money was condemned, and selfish accumulation and conspicuous consumption were denounced in no uncertain terms. Moderation was the rule by which the good life was to be lived, and this curb to whatever acquisitive spirit there may have been in early modern England was reinforced not only by puritan sermons, but also by the immensely popular Stoic literature which, as part of the Erasmian legacy, filled early modern libraries.[142] Seneca's exhortation to be content only 'to have what is necessary'

[138] Samuel Ward, *The wonders of the load-stone* (1640), pp. 9–10, 136–7.
[139] Perkins, *Cases of Conscience*, p. 189; *cf.* Robert Cleaver, *A Godly Forme of Householde Government* (1598), p. 62. The increasing fluidity of the social hierarchy during the sixteenth century, and the importance of money in gaining entrance to a higher status group, may have made this rule more open-ended than its author intended (Wrightson and Levine, pp. 103–9). But the *intent* of the preachers' definition of legitimate gain as necessary income was apparent, and warnings against ambition – lack of contentment with one's own estate (*Cases of Conscience*, p. 193) – must have given second thoughts to aspiring entrepreneurs of a religious bent.
[140] O'Connell, pp. 6–7; Perkins, *Works*, vol. 2, p. 126; Ward, *Wonders*, p. 214, emphasis original.
[141] BL, Harl. MS 3230, fol. 90; William Ames, *Conscience with Power and the Cases Thereof*, p.253; *cf.* John Ball, *The Power of Godliness* (1657), *passim*. Richard Sibbes, *Light from Heaven* (1638), p. 101, also suggested the moral neutrality of material goods, as did Simonds D'Ewes, BL, MS Harl. 227, fol. 9. Robert Hill, *The Pathway to Prayer and Pietie* (1613), pp. 78–83, advocated a 'modest prosperity.'
[142] See my 'Seneca and the Protestant Mind: The Influence of Stoicism on Puritan Ethics,' *Archiv für Reformationsgeschichte*, 74 (1983), 182–99.

Seneca's exhortation to be content only 'to have what is necessary' was read with approval by Brilliana Conway, Oliver St John and D'Ewes, as it had been by Seneca's Christian humanist editors and translators early in the sixteenth century.[143] The warnings of Stoics, Erasmians and puritans alike against the dangers inherent in excessive wealth were taken seriously. The economically successful were, after all, among those Parliamentarians who legislated against luxury and excess and the oppression and fraud which produced them. It was the puritans who had 'made it' in the community of Terling, moreover, who outlawed Sunday work – a move hardly calculated to line their purses further.[144]

Material abundance was regarded not as a sign of justification, but as a temptation to other forms of excess. While an adequate income was cause to thank God, riches were generally interpreted as a test all too likely to be failed. God may grant material blessings in his wrath, Perkins warned, observing that the hearts of rich men were generally enslaved to the joys of hawking, hunting, riotous gaming, fine apparel and good cheer, rather than to God.[145] Bedel, Gataker and Greenham all saw wealth as a trial to faith.[146] Greenham argued that riches 'have been ever greater causes of harm than of good.' Poverty, he said, 'hath been the decay of many a man, but riches of a far greater number... [for they] are evil commonly in either getting, or in keeping, or in using, or in loving them... Riches are not signs of God's favor.' He commended instead the mean between austerity and excess, the humanist ideal of mediocrity.[147]

Puritans also concerned themselves with godly methods of getting and spending 'necessary wealth'. Wallington's confession illustrates their approach to business:

I must one day give account before the great God as how I have got my money. So I must give an account how I have improved and laid out every penny I have got. My conscience tells me I have been very remiss and unwise in some kind both in getting and in spending. But I hope and trust the Lord hath forgiven me this and all other of my sins... It is the desire of my heart

[143] Seneca, *Epistle*, 2, tr. Richard Gummere (Cambridge, Mass., 1953), vol. 1, p. 9; Nottingham University MSS, Box 166 (Conway), fol. 115; BL, Add. MS 25,285, fols. 19v, 37v; Simonds D'Ewes notebooks, BL, Harl. 121, fols. 50v–51; *cf.* fols. 22 (an essay on Horace's *Dives miser est*), 25, 41; BL, Harl. 182, fol. 24v.
[144] F&R, vol. 1, p. 80 (15 February 1643); Wrightson and Levine, p. 157.
[145] Perkins, *Works*, vol. 1, pp. 754, 769; *cf.* D'Ewes' equation of riches with snares to sin, BL, Harl. MS 227, fol. 17v.
[146] Henry Bedel, *A sermon exhortyng to pitie the poore* (1572), sig. Aiii; Gataker, *Certaine sermons* (1637), p. 155; Richard Greenham, *Workes* (1601), p. 30.
[147] Greenham, pp. 269, 392. *cf.* Brilliana Conway, who said that the wealth of wicked men is 'poison, and serves to make them more inexcusable' (fol. 115).

that in everything I either buy or sell that I take God with me in the lifting up of my heart to God saying shall I buy this or shall I sell that, or thus, Lord give me wisdom in my buying and my selling... to deal with an upright heart as I would have others deal with me, not seeking my own ends only, but as the good of them I deal with.[148]

The most basic of the guidelines which were established was a clear sense of priorities in which work and wealth were firmly subordinated in importance to godly living. Again, Wallington's diary provides the best illustrations. Despite his concern with his income and indebtedness, Wallington recorded numerous instances of closing his shop in order to attend public fasts or lectures; one Monday morning he decided to stay home from work in order to pray, having discovered during his 4.00 a.m. devotions that he 'did find... more sweetness to tarry at home and solace my soul with the Lord than there could be in going abroad and taking all the delight and pleasure the world could afford me.' He realized that the 'rich fall into temptation and snares and into many foolish and noisome lusts which drown men in perdition and destruction. For the desire of money is the root of all evil.' He prayed to be neither rich nor poor, for 'outward comforts are vain and will fail us.'[149] He was in fact well on the way to losing what comforts he had by reducing his prices so as not to blemish the godly name of puritan.[150]

Wallington was extremely concerned with business ethics, scrupulously avoiding such 'sins of buying and selling' as false advertising of his wares. On one occasion he refunded the price of some trenchers which his servant had misrepresented to a customer as being of maple, and he repeatedly reprimanded his servants for 'lying, though it be for my profit.' During his self-examination, however, he once confessed that he had himself 'multiplied more words than I need with some lying words' in order to sell his goods. He found it altogether just that 'I should lose my customer for it,' and he seems to have regretted this loss less than his having offended God. Far from separating the duties of the Two Tables of the Law, Wallington's goal was 'to see my God in the fire, in the water, in the air, in Liberty, in peace, in health, in kindness of friends... in my buying and selling.'[151]

The puritan guidelines for proper business behavior include traditional denunciations of all forms of economic exploitation, by unqualified physicians, greedy magistrates, merchants using gloss or inadequate lighting to disguise faulty merchandise, rack-renting

[148] BL, Add. MS 40883, fol. 15v.   [149] *Ibid.*, fols. 24, 32.
[150] *Ibid.*, fol. 9.   [151] *Ibid.*, fols. 7v, 32v, 29v.

landlords, enclosers (driven by 'want of sobriety and temperance in diet and apparel,' according to Perkins), grain-hoarding husbandmen ('shedding the blood of the poor'), or printers of unprofitable books.[152] But the basis for these censures is not traditional: it is the humanist conviction that a secular vocation need not be less holy than a clerical one, just as marriage is not inferior to celibacy. Perkins criticized usurers, oppressors, engrossers and users of fraudulent weights and measures because they fail to unite their two callings, the general (to Christian faith) and the particular. 'They prophane their lives and callings,' he charged, 'that employ them to get honours, pleasures, profits, worldly commodities, etc.' because they thereby serve themselves, not God or their fellows.[153] His aim was not to denigrate business, however, but to sanctify it by bringing its benefits to church and commonwealth. As Bucer had reasoned earlier, 'Marketing is a business which is honest and necessary for the commonwealth if it confines itself to the import and export of things that are advantageous to the commonwealth for living well and in a holy way, but not those which encourage and foster impious pomp and luxury.' Only the 'crooked kind of merchants and tradesmen,' those so highly regarded by Erasmus' Folly, placed their own profits over the welfare of the community.[154]

Some historians have suggested that the subordination by Wallington and his advisers of money-making to godly living for the common good reveals the traditionalism of puritan economic attitudes.[155] Certainly, the evidence of Wallington's diary, in combination with the advice literature and sermons to which he was exposed, militates against the notion that puritanism sanctified economic expediency and argued justification by success. Puritans were manifestly equivocal about their profit-making. If we can venture onto the uncertain ground of dream interpretation, Wallington's nightmare of having a large volume of business but experiencing 'no peace with it' – a dream from which he was startled by a vision of a man in black – illustrates the psychological effects of their misgivings.[156] On the other hand, as part of the Erasmian tradition, puritans represent a departure from medieval economic traditionalism in their concerted efforts not simply to justify, but to sanctify, the diligent, hard-working life of the entrepreneur. Wallington, well aware of the role of his own labor, none the less credited God for

---

[152] Perkins, *Works*, vol. 1, p. 771.   [153] *Ibid.*, vol. 1, p. 757.
[154] *Ibid.*, vol. 1, p. 773; Bucer, pp. 342–3, 344.
[155] Seaver, 'Puritan Work Ethic,' *passim*, and his *Wallington's World* (Stanford, 1985), ch. 5; Green, pp. 283–7.   [156] BL, Add. MS 40883, fol. 9v.

every shilling he earned; he apparently had no second thoughts about this confluence of the sacred and the mundane.[157] Earnings from business were far from evil in his eyes.[158] Perkins was quick to preach what godly entrepreneurs had learned in practice, that ethical business activity (work for the glory of God rather than personal gain) was actually more profitable for the worker in the long run; he thereby encouraged honest entrepreneurship on practical as well as theological grounds.[159] Recent research on seventeenth-century Scottish capitalist practice reveals the considerable encouragement given by Calvinist preachers to entrepreneurial callings there. The stimulation of business was understood on both sides of the northern border to be of potential benefit to the whole realm, so that business loans at interest were justified by protestants as they had been by Erasmus.[160] The point of departure was obviously pre-Reformation; puritans were simply expressing what had become the consensus of economic moralizers by their day. By examining motives, setting priorities and establishing ethical guidelines, the theorists of Renaissance and Reformation provided a Christian mean between medieval economic traditionalism and modern capitalist aggression.[161]

Their mean clearly allowed considerable profit-making, so that in addition to defining Christian getting, puritans also addressed themselves to Christian spending. Like their Catholic mentors, they preached the doctrine of stewardship. The wealth which men held was a trust from God, and to spend it on 'things contributing more to the delight of the flesh than to the virtue of the spirit and the true utility of the commonwealth' was 'unworthy of those who profess piety,' and, for that matter, 'the greatest pitfall for healthy indus-

---

[157] *Ibid.*, fols. 9, 12–14, 26, 29, 34v, 45, 78v, 87v, 115, 117v, 120v, 129v–131v.
[158] Seaver, *Wallington's World*, describes the transitional position of Wallington on economic issues: 'If Wallington was suspicious of economic success, he was equally dubious about the moral worth of economic failure, and he alternated in explaining his periodic bouts of poverty between attributing them to his own "idleness and negligence" in his calling, and attributing them to God's attempt to wean him from an inordinate love of the world.' Seaver concludes that his 'values and attitudes neither preserved the past nor anticipated the future'; he might as well have said that they did both (p. 130).
[159] Perkins, *Works*, vol. 1, p. 757.
[160] Martin Bucer argued for this in the Marburg Disputation of 1538, tr. F. H. Littell in *Reformation Studies* (Richmond, Va., 1962), p. 156. On Scottish Calvinism and capitalism, see Marshall, *Presbyteries and Profits*.
[161] Renaissance thinkers were not, of course, the first to justify business loans at interest. See, for example, Baldwin, *Just Price* and his *Masters, Princes and Merchants*, and Little, *Religious Poverty*. But even in the most forward-looking theorists, the life of the merchant was second in sanctity to that of the cleric, particularly the voluntarily poor monk or friar.

try.'[162] God's stewards, said Cartwright, are to 'live soberly with our own, not lavishing, nor greedily keeping goods gotten, but to be liberal to the poor.' The wealthy are to be honored 'not for their riches simply, but for the right use of riches; namely, as they are made instruments, to uphold and maintain virtue.'[163] As William Jones warned, the successful businessman will be required to give an account of his stewardship (of goods no less than time) before God's judgment seat.[164] Accordingly, a Christian's wealth must be used as the Christian humanists had prescribed, with prudence, discrimination and generosity. The most obviously Christian use of excess profits – the relief of poverty – was regulated by all of these considerations.

Prudence and discrimination were not, as we have seen, characteristics of medieval hospitality. But puritans were apparently convinced by humanist arguments that the result was not truly generous, that is, genuinely beneficial to the poor. Their stress on prudence and discrimination by no means eliminated their compassion. Sympathy and liberality were still considered virtues. The 'living affection to the poor' shown by Chaderton was held up by Samuel Ward for emulation as a 'certain token of a sound Christian'; Ward recognized his own failures to remember the poor as a serious sin.[165] Richard Rogers recorded visiting the poor in Bridewell, and he exhorted the prosperous among his parishioners to give interest-free loans to their impoverished neighbors and to remit the principal if they proved unable to pay.[166] It was said that Richard Greenham 'approached fanaticism in his zeal for charity.'[167] Countless puritan preachers exhorted their congregations to give generously to their unfortunate brethren.[168] Research on poor relief during periods of

[162] Bucer, p. 354.   [163] *Cartwrightiana*, p. 165; Perkins, *Cases of Conscience*, p. 237.
[164] Jones, *A pithie and short treatise whereby a godly Christian is directed how to make his last will* (1612), pp. 20–1; *cf.* Richard Rogers, *A Garden of spirituall flowers*, Part II, sigs. Avi, Bv; Gataker, p. 300; and Perkins' argument that works of charity enable the rich man to 'lay up a good foundation in conscience, against the evil day' (*Cases of Conscience*, p. 196).
[165] Ward, *Diary*, in *Two Elizabethan Puritan Diaries*, pp. 107–9, 116.
[166] Rogers, *Diary*, p. 77; Hunt, p. 138.
[167] M. M. Knappen, *Tudor Puritanism* (Chicago, 1939), p. 382, *cf.* p. 344.
[168] Henry Arthington, *Provision for the Poore* (1597); Laurence Chaderton, *An Excellent and Godly Sermon preached at Paules Crosse the xxvi Day of October 1578* [1580], sigs. Cvi, verso-Cvii; John Dod, *Bathshebaes Instructions*, pp. 48–9; Dent, p. 197; Greenham, *Workes*, p. 41; Rogers, *Spirituall flowers*, Part II, sig. Fv; George Walker, *Exhortation for contributions* in *Miscellany*, ed. C. W. Sutton (Chetham Society, Machester, 1902), n.s., 1, p. 47; John Milton, *Commonplace Book*, in *Complete Prose Works* (New Haven, 1953), vol. 1, p. 418 – among many other examples. See also Collinson, *Religion of Protestants*, p. 159, on the generosity of West Suffolk puritans in the Elizabethan period.

puritan ascendancy has demonstrated that local relief during the Civil War and Interregnum was dispensed on a scale unmatched in previous decades: JPs in Warwickshire handled nearly three times as many relief cases from 1649 to 1660 as they had from 1630 to 1641.[169] The poor also received a higher percentage of total charitable contributions in that county from 1641 to 1660 than ever before.[170]

As means to encourage giving, the preachers used not only the doctrine of stewardship and the argument that generosity to the poor provides evidence of election, but also the compelling notion of celestial usury which Vives had used to good effect decades earlier. 'He that giveth to the poor lendeth to the Lord, a sure discharger of his debts to the uttermost,' Edwin Sandys preached in 1585. His text, Proverbs 19.17, was a favorite of preachers on charity from the Church Fathers to the seventeenth century. Robert Allen quoted St John Chrysostom in his *Treatise of Christian beneficence*: 'He that hath mercy on the poor, lendeth to the Lord, as it were upon usury. He that receiveth, that is, the poor man, is altogether another from him who bindeth himself to pay the loan, to wit, God.'[171] Richard Sibbes used the same biblical text, buttressed by patristic approval, in a 1637 sermon; D'Ewes included it in a list of his favorite classical quotations on giving; and Wallington used it in 1642 to reason that he should give to the poor even though he was himself in debt, since 'there is never anything lost in doing for God (or his children).'[172] There was, of course, a negative version of the commonplace. It was expressed by the English translator of Bucer's work on poor relief: 'Remember the poor, and God will remember you; forget the poor, and God will not forget you.'[173]

The final argument used by the preachers was that alms were the poor man's due. William Bright expressed it in connection with stewardship:

Though God hath not disposed so immediately to the poor, yet he gives them as it were bills of assignment upon the plenty of the rich ... If a rich

---

[169] A. L. Beier, 'Poor Relief in Warwickshire 1630–1660,' *P&P*, 35 (1966), 3–29, p. 78. The difference is surely too great to be explained solely by the dislocation resulting from the Civil War: *cf.* Valerie Pearl, 'Puritans and Poor Relief: The London Workhouse, 1649–1660,' in *Puritans and Revolutionaries*, ed. Donald Pennington and Keith Thomas (Oxford, 1978), 206–32. See also chapter 7, below.

[170] Beier, pp. 84, 98.

[171] Sandys, *Sermons*, (1585), sig. Niii, verso; Allen, *A Treatise* (1600), p. 221, citing Chrysostom, Hom. 3 on the first chapter of Genesis.

[172] Sibbes, pp. 144–5, explained that although the giver 'hath cast away his bounty, yet he hath cast it upon God, and Christ, that will return it again; he knows he doth but lend to the Lord.' D'Ewes, BL, Harl. MS 182, fol. 25; BL, Add. MS 40883, fol. 16v. [173] *Christian mens Almose*, p. 29.

man leaves the poor destitute, and suffers either his riot, or courteousness [pleasure, or hospitality] to feed upon their portions, what more detestable falseness can be committed, not only in respect of them whose *right* he thus invades, but of God also whose trust he abuses.[174]

Christians are bound to give to the poor, according to Perkins, since 'it is God's will that the poor should have title to a part of every man's goods; and for this cause it is a shame if they have not relief without roving, begging, or crying.'[175]

The poor were not to be despised, but rather accepted as brothers and co-heirs of Christ, so that, far from denying them their rights, Christians should share their goods with them willingly and without condescension. The popular tendency to regard the poor as accursed and despicable was criticized by Sibbes, who observed that 'the poor man is trod on at all hands; men go over the hedge where it is lowest.' This was clearly sinful: Sibbes urged Christians 'not to despise the brother of low degree.'[176] Bedel likewise charged his congregation to respect as well as care for the poor, and his sources were not limited to the Scriptures: 'Let Christians learn a lesson of the heathen orator Tully . . . poverty (saith he) compelleth many a good and honest man to take in hand vile and slavish businesses, for which cause they deserve mercy and succour, rather than destruction.'[177]

This perspective stemmed partly from the puritans' understanding of the nature of poverty. Just as wealth was not considered a sign of divine approval, so poverty was not presumptive evidence of reprobation. 'We may not ask earthly blessings as signs of God's favour; neither must we esteem the want of these things as tokens of his displeasure,' Greenham taught. Poverty was understood to be an affliction, but affliction was in some senses 'proper to the godly.'[178] It could actually be of more help to salvation than riches could. 'God sanctifies outward affliction and poverty,' according to Sibbes, 'to help inward poverty of spirit . . . he takes away the fuel that feeds pride.' Indeed, for the haughty rich to be brought low may be their only means to salvation: if we use wealth 'as clouds to keep God from us, and to fasten, and fix upon the things themselves,' there may be 'no other remedy, but God must strip us naked of them.'[179] Even in

---

[174] CUL., Add. MS 6160, p. 231 (emphasis Bright's). This passage occurs in a discussion of the evils of luxury and self-indulgence (pp. 230–2).
[175] Perkins, *Cases of Conscience*, p. 224; *Workes*, vol. 1, p. 775.
[176] Sibbes, pp. 98, 103.   [177] Bedel, sigs. Aiv, Div, verso.
[178] Greenham, *Workes*, p. 270; D'Ewes, *Theological Observations*, BL, Harl. 227, fol. 21; *cf.* Dent, p. 197. Job provided a ready example for the preachers of a godly man oppressed by poverty.   [179] Sibbes, pp. 98–9.

this case, poverty was not so much a punishment for sin as God's device to rescue those who might otherwise be drawn to perdition by their excesses.

But poverty was not automatically interpreted as a result of or remedy for the wickedness of the victim. Sometimes it was the end product of the rapaciousness of the wealthy or of the evil in the economic system itself. The duty of the Christian, whether puritan, Anglican or Catholic humanist, was to analyze the causes of poverty in every particular and to address the problem at its source. Accordingly, Perkins found the true 'bane and plague of a commonwealth . . . they that make beggars and vagabonds' in those who lend money at interest to the poor 'till they have sucked their bones'; it is usury which should be repressed, rather than the poor who are created by it.[180] In 1603, Richard Stock attacked poverty in a sermon at Paul's Cross by charging the Lord Mayor and aldermen of the city with oppression of the poor:

I have lived here some few years, and every year I have heard an exceeding outcry of the poor that they are much oppressed of the rich of this city, in plain terms, of the Common Council. All or most charges are raised by your fifteenth, wherein the burden is more heavy upon a mechanical and handi-craft poor man than upon an alderman, proportion for proportion... You are magistrates for the good of them that are under you, not to oppress them for your own ease.[181]

In early Stuart Salisbury, the puritan magistrates recognized the unemployed and under-employed as a legitimate category of deserving poor, able-bodied but deprived of work by social and economic dislocation beyond their control. Their approach to poverty thoroughly accorded with that of the humanists, expanding and adapting the conventional categories of 'sturdy' and 'impotent' as the scale and nature of the poverty problem changed.[182] In 1649, the puritan Council of State launched a two-pronged attack on the problem of poverty, one aimed at employing the poor, the other at abating the price of corn.[183] Their action, reminiscent of the 1630/31 Book of Orders, illustrates that in both puritan and non-puritan eyes, if poverty resulted from evil, that evil did not necessarily characterize the poor themselves.

Puritans saw the poor as unfortunates to be served, vindicated and protected, rather than despised. Lucy Hutchinson included in her

---

[180] Perkins, *Works*, vol. 1, p. 774.
[181] Richard Stock, *A Sermon preached* . . . in *HMC Salisbury* (1910), vol. 12, p. 672.
[182] Slack, pp. 173–8, 180–1.
[183] *CSPD*, 22 November 1649, ed. M. A. E. Green (London, 1875), p. 402.

definition of a puritan the qualities of being 'grieved at the gripping of the poor' and devoted to their relief and protection, and however idealized her view, it may well be a more accurate portrait of the puritan than is the usual image of repressive, ungenerous individualism.[184] Puritan concern for discipline, prudence and discrimination must not be construed to imply a negative attitude toward either charity or its recipients. As Paul Slack has observed of the godly magistrates of Salisbury, puritans were 'reasonable' rather than 'harsh' in their attitudes toward the poor; if they are to be criticized, it must be for their 'liberality and forwardness in well doing.'[185] Their view of the impotent poor was that expressed by Thomas Gataker when he urged his auditors at Sergeants' Inn to be especially diligent in meting out justice to the poor and oppressed, since God 'hath a special interest in them. God created, redeemed, and protects the poor and rich alike. But special protection is given to the poor, the widow, the orphan. . . He will glorify the poor as well as the rich, and make them Kings and Judges.'[186]

But as always, there was no single-minded approach to social facts. Poverty was not regarded as intrinsically good. It hardly needs saying that protestants were as ruthlessly critical as Erasmus had been of that 'popish conceit,' voluntary poverty, and of the poverty which resulted from idleness. Christ may have lived by alms, Perkins said, but not by begging, 'as the Papists affirm, but by the voluntary ministration and contribution of some, to whom he preached.' When Whitgift charged Cartwright with living like a lazy mendicant friar, 'going up and down idly, doing no good, but living at other men's tables,' Cartwright responded similarly that his support was given him in exchange for his labor in teaching the children of his hosts, partly in the principles of religion, partly in other learning.[187] Neither Anglican nor puritan attached any sanctity to poverty *per se*

---

[184] Lucy Hutchinson, *Memoires of the Life of Colonel Hutchinson,* ed. Julius Hutchinson (1822), vol. 1, p. 122. It should be noted that she lists this quality before that of being 'zealous for god's glory or worship'; *cf.* Sears McGee on the supposed priority of First Table duties, in *The Godly Man in Stuart England 1620–1640* (New Haven, 1976), ch. 4. Further discussion of this issue occurs in chapter 6, below. *cf.* Hill, *Puritanism and Revolution*, ch. 7; Margaret James, *Social Problems and Policy during the Puritan Revolution* (1930), p. 301.

[185] Slack, pp. 185–6 *et passim*; Pearl, pp. 206–32; E. M. Hampson, *The Treatment of Poverty in Cambridgeshire, 1597–1834* (Cambridge, 1934), p. 44; W. K. Jordan, *Philanthropy in England, 1480–1660* (1959), *passim*; Beier, p. 99, notes 'occasional egalitarian undertones' in the language used toward the poor by puritan JPs in Warwickshire.

[186] Gataker, *Certaine Sermons* (1637), pp. 110–11, 112.

[187] Perkins, *Cases of Conscience*, pp. 195, 224; John Strype, *Life and Acts of John Whitgift* (Oxford, 1882), vol. 1, p. 130.

or to religious mendicity. Rather, like Erasmus, they held *mediocritas* as the ideal in regard to possessions. They recognized that poverty, like riches, carried its own set of snares to sin. Richard Rogers found his poverty sufficiently oppressive that his thoughts were drawn by it from the worship of God to idolatry of the money he lacked. 'I have been set on such untemperate thoughts about becoming rich,' he confessed, 'that for that time nothing heavenly might be looked after.'[188] Furthermore, while the rich are more susceptible to the sin of pride than are the poor, the latter are by no means immune to it:

for we see a world of poor and proud. A man as he goes along in the street, shall hear a company of poor that are the greatest rebels in the world against God, that blaspheme, and swear, that rail against magistrates and governours, they are the most unbroken people in the world: the poorest and beggarliest, the refuse of mankind; as they are in condition, so they are in disposition... [these are] the devil's poor, such as are poor every way, outwardly and inwardly, and have their poverty as a just punishment of their wicked lives, and continue in that wicked life, having it not sanctified to them to make them desire better riches. Doth God esteem such poor? No...[189]

Because of the obvious distinction between 'the devil's poor' and those to whom God has sanctified poverty, protestants saw the need to follow the Vivesian pattern of categorizing the poor. Like the Christian humanists, they saw themselves in the venerable tradition of Seneca and Cicero in their drive for discriminate almsgiving. Robert Allen even found it necessary to apologize for his extraordinarily heavy reliance on the Stoics and other ancients for advice on this subject, by pointing to the 'special light of nature' which they had obviously been given.[190] The puritan fear was that the alms, of which men were, after all, only stewards, would fall into unworthy hands.[191] They argued, as had the humanist *Forma Subventionis Pauperum* a century earlier, that such carelessness would not only offend God, it would also deprive the true poor of that which was rightfully theirs and encourage all manner of vice in the unworthy poor. It was, for instance, Anthony Parker's concern for those who

[188] Rogers, *Diary*, pp. 66, 86; *cf*. p. 94.   [189] Sibbes, pp. 98–9.
[190] Robert Allen, *A Treatise of Christian beneficence* (1600), p. 240 (mispaginated 342) *et passim*. The final section of the treatise (pp. 199–240) consists entirely of 'sentences chosen out of sundry writers, Christian and pagan,' but mostly pagan. *cf*. Bucer, p. 306, quoting Cicero's *De Officiis* (I, 14; II, 18) to argue that 'kindness... should be rendered according to the worthiness of each individual.'
[191] Greenham, *Workes*, p. 408; Milton, *Commonplace Book*, p. 417; Rogers, *Spirituall flowers*, sig. Avi.

'stand in need and are not able to work' that incensed him against those who 'give to the jesters and scoffers, the stageplayers and idle persons, though it had been better bestowed on them that lack meat and drink and other necessaries.'[192] Careless benevolence deprives the truly impotent of the limited resources which are their due. Perkins analyzed it in precisely the same terms as had the authors of the *Forma* and the 1531 humanist reform proposal, when he described it as a 'great disorder in commonwealths. For the boldest and most clamorous beggar carries away all the alms from the rest, and so relief is distributed both unwisely and unequally.'[193] To give alms without discretion was to support those 'better instructed at begging, indeed, extorting, the alms which should be dispensed to the poor alone.'[194] In the eyes of the reform-minded, misplaced benevolence was in effect evil-doing. Instead, as Bucer had told King Edward, deacons should be assigned to 'investigate how many really indigent persons live in each church for whom it is equitable for the church to provide the necessities of life.'[195]

Indiscriminate almsgiving was also evil in its maintenance of 'lusty beggars' and vagrants in their idleness, loose living and wickedness. Those who gave themselves over to beggary when they might work were 'men prone to every crime . . . harmful pests of society,' and it 'certainly is not the duty of the church to foster such people in their godless idleness.'[196] Robert Allen saw vagrants as 'a most dangerous and harmful sort of people,' prone to fornication, bastardy, drunkenness, infanticide, kidnapping and robbery, and certainly unworthy of alms.[197] The customs of begging and of private, personal almsgiving served to perpetuate the corruption of the idle poor: Perkins saw mendicity itself as 'the very seminary of vagabonds, rogues, and straggling persons, who have no calling . . .'[198] He was expressing an opinion not peculiar to puritanism, but one which had become a commonplace in sixteenth-century England. It is revealed, for instance, in the regulations for the relief of poverty which were instituted by the city of Norwich in 1570. The city

[192] Parker, *Collectanea Theologica* [1581], BL, Harl. MS 4048, p. 90.
[193] Perkins, *Cases of Conscience*, p. 226; Bucer, p. 306.   [194] Parker, p. 90.
[195] Bucer, pp. 257–258, 307; cf. Perkins, *Cases of Conscience*, p. 225.
[196] Bucer, pp. 258, 307. Bucer insisted that they should be excluded from communion, as well as from relief (pp. 307 and 334: 'Just as the churches, therefore, ought to exclude from their communion whoever lead idle lives, neither should a Christian state [*Respublica Christiana*] tolerate anyone who does not dedicate himself to some honest work or labor which is useful to the commonwealth').
[197] Allen, Epistle Dedicatory.
[198] Perkins, *Cases of Conscience*, p. 226, and *Works*, vol. 1, p. 755.

fathers there, in an action precisely parallel to that of their Catholic counterparts in Ypres and Lyon, officially condemned the 'foolish pity' which moves 'many to make provision at their doors' so that 'it hath made the greatest number [of poor] to leave their works to attend such alms as thereby they have achieved to such idleness and have found it (as they think) more profitable to them than to do any work at all.' Personal, direct almsgiving does not allow for proper investigation of the recipient and his need, and as long as this medieval practice is allowed to continue, the unworthy will be maintained in their wickedness. It was to lack of discretion on the part of benefactors that the Norwich legislators attributed 'the victualling houses ... stuffed with players and drunkards that so tended their drink all day that they could not incline to work.'[199] Accordingly, the city adopted a highly rationalized, discriminate system of relief which prohibited begging and personal almsgiving altogether. They appointed overseers of the poor, levied a poor rate on all householders, and distinguished among several categories of poor. Among the deserving poor were listed not only the physically disabled, but also untrained youth, the unemployed, and the underemployed who were willing to work if given the opportunity. The undeserving – loiterers, vagabonds and strong beggars – were not to be given doles, but were to be trained and set on work, or (if unwilling to labor) punished and expelled from the city.[200]

This legislation was a continuation of the earlier sixteenth-century trend among municipalities to implement Vives' discriminate poor relief scheme. Similar regulations dot the records of both local and central government for the next century.[201] Enforced discrimination between the truly impotent and able-bodied idlers was the intent of the 1597 Poor Law, which Perkins praised as 'an excellent statute and being in substance the very law of God, is never to be repealed.'[202] Allen agreed, calling it a 'gratulatory monument' which has served to 'shut the door against idleness and all unthrifty and wasteful misplacing of alms.' Writing in 1600, he was convinced that the law already 'hath so prosperously, and with so speedy success prevailed, that God hath, to the great comfort of all that love true judgment and mercy, showed evidently, that his good hand

---

[199] *TED*, vol. 2, pp. 317, 318; *cf.* Bucer against begging, p. 257.
[200] *TED*, vol. 2, pp. 313–19.
[201] Note, for example, acts passed in London in 1647 and 1649 to relieve the impotent poor and punish rogues and vagrants (F&R, vol. 1, pp. 1042–5; vol. 2, pp. 104–10). They were a response to the economic dislocations of the war years, but a response which was humanist in inspiration.   [202] Perkins, *Works*, vol. 1, p. 755.

went with the execution of it.'[203] The poor law was reaffirmed and strengthened in 1601. But it is worth noting that, while puritans praised both laws, they could not claim sole authorship of them, for the Parliaments which passed them were by no means exclusively puritan gatherings. The presbyterians of the Dedham classis, who had in the 1580s agreed that their town should not support idlers, had been suppressed,[204] but as Conciliar directives of the 1590s show, their principles of selective poor relief were held in common with non-puritan authorities. Puritans and Anglicans were both proponents of the discriminate, rationalized poor relief system which Catholic humanists had implemented decades earlier.

The lusty beggars against whom protestants discriminated in their giving were the objects of a concerted effort to inculcate discipline. The effort was, at least in intent, reformist rather than punitive, and as such is another protestant continuation of a Christian humanist innovation.

Work itself was, of course, considered a form of discipline and a means of self-improvement, so that by forcing the able to work, magistrates hoped to reform their attitudes, habits and lifestyle. Forced work was described by the puritan magistrates of Warwickshire as a positive, preventive measure; in Salisbury a Bridewell was established in 1602 'for the *correction* of the idle and the setting to work of the able poor'; and Bacon commended 'houses of relief *and correction* which are mixed hospitals, where the impotent person is relieved, and the sturdy beggar buckled to work, and the unable person also not maintained to be idle, which is not ever joined with drunkenness and impurity, but is sorted with such work as he can manage and perform ...'[205] Work was clearly perceived to be therapeutic, tending to the moral reform of the worker. As Edward Hext wrote to Burghley in 1596, if 'every prisoner committed for any cause and not able to relieve him self [were] compelled to work ... I dare presume to say the tenth felony will not be committed that now is.'[206] On this assumption, the Salisbury workhouse was enlarged in 1623 to include rooms where the 'lewder and baser sort' might be corrected, and where poor children could be lodged and

---

[203] Allen, Epistle Dedicatory.
[204] *Minute Book of the Dedham Presbyterian Classis, 1582–1589*, ed. R. G. Usher (1905), p. 100.
[205] Beier, p. 99; Slack, p. 180 (emphasis mine); Francis Bacon, *Letters and Life*, ed. James Spedding (1868), vol. 4, p. 252 (emphasis mine). The use of the term 'correction' is surely indicative of the initially reformist intent of these establishments.   [206] *TED*, Vol. II, p. 342.

taught a trade before being bound out as apprentices. The puritan magistrates of that city also sought outside employment for the 'respectable' poor of the town during the 1625 depression by asking clothiers, spinners and knitters to certify how many poor they could employ. The ever-present aim of their focus on work was to set and keep the poor on a proper course of life by forcing the idle to discipline themselves and providing the willing with regular employment. Such official attempts to locate jobs for the poor are reminiscent of Bucer's suggestion that the law should encourage gardening, spinning and mining to employ the idle, as they are of More's and Starkey's proposals. Bucer had explicitly advocated mining as a deterrent from and correction of idleness and its attendant crimes.[207]

The language of punishment is not absent from the work orders of the period, however. While the Elizabethan poor law of which the puritans approved so heartily required the poor to be set on work, it also allowed the flogging of those who refused to work. But the assumption in this and other legislation was that punishment was reserved for extreme cases of refusal to accept proffered employment. The 1571 Norwich Orders for the Poor provided for both the 'setting on work of loiterers' and 'the punishment of vagabonds,' and the 1576 and 1597 Poor Laws ordered those refusing to work to be incarcerated in a house of correction, 'there to be straightly kept, as well in diet as in work, and also punished from time to time,' or gaoled until the next Quarter Sessions, when they might be banished from the realm.[208] The pious hope was that this extreme measure would not be needed, but that the sturdy rogue would be 'corrected' through work and punishment. It is noteworthy that the 1597 Poor Law abolished the branding of vagrants – a clear indication of the shift away from medieval consignment of an individual to an unchangeable social status in favor of the Renaissance drive to reform the offender. The ferocity of pre-sixteenth-century vagrancy laws should be kept in mind when charges of capitalistic oppression

[207] Slack, p. 181; Bucer, pp. 339–40; *Utopia*, p. 69; Starkey, p. 173; *cf.* also the *Discourse of the Commonweal of this Realm of England*, pp. 92, 126ff. Note, too, Karlstadt's tract on the encouragement of vocational skills in the poor as a preventive poor relief policy: Carter Lindberg, ' "There Should Be No Beggars Among Christians": Karlstadt, Luther, and the Origins of Protestant Poor Relief,' *CH*, 46 (1977), 313–34, p. 323.

[208] *TED*, vol. 1, pp. 316, 333–4; *cf.* Perkins, *Cases of Conscience*, p. 226; F&R, vol. 1, p. 1044 and vol. 2, pp. 107–9, on the 1647 and 1649 London orders which decreed both punishment of rogues, vagrants and beggars, and provision of work for the willing poor. On the penal nature of the London Bridewell, see Pearl, p. 212.

of the poor are leveled at sixteenth- and seventeenth-century protestants.

Puritans seem to have been among the most ardent protestant supporters of work schemes for the poor. Valerie Pearl has remarked that, while plans to provide stocks of material for work were put forward in London from the Common Council's 1579 Orders for the Poor to the Proclamation of 1629, none were as ambitious as the schemes proposed in the 1640s.[209] Among these were the Corporation of the Poor, which had the power to apprehend vagrants and offer them a choice between work and whipping, and Samuel Hartlib's Office of Address, which was intended to be as much an employment agency as the center of technological information into which it actually developed. Both had counterparts on the continent, for both were implementations of those Christian humanist ideals which had made such an impact on sixteenth-century municipal poor relief.[210] In Salisbury, innovative employment schemes for the poor were the work of the puritan mayor John Ivie, and of zealous puritan councillors known also for their opposition to morris dances on the sabbath, church courts, episcopacy and stained glass. The city's Recorder, Henry Sherfield, fined in Star Chamber in 1633 for breaking the stained glass window at St Edmund's, might have been more severely dealt with had it not been reported that 'he hath done good in that city . . . so that there is neither beggar nor drunkard to be seen there.'[211]

Work was not the only method by which puritans wished to discipline the poor. Like the Catholic humanists, they also relied on the withholding of alms from the undisciplined, on diligent oversight and regulation of behavior by special officials, and most importantly on the redemptive value of education. The withholding of alms, like the threat of whipping, need not be interpreted as primarily punitive[212] – as we have seen, it was in part an attempt to protect the rights of the deserving poor and a guarantee of good stewardship for the benefactor. However it was also a strong incentive to good behavior; and it was one which characterized every early modern poor relief scheme, both public and private, from Vives' through the Interregnum. The Dedham classis provided in the 1580s, for instance, that two of their number, along with two or three aldermen and a

[209] Pearl, p. 210; cf. Jordan, Charities of London, pp. 177–9.
[210] Pearl, p. 211; Webster, pp. 67–75; cf. Solomon on Theophraste Renaudot's Bureau d'Addresse in Paris. The London Office of Address was headed by Henry Robinson from its foundation in 1647; it was abolished in 1659.
[211] Slack, p. 184.   [212] cf. Hill, Society and Puritanism, pp. 293ff.

constable, visit the poor monthly, 'and chiefly the suspected places, that understanding the miserable estate of those that went and the naughty disposition of disordered persons, they may provide for them accordingly,' withholding aid until the disorderly should reform.[213] And when the Essex puritan Henry Smith established a charity in 1626 for the relief of the able-bodied poor, he disqualified those 'guilty of excessive drinking, profane swearing, pilfering or other scandalous crimes,' along with vagrants and 'incorrigible servants', from received aid.[214] Presumably the truly destitute would conform to puritan discipline rather than forego assistance, so that such criteria for relief would tend to the moral improvement of individual and community.

Careful oversight by those officers labeled by Vives overseers of the poor aided in maintaining circumspect behavior by recipients of alms, as would the strict control of such temptations to undisciplined activity as alehouses and communal festivities.[215] The magistrates of Salisbury, intent on eliminating the disorderly behavior which created and perpetuated poverty, carefully controlled alehouses, required recipients of alms to attend church, regulated the diet of the poor, and provided a weekly examination of paupers by the churchwarden and overseers of the poor to verify that they had reformed their conduct.[216]

One of the duties of overseers in most relief schemes was to supervise the education and vocational training of the poor and their children.[217] Because puritans saw lack of proper education as a cause of poverty no less than Starkey and Morison had done, so they viewed the proper training of young people in moral behavior and practical skills as the most effective single means of correcting the problem. The influence of Christian humanism here is obvious. 'Ignorance' was defined by Arthur Hildersham, as by Erasmus, as 'darkness, which is breach of the law, or sin.'[218] To eliminate

---

[213] *Dedham Minutes*, p. 100.   [214] Wrightson and Levine, p. 179.
[215] Wrightson, *English Society, 1580–1680* (New Brunswick, New Jersey, 1982), pp. 206–21, and *Reformation of Manners*, pp. 35–42 (on dancing) and chs. 4–5 (on drunkenness). Note that the legislation being administered by puritan magistrates was not the work of predominantly puritan Parliaments (e.g., 4 Jac. I, c.5; 7 Jac. I, c.9 and 10; 21 Jac. I, c.7; I Car. I, c.4), although the zeal with which it was enforced by puritans is certainly noteworthy. *cf.* Dent, pp. 165–6.
[216] Slack, pp. 182, 185.
[217] For example, in the Norwich Orders, *TED*, vol. 2, p. 316, the authors declared their intent that youth 'be trained in work, in learning, and in the fear of God, so as no person should have need to go abegging'; *cf.* p. 324; on the apprenticing of poor children by the 1597 Poor Law, *TED*, vol. 2, p. 347.
[218] BL, Harl. MS 3230, fol. 102v; Allen, Epistle Dedicatory.

ignorance was to attack sin and eliminate its manifestations – idleness, drunkenness, frivolity, and the poverty they produced. Puritans were, therefore, in the forefront of the sixteenth-century drive to endow schools and scholarships as a means of reformation.[219] Elizabethan presbyterians allocated half of all communion offerings for 'the teaching of . . . poor men's children'; early Stuart puritans praised humanist educational foundations for the poor; and London in the 1640s was the scene of charitable educational experiments which would have delighted Erasmus.[220] Included among puritan suggestions for poor relief in London was William Petty's proposal of 'literary workhouses' for all children over seven years old, a clear connection between the exaltation of work and the hope for reformation through education which united humanist and puritan.[221]

The incorporation of education and vocational training into poor relief was one of several imaginative approaches to solving the problem of poverty. In seeking to address the causes of the problem, puritans frequently reflected the Christian humanists' willingness to

[219] Wrightson and Levine, p. 15; cf. p. 17 on the influence of Erasmus' works on puritan yeomen. Jordan, *Philanthropy in England*, p. 154, attributes this drive to broaden 'the ambit of opportunity . . . in the conviction that poverty bred and perpetuated itself in the slough of ignorance' to the protestant Reformation; however, the common impulse for both puritan and non-puritan educational reformers was Erasmian humanism. cf. Joan Simon, *Education and Society* (Cambridge, 1966), and Lindberg, pp. 320–1, on the influence of late medieval protest on Karlstadt. The Wittenberg Church Order (1522) prescribed subsidized education for the children of the poor (Lindberg, p. 322).

[220] *Dedham Minutes*, p. 100; Gataker, *Certaine sermons*, p. 10; Pearl, pp. 211–19. Pearl discusses the link between London's Corporation of the Poor and Hartlib's educational and vocational training schemes. She puts the penal nature of Bridewell into the context of these more positive attempts to eliminate poverty and sees the overall plan to train and employ the poor as a continuation of the policies of Henry VIII and Edward VI by puritans intent on godly service to the commonwealth. Puritan sponsors of the London ordinances included aldermen Thomas Andrews and George Witham, Lieutenant-Colonel Walter Lee, Hartlib, Dr Edward Odling and the radical Lord Mayor John Warner (Pearl, p. 217). cf. Webster, pp. 114, 207 (tracing the influence of Bucer on seventeenth-century educational reformers); and Quentin Skinner's interpretation of these plans as utopian (*TLS*, 2 July 1976).

[221] William Petty, *Advice . . . to Samuel Hartlib for Advancement of . . . Learning* (1648). Petty was aware of the social detriment caused by limiting educational opportunity to the well-born: not only did poverty and crime abound, but the commonwealth was deprived of leaders, since 'many are now holding the plough, which might have been made fit to steer the state.' By the same token, universal education was potentially disruptive of the hierarchical *status quo*; therefore its strongest supporters, both humanist and puritan, were those who least feared social change in their drive for reformation. See chapter 6, below, on the humanist/puritan challenge to the Great Chain of Being.

try non-traditional methods. No- or low-interest loans to impoverished artisans exemplify one such technique developed by Catholic humanists and used to good effect by their protestant progeny.[222] Another is the concept of outdoor relief (the administration of a dole to disabled or under-employed poor living in their own homes), which offered a more humane mode of existence to the poor at the same time as it prevented mendicity and reduced the cost of maintaining a large workhouse.[223] Support for these measures was not limited to puritans; however, puritans are especially visible in the more imaginative municipal plans to develop new employment opportunities for the poor and new methods of financing and administering relief. In London it was the puritan Sir Thomas Middleton who in 1623 tried to persuade parishes jointly to finance and build hemp and flax houses to provide local employment for the poor. This plan won the favor of non-puritans, too: Sir Francis Bacon, among others, pointed out the 'abatement of the tax' which would result from such an attempt to give the poor a means of self-support.[224] In Salisbury, puritans got the Corporation itself to invest in the brewing trade and use the profits to employ the poor; in 1628, they founded a municipal storehouse and developed a truly original token system whereby the poor could purchase food at cost and be spared the temptation to spend a money dole on drink.[225] The puritan magistrates of Warwickshire were both efficient and forward-looking in administering poor relief: they adjusted the size of the dole in accord with price fluctuations, appealed for 'general collections' on a county-wide basis to aid disaster-stricken families or towns, and reformed taxation by ordering more equitable direct assessments and extending the tax base in order to pay for poor relief.[226] And the Norfolk assize of 1620 encouraged the growing of

---

[222] *TED*, vol. 2, p. 297; *cf.* Bucer, p. 315, and William Hunt, *The Puritan Moment* (Cambridge, Mass., 1983).

[223] Perkins, *Cases of Conscience*, p. 226, supported this concept, as did Sandys in the 1572 Commons debate. Sandys noted both the humanity of the system and its practicability as evidenced by the success which had attended the adoption of such measures in Worcester (D'Ewes, *The Journals of all the Parliaments during the Reign of Queen Elizabeth* (1682), Part I, p. 165 (13 April 1572); *TED*, vol. 2, p. 333 (18 El., c.3, 1576). Indoor relief was a feature of English poor relief until prohibited by the notorious 1834 Poor Law.

[224] Pearl, pp. 214–15. Middleton, president of Bridewell, was unfortunately not persuasive enough to get his plan implemented; however, both national and local relief measures frequently included orders to provide at public expense a stock of raw material upon which the poor could work: e.g., D'Ewes, *Journals*, Part I, p. 254; *TED*, vol. 2, pp. 332, 347. For Bacon's argument, see *Letters and Life*, p. 252.

[225] Slack, pp. 182–3.   [226] Beier, pp. 82, 96–7.

root crops by the poor by paying them twopence a day for their gardening work.[227]

Developments like these were possible in the seventeenth century
because puritans had absorbed from the sixteenth-century Christian
humanists the principle that employment of the poor would do
more than either doles or punishment to correct the problem of
poverty. Like Vives, they saw more potential reformation in a poor
man laboring in his own garden than in a beggar whipped and
expelled from the city, and like the magistrates of Ypres and Lyon,
they were willing to try new methods of providing work in order to
achieve that reformation. The real innovators were the Catholic
humanists who established the patterns elaborated upon by
seventeenth-century protestants.

Puritan schemes were made possible, too, by the fact that both
puritans and non-puritans agreed with the Renaissance laicization of
charity. Secular administration was part of the rationalized, insti-
tutionalized, less personal approach to social problems which had
been advocated by the Christian humanists out of concern for the
welfare of the poor. Lay overseers and constables were more strictly
accountable for administering relief than medieval clergy had been –
an advantage recognized by the magistrates of Norwich, Salisbury
and London, and by Elizabethan JPs, as it had been by Vives and the
author of the Ypres scheme.[228] A secularized administration also
possessed the requisite authority to enforce a rate, obviously an
advantage for regular and consistent relief in times of economic fluc-
tuation.[229] Oversight by JPs provided a means by which geographic
variations in wealth could be equalized, too: the 1597 Poor Law decreed that JPs were to rate wealthy parishes more heavily to pay for
relief in impoverished ones.[230] Puritans were in sufficient agreement
with their contemporaries on the merits of secular relief for
Elizabethan presbyterians to rule against calling for reform of poor
relief as members of a classis; such action could only be appro-

---

[227] Norfolk and Norwich Record Office, Walsingham MS XVII/2, De Grey Letter
Book, no. 5, Norfolk Assize Orders of Montague and Doderidge, n.f. I am grateful
to Derek Hirst for this reference.
[228] F&R, vol. 1, p. 1045, vol. 2, p. 109; *TED*, vol. 2, pp. 322, 346–9, 354; Beier, p. 97;
Slack, p. 180.
[229] The rate, for which Bucer had given an apology (*Marburg Disputation*, p. 156), was
established on a national level by the 1572, 1576 and 1597 Acts (*TED*, vol. 2, pp.
330–2, 347), although the county rates were in actuality only rarely used.
[230] *TED*, vol. 2, p. 348; *cf.* the similar arrangement for the three parishes of Salisbury
in 1599 (Slack, p. 180).

priately taken as 'private men,' since the oversight of charity was the responsibility of the magistrate, rather than of the church.[231]

Puritans, then, carried on both in theory and in practice the Christian humanist tradition of discriminate, disciplined, rationalized and secularized poor relief. They were, moreover, part of an early modern English consensus on the proper nature of charity – a consensus of Catholic and protestant, of Anglican and puritan. Protestants acknowledged, albeit with chagrin, that

> the right care of the poor has already been restored [to the presumed ideal of the primitive Christian church] in very many regions which still serve Antichrist, whereas the very ones who glory in the reception of the gospel of the Kingdom of Christ, although they are not unaware how necessary this practice [of discriminate relief] is, and how much it is a part of the salutary religion of Christ, still fail to re-establish it.[232]

Puritans supported and praised the legislation which was finally passed by not necessarily puritan Parliaments to correct this situation. They agreed with Anglicans like Henry Hammond that the poor should not be despised, with George Herbert that social ills are due to lack of education and idleness, and with Robert Sanderson that the idle should be set on work. Their agreement is to be expected, since the authority cited by Sanderson – Erasmus – was no less an authority for puritans.[233] Anglicans and puritans were in substantial agreement on the theory of poor relief because they relied on a common tradition, that of Erasmian humanism. Both were motivated by a Renaissance sense of civic responsibility as well as by private piety.

---

[231] *Dedham Minutes*, p. 32 (1583); Bucer (pp. 182, 310) agreed; *cf.* R. W. Henderson, 'Sixteenth Century Community Benevolence: An Attempt to Resacralize the Secular,' *CH*, 38 (1969), pp. 421–8, arguing that the late medieval trend toward laicization of poor relief was reversed in Calvin's Geneva by the Ecclesiastical Ordinances of 1541, establishing diaconal oversight of charity. Aside from the absence of a parallel definition of the office of deacon in England, the distinctions between sacred and secular spheres were somewhat blurred in both Christian humanist and protestant social thought; it is not clear that there was any significant difference between the *procureurs* and *hôpitaliers* of fifteenth-century Geneva and the deacons of the Reformed city. [232] Bucer, p. 258.
[233] Henry Hammond, *Sermons* (1695), p. 121. Hammond also condemned the pride of the rich (p. 258, citing Aristotle) and urged generous almsgiving (pp. 140, 251). *The Poems of George Herbert,* ed. F. E. Hutchinson (Oxford, 1961), pp. 7, 14; *cf.* p. 26 on thriftiness and p. 28 on wealth as 'the conjurer's devil'; Robert Sanderson, *XXXIV Sermons* (1661), pp. 107 (citing Cicero and Seneca, among others), 246, 249 (quoting Erasmus' opinions of idle rogues), 251. Note also the essentially Christian humanist positions of Thomas Fuller, *Works,* ed. M. G. Walter (New York, 1938), vol. 2, p. 154, and Lancelot Andrewes, *Works* (Oxford, 1854), vol. 5, p. 43, on this issue. On puritan and Anglican agreement, see Breen, *passim*; Jordan, *Philanthropy in England*, p. 155.

Both were animated by the desire which John Ivie expressed 'to advance God's glory and to settle a livelihood for the comfortable living of poor souls.'[234]

The attitudes of both protestants and humanists to poor relief, like their theories of work, wealth and poverty, occupy an intermediate position between the medieval and the modern. Theirs was a partial sanctification of the market-place– encouraging discipline, productivity and thrift, but suspicious of profit-making and accumulation. Poverty was no longer praiseworthy, but neither was financial success. Both prudence and generosity were enjoined, and social responsibility rather than personal gain was to determine the direction of economic activity. Progressive methods were to be employed in reforming the social order, but that reformation was aimed at the greater glory of God and the establishment of Christ's Kingdom on earth. The economic theory held by early modern Englishmen was, in short, a transitional one; but what is apparent in all its aspects is that its transitional nature was not determined by the protestant Reformation. Its direction had been set before the Reformation, by Christian humanists intent on applying ancient wisdom to contemporary problems.

Undeniably, the theories which emerged were responses to actual socio-economic circumstances: a basic tenet of Christian humanism was the need to devise practicable solutions for mundane problems. It was the combination of demographic and urban expansion, commercial changes, rising prices, periodic dearth and unemployment which stimulated the development of new social and economic attitudes in the sixteenth century. It was this combination which gave rise to the vagrancy problem and to the polarization of wealth and poverty with which contemporary theorists were confronted. Social change conditions social ideology, and if Catholics and protestants in early modern England shared a social outlook, it was at least in part because they were responding to common circumstances. They were not so much theologically casuistic as simply troubled. Both legislated against idleness because both were faced with the problem of vagrancy and mendicity; both criticized drunkenness because both witnessed its increase during periods of dearth and understood it as a secondary cause of poverty.[235]

---

[234] Quoted by Slack, p. 184.
[235] John Walter and Keith Wrightson, 'Dearth and the Social Order in Early Modern England,' *P&P*, 71 (1976), pp. 22–42; Wrightson, 'Reformation of Manners,' pp. 179–90 (on the interaction of dearth and piety in spurring puritan enforcement activities); Charles Phythian-Adams, *Desolation of a City: Coventry and the Urban Crisis*

The nature of their response, however, was conditioned no less by ideas than by circumstances, and as the century progressed, ideas gradually came to the forefront as the determinants of action. While puritans and their opponents agreed on the need to enforce social discipline, by the seventeenth century it was becoming clear that puritans were in fact more diligent in doing so. Wrightson has found, for instance, that while dearth stimulated magisterial repression of alehouses, this phenomenon was much more pronounced in puritan Essex than in Lancashire.[236] Puritan reformers in Salisbury were eventually opposed by the dean and chapter of the cathedral in their attempts to implement innovative and non-punitive solutions to the problem of unemployment.[237] It will be shown that by the 1630s, many Anglicans were beginning to opt for a more 'hard-hearted' policy toward the idle, for the doctrine of poverty as a punishment for wickedness, and for a penal approach to poor relief, and that they were herein following a pattern which had been set by European Catholics at the end of the sixteenth century.[238] Catholics in the six-teenth century and Laudian Anglicans in the seventeenth were obviously addressing the same problems as their ecclesiological opponents were. The differences which had developed in their social and economic theory must be traced, then, to an ideological shift – a shift away from the Christian humanist consensus, in favor of a more conservative, conformist approach to social problems. Tridentine Catholics and Laudian Anglicans espoused a new ideology of authority and control which gave rise to new interpretations of social order. Before the changes which occurred in their attitudes toward poverty and wealth and toward marriage and the religious functions of the household can be analyzed, then, it is necessary to investigate that fundamental aspect of social theory on which protestants and Catholics, puritans and Anglicans, first diverged – the nature of social hierarchy and the locus of authority in the Chris-tian commonwealth.

---

of the Late Middle Ages (Cambridge, 1979), ch. 20, has also noted the correlation of drunkenness laws with periods of unemployment and compensatory drinking.

[236] Wrightson, *Reformation of Manners*, pp. 188–90.

[237] Slack, pp. 186–8.

[238] Slack, p. 185; Hill, *Society and Puritanism*, p. 267; Breen, p. 281; Beier, pp. 83–4, 99, Table 3; chapter 7, below.

6

◁ ══════════════════════════════════ ▷

Conscience and the Great Chain of Being

Inferior authority cannot bind the superior: now the
courts of men and their authority are under
conscience. For God in the heart of every man hath
erected a tribunal seat, and in his stead he hath placed
neither saint nor angel, nor any other creature whatsoever, but conscience itself, who therefore is the
highest judge that is or can be under God.

William Perkins, 1596[1]

Thou must not rest upon the testimony and suggestions of thine own conscience ... Why should you
think yourselves born, or grown so good divines, that
you need no counsel; in doubtful cases, from other
men? ... For our Judge, which is the conscience, let
that be directed before hand, by their advice whom
God hath set over us.

John Donne, 1622[2]

The conflict between Anglicans and puritans over so basic a
Reformation assumption as the authority of conscience represents
more than a theological disagreement. When Donne cast
conscience down from the lofty height where it had been enthroned
in the previous century and substituted for it the authority of the
hierarchy, he was articulating not so much an ecclesiological position as an approach to the problem of social order – one which

[1] *A Discourse of Conscience*, ed. T. F. Merrill, in *William Perkins: His Pioneer Works on Casuistry* (The Hague, 1966), p. 32.
[2] *Sermons*, ed. G. R. Potter and E. M. Simpson (Berkeley, 1957), vol. 4, pp. 221, 223.

seems to have had very little to do with his theology. It was in fact a Catholic approach, and Donne adopted it not because of any identification with the doctrine of his popish foes, but because it happened that Catholics had recognized before protestants the anti-authoritarian possibilities inherent in the exaltation of conscience. It was the similar concern of the Anglican and Catholic hierarchies with social order which prompted them to re-emphasize the primacy of constituted authorities.

However, in affirming the sovereignty of conscience over the guidance of social and ecclesiastical superiors, Perkins was no less concerned with the maintenance of social harmony than was Donne. His statements concerning conscience occur within the context of the first significant English protestant work of casuistry, a treatise whose purpose was to exhort Englishmen so to regulate their behavior that a godly, well-ordered commonwealth would be produced. If Catholics, Anglicans and puritans found themselves agreed on anything, it was on the need for social regulation and on the responsibility of preachers to provide an ideological guarantee for order in the commonwealth. Political rebellion, democratic ideas, and social levelling were anathema to all; they were equally concerned with questions of authority and obedience. The differences among them which emerged by the end of the sixteenth century on the issue of social order arose not so much from their aims, then, as from their means, for there was more than one approach to the problem of social order available to Elizabethan and Stuart theoreticians.

The issue expressed by Perkins and Donne in terms of the role of conscience may be broadly conceived as a conflict between two methodologies of social control – the one humanist-inspired and progressive, the other medieval, static and ultimately repressive. The question for the preachers, convinced (as were most of their contemporaries) of the danger of imminent social breakdown, was whether to insure the maintenance of order and stability in the realm by demanding a reformation of behavior dictated at the level of the individual conscience, as Perkins (following the humanist model) did, or by asserting that the road to salvation lay in unquestioning obedience to constituted authority, the solution for which Donne opted.

Neither Perkins' approach nor Donne's was distinctively protestant. Part of the reason that the controversy over authority in seventeenth-century England presents such a complex problem for historians is the fact that the length of its pedigree has never been clearly recognized. The intellectual roots of the conflict must be sought before the Reformation, in late medieval anticlericalism and particularly in the social criticism of the Christian humanists, where an alternative to the hierarchical conservatism of medieval society first appeared in a reformist ethic. The protestant emphasis on conscience was actually one aspect of Erasmian social ideology, a 'grass roots' approach to the problem of order in the common-wealth. Reasoning along classical lines that the common weal was to be achieved not by authoritarian means, but by inculcating virtuous behavior in the individual citizen, the Christian humanists had demanded a continuous, dynamic confrontation of the informed individual conscience with moral issues in a civic environment. The commonwealth was to be reformed from below by an emphasis on behavior, rather than repressed from above by an insistence on obedience to prescribed outward forms. The humanist goal was a godly society, not just without disorder, but even without tension– a state in which order was guaranteed by the government of rightly-informed individual conscience.

The humanist vision was readily taken over by protestant re-formers, who had necessarily abandoned the rule of metaphysical hierarchies in favor of direct individual access to God. The social concomitant of their theological position was precisely the com-monwealth ideal of the Christian humanists. The civic responsibility of the humanist citizen corresponded to the religious accountability of the protestant saint; just as the well-ordered commonwealth was to be achieved by individual reform, so the peace and harmony of the elect nation was to be insured by a reformation of manners. Nor was this an assumption disputed by most Anglicans, at least until the 1620s. The common humanist heritage of English protestants guaranteed a relatively high degree of cooperation in urging moral reformation.

This is not to say that protestants and Catholic humanists were not in substantial disagreement on theological questions, even as they pertained to moral reform. The Erasmians defined the good man as one who led an exemplary life in light of the *vita Christi* and the moral advice of the ancients; protestants defined the good man as one redeemed by Christ. In humanist eyes education could achieve a great deal nearly unaided; protestant theology required spiritual intervention for education to make a genuinely effective contri-bution to the sanctifying process. Ultimately, of course, the quarrel over free will divided humanist from protestant. But despite the dif-ferences, both acknowledged the power of sin and the need to overcome its effects individually and socially. And despite the protestant focus on redemptive history in the Scriptures, their stress on Christ as moral exemplar and on the usefulness of classical ethics was no less than Erasmus'. While the protestant saint did not win salvation by good works, those works were none the less required as a response to election. Whatever their theological differences, protestants were able to use humanist moral guides and social advice to good effect. And because their Reformed theology rejected mediation between man and God by priests and saints, the Christian humanist emphasis on individual responsibility to the guidance of rightly informed conscience was all the more palatable.

It was a common, humanist approach to social order, then, which established the consensus of Catholics and protestants for most of the sixteenth century on the nature and aims of family life, education, economic conduct and poor relief. Only as the century progressed did it gradually become apparent, first to Catholics, then to Anglicans, that the humanist and Reformed approach was fraught with danger for upholders of hereditary status and social stasis. It was the reformation of individual behavior through godly self-discipline which humanists regarded as the means to social order, and underpinning this assumption was an explicit critique of the opposing approach to social harmony, the Great Chain of Being.

The concept of the cosmos as a hierarchy of essence and degree derived originally from Neo-platonic theory, and it seems never to have been absent from medieval thought. It combines the Platonic principle of plenitude, the notion that no genuine potentiality of being in the multi-leveled universe can remain unfilled, with its logical (although not strictly Platonic) implication, an absolute cosmological determinism. A vaguely Aristotelian notion of ontological scale is also incorporated.[3] What is posited, then, is a harmonious, hierarchical order of things which is by its very nature unalterable. The Chain of Being divides aetherial from aerial beings, and aerial from terrestrial, placing each in its proper sphere. In parallel fashion, it separates reason from appetite, soul from body, king from commons, and fills the space in between with a hierarchical arrangement of intermediaries. What is important is that

[3] Macrobius, St Augustine and the Pseudo-Dionysius are the most important fifth-century Neoplatonic shapers of medieval cosmology; they used elements drawn from both Plato and Aristotle, with varying degrees of fidelity to the original contexts of their ideas. Arthur O. Lovejoy's *The Great Chain of Being* (Cambridge, Mass., 1936) is the classic study of the genesis of this idea; see pp. 52–66 for a summary of its sources.

not only the arrangement itself, but the precise position of each
element within it is part of the nature of the cosmos; that is, it is
determined not by any action or behavioral merit of the element,
but by the natural essence with which it had been endowed. What
this means at the level of human society is that the essential inequality of persons is ensconced in a theoretically rigid hierarchy of
birth in which movement of an individual out of his allotted social
space is necessarily regarded as his attempt to flout the authority of
the Forger of the Great Chain – a challenge to the natural order of
the universe.[4] Virtue is regarded as inbred, not inculcated; hence
hereditary aristocracy is a precise reflection of the cosmic order
within the sphere of human relations. Similarly, vice in a member of
the lower social orders is treated as an essential characteristic, rather
than as a behavioral lapse; thus reform is not to be considered an
alternative to or an end of punishment.

Against these presuppositions of their late medieval environment,
the Christian humanists stand out as staunch opponents of the most
basic elements of the social order. In the contrast between their
reformist ethic and the more complacent social theory of the Middle
Ages can be seen the unintended revolutionary implications of the
humanist approach, those aspects of Erasmian theory which were
ultimately to be perceived as a threat to social order, rather than a
guarantee of it, first by Catholics, then by those conservative seg-
ments of English protestantism which would be distinguished as
'Anglican.'

These supporters of hierarchical authority in church and state
were not deceived in their apprehension of the humanist challenge
to the established order. Humanists, while not actually the levelers
that some apparently feared them to be, none the less posed a threat
to the bases upon which the sixteenth-century social hierarchy – lay
as well as clerical – was established. They were, after all, part of that
late medieval anticlericalism which not only exposed the ignorance
and immorality of the clergy, but also labeled 'superstitious' the
whole medieval apparatus by which God's favor was mediated to
humanity by a multi-leveled celestial hierarchy of saints and angels.[5]

[4] In the words of a later adherent of the theory of the Great Chain of Being, 'Take
but degree away, untune that string/ And hark! What discord follows!' (Shakespeare, *Troilus and Cressida*, I.iii).
[5] For example, *Coll.*, p. 38; *Praise of Folly*, tr. Betty Radice (New York, 1971), pp.
128–30, 139; *cf.* pp. 177–83; *Liber de Sarcienda Ecclesiae Concordia*, in *The Essential
Erasmus*, tr. John P. Dolan (New York, 1964), pp. 369, 380. In the *Institutio principis
Christiani*, tr. L. K. Born (New York, 1936), p. 196, Erasmus argued against a
mediating position for the stars.

Proposing instead the possibility of direct access to God through Scripture, they reduced the semi-magical role of the cleric to the level of spiritual guide. Ridiculing the cults of saints and relics, pilgrimages and indulgences, they posed a serious threat to the authority of the ecclesiastical hierarchy. Demanding an end to the double standard of behavior for laity and clergy, and declaring the market-place rather than the cloister the proper place to live out the precepts of Scripture, they denied the inherent superiority of the clerical estate and so shattered an important hierarchical assumption. But it was their emphasis on behavior and their demand for change which brought them into conflict with the foundations not only of clerical, but also of lay hierarchy.

The argument that change within the social order is possible and even good is perhaps one of the most significant innovations of Christian humanist social theory. Change has been called the 'perennial bugbear of the Great Chain'; it ultimately spelled the defeat of a model in which the social order, like the cosmological, is a *given*, a matter of being.[6] The humanist understanding of change springs both from the theory of behavior rather than birth as the determinant of degree, and from humanists' observations of the changes which were taking place within their own world. Such circumstances as the augmenting numbers and influence of the mercantile elements of society, rising popular disillusionment with old authorities (especially religious authorities), the apparent rise in the numbers of poor and vagabonds – all were duly noted by humanists and set forth as evidence that the cosmos is not, in fact, a static entity. In Richard Taverner's 1539 translation of the *Adages*, this sense of flux is expressed clearly: 'There is an alteration of all things . . . in men's things nothing is perpetual, nothing stable, but all pass and repass even like to the ebbing and flowing of the ocean sea.'[7] New problems arise; new solutions are required. And it was the humanists' sincere hope that with the spread of the New Learning, humankind would be enabled to construct a new, rational, humane social order in the changing world.

[6] Lovejoy, pp. 329–31. Hence Langland's conviction that evil will result from any change in the social order (*Piers Plowman*, C. vi, 65–81). *cf.* Arthur Ferguson, *The Articulate Citizen and the English Renaissance* (Durham, NC, 1965), pp. 42–69, on Langland and Gower.

[7] *Proverbes or adagies with newe addicions gathered out of the Chiliades*, fol. xxiv; *cf. Formulae, Coll.*, pp. 581–2. Ferguson has argued that it is this 'new historical consciousness, marked in varying degrees by a new sensitivity to the implications of social change' which distinguished humanist thought in sixteenth-century England: *Clio Unbound: Perceptions of the Social and Cultural past in Renaissance England* (Durham, NC, 1979), pp. x, 179.

For Erasmus, war, ignorance, crime and poverty are among the social evils which result not merely from individual moral failure, but from a static rather than a progressive view of human society.[8] In his reckoning, these evils both can and must be changed. Change may be in and of itself good; stagnation always spells defeat. The enemy on whom he declared his own war, therefore, was custom, the ultimate barrier to social change, the guardian of all that is archaic. It is custom, he said, which allows the proliferation of holy days which results in idleness and its attendant evils, gluttony, drunkenness and lechery: 'and why should it be an offence against religion to change the custom, for the very same reason for which our ancestors established it?'[9] It is custom, moreover, which prevents bad laws from being amended.[10] Custom, the real ruler of early modern society, is 'the fiercest tyrant of them all,'[11] a tyrant who must be overthrown for a truly rational and godly society to be constructed.

In the Christian humanist scheme, then, a godly social order, far from eschewing change, requires it. At the individual level, one is born no more to poverty and ignorance than to virtuous leadership. The individual is expected to rise above the circumstances of low birth and not to take for granted the advantages of high birth; he is to exercise self-discipline, to pursue wisdom, to know the Scriptures, and to behave uprightly. At the social level, high regard is to be re-served not for the well-born, but for the virtuous. It was this doc-trine, combined with the positive conception of change, which developed in Christian humanist literature into a frontal assault on the medieval theory of a natural hierarchy of being.

Erasmus may again be taken as a representative figure. The notion of an aristocracy of birth was repugnant to him, and he bestowed some of his most caustic social commentary on what he regarded as

---

[8] Robert P. Adams, 'Designs by More and Erasmus for a New Social Order,' *Studies in Philology*, 62 (1945), 131–46. On Erasmus' pacifism, see the adages *Dulce bellum in-expertis, Spartam nactus es, hanc orna,* and *Sileni Alcibiadis,* in *The 'Adages' of Erasmus,* tr. Margaret Mann Phillips (Cambridge, 1964), pp. 269–353; the colloquy *Charon,* (*Coll.,* pp. 388–94); and the *Querela pacis* (1517). A facsimile of the 1559 English translation of the latter, *The Complaint of Peace,* by Thomas Paynell, is available with an introduction by William James Hirten (New York, 1946).

[9] *Ignavis semper feriae sunt, Adages* (1964), p. 268; *cf. Liber de Sarcienda Ecclesiae Concordia,* Dolan, p. 385. (It was precisely this line of reasoning which puritans would follow when, during the Interregnum, they abolished holy days, including Christmas.)

[10] *Institutio,* p. 229. Thomas Starkey similarly argued against the acceptance of tra-dition *per se;* his emphasis on the 'process of time' is discussed by Ferguson, *Clio Unbound,* pp. 174–8.

[11] *Convivium profanum, Coll.,* p. 600; *cf. Franciscani, Coll.,* p. 214: 'There is nothing too ridiculous for custom to sanction'; *Abbatis et eruditae, Coll.,* p. 221: 'Why tell me of custom, the mistress of every vice?' *Puerpera* and *Synodus grammaticorum (Coll.,* pp. 270, 272, 398) express very similar sentiments.

one of the most unfortunate outcomes of it – hereditary monarchy. Just as he denied the necessity for intermediaries between man and God, so he rejected the links of the Great Chain of Being which correspond to the celestial hierarchy in human society. And his rejection incorporated a very basic critique of the medieval/ Neo-platonic model of the cosmos: it insisted that degree is not properly a matter of being, or natural essence. Degree in society should correspond rather to virtue, and virtue, in Erasmus' experience, seemed all too often to bear an inverse relationship to exalted birth. In early modern Europe as Erasmus perceived it, the aristocracy was seldom composed of the *aristos*.

This thesis is perhaps most forcefully argued in Erasmus' lengthy commentary on the adage *Scarabeus aquilam quaerit*, which first appeared in the 1515 edition of the *Adages*.[12] Here the natural hierarchy of the animal kingdom, presided over by the eagle and the lion, is presented as the precise counterpart to the domination of the human social and political order by king and nobles. Erasmus' conclusions are devastating to the honor and prestige accorded to royalty and nobility as such. According to the traditional conception, the inherent nobility of the eagle won it its royal title, and the status of the beetle (popularly thought to dwell and feed on dung) was likewise determined by its natural position in the Chain of Being, its inherent lowliness. But Erasmus saw the irony of this order:

The eagle alone has seemed suitable in the eyes of the wise men to represent the symbol of a king – the eagle, neither beautiful, nor songful, nor good to eat, but carnivorous, greedy, predatory, ravaging, warring, solitary, hated of all, a universal pest, the creature who can do the most harm and would like to do even more than it can. It is exactly on the same grounds that the lion is appointed king of the animals – when there is no other great beast which is fiercer or more noisome... Obviously it must be a royal creature, just like the eagle.[13]

Other animals, even the lowliest, are by contrast positive contributors to the common weal: dogs watch over men's possessions, oxen till the soil, mules carry heavy loads. And it is the occupant of the humblest position of all in the animal realm, the beetle, which receives the highest praise from Erasmus for its diligence, reliability, and ingenuity: 'What valour of spirit the beetle has! What mental power, worthy of heroes!'[14]

A more complete inversion of the traditional hierarchy can hardly

[12] *Adages* (1964), pp. 244–63.   [13] *Ibid.*, p. 245.   [14] *Ibid.*, p. 249.

be imagined. If kings are universal pests, and the least of commoners heroes, what must Erasmus' readers have concluded about their own social order? Obviously, the Erasmian approach is antipathetical to the enforcement of social order on the basis of the inherent authority of the well-born. Elsewhere, Erasmus was even more blatant in his castigation of those born to prominence. In the *Institutio principis Christiani*, Erasmus compared the hereditary succession of his own time with barbarian practices of old and argued that 'kings who have the inclination of brigands and pirates should be put in the same class with them. For it is the character, not the title, that marks the king.'[15] It is absurd to place the slightest value on birth in determining who should rule, given the evidence of history and observation that even if kings in the present system are not found to be downright evil, they create mischief in their realms by their lack of understanding: 'You merely have to turn over the chronicles of the ancients and the moderns, and you will find that in several centuries there have been barely one or two princes who did not by sheer stupidity bring disaster to human affairs.' Folly obviously maintains her empire even over emperors.[16]

It is hardly surprising to find Erasmus' socially conservative contemporaries describing his 'wanton pen.' 'Whatsoever might be spoken to defame princes' government is not left unspoken,'

---

[15] *Institutio*, p. 169; *cf*. p. 248. In the adage *Civitas non civitas* Erasmus' republican sentiments emerge; acknowledging, however, that monarchy was an unavoidable evil in his own day, he argued for elective rather than hereditary kings. See *Ut fici oculis incumbunt, Adages*, p. 359. Contrast, as an example of the medieval view, the opinion of Aegidius Romanus, a pupil of St Thomas, that hereditary monarchy is the best form of government, in *On the Governance of Princes* (1287) (noted by L. K. Born, *Institutio*, p. 118). Erasmus was willing to compromise his ideals by writing tactful advice to monarchs of both types in hopes that a bad system could thereby be ameliorated. In a letter of 1504 to Jean Desmarez, he gave an apology for his 1503 *Panegyricus* for Prince Philip: such a composition

> consists in presenting princes with a pattern of goodness, in such a way as to reform bad rulers, improve the good, educate the boorish, reprove the erring, arouse the indolent, and cause even the hopelessly vicious to feel some inward stirrings of shame . . . How much better to improve matters by compliments rather than abuse. And what method of exhortation is more effective . . . than to credit people with possessing already in large measure the attractive qualities they urge them to cultivate? *CWE* 2, no. 180, p. 81.

cf. More's reluctance to follow suit in *Utopia*, pp. 87, 103. Quentin Skinner offers a useful discussion of 'mirror-for-princes' writers in *Foundations of Modern Political Thought* (Cambridge, 1978), vol. 1, pp. 213ff. On Erasmus' political thought, see James D. Tracey, *The Politics of Erasmus* (Toronto, 1978), esp. pp. 23–48.

[16] *Aut fatuum aut regem nancisci oportere* (1515), *Adages*, p. 216. Note that the beetle in *Scarabeus aquilam quaerit* is credited with 'no common brains' (p. 249). *Folly*, pp. 113, 117, 173–5; *cf. Meliores naucisci aves, Adages*, p. 23, in which Erasmus argued that kings are as susceptible as 'the vulgar' to superstition. Erasmus, always desperate for patronage, none the less refused an offer from Francis I to join the court at Paris: Johan Huizinga, *Erasmus and the Age of Reformation* (New York, 1957), p. 94.

charged Stephen Gardiner. But Bishop Gardiner also correctly located the basis of Erasmus' radical social theory in his insistence that 'every man must come to the high prick of virtue, or . . . be extremely nought.'[17] In his insistence on individual virtue and the rule of conscience as the foundations of order in the commonwealth, Erasmus implicitly destroyed the basis for the medieval methodology of control, the inherent authority of the well-born.

Nor did Erasmus restrict his criticism to the summit of the nobility, the king. Having noted in another adage the obscure social origins of Jesus and the Apostles, 'lowest of the low, the objects of everyone's scorn,' he contrasted those who receive honor as noblyborn:

> You would find in no one less real nobility than in those Thrasos with their long pedigrees and collars of gold and grand titles, who brag of their noble blood; and no one is further from true courage than those who pass for valiant and invincible just because they are rash and quarrelsome. There is no one more abject and enslaved than those who think themselves next to the gods, as they say, and masters of all.

'Noble birth,' he concluded, 'is simply laughable, an empty name.'[18] If society were scaled according to true virtue, the present nobility would surely occupy the lowest position, since they are in practice the deliberate destroyers of the common good. In his commentary on *Ut fici oculis incumbunt*, he portrayed the great lords and grandees as 'insatiable in their greed, most corrupt in their appetites, most malignant in their cruelty, inhuman in their despotism – real enemies of the public weal, and highway robbers . . . who fatten on public misfortune.'[19] The Chain of Being is thus regarded as inimical to the common weal, rather than the guarantee of it.

Nobles were seen as no less despicable in their personal conduct. In the colloquy *De rebus ac vocabulis*, Erasmus defined a knight as one who has possessed himself by inheritance or by purchase of a title, and who 'never does a good deed . . . dresses like a dandy, wears rings on his fingers, whores bravely, dices constantly, plays cards, spends his life in drinking and having a good time . . .'[20] How absurd it is to bestow honor and power on such an unworthy class; none the less,

---

[17] *The Letters of Stephen Gardiner*, ed. J. A. Muller (Cambridge, 1933), pp. 386–7.
[18] *Sileni Alcibiadis, Adages*, pp. 273–4, 278.   [19] *Adages*, pp. 258–9.
[20] *Coll.*, p. 388. See also *Folly*, pp. 105, 123, 176, and the colloquies *Ementita nobilitas* and *Coniugium impar*, pp. 424–32 and 401–12 in Thompson's edition. In the latter colloquy, the parents of a young, beautiful woman are denounced for marrying her to a notorious gambler, whoremonger and drunkard, a thief and a bankrupt, a poxridden corpse whose 'breath is sheer poison, his speech a plague, his touch death,' all for the sake of 'his glorious title of knight.'

Erasmus observed such absurdity in daily practice. Title is normally placed in high regard in the choice of marriage partners, a practice which Erasmus deplored. On a less serious level, part of his highly entertaining critique of German inns was pointed at the preferential treatment given to nobles over commoners.[21] Yet if preference is to be given, it should go to the latter, since one who glories in his ancestry is in reality 'low and base-born because he is so far from virtue, the only true fount of nobility.'[22] Neither should wealth or position be regarded as proper determinants of social status, since heaven grants wealth, palaces and kingdoms to the slothful and the worthless, and wealth, honor and descent make one neither better nor happier.[23]

The strongest second to Erasmus' disdain for hereditary nobility came from Sir Thomas More. Erasmus remarked with obvious approval in a biographical sketch of More that the latter was disinclined to life at court and to intimacy with princes, so great was his liking for equality.[24] More's egalitarian tendencies are most apparent, of course, in the social structure of Utopia, which provides a vehicle for the most pervasive attack on chivalric aristocracy of the period. More attacked both lords and their retainers as idlers, condemned princes as war-mongers, and denounced virtually every aspect of aristocratic living as destructive of the common weal. His denunciation of chivalric values was complete.[25]

Thomas Starkey followed in the same tradition: 'Princes and lords,' he accused, 'seldom look to the good order and wealth of their subjects; only they look to the receiving of their rents and revenues of their lands.' Nobles and prelates maintain in their houses 'an idle rout . . . which do nothing else but carry dishes to the table and eat them when they have done; and after, giving themselves to . . . idle pastimes and vain, as though they were born to nothing else at all.'[26] As for monarchy, while it is the rule 'most convenient' for England, 'princes commonly are ruled by affects rather than by reason and order of justice,' so that 'seldom it is that they which by succession come to kingdoms and realms are worthy of

---

[21] *Coniugium impar, Proci et puellae*, and *Diversoria, Coll.*, pp. 401–12, 86–98, and 147–52; cf. *Institutio*, p. 241; *Folly*, p. 131.   [22] *Folly*, p. 38; cf. p. 59.
[23] *Ars notoria* and *Abbatis et eruditae*, in *Coll.*, pp. 220, 460.
[24] Erasmus to Ulrich von Hutten (23 July 1519) in *Opus Epistolarum Des. Erasmi Roterodami*, ed. P. S. Allen (Oxford, 1922), vol. 4, no. 999, p. 15.
[25] *Utopia*, pp. 57, 62–3, 66, 128, 131, 138, 146, 150–2, 166–70, 204. See Hexter's introduction, pp. l-liv; his 'The Loom of Language and the Fabric of Imperatives: The Case of *Il Principe* and *Utopia*,' *American Historical Review*, 69 (1964), 945–68, pp. 960–2; and Skinner, vol. 1, pp. 257–60, for more complete discussions of More's radical stance on the nature of aristocracy.   [26] Starkey, pp. 79, 86; cf. 123–5.

such high authority.' Hereditary succession is judged to be 'contrary to nature and all right reason.'[27]

Birth, then, was not deemed a proper determinant of status by humanist theorists. While those born to nobility are too often the most ignoble of men, people of lowly birth who apply themselves to virtuous behavior and education may well be worthy to rule. The disdain which humanists evinced for the 'common sort' rested on an Erasmian re-definition of the term. For Erasmus, the appellation 'common' or 'vulgar' was related not to social class, but to level of understanding and moral uprightness. The 'stupid generality of men' are those who 'blunder into wrong judgments because they judge everything from the evidence of the bodily senses.'[28] The 'common people' include all those who are fooled by the false opinions of astrologers and other superstition-mongers, but these include kings and emperors.[29] In his paraphrases on the Sermon on the Mount, Erasmus identified the 'common sort' as those whose concern is with material possessions, rather than with learning righteousness; again, however, this is not a criterion which corresponds exclusively to low social estate.[30] To value gems, gold, royal purple, the pomp of heralds and an exalted genealogy is one characteristic of the 'base, vile, and unbecoming' thought of the vulgar. But Erasmus found this trait typical of the opinions of the princely estate. 'How ridiculous it is,' he exclaimed, for one possessed of these superficial benefits to regard himself as 'so far superior to all because of them, and yet in light of real goodness of spirit to be found inferior to many born from the very dregs of society.'[31] Erasmus would have concurred heartily with Archbishop Cranmer's judgment that the children of the poor are often more gifted than gentlemen's sons.[32] When he did use the term 'common' in its more usual sense of low social estate, he was as often as not alluding to the wisdom of simple folk.[33]

[27] *Ibid.*, pp. 99, 104, 165.
[28] *Sileni Alcibiadis, Adages*, p. 276; *cf. That chyldren oughte to be taught . . .*, a treatise by Erasmus included in Richard Sherry's *A Treatise of Schemes and Tropes* (London, 1550), fol. Giii; *Apophthegmes*, tr. Nicolas Udall (London, 1542), fol. 21.
[29] *Institutio*, p. 196; *cf. Adages*, p. 23; *Folly*, pp. 113, 117.
[30] *The First Tome or Volume of the Paraphrase of Erasmus upon the Newe Testamente* (London, 1548, Scholars' Facsimiles, 1975), fol. xix; *cf. Apophthegmes*, fol. 51, where the wealthy classes are obviously in Erasmus' mind as he labels 'common' those who spend money on their horses and stables, rather than on their children's education.
[31] *Institutio*, pp. 145–50; in *Apophthegmes*, fol. 47, he deems a beggar superior to an ignorant or unwise man.
[32] Thomas Cranmer, *Works* (Cambridge, 1844–6), vol. 2: *Miscellaneous Writings and Letters*, p. 398, from BL, MS Harl. 419.
[33] For example, *Festina lente, Adages*, p. 188, notes that 'the common people' are in agreement with Quintilian in regard to certain child-rearing practices.

Birth, therefore, has nothing to do with the virtue of the
individual, which is for the humanists the proper determinant of
status. John Colet articulated their aspiration that 'all the old diversity might be abolished . . . and one new and simple and like form of
Christ be put on by all.' The aim of Christian behavior on the part of
men of all social levels Colet regarded as 'the closer of the grovelling
eye which regards only the inequalities of earth.'[34] Erasmus was
clearly an accurate spokesman for Christian humanism when he
boldly asserted in the *Institutio* that 'Nature hath created all men
equal, and slavery was imposed on nature.'[35]

This should not be construed to imply, however, that the
humanists were completely anti-hierarchical or in any sense of the
word democratic in their social outlook. They were, after all, early
modern men, and they shared the concern of their contemporaries
with the ever-present threat of social chaos should degree be
abolished. Erasmus was particularly affected by the German Peasants' Revolt, which inspired in him a horror of anarchy: 'The peasants raise dangerous riots and are not swayed from their purpose by
so many massacres. The commons are bent on anarchy . . . the whole
earth is pregnant with I know not what calamity'; in the adage *Ut fici
oculis incumbunt* he commented that princes are to be endured 'lest
anarchy – on the whole a worse evil – take the place of tyranny. The
experience of public events has often proved – and the recent
peasants' revolts in Germany show us– that the harshness of princes
is to some degree more tolerable than the confusion of anarchy.'[36] As
a result, the ideal social order which they would oppose to the
'slavery' of the Chain of Being does incorporate hierarchy, but it is a
hierarchy determined by behavior – active evidence of virtue.[37]
Equality at birth simply allows for the potential of wisdom, moral
uprightness and ruling ability in a given individual, irrespective of
class or condition of birth. It is an allowance not particularly surpris-

[34] *Ioannis Coleti Enarratio in Primam Epistolam S. Pauli ad Corinthios*, tr. J. H. Lupton
(London, 1874), p. 97.
[35] *Institutio*, p. 177; the adage *Festina lente* urges masters to treat their servants like
men, not beasts of burden, on this basis. *Adages*, p. 184.
[36] *Puerpera, Coll.*, pp. 269–70; *Adages*, p. 359; *cf. Adages*, p. 378 and *Proverbes*, fol. liii.
Luther's response to the Peasants' Revolt was similar, if more strongly expressed.
[37] Clarence Miller, 'Some Medieval Elements and Structural Unity in Erasmus' *The
Praise of Folly,' Renaissance Quarterly*, 27 (1974), 499–511, finds in Erasmus' hierarchical concepts evidence of 'medievalism'; however, whereas medieval social
critics sought restoration of a diseased social organism to health, Erasmus wished
to see it replaced with an ideal entity in which different criteria for status are
employed, republicanism is held to be preferable to monarchy, etc. Complete
social reform for Erasmus would require reversion not to a medieval Golden Age,
but to a classical schema worked out in a Christian context.

ing to discover in the theory of a man ever-conscious of his own base birth, but one which none the less pervaded the thought of other humanists as well. Their admiration for classical Stoicism is perhaps nowhere more evident.

Given, then, that the combination of birth, wealth and honor corresponds neither to understanding nor to virtue, it is not a proper criterion for the designation of a ruler or ruling class. Rather, wisdom, learning and moral excellence – possibilities at any social level – should be the sole considerations:

In navigation the wheel is not given to him who surpasses his fellows in birth, wealth, or appearance, but rather to him who excels in his skill as a navigator, in his alertness, and in his dependability. Just so the rule of a state: most naturally the power should be entrusted to him who excels all in the requisite of kingly qualities of wisdom, justice, moderation, foresight, and zeal for the public welfare.[38]

It is implied that those who do the choosing are also to be qualified for their important position in the hierarchy by their virtue and learning; they are to rule with the prince and receive honor from the ruled. But in the humanist order, 'there is no real honor except that which springs from virtue and good deeds.'[39]

Erasmus's system is thus not without a nobility. But 'noble', like 'common', is redefined:

There are three kinds of nobility: the first is derived from virtue and good actions; the second comes from acquaintance with the best of training; and the third from an array of family portraits and genealogy or wealth. It by no means becomes a prince to swell with pride over this lowest degree of nobility, for it is so low that it is nothing at all, unless it has itself sprung from virtue. Neither must he neglect the first, which is so far the first that it alone can be considered in the strictest judgment.[40]

---

[38] *Institutio*, p. 140; *cf.* pp. 203–4; an abstract of this passage was translated and presented to Edward VI in 1550 by John Lumley (BL, Royal MS 17.A.XLIV, fols. 2–2v). *cf. Apophthegmes*, fol. 6; *Enchiridion militis christiani*, tr. and ed. Raymond Himelick (Bloomington, Indiana, 1963), p. 65. It is noteworthy that when discussing the problem of who should rule, Erasmus consistently rejected the traditional literary image of society as an organism in favor of the more flexible image of the ship. This allows choice of a captain on the basis of merit, not birth, or *essential* headship, as in the organic metaphor. *cf.* Michael Walzer, *Revolution of the Saints* (New York, 1972), pp. 171–83.

[39] *Institutio*, pp. 203–4: 'During a great tempest even the most experienced navigators will listen to advice from a layman. But the ship of state is never without a storm.' *cf.* pp. 198, 224; *Enchiridion*, pp. 198–90.

[40] *Institutio*, p. 151; *De rebus ac vocabulis* and *Ementita nobilitas*, in *Coll.*, pp. 382–8, 424–32. The educational element is further stressed by Erasmus in *De Civilitate Morum Puerilium*, translated by Robert Whittington as *A lytell booke of good manners for chyldren* (1532). See Foster Watson, *The English Grammar Schools to 1660* (Cambridge, 1908), p. 106, for the widespread influence of this work.

Elsewhere, Erasmus added a spiritual dimension to the definition of 'nobility'. The *Enchiridion* counts as true nobility a sort of spiritual elite composed of those who imitate Christ most nearly, and the *Liber de Sarcienda Ecclesiae Concordia* (1533) describes society as a spiritual hierarchy in which status is determined by conquest of sins: 'To be born from a father who is a servant is not base, while to be a slave to lust, avarice, and other vices is most base; to beg one's bread when necessity requires is not shameful, but to refuse the necessities to the poor or to live on what has been stolen from them is a contemptible crime.'[41] Clearly, the reformist concerns of Christian humanism are uppermost in this denial of one of the central tenets of medieval social theory, that status is a matter of being, not behavior.

The Erasmian position is visible in its most idealized form in *Utopia*, where there are no distinctions of birth. Here it is the most virtuous and learned men who are elected rulers. More's epigrams reveal his disapproval of monarchy: Epigram 182, on the best form of government, promotes the rule of an elected senate rather than that of a monarch chosen by the 'blind chance' of birth.[42] Likewise, Starkey raised the possibility of elective rather than hereditary rule as a means of insuring that the best men, rather than the highest-born, are placed in positions of authority: 'that country cannot be long well governed nor maintained with good policy', observes Pole in the *Dialogue*, 'where all are ruled by the will of one not chosen by election but come to it by natural succession.'[43]

For Starkey, as for Erasmus and More, such a proposition was purely theoretical; however, the underlying assumptions about the proper nature of social hierarchy were there in their published writings for subsequent generations of readers to consider in light of their own political situations. And in the meantime, both Catholic and early protestant humanists would maintain those assumptions even when called upon to defend the established political order. While the event of rebellion would seem the logical context for a demand for unquestioning obedience to constituted authority, Richard Morison found himself justifying the obedience due to

---

[41] In Dolan, pp. 338, 365; *Enchiridion*, pp. 189–91 *et passim*. The parallels between those considered reprobate in puritan theology and the vulgar in the humanist scheme are obvious. But puritans and humanists would admit that some people seem to be beyond reformation; both saw repression as the only means to insure social order in such extreme cases.

[42] More, *Utopia*, p. 122; James McConica, 'The Patrimony of Thomas More,' *History and Imagination*, ed. Hugh Lloyd-Jones, Valerie Pearl and Blair Worden (New York, 1981), 56–71, p. 67.   [43] Starkey, pp. 99, 104–5, 154.

Henry VIII in the wake of the Pilgrimage of Grace on the basis not of the king's birth and position, but of his virtue and courage in the defense of truth and the common weal. Disobedience would be an act of ingratitude for the king's virtuous behavior. Depicting the present struggle as a conflict between an anti-Christian foreign power and the representatives of the true faith, Morison issued an appeal to conscience to come to the defense of right. In his officially sanctioned treatise, he presented the humanist formulation that the authority of the ruler is not absolute, but is conditioned by his virtuous actions: 'God standeth with kings that stand with him.'[44]

Even more striking was the use of a similar argument in the next decade against rebellion not by the aristocracy, but by a 'rabble of Norfolk rebels' claiming a political voice. Those who would contemplate such a rebellion were exhorted to obedience by the humanist Sir John Cheke not with an appeal to the Great Chain of Being, but with an Erasmian theory of rightly determined rule. Cheke did not deny hierarchy, but replaced hierarchy of birth with that of merit: 'they that have seen most, and [are] best able to bear it, and of just dealing besides, be most fit to rule.'[45] Obedience is owed the king not because of his exalted birth, his position next to God in the cosmological order, but rather because of his virtue. The present king is ruled by informed conscience; therefore, conscience dictates that obedience is due him.

Thus, in expanding their doctrine that reform is the key to social control and that virtuous behavior is the foundation upon which the godly commonwealth must be built, the Christian humanists developed an approach to social order diametrically opposed to the medieval conception. The Erasmian focus was on the informing of conscience; the Great Chain of Being subjected conscience to essential hierarchical authority embodied in king, lords and bishops. Both aimed at social order, but one approached it from below, while the other imposed it from above. The lines were drawn, the conflict apparent, by the time protestantism appeared on the scene. In their reformist zeal to achieve a godly commonwealth, the early Re-

---

[44] Richard Morison, *An Exhortation to styire all Englishmen to the defence of theyr countreye* (1539), sig. Bviii; cf. Biiii ff, Diii–Diiii; *An Invective agenste the great and detestable vice, treason* (1539), sig. Ai–Biii et passim.

[45] [Sir John Cheke], *The Hurt of Sedicion howe Greveous it is to a Commune Welth* (1549), sig. Avii. On Ket's Rebellion, see S. T. Bindoff, *Ket's Rebellion, 1549* (Historical Association, G.12, 1949); Stephen K. Land, *Kett's Rebellion: The Norfolk Rising of 1549* (Ipswich, 1977); Diarmaid Macculloch, 'Kett's Rebellion in Context,' *P&P,* 84 (1979), 36–59; and Barrett L. Beer, *Rebellion and Riot: Popular Disorder in England during the Reign of Edward VI* (Kent, Ohio, 1982).

formers naturally seized upon their humanist heritage. One must agree in principle with the historian who has observed that 'Commonwealth, Protestantism and Christian humanism' were indeed 'jumbled together in a splendid porridge of reformist yearnings,' and that this 'cross-play of beliefs, weighing differently in different men, strikes much more convincingly than a distinction of categories.'[46] That porridge would nourish Anglicans and puritans alike in Elizabethan England.

Protestant adoption of the humanist approach to social control followed logically from the reformist orientation which they shared. Both reform movements were founded on an optimistic vision of a true stability to be achieved through change, a conviction that a godly society is to be achieved not by enforcing obedience to hierarchy, but by a concerted attack on the reasons for disorder in the commonwealth – individual sin, moral ignorance and civic irresponsibility. If the protestant believer was a 'citizen by calling,'[47] he was indebted to his Christian humanist forebears; his duty to the commonwealth involved him in the same confrontation between conscience and sin which Erasmus' Christian knight had faced. Protestant preachers addressed congregations trained in the humanist assumption of the importance of individual virtue to the common weal. That order in the realm was to be achieved by individual reformation of behavior was beyond debate in the mid-sixteenth century. It was this presupposition which conditioned the preaching of Bishops Latimer and Bale as it would that of puritans for the next century and more. It helped to define the Elizabethan mainstream in which puritans and conformists labored to realize the godly commonwealth.

Protestant acceptance of humanist social theory was also conditioned by their consensus on the authority of Scripture and the need to apply its precepts to the practical problems of daily living. In combination with their common rejection of the need for clerical, saintly and angelic mediation between man and God, this biblicism

---

[46] G. R. Elton, *Reform and Renewal: Thomas Cromwell and the Common Weal* (Cambridge, 1973), p. 1; *cf.* Gordon Zeeveld, *Foundations of Tudor Policy* (Cambridge, Mass., 1948); James McConica, *English Humanism and Reformation Politics* (Oxford, 1965); Arthur B. Ferguson, *Articulate Citizen*. J. G. A. Pocock has suggested that the difficulties encountered by Ferguson's 'commonwealth' humanists in achieving their ends after the Reformation can be attributed to the 'sheer fear of disorder [which] compelled an obstinate adherence to the vision of England as a hierarchy of degree.' *The Machiavellian Moment* (Princeton, 1975), pp. 348–9.

[47] C. H. and K. George, p. 18.

naturally resulted for both humanists and protestants in an elevation of the role of individual conscience in interpreting and acting on scriptural injunctions. Reform was to be channeled to society through conscience.

Zealous protestants, like Catholic humanists, wrote handbooks for self-improvement, domestic conduct manuals, treatises on education and diatribes against idleness, drunkenness, dancing and other deadly sins not because of any intrinsic value in such endeavors, but because of their larger social vision. Their remarkable literary output was rather aimed at the goal of social order and the common weal. The demands on conscience which they made of gentlemen and servants alike comprised their method of achieving social control. Reasoning along humanist lines, for example, that crime is the result not of disobedience to superiors, but of idleness in the lower orders and greed at the top, non-conformists, moderate puritans and reforming bishops alike preached against idleness and avarice, and supported workhouse legislation and the regulation of enclosures, rents and prices. Their goal was the common weal, the abolition of social disorder as it is manifest in crime. Likewise, their shared sabbatarianism was not an end *per se*, nor an obsession with Old Testament legalism, but a conviction that want of regular church attendance 'is the cause of so many wicked and rebellious children, untrusty and disobedient servants, nay, unfaithful and unkind wives everywhere.'[48] Social harmony would result only from a reformation of manners, and this reformation would be achieved through the vehicle of preaching. The drive to move the ungodly multitude from alehouse to church on Sunday was fuelled by a conviction that the instruction and exhortation received there would awaken lax consciences and guide behavioral reformation. When the godly laity of Elizabethan Essex protested against the suspension of their puritan ministers, they noted the preachers' promotion of social discipline by means of sermons.[49] The publication of sermons on practical social reform had the same goal: the puritan William Jones' essay on household government was explicitly written as a means of amending disorders in the commonwealth.[50]

Protestants emulated the humanist preference for moderation

---

[48] Robert Cleaver, *A Godly Forme of Householde Government* (London, 1598), p. 31; *cf.* the sabbatarianism of the Catholic humanist Richard Whitforde, *The Werke for housholders* (n.p., 1537), sigs. Dviii–Eii.

[49] William Hunt, *The Puritan Moment* (Cambridge, Mass., 1983), p. 98.

[50] William Jones, *A Briefe Exhortation to all men to set their houses in order* (1612), p. 3.

and self-control in all things out of a concern for the common weal.[51] Puritan opposition to tippling rested similarly on their charge that it resulted in social disorder. Nor do drunkards make any positive contribution to the commonwealth: William Perkins, in his *Treatise of the Vocations* (1597), condemned drinking, feasting and idle sports and pastimes because they prevented men from 'employing themselves in service for Church or commonwealth,' not because they were inherently evil. Perkins is in this treatise representative of puritanism's inheritance of the humanist commonwealth ideal: every action of a Christian, including his choice of vocation, should be determined by a desire to contribute to the common good, the edification of a godly and well-ordered society.[52] Puritan casuistry from Perkins and William Ames to Richard Baxter should thus be interpreted as evidence of the consensus among humanists and protestant reformers that since individual sin is the root of England's troubles, individual reform will assuage the turmoil. And the protestant, like the Erasmian, requirement for spiritual self-examination may therefore be understood as a technique of social control.[53] Elizabethan

[51] Following the advice, for instance, of Ulrich Zwingli's *Of the Upbringing and Education of Youth in Good Manners and Christian Discipline* (1523) in *Library of Christian Classics*, vol. 24, tr. G. W. Bromiley (Philadelphia, 1953), p. 114. Zwingli here shows a humanist-inspired respect for Seneca, citing him in connection with the contributions of individual self-control to the common weal.

[52] William Perkins, *A Treatise of the Vocations, or Callings of Men* in *Workes* (1616), vol. 1, pp. 758, 773, *et passim*. Keith Wrightson, in 'The Puritan Reformation of Manners with special reference to the Counties of Lancashire and Essex, 1640–1660' (unpublished Ph.D. thesis, University of Cambridge, 1973) has effectively challenged puritan exaggeration of the extent of the problem of drunkenness, as well as their charges that it led to more serious crimes. But while he admits that puritan bombast against drink was heavily, if not correctly, fortified by appeals for order and social responsibility, he sees this as a popular ideological disguise for their real concern with drink as a barrier between the individual and his awareness of his sins (pp. 78–82). I would argue rather that puritan concerns were both individual and social. If drink numbs conscience, it does so to the detriment both of the drunkard and of his community in puritan eyes. The godly commonwealth is the one in which order is achieved at all levels through the control of sinful behavior by individual conscience.

[53] Perkins, *The Whole Treatise of the Cases of Conscience*, in Merrill, pp. 79–240; William Ames, *Conscience With the Power and Cases Thereof* (1639), *passim*; Richard Baxter, *Practical Works* (1838), vol. 1, pp. 902–4 *et passim*. Self-examination was preached, for example, by William Perkins and George Webbe in *A Garden of spirituall Flowers* (1610), sigs. Biiii–Bv, Fiii–Fiiii, and by Luke Rochfort in *An antidot for laziness* (Dublin, 1624), p. 20, in the latter case with more classical than biblical citations. It was recommended by James Duport to his students at Trinity, Cambridge, complete with the Pythagorean questions so highly thought of by Erasmus and Cranmer (Trin. MS O.10A.33). It was practiced by Richard Rogers and Samuel Ward (*Two Elizabethan Puritan Diaries*, ed. M. NM. Knappen (Gloucester, Mass., 1966)), Lady Margaret Hoby (*Diary*, ed. D. M. Meads (1930)), and Sir Simonds D'Ewes (*Autobiography*, ed. J. O. Halliwell (1845)), vol. 1, pp. 353–63, to name a few. The correspondence of Thomas Gataker, moreover, reveals the concern of puritan divines with guidance of their parishioners in the process of self-examination (CUL, MS Dd. 3.83,19, dated 1631).

protestants and puritans in the next century were in full agreement with humanists that the problem of order in the commonwealth was to be approached at the level of individual conscience.

The implications of this approach for the authority of the social and ecclesiastical hierarchy is as apparent in protestant as in humanist social theory, and here the first divergence of puritan from conformist social understanding begins to emerge. Just as Erasmian critics had subjected the behavior of kings, nobles, and clerics to the scrutiny of morally informed conscience, so the hotter sort of prot-estants would demand the imposition of a disciplined life style on their social superiors. Andrew Melville, who identified uneducated nobles as enemies of godliness, threatened James VI in 1597 'with fearful judgments if he repented not'; he was denounced by Richard Bancroft for charging 'the greatest men of the land with God's heavy punishments' should they fail to conform to standards of godly living. Thomas Cartwright called magistrates to govern according to God's rules, and 'to submit their sceptres, to throw down their crowns before the church,' a church in his vision directed by godly laymen no less than by ministers.[54] Laurence Humphrey wrote to the queen and bishops criticizing the royal policy whereby 'the learned man without his cap is afflicted, the capped man without learning is not touched' merely because the latter conforms to the demands of tradition. He charged bishops and priests in Erasmian style with neglecting their true duties of caring for the poor, preaching, seeing vagabonds disciplined and pulling down 'monuments of super-stition', and boldly announced to Elizabeth that while he believed in obedience to the prince, 'it is most right and convenient that the mind and conscience of any, be not forced or compelled.'[55] The Cambridge puritan, Samuel Ward, numbered the sins of princes and primates (including bull-baitings on the Sabbath and indulging papists) among reasons for the ills of the nation.[56] And puritans such as Laurence Chaderton and Henry Smith would wholeheartedly agree with Colet that 'God has no respect of persons' in his demands on conscience: the commandments of Scripture are directed to pauper and lord alike.[57] In the next century, the puritan Thomas Gataker warned nobles not to rely on their birth to give them status

[54] Andrew Melville, *Diary* (1556–1601), ed. James Melville (Edinburgh, 1844), pp. 130, 274; Richard Bancroft, *Dangerous Positions* (1593), n.p.; Cartwright is quoted in H. C. Porter, *Reformation and Reaction in Tudor Cambridge* (Cambridge, 1958), p. 142.

[55] BL, Harl. MS 7033; *cf.* Humphrey's debate with Sanderson, recorded by a puritan student at St John's, Cambridge (MS S.20), pp. 107–30.

[56] Sidney Sussex College, MS Ward B, fol. 31.

[57] Colet, p. 96; Laurence Chaderton, *An Excellent and Godly Sermon . . . preached at Paules Crosse* (1578), sig. Biiii; Henry Smith, *Sermons* (London, 1593), sig. Yy5.

in God's kingdom, but to look to their actions, since 'It is with men as with counters: howsoever while the account lasteth one standeth for a penny and another for a pound, yet are they all counters alike before and after the account, when they are together in the bag.' Rulers who neglect the common good in their pride of birth 'are more dangerous to Crown and State, I say not than idle vagrants, or than whoremasters and adulterers, or than thieves and murderers. . . but even than popish traitors and conspirators.'[58] Preachers such as Thomas Hooker and William Gouge thundered warnings against magistrates and the king himself, threatening them and the nation with divine retribution for their sins.[59] Even John Preston, as chaplain to Prince Charles, managed tactfully to criticize the king's foreign and religious policies in court sermons, calling for the prince to submit his politics to the direction of instructed conscience. In one such sermon, Preston went so far as to comment that God 'doth not need princes' to care for his people, and that the believer would do well to distinguish between God's cause and the king's.[60] Protestant disregard of hierarchy of birth in relation to virtuous action, like that of the humanists, is evidence of their 'grass roots' approach to the problem of order in the commonwealth, their conviction that order is to be exhorted on the level of the individual conscience, whether noble or common, not imposed by force from above.

That Calvinist theology contributed to the implicit opposition of English puritanism to hierarchy of birth is undeniable. But at least part of the appeal of Calvinist social theory to English protestants even before the rise of puritanism must be located in their predilection for Christian humanist social criticism.[61] The Erasmian Reformer Martin Bucer had told English divinity students that virtue is a more vital quality than exalted genealogy in a ruler, that the Kingdom of Christ ought to be governed by a 'person who excels the others in wisdom and every virtue'; the responsibility of rule should

---

[58] Thomas Gataker, *Certaine Sermons* (1637), p. 103; *cf.* pp. 73, 87–90, and 110, frequently citing Seneca.

[59] Hunt, pp. 199–208, provides numerous examples and notes that geographically, resistance to the Forced Loan in Essex is found precisely in those areas where puritan preachers were most active (p. 202).

[60] Irvonwy Morgan, *Prince Charles's Puritan Chaplain* (1957), *passim*; Preston, *Life Eternall*, p. 126.

[61] Walzer, pp. 148–83, attributes puritan anti-hierarchical tendencies exclusively to Calvinist theology, rather than acknowledging the Christian humanist precedent. Furthermore, in his focus on revolution and radical politics, he fails to see that a desire to achieve social order and harmony lay at the heart of the puritan reformist program and that their critique of the behavior of nobles and prelates was necessitated by their thesis that conscience is the proper agent of social control. *cf.* Patrick Collinson, *The Religion of Protestants* (Oxford, 1982), pp. 150–88.

not be assigned to 'any particular class of men, much less to hyp-ocrites with empty titles.' He used nautical imagery just as Erasmus, his predecessor at Cambridge, had used it: 'No one willingly entrusts himself to a ship whose master has only the name and income of a navigator, but who does not know how to navigate; but everyone prefers to sail with a man who, although his name is unknown and his talents modest, nevertheless has all the knowledge and experience necessary for sailing a ship.'[62] While extreme protestants pragmatically convinced themselves that these behavioral requirements were met by the then King Edward VI, their doubts about nobles and prelates remained, and were embodied in an Erasmian critique of these estates as detractors from the common weal and ultimately breeders of disorder through vice. Nobles in Bucer's view were far from being 'a shining example to the common people, as they should be'; rather, 'the effort they make for the advantage of the common-wealth' is paltry compared to that of citizens of less birth but more virtue.[63] The critique of aristocracy embodied in Thomas Becon's tracts likewise parallels Erasmus' at every turn, and evinces the same attitude toward hierarchy even before the full impact of Calvinism had been felt in England. In a 1560 sermon, Becon asked Seneca's question, 'Seeing, then, that as touching our corporal creation there is no difference, no prerogative, what nobility or worthiness of blood can there be more in the noble personage than in the base slave?' Virtue, he argued, is the sign of true nobility, a sign too often absent from the titled.[64] In the next century, Bulstrode Whitelocke told his children that 'no birth will make one noble' without righteous behavior.[65]

This principle was firmly established in the minds of Elizabethan and early Stuart puritans. They learned it, either directly from Seneca or through the mediation of Christian humanists, in the course of their university studies,[66] and they applied it to increasingly virulent attacks on a frivolous and ungodly aristocracy, on the reign of custom, and on the insistence of the conformist hierarchy that conscience must be subject to temporal authority. William Bright, having copied large portions of More's *Utopia* into his commonplace book, called for rule based on virtue and ability, and Simonds D'Ewes could only wish 'that it might be truly said. . . *Omnus magnus est*

---

[62] Bucer, pp. 176–7, 267–8.   [63] Bucer, pp. 341, 360.
[64] Thomas Becon, *The Jewel of Joy* (1560), sig. CCc6.
[65] *Memoirs of Bulstrode Whitelocke*, ed. R. H. Whitelocke (London, 1860), p. 36.
[66] For example, Trin. MSS R.16.6 (pp. 529–30), R.16.12 (fol. 87v), R.16.17 (fol. 34), R.16.18 (fols. 105, 115); Pembroke, Cambridge, MS LC.II.16 (n.f.).

bonus, the greatest are the best.' Enamoured as he was of his own genealogy, D'Ewes admitted that 'Every beggar comes from a king,' and that we all trace our lineage to Noah; he saw pride in birth, as in riches, as a hindrance to his progress toward heaven.[67] By the 1640s, the tendency to locate responsibility for social disorder in an idle, vice-ridden courtly class, reliant on its birth rather than laboring to attain true wisdom and virtue, had become part of the definition of a puritan:

> if any were grieved at the dishonours of the kingdom, or the gripping of the poor, or the unjust oppression of the subject, by a thousand ways, invented to maintain the riots of the courtiers... he was a Puritan... in short, all that crossed the views of the needy courtiers, the proud encroaching priests, the thievish projectors, the lewd nobility and gentry, whoever could endure... modest habit or conversation or anything good, all these were Puritans; and if Puritans, then enemies to the king and his government.

Lucy Hutchinson, who thus defined puritanism, praised her husband because 'he was above the ambition of vain titles... he loved substantial and not airy honor... [and] pitied those that took a glory in that which had no foundation of virtue.'[68] Other puritan women would go much further: Lady Brilliana Harley proclaimed in 1641 her 'belief that hierarchy must down, and I hope now.'[69]

Until the Civil War, most puritans were sufficiently fearful of disorder to go no further than expressing criticism of the blatantly irreligious among the aristocracy and fear of divine retribution on the nation, and urging individual moral reform to create the godly commonwealth. Far from wanting to level society, they readily adopted the alternative hierarchy of merit proposed by the humanists. They were no more egalitarian than Erasmus had been; they saw a need for society to be structured along hierarchical lines. But they re-formed those lines as Erasmus had. They recommended that Englishmen 'honour all men in their places, but no man so much for his greatness as for his goodness, and thus shall you imitate the Lord himself, who accepteth not persons, but in every nation accepteth him that feareth him.'[70] Richard Sibbes' description of

---

[67] CUL, Add. MS 6160, pp. 21, 33, 48; BL, Harl. MS 182, fol. 38v; Harl. 186, fols. 54v–58v; *cf.* D'Ewes, *Autobiography, passim.*

[68] Lucy Hutchinson, *Memoires of the Life of Colonel Hutchinson*, ed. Julius Hutchinson (1822), pp. 122–3; *cf.* pp. 175–6.

[69] *Letters of Lady Brilliana Harley*, ed. T. T. Lewis (Camden Society, 1884), p. 111. Lady Brilliana was admittedly given to overstatement– she is the same Brilliana who had earlier elevated parents to divinity; however, it should be recalled that she lost her life beseiged by the forces of her king, against whom she and her family waged determined war.

[70] *A Garden of spirituall Flowers Planted by Ri. Ro[gers], Will. Per[kins], Ri. Gree[nham], M. M., and Geo. Web[be]* (1610), Part II, sig. Av.

degree ignores birth altogether in favor of behavior as the sole determinant of status; other puritans recognized various kinds of nobility, but reckoned that of birth inferior to that 'which a man doth
purchase by virtue and good living.'[71] That 'distinction which God
maketh between man and man in every society' was paralleled to the
angelic hierarchy by Perkins in a sense diametrically opposed to the
essential hierarchy of the Great Chain of Being: distinctions for
angels and for men are based not on being but on behavior, on
obedience to God's commands under the guidance of conscience.
The dictates of conscience could even release the godly from
ordinary social obligations: rather than violate the dictates of conscience, a servant could legitimately leave his master, according to
Perkins.[72] Others expressed the logical implications of the notion of
an alternative hierarchy of virtue in politically reformist terms: the
godly vestry of Braintree issued in 1619 a new set of regulations for
the town's government, requiring that its governing body be chosen
not only on the traditional basis of social status, but also on grounds
of virtuous behavior – they must be 'unreprovable in their lives'
rather than merely wealthy or of the highest status.[73]

In Cambridge, a notorious case tried in the Vice-Chancellor's
court in 1628 reveals that the implications of the alternative
hierarchy could be more alarming to constituted authorities. When
the puritan Thomas Edwards of Queens' preached at St Andrew's on
obedience to the dictates of conscience, he told his auditors that
when they had difficulty understanding the word of God,

When there arise any doubts about the way, and thou knoweth not well
which way to take, if thou beest a servant, thou must not go to thy carnal
master to enquire of him; if thou beest a wife, thou must not go to thy carnal
husband to ask him; if thou beest a son, thou must not go to they carnal
father; if thou beest a pupil, thou must not go to thy carnal tutor to ask him,
but thou must find out a man in whom the Spirit of God dwells, one that is
renewed by grace, that he shall direct thee.[74]

[71] Richard Sibbes, *Beames of divine light* (1639), Part I, p. 156. Francis Rogers, *A sermon preached . . . at the Funerall of William Proud* (1633), sig. Bii–Biiii; Perkins, *Cases of Conscience*, pp. 236–7.

[72] Perkins, *Vocations*, p. 755, and *Works* (Cambridge, 1608), vol. 1, p. 734; *cf.* Walzer, pp. 161–6. That Perkins passed such opinions on to his students at Christ's College is evident from the moderate William Bedell's counsel to Samuel Ward in 1607 that 'so often as a man doth not follow the dictamen of his conscience (yea though erring) inciting him to do that which may be most for God's glory, all things considered, he sins; that being the highest reason of doing that may be and to be crossed or hindered by nothing under it' (Bodl., MS Tanner 75, fol. 354, 23 July [1607]). [73] Hunt, p. 82.

[74] CUL, MS CUR 6.1, it. 39, fols. 21–21v; *cf.* fols. 21–25; and CUL, MS VC Ct. I.49, fols. 25–26. Edwards was later suspended by Archbishop Laud, but he was an active preacher under Parliamentary rule. He is known primarily as the author of *Gangraena* (1646).

The Edwards case illustrates both the radical potential of the alternative hierarchy and the fear of both the conformists and the moderate puritans on the court about the possible outcome of such a doctrine. If virtue is to determine status, then patriarchy is as endangered as monarchy and aristocracy. Edwards was required to clarify to the parishioners of St Andrew's that he had not intended to justify 'disobedience to superiors.' That he was ordered to do so even by those puritan heads who had themselves denounced princely and clerical sins[75] is an indication of the fear of disorder and conflict that bound the early Stuart church together. At this date even the later politically radical Stephen Marshall was behaving circumspectly, and Jeremiah Burroughs was keeping his theories of popular sovereignty to private conversations.[76] When the sins of the well-born became intolerable, the alternative hierarchy would become a revolutionary possibility. That the destruction of royal patriarchy was held off until 1649 owes more to puritan fear of social chaos and their humanist hope for reformation (particularly in view of that already achieved by godly magistrates and bishops in the preceding generation) than to any theoretical conservatism. Bastions of order they were, but of a reformed and reforming order.

In their concern for order in the commonwealth, puritans followed closely the humanist tradition of calling for individual moral reform at all levels, rather than unquestioning obedience to constituted authority. In so doing, they repudiated the Chain of Being to the extent that theoretically the guidance of individual conscience was elevated above the demands of human authority and laws, which 'bind not simply of themselves, but so far forth as they are agreeable to God's word, serve for the common good, stand with good order, and hinder not the liberty of conscience.' It is conscience which judges human authority in particular cases, the standards being provided by Scripture, order and the common weal. Even the authority of princes, fathers, priests, tutors, saints and angels is subject to review by conscience.[77] What is important is that in the puritans' stress on conscience their objectives, like those of the Christian humanists, were not primarily spiritual or other-worldly,

---

[75] Samuel Ward was a member of the consistory and supported the judgment of the court; Laurence Chaderton was one of the members assigned to follow up on Edwards' subsequent performance at St Andrew's. Sidney Sussex, MS Ward B, fol. 31; CUL, MS CUR 6.1, it. 39, fol. 22v.   [76] Hunt, pp. 276, 278.

[77] Perkins, *Discourse of conscience*, pp. 34, 26–35; on the relative authority of the clergy, p. 23; *cf.* Arthur Hildersham, BL, Harl. 3230, p. 44. Brilliana Conway quoted Perkins' opinion in her commonplace book (Nottingham University MSS, Box 166), fol. 85.

nor were they aimed at destroying social order. Puritans were in fact carrying on the reformist tradition of humanist commonwealthmen. While William Fulke was charged with having 'diminished the laws of the realm, referring all things to conscience,' his aim was to strengthen social order from the bottom, and to attack authority at the top only insofar as he perceived it to diminish the common weal.[78] Laurence Humphrey concluded his debate with Bishop Sanderson over the relationship between conscience and obedience to authority with the humanist principle that 'It is a matter of conscience to seek or procure the good of the commonwealth . . . 'tis a matter of conscience to obey good or profitable laws *so far as we are persuaded our obedience is profitable.*'[79] Puritan concern was for the establishment of social order on the basis of rightly informed individual conscience.

A Paul's Cross sermon preached in 1616 by Samuel Ward of Ipswich may illustrate the connection most graphically. In *A Balme from Gilead to Recover Conscience,* Ward defined conscience as

in man the principal part of God's image, and that by which he resembleth most the autarchy and self-sufficiency of God, which I grant is proper to his infiniteness, to be content and complete within itself; but under him, and with his leave and love, this faculty makes man self-sufficient and independent of other creatures, like unto those self-moving engines, which have their principle of motion within themselves . . . [Conscience is] God's lieutenant, and under him the principal commander and chief controller of man's life, yea every man's god in that sense that Moses was Aaron's.

Conscience is 'wonderful in the greatness and sovereignty of it,' and Ward exhorted his readers to remember 'Paul's rule, to follow the dictate of conscience, rather than of angel, potentate, or prelate, yea of apostle.'[80] What is significant is that, having given sovereignty to conscience, Ward continued his sermon by informing the consciences of his readers as to the social behavior which they should require of the individual. He warned that obsession with business and accumulation may 'choke the conscience':

Mark, then, you that have mills of business in your heads, whole Westminster-Halls, bourses, exchanges, and East Indies (as I fear many of you have whilst I am speaking to your conscience), that making haste to be rich, overlay your brains with affairs, are so busy in your counting house and books, and that upon this very day [the sabbath], that you never have once in a week, or year, an hour's space to confer with your poor consciences; yea, when did you?[81]

---

[78] Porter, p. 125.
[79] St John's, Cambridge, MS S.20, p. 130; the debate is recounted on pp. 107–30.
[80] Samuel Ward, *A Balme from Gilead*, pp. 17–18, 21, 47.   [81] *Ibid.*, pp. 27–8.

He continued with instructions in family religious duties, proper use of recreation time, honest business practices, and charity as well as fighting against popery and Arminianism and encouraging a preaching ministry.[82] Whatever the radical potential of the doctrine of sovereign conscience, Ward's concern was to edify, rather than undermine, social order, by demanding reformation based on the guidance of informed conscience.

Puritans were convinced that social order required social change. The process of informing and guiding conscience involved practical reform endeavors. While it has been suggested that puritans were concerned with 'the inward peace of a good conscience' even at the expense of social harmony and so concentrated on 'First Table duties,' their endless tracts, treatises and sermons on family government, education, recreation, vocation, economic behavior, poverty, drunkenness, idleness, etc., were aimed precisely at the goal of a well-ordered commonwealth.[83] As Simonds D'Ewes argued, we know our holiness toward God is genuine 'if we make conscience of our duties towards our neighbors, by the careful performance of family duties, relative duties, and calling duties.' He noted that only four of the Ten Commandments relate to our obligations to God; the rest relate to our social callings.[84]

So that they might perform those callings effectively, the godly were obliged to reform the social order. The rule of custom condemned by Erasmus as an upholder of evil, was no less an enemy of his seventeenth-century followers. They charged that the ungodly justify themselves by an appeal to tradition: 'if all other things fail, they say, "these things pleased our ancestors" . . . as if they had wittily concluded the matter [and] with this answer stopped every man's mouth.'[85] William Hull quoted from Erasmus' Adages and cited them frequently in the marginal notes to his sermon criticizing custom as a guide.[86] The preachers argued from the mutability of all nature that 'custom is an idiot, and whosoever dependeth wholly upon him,

[82] Ibid., pp. 49–54, 78–9, 81–2.
[83] J. Sears McGee, The Godly Man in Stuart England: Anglicans, Puritans, and the Two Tables, 1620–1640 (New Haven, 1976), p. 135, and chapter 4, passim. It should hardly be necessary to count the number of pages devoted by puritans not mentioned by McGee to practical Christian behavior in a social context to demonstrate the primacy of their devotion to Second Table duties. One wonders whether McGee began his investigation after 1620 in order to avoid such representative figures of puritan social theory as Perkins, Dod, Cleaver, Ames and Rogers—whose works were in any case reprinted throughout the seventeenth century.
[84] BL, Harl. MS 227, fol. 16.   [85] CUL, Add. MS 6160, p. 21.
[86] Repentance not to be Repented Of, fols. 16v, 63v–64.

without the discourse of reason, will . . . become a slave.'[87] This was one of their bases for accusing rulers of using 'ceremonies and false opinions to keep the people in awe.'[88] Godly magistrates like Henry Sherfield accordingly participated in iconoclasm as easily as in constructing innovative schemes for poor relief: both had the same end, the reformation of society by the casting down of 'ungodliness,' defined in the humanist tradition to include both 'superstition' and poverty. Sherfield was certainly a supporter of established order; but it should not be overlooked that the established order in his Salisbury was a reformist one. When, under the pressure of Laudian clericalism, it ceased to be so, Sherfield, like other godly magistrates, found himself in opposition to authority – and prosecuted by the new establishment for his reformist pains.[89] But this is looking ahead. While the Erasmian consensus prevailed, social reform sponsored by godly magistrates was the order of the day.

This is the context in which the reformation of manners belongs. The puritan magistrates of towns like Salisbury and Exeter and Ipswich took precisely the Christian humanist tack on social reform: it was to be accomplished by appeal to reason through education and to conscience through sermons, and by eliminating problems like poverty that led to disorder. The puritan impetus for educational expansion illumined by John Morgan was directed toward the goal of a biblically literate laity capable of educating their own households in godly behavior and of a preaching clergy able to direct the building of the New Jerusalem.[90] Only when these means fail should force be applied, and then in hopes that an enforced discipline will provide an atmosphere conducive to moral improvement (hence, for example, the incorporation of education and religion into work-

[87] CUL, MS Add. 6160, p. 21; *cf.* fol. 135, deriding 'grey-headed errours.'

[88] Trin. MS R.16.7, fol. 123v. There is inadequate evidence in the MS to identify this author as puritan or non-puritan; 'ceremonies' in this context are not limited to the liturgical. But the commonplace book is heavily Erasmian, and is an indication that Christian humanism was one source for such seventeenth-century critiques of tradition by university-trained divines.

[89] See chapter 5, above, for the Salisbury scheme to support the welfare program with a municipal brewhouse; also Paul Slack, 'Poverty and Politics in Salisbury 1597–1666,' in *Crisis and Order in English Towns*, ed. Peter Clark and Paul Slack (London, 1972), pp. 164–203. *cf.* Collinson, *Religion of Protestants*, pp. 147–50, with Paul Seaver's view of Sherfield as a radical in *The Puritan Lectureships: The Politics of Religious Dissent 1560–1662* (Stanford, 1970), p. 90.

[90] John Morgan, *Godly Learning: Puritan Attitudes towards Reason, Learning, and Education, 1540–1640* (Cambridge, 1986); *cf.* Keith Wrightson and David Levine, *Poverty and Piety in an English Village: Terling, 1525–1700* (New York, 1979), pp. 142–54; and Wrightson, *English Society 1580–1680* (New Brunswick, New Jersey, 1982), pp. 206–21.

houses). The reformation of manners in practice looks very much like the vision of Thomas More for the ideal society.[91]

It was not the intent of most puritans, any more than of Christian humanists, that the resultant social progress should involve revolution or regicide. They were not, as their Anglican opponents charged, enemies of social order. If their emphasis on conscience carried with it the seeds of rebellion, it should not be concluded that they lacked devotion to the good order of the commonwealth. Their hope was for order through reform. On the other hand, it cannot be denied that in their journals, sermons and treatises is found the transmission of a theoretical basis for opposition to king, lords and bishops. It was a theory derived, sometimes unconsciously, from humanists no more revolutionary than most protestants, but it would be taken up in the 1640s by radicals like Christopher Feake, who located 'an enmity against Christ' in aristocracy and monarchy.[92] It would be used by the more moderate puritan settlers of Massachusetts to discourage the establishment of a hereditary aristocracy in their colony of saints.[93] It would inspire Stephen Marshall, in a sermon of 1642, to observe that all too often it is the mighty who

engage all against the Lord, his church and cause. The Lamb's followers and servants are often the poor and off-scouring of the world, when kings and captains, merchants and wise men, being drunk with the wine of the whore's fornications, proceed to make war with the Lamb . . . When the might of the world do oppose the Lord, God's *meanest servants* must not be afraid to oppose the *mighty*.[94]

Shades of Erasmus' eagle and beetle can be discerned in this passage. Nor were puritans always unaware of either the origins or the implications of their reformism. D'Ewes opined that while Erasmus doubtless left some of his more dangerous principles out of his

---

[91] More, *Utopia, passim*; J. C. Davis, *Utopia and the Ideal Society* (Cambridge, 1981), notes that the utopians depended not only on education and good will to form a rational society; they also depended on total discipline and enforcement. *cf.* Wrightson, *English Society*, pp. 168–70, 181–2, 210–19; and Wrightson and Levine, *Poverty and Piety*, pp. 156–63. [92] Quoted by Thomas Edwards, *Gangraena* (1646), pp. 147–8.
[93] When Lords Saye and Sele and Brooke were considering emigration to New England, the official response from the puritan magistracy there was a warning that exalted birth would be no guarantee of political status in their godly commonwealth: should their lordships' progeny not be endowed with virtue and ability to rule, the colonists warned, 'We should expose them rather to reproach and prejudice and the commonwealth with them, than exalt them to honour, if we should call them forth, when God doth not, to public authority.' Quoted by Lawrence Stone in *The Crisis of the Aristocracy* (Oxford, 1965), p. 745.
[94] *Meroz Cursed* (1642), p. 8, quoted by Hunt, p. 296.

published works, a few remained that could be construed to call for 'dethroning kings and princes.' Still, he purchased Erasmus' *Adages* for his children and maintained an obvious respect for the humanists' neo-Stoicism. And while he insisted that 'I have ever maintained obedience to the magistrate in all lawful things,' he added the standard humanist/puritan qualification, 'that the conscience ought not to be enforced.'[95] He was fearful of disorder, but convinced that a truly godly order would be achieved not by demanding absolute obedience to traditional authority, but by informing and exhorting individual conscience to take responsibility for godly behavior. Ultimately, when the lines were drawn between conscience and authority by the requirements of king and bishops, the critique of established authority implicit in the humanist reformism of puritanism would force the hotter sort into a choice which many would have preferred to avoid. However reluctant they had been earlier to admit the implications of their opposition to the Great Chain of Being, those who opted to fight for Parliament found that they had readily available a theoretical basis for their action in the Erasmian challenge to existing authority structures.

The opponents of puritanism had recognized long before the Civil War the radical implications of the Erasmian approach to social order. Anglicans, especially the new Laudian strain, were by the seventeenth century realizing as Catholics had in the sixteenth that Christian humanist social theory was ultimately inimical to the traditional, hierarchical authority structure to which they were committed. Accordingly, they required that conscience 'be directed before hand, by their advice whom God hath set over us.'[96] In so doing, they repudiated what had become by the mid-sixteenth century a reformist consensus among social theorists, in favor of a different approach to social order – a demand for obedience and conformity.

[95] D'Ewes, *Autobiography*, Part II, pp. 64–5, 113; *cf.* Watson, *The Library of Sir Simonds D'Ewes* (1966), pp. 101, 139.
[96] Donne, *Sermons*, vol. 4, p. 223.

7

The conservative reaction: Trent, Lambeth and the demise of the humanist consensus

Erasmus encountered opposition from conservative Catholic theologians as soon as the core documents of his social criticism had become available. The University of Paris waged unremitting warfare on the *Colloquies* and the *Moriae Encomium* in particular; the theologians of Louvain attacked among other works the *Encomium Matrimonii* in 1519; 1527 saw a conference of theologians at Valladolid condemning Erasmian 'heresies'; and in 1533 a vigilant group of theologians raided a Paris bookshop and confiscated Erasmus' *Colloquies*, the *Moriae Encomium*, the *Encomium Matrimonii*, the annotated translation of the New Testament, and even (surely by mistake) the *De Copia verborum*.[1] The heaviest fire was consistently drawn by those works most critical of ecclesiastical authority and most insistent on the availability of the Scriptures to the laity. And the attacks increased dramatically in frequency and virulence after the appearance of Luther on the scene. The hierarchy clearly perceived Erasmus' works as a threat to clerical privilege and authority, to the church's monopoly on learning and interpretation, and ultimately to the unity and order of Christendom.

With the earliest opposition to Erasmus, the Catholic Reformation can be seen transforming itself into the Counter-Reformation.

[1] *The Correspondence of Erasmus*, tr. R. A. B. Mynors and D. F. S. Thomson (Toronto, 1977–), *CWE*, 6 (1982), no. 948 (Erasmus to Petrus Mosellanus, 22 April 1519), pp. 310–18; *Opus Epistolarum Des. Erasmi Roterodami*, ed. P. S. Allen, H. M. Allen and H. W. Garrod (Oxford, 1906–58), no. 1784, vol. 6, pp. 459–61 and no. 2868, vol. 10, pp. 301–3; G. Van Calster, 'La Censure louvaniste du Nouveau Testament et la rédaction de l'index érasmien expurgatoire de 1571,' in *Scrinium Erasmianum*, ed. J. J. Coppens (Leiden, 1969), vol. II, pp. 379–436; Marcel Bataillon, *Érasme et l'Espagne* (Paris, 1937), pp. 264–6. On the Valladolid conference, see Bataillon, pp. 309–35.

The fear of a critical and potentially disobedient laity drew from the threatened hierarchy a reaction against innovation, against lay initiative, against any new developments which could detract from the authority vested in the clerical estate. Christian humanists had gone too far in their criticism; church control of Christian society was perceptibly weakening, and the response of the hierarchy was to repress those humanist ideas thought to be potentially subversive, to demand new conformity and obedience to constituted authority, and to give official sanction to the revival of both Thomistic theology and its counterpart in social theory, the Great Chain of Being.

The Thomists of the sixteenth century, led by Francisco de Vitoria, Fernando Vasquez, Domingo de Soto and (in the next generation) the Jesuits Robert Bellarmine, Luis de Molina and Francisco Suarez, aimed their attack at the two aspects of Erasmian humanism which most threatened the authority of the ecclesiastical hierarchy: its demand for accurate, vernacular translations of the Greek and Hebrew Scriptures, and its ideal of a religiously educated laity. The first gave rise to the Lutheran doctrine of *sola scriptura*, the second to the protestant views of the church as *congregatio fidelium* and of the priesthood of all believers.[2] Both were obvious affronts to Roman clericalism and tradition; both pointed logically to a social order dominated by the godly laity, and to a political order in which, as Suarez warned, 'the power to make laws depends on the faith or morals of the prince.'[3] In such an order, the ecclesiastical establishment would be constantly subject to the reforming enthusiasm of lay householders, and monarchy would be in perpetual dread of the sort of revolutionary ideology developed by French Huguenots in the sixteenth century and English Parliamentarians in the seventeenth.

Recognizing this potential in Christian humanism, the defenders of orthodoxy returned to the *via antiqua* in defense of tradition. St Thomas' incorporation of Aristotelian natural hierarchy into Roman Christianity was reaffirmed, providing a philosophical basis for the restoration of nobility to 'their ancient honours, dignities and privileges' (including special preferment to the church) and of the commons to the 'old simplicity' from which heresy had lured

---

[2] Quentin Skinner, *The Foundations of Modern Political Thought* (Cambridge, 1978), vol. 2, pp. 135–73.   [3] *Ibid.*, p. 140.

them.[4] Even more important, the natural mediatory position of the clerical hierarchy in the Thomistic scheme allowed the Jesuits to demand absolute, unquestioning obedience to the papal establishment. 'To be right in everything,' Ignatius Loyola told his followers, 'we ought always to hold that the white which I see, is black, if the Hierarchical Church so decides it.'[5] Catholic universities in the sixteenth century, especially those dominated by Dominicans and Jesuits, became centers of militant scholasticism in which the humanist language of persuasion and analysis was replaced by Thomistic definitions and a systematic conceptual exactitude altogether absent from the writings of Catholic humanists.[6] These universities produced such conservative crusaders as Robert Bellarmine, who defended the Vulgate against Erasmus' 'manifest lying', and later in the century the English Jesuit Robert Parsons, who charged that 'wheresoever Erasmus did but point with his finger, Luther rushed upon it; where Erasmus did but doubt, Luther affirmed.'[7]

At the Council of Trent (1545–63) the Neo-scholastic campaign against Erasmus reached its culmination. Assembled in direct response to the spread of protestant heresy, the cardinals at Trent were immediately confronted with the opposition of Thomistic orthodoxy to humanist reformism and forced to decide between the two. Compromise was impossible, as the advocates of a humanist Catholic, rather than Counter-, Reformation soon discovered. Led by Pole, Contarini, Valdes and Morone, their call for reformation through interior regeneration and the spread of biblical understanding to the laity was decried by their Jesuit and Dominican adversaries as Lutheran. The lines were clearly drawn between these *spirituali* and the *zelanti* (led by Carafa), and the fact of the Reformation erased

[4] Robert Parsons, *Memorial for the Reformation of England* (n.p., 1690), p. 220; *cf.* pp. 220–4. Parsons' treatise was written in Seville in 1596 and is analyzed by T. H. Clancy, 'Notes on Parsons's "Memorial",' *Recusant History*, 5 (1959), 17–34, and by J. J. Scarisbrick, 'Robert Parsons's Plans for the "true" Reformation of England,' in *Historical Perspectives: Studies in English Thought and Society in honour of J. H. Plumb*, ed. Neil McKendrick (London 1974), pp. 19–42. See also Clancy's *Papist Pamphleteers* (Chicago, 1964).
[5] *The Spiritual Exercises*, tr. Elder Mullan (St Louis, 1978), Part II, Rule 13, p. 234.
[6] In all fairness, the protestant scholasticism which blossomed in the seventeenth century was also committed to rigid definition and philosophical systematization, but in protestant universities the new scholastics, protestant and Catholic, were injected into the old humanist curriculum rather than used to replace humanist and expurgated classical authors. See chapter 3, above.
[7] Bellarmine, *De Verbo Dei*, in *Opera Omnia*, ed. Justin Fèvre, 12 vols (Paris, 1870–4), vol. 1, pp. 109–10, *cf.* pp. 138–9; Parsons' *A Treatise of Three Conversions of England* ([St Omer], 1604), Part III, pp. 307–8.

any middle ground between the two.[8] The question before the cardinals was whether to continue to allow the sort of internal criticism which in the *zelanti*'s view had given rise to the Reformation, or whether to opt for the new, militant approach of Carafa and the Roman Inquisition and repress all dissension. In view of the apparent failure of the moderate approach recommended by Pole and Contarini to bring protestants back into the fold, the decision reached by the majority at Trent was to enforce orthodoxy by actively repressing heresy, to demand conformity to narrowly defined dogma, and in the process to repudiate Erasmian humanism in no uncertain terms.

Accordingly, the Council of Trent located truth both in the 'written books and in the unwritten traditions' of the Church, and in order to 'check unbridled spirits' directed Christians to rely not on their own judgments of the Scriptures, but on the understanding mediated by the 'holy mother church, to whom it belongs to judge of their true sense and interpretation.'[9] Sir Edwin Sandys, for all his virulent anti-popery, was thus by no means wide of the mark when he observed to the 1599 Parliament that the Roman church required each individual to 'submit his own reason to the Church's authority.'[10] As for the role of the Scriptures in social reformation, the Council decreed the Vulgate to be the only admissible translation, and only clerical instruction in its meaning was to be allowed. At the fourth session of the Council (1546), de Soto condemned the individual lay Bible-reading enjoined by Christian humanists as 'a heretical individualism.'[11] The instruction which was to replace it would combat that heresy with precisely defined Thomistic orthodoxy and replace its incipient individualism with strict hierarchical control.

The most explicit Tridentine repudiation of Erasmus came when the Index of Prohibited Books was compiled by Pope Paul IV in 1559. Erasmus was here included in the highest category of heterodoxy, the entire corpus of his writings being wholly condemned. And although the 1564 Tridentine Index exempted some of his educational works from this blanket censure, Pope Sextus V's 1590 Index reverted to the 1559 ruling and again banned all of his works. Such was the Counter-Reformation concern for conformity

---

[8] Dermot Fenlon, *Heresy and Obedience in Tridentine Italy: Cardinal Pole and the Counter Reformation* (Cambridge, 1972), pp. 100–60 *et passim*.
[9] *Canons and Decrees of the Council of Trent*, ed. H. J. Schroeder (St Louis, 1941), pp. 17, 18–19.
[10] Quoted by Marc Schwarz, 'Lay Anglicanism and the Crisis of the English Church in the Early Seventeenth Century,' *Albion*, 14 (1982), 1–19, p. 6.
[11] *Canons and Decrees*, p. 18; Skinner, p. 147.

to orthodox doctrinal definitions that even such innocuous educational treatises as *De copia* and the orthodox production of Erasmus' youth, *De contemptu mundi*, were included.[12] The apparent fear was that by admitting some of the humanist's works to be legitimate fare, the church might inadvertently mislead the literate layman into reading works critical of authority and tradition.

The Tridentine decrees and Indices communicate to modern readers a distinct impression of the desperation felt by the cardinals in the face of first the Lutheran and then the Calvinist threats. The Counter-Reformation was dogmatic, repressive, and uncompromising in its demands for strict formulations and absolute obedience to authority because it saw both religious and political disunity and social chaos as the inevitable results of diversity and tolerance of criticism. At the level of popular culture, this conviction is apparent in the methods used to carry out the intentions of the Council: all were aimed at increasing ecclesiastical control over all aspects of life, occasionally in the face of lay resistance, but generally without significant compromise. Late medieval confessional summas were resurrected and used as instruments of social control, and the religious confraternities which drew the most zealous lay people were established under clerical auspices to enforce Counter-Reformation orthodoxy.[13] When the confraternities got out of line, as happened occasionally in Spain and in Venice, particularly in the context of welfare administration, clerical authorities responded immediately by re-affirming the official line promulgated at Trent. One historian has described Spanish confraternities as 'a thorn in the side of ecclesiastical authorities,' whose drive to 'control their growth and eliminate some of their secular activities' was largely successful.[14] On another front, the educational institutions which had

---

[12] F. H. Reusch, *Der Index der verboten Bücher* (Bonn, 1883–5), vol. 1, pp. 347–55; *Die Indices librorum prohibitorum der sechzehnten Jahrhunderts* (Tubingen, 1886), pp. 183, 259, 477.

[13] Thomas N. Tentler, 'The Summa for Confessors as an Instrument of Social Control,' in *The Pursuit of Holiness in Late Medieval and Renaissance Religion*, ed. Charles Trinkaus and Heiko A. Oberman (Leiden, 1974), pp. 103–26. Tentler has defended his use of the term 'social control' against the objections of Leonard Boyle (*Pursuit of Holiness*, pp. 126–30, 134–7). John Bossy's review, 'Holiness and Society,' *P&P*, 75 (1977), 119–37, pp. 127–8, argues that the primary social function of confession was rather 'to restore damaged relations between the sinner and others,' and that social control was of secondary importance. Tentler's argument may be somewhat overstated, but it is a substantial and thought-provoking elaboration of the thesis briefly argued by Christopher Hill in 'Protestantism and the Rise of Capitalism,' in *Essays in the Economic and Social History of Tudor and Stuart England in honour of R. H. Tawney*, ed. F. J. Fisher (Cambridge, 1961), 15–39, p. 27.

[14] Linda Martz, *Poverty and Welfare in Hapsburg Spain* (Cambridge, 1983), p. 48.

burgeoned in Catholic as in protestant countries during the Renaissance were increasingly either brought under church control or abolished, and in either case humanist elements in the curriculum were suppressed as threats to tradition and authority. And, as we shall see, Erasmian ideas about the family and humanist plans for poor relief were either suppressed or significantly modified to meet the regulative aims of Trent.

It is, of course, possible to overdraw the distinction between humanist and later sixteenth-century Catholic social thought. It will be suggested below that post-Tridentine Catholics – lay people in particular – were by no means unaffected by their humanist heritage as they tackled the social problems which faced early modern Europeans of all persuasions. The official line of the victorious cardinals and the actual practice of post-Tridentine Catholics were not always identical, and particularly in the area of welfare reform, the practicality of humanist proposals was not overlooked even by the opponents of Erasmus and Vives. But the official line is clear enough. However wary we ought to be of arbitrary periodization, the fact remains that the Church at Trent deliberately and formally rejected the Christian humanist heritage in its blanket condemnation of the prince of humanists, and that this institutional move reflected a profound intellectual shift which would necessarily effect modifications of Catholic social reform programs from the later sixteenth century onwards. In its banning of Erasmus' works, the Church recognized fully that the humanist approach to reform by appeal to individual conscience was a risky business at best for an institution whose claim to authority had been severely undermined by Luther's revolution. The Council of Trent thus presents an unavoidable watershed in the history of Catholic social thought in the early modern period. The Council in itself was not an innovator: Domingo de Soto was occupying himself in opposing Vivesian welfare reforms in Spain decades before the Council offered him a forum for his criticism of humanism. But it was during the course of the Council that the Roman hierarchy adopted and consolidated the conservatism represented earlier by the theologians of Paris and Louvain, Valladolid and Salamanca, and defined it as orthodox. The fathers at Trent firmly and explicitly departed from the humanist consensus which had earlier united protestants and Catholics on a myriad of social issues, and demanded that the orthodox follow suit. Whatever the pitfalls of periodization, where anomalies congregate an attempt at description and explanation is in order.

One illustration of the highly selective survival of humanism in the hostile environment of Catholic Europe after Trent is provided by shifts in pedagogy and curricula in Counter-Reformation colleges. Numerous and detailed studies of French urban *collèges*, established by townsmen from 1500 on humanist lines and taken over by bishops or Jesuits in the early seventeenth century, suggest that the clergy's interest in humanistic education was not so great as their commitment to the propagation of Tridentine orthodoxy and ecclesiastical authority, and that this commitment in fact shaped an approach to education to which Erasmus would have taken great exception. While many elements of the humanist curricula of the early sixteenth century remained, modifications in the objectives and the methods of the *collèges* reflect the authoritarianism of Trent and may serve as an introductory glimpse into the effects of Tridentine conservatism on the humanist vision of social order.

The Tridentine clergy apparently waged constant and ultimately successful battles with French aldermen in the second half of the sixteenth century, over whether the aim of education was the proliferation of clergy or the provision of opportunity for children of the poor to attain the status of *gens de biens* and for children of substance to learn to serve the commonwealth in secular callings as good citizens. A recent study of the 'geography of humanism' shows that Latin schools flourished in sixteenth-century parlementary and commercial towns like Amiens, where they had been founded for the sons of magistrates and merchants to be trained as good governors in the classical tradition and for gifted sons of the poor to learn the values of productive citizenship. It was in these same towns that *bourgeois* opposition to the Jesuits in the seventeenth century was virulent, as the followers of Loyola seized control of the often financially troubled institutions and attempted to replace much of the literary portion of the curricula with scholastic theology and philosophy.[15] By the 1620s, when either bishops or Jesuits had been largely successful in seizing control of the *collèges*, parents were complaining that graduates of the institutions looked down on the mercantile life and had learned nothing useful to the community.[16]

---

[15] George Huppert, 'The Social Function of Classical Education in Renaissance France,' (unpublished paper read at the Sixteenth-Century Studies Conference, 25 October 1980) has discussed the intervention of both the secular clergy and Jesuits in the *collèges*, and especially in the Amiens Collège de la Ville. On methods of Jesuit takeover, see Pierre Delattre, *Les Établissements des jésuites en France depuis quatre siècles* (Enghien, 1949), vol. 1, ix, and entries for (e.g.) Amiens, Bordeaux.

[16] François de Dainville, *L'éducation des jésuites (XVIe–XVIIIe siècles)* (Paris, 1978), pp. 25, 36.

Education for virtuous participation in forum and market-place had given way to education for the cloister, leading English commentators like Sandys to conclude that the Roman church had returned to her historic practice of enclosing 'all learning within the walls of their clergy, setting forth Lady Ignorance for a great saint to the laity.'[17] His conclusion is exaggerated, perhaps, but not groundless.

Despite their reputation for having a primary commitment to education, moreover, sixteenth- and early seventeenth-century Jesuits seem in fact not to have been terribly interested in teaching. Even Jesuit historians admit that the educational process in the *collèges* was subordinated by most of the resident clergy to other activities, particularly preaching and missionary efforts in the countryside.[18] Of the twenty-five Jesuits in residence in the Collège Sainte-Marie at Aire-sur-la-Lys in 1636, only six were occupied with teaching.[19] Delattre remarks that it was not unusual for the entire teaching enterprise in a *collège* of 1400 to 1600 students to depend on only one prefect of studies and six regents. This was the case at Amiens in 1629, and Dijon provides a similar case; the Bordeaux Collège de la Madeleine was fortunate to have thirteen professors for 1,200 students in 1610.[20] Dainville found grammar classes of 200 students per master typical in the sixteenth century.[21] Clearly there was ample manpower in the Society sufficiently unencumbered by teaching duties to pursue the political and propagandistic efforts on behalf of papal authority to which Loyola had been primarily committed.

Finally, the curricula of Jesuit and episcopal *collèges* reveal both the survival of a humanist corpus and the ravages inflicted by Trent in the name of orthodoxy and order. Much of the classical literature prescribed by the humanists remained in the grammar and rhetoric courses, but approved versions of Cicero, Quintilian, Virgil and Horace were read only alongside Christian 'explanations' of them; Ovid was read only in expurgated versions; Terence was officially expelled from the *collèges* by an absolute decree in 1575; and masters found it difficult to restrain students tantalized by the blank spaces in their texts of Lucretius from seeking uncensored editions.[22] Again, even Jesuit historians of education bear witness to the extensive censorship of classical as well as contemporary texts which in some cases all but eliminated poetry from the study of humane letters altogether in the sixteenth century.[23] The late sixteenth-century

[17] Quoted by Schwarz, p. 6.   [18] Delattre, vol. I, p. viii.   [19] *Ibid.*, vol. 1, p. 33.
[20] *Ibid.*, vol. 1, pp. viii, 734–51 (Bordeaux).
[21] Dainville, p. 175.   [22] *Ibid.*, pp. 169, 180–83.   [23] *Ibid.*, p. 170.

214	CHRISTIAN HUMANISM AND THE PURITAN SOCIAL ORDER

Toulousan library inventories which have been examined by Dainville tell much the same story: they include approved texts of Cicero, Quintilian, Virgil, Ovid and Horace, but never Terence or Plautus. The only Christian humanist works are Erasmus' *De copia* and *De conscribendis epistolis*; Aristotle is much in evidence but Plato is obviously suspect; and only Latin Bibles are found.[24]

Clearly the Jesuits were not so dogmatically philistine as those Louvain theologians who in 1519 had condemned 'classical languages and the humanities, repeating that these are the springs from which heresies flow.'[25] But they were sufficiently devoted to orthodoxy and ecclesiastical authority to exercise the sort of heavy-handed censorship and approval of corrupt texts which Erasmus would have found reprehensible and which seems not to have happened in English education. The issue here, of course, was the old debate about Athens and Jerusalem, and it was a debate of which Erasmus had been as aware as his detractors were. But whereas Erasmus had acknowledged the problem but opted for Athens uncensored as an appropriate foundation for the teaching of Christian truth, the Jesuits found the implications of such free inquiry ominous. Preserving what they felt was safe in the pagan corpus edited by Erasmus and his colleagues, they none the less irretrievably compromised their humanism by sacrificing the principle of exegesis based on complete, unexpurgated, and critically edited texts in favor of clerical censorship. Not only in the case of the Bible, where retention of the Vulgate was an obvious rejection of humanist textual advance in favor of the authority of tradition, but also in the case of classical authors who might too easily corrupt the young conscience not adequately submissive to constituted authority, the Jesuits adopted the role of selectors and mediators of truth. Tridentine Catholics seem to have had less trust of the individual student's informed moral judgment than even those protestants who held total depravity to be an article of faith. Ironically, it was the latter who carried on the humanist tradition of presenting entire texts – pagan and Christian – with all of their problems, to the judgment of the individual. As for Erasmus' own works, even if they had not been included in the Index, the Jesuits' commitment to Tridentine positions on the merits of celibacy, of pilgrimages, of the veneration of images, of indulgences, etc. would have resulted in their purging most of his works from the curricula of the *collèges*.

It is surely not to be expected that Catholics trained in such a tra-

[24] *Ibid.*, pp. 270–4.   [25] *CWE*, 6, p. 313 (Erasmus to Petrus Mosellanus).

dition would adopt a Christian humanist approach to the social order without significant modification. We must expect, then, that Trent as watershed must substantially qualify, if not entirely negate, our stress on the continuity of Erasmian humanism as a shaper of social thought in early modern Europe.

In England, the response of humanists to such Counter-Reformation tendencies was varied. The greatest of English humanists, Sir Thomas More, had of course been faced with his decision long before the Council of Trent, and his choice was a reluctant but clear repudiation of his humanism. It has been suggested that as early as 1516 More had begun to question the possibility of joining the *philosophia Christi* with public life; certainly between the publication in that year of *Utopia* and the 1523 *Responsio ad Lutherum*, More retreated from his humanist criticism of church and society into a reactionary stance rooted in fear of the social and political anarchy which could result from over-zealous reformism.[26] The Lutheran Reformation was for More, as for the majority of Tridentine cardinals, sufficient reason to repudiate humanism, with its 'ideal of an enlightened society of earnest saints on earth' in favor of 'the safety of a society so regulated by earnest saints as to include nobody but themselves.'[27] It was in the light of growing heresy that More said he would burn *Utopia* rather than see it translated into English. Members of the More circle, however, did not necessarily follow in the martyr's footsteps, and the diversity of their responses was mirrored by that of the *spirituali* at Trent. Some were sufficiently committed to the biblical reformation of church and society to ally themselves with protestantism rather than remain loyal to an increasingly Neo-scholastic, conformist Catholicism. More's daughter Margaret may be an early example of this group, along with those of the commonwealth men who did not take the Oath of Supremacy simply for con-

[26] D. B. Fenlon, 'England and Europe: *Utopia* and its Aftermath,' *TRHS*, 5th ser., 25 (1975), 115–35, and especially pp. 124–8, 133; 'The Counter Reformation and the Realisation of Utopia,' *Historical Studies: Papers Read at the Ninth Conference of Irish Historians*, ed. J. Barry (Dublin, 1973); *Heresy and Obedience*, p. 41. On More's conservatism, see Alastair Fox, *Thomas More: History and Providence* (Oxford, 1982) and G. R. Elton, 'The real Thomas More?', *Studies* (Cambridge, 1983), but *cf.* Brendan Bradshaw, 'The Controversial Sir Thomas More', *JEH*, 36 (1985), 535–69.

[27] William A. Clebsch, *England's Earliest Protestants* (New Haven, 1964), p. 301, commenting on More's *Apology* (against St Germain); *cf.* Bradshaw, pp. 566ff, who believes that More repudiated protestantism in order to maintain Erasmus' stand on free will. Bradshaw may be right as far as he goes, but there is no evidence that More maintained other Erasmian positions after the Reformation, and in the area of social criticism, the evidence – e.g., his statement about burning *Utopia* – tends to the opposite conclusion.

venience.[28] Others did, like More, give their lives for the authority of the Roman church, although the implications of Counter-Reformation for Christian humanism may not have been as apparent to them as it was to More.[29] Still others took the Oath but lived as recusants or fled to the continent. Of these, many were confronted with the choice between maintaining their humanism and risking the wrath of Tridentine conservatives or conforming to the anti-Erasmian stance of the church in order to restore the unity of Christendom. Pole is an example of those who maintained a compromise between loyalty to Rome and Christian humanism as long as possible but finally succumbed to pressure and abandoned their reformist middle ground to align themselves with Tridentine orthodoxy.[30] Richard Smith, who became a professor of theology at Douai, similarly reneged on his humanism in favor of conformity. Other members of the More circle seem to have arrived more gradually at the realization that the social and religious reforms of Christian humanism would have to be set aside if loyalty to Rome were to be maintained.[31]

But after the generation of John Harpsfield, George Etherige, John Seton and Thomas Watson, English Catholics no longer had a choice to make. After Trent, full-blown Christian humanism was simply no longer an option; Erasmus had virtually disappeared from the orthodox Catholic scene.[32] Elizabethan recusant scholarship presents us with a completely different set of concerns from Erasmus' or Whitforde's or Pole's. The themes being argued by Nicholas Sander, Thomas Stapleton, Edmund Campion and Robert Parsons are reformation for the clergy, conformity for the laity, and restoration to Rome for England.[33] No longer is there an insistence

[28] James Kelsey McConica, *English Humanists and Reformation Politics* (Oxford, 1965), p. 264, points out that Margaret More Roper not only took the oath, but also attempted to get the protestant Roger Ascham to tutor her children. Among continental humanists who opted for protestantism and maintained their humanism were Ochino and Vermigli, who embarrassed their patron, Pole, and incidentally fed the anti-humanist fires of Trent by their choice (Fenlon, *Heresy and Obedience*, pp. 45, 50–1).

[29] By 1543, John More, William Roper, William Daunce and other members of the More household had formed the 'Plot of the Prebendaries' against Cranmer.

[30] Fenlon, *Heresy and Obedience*, pp. 174–95, discusses Pole's reluctant acquiescence in the face of a widening theological gulf between protestantism and Catholicism during the course of the Council. His acceptance of the decrees Fenlon describes as an act of obedience rather than conviction (p. 208).

[31] McConica, pp. 266–78, 285–92.

[32] Thomas Stapleton's account of More's life makes no mention of More's Erasmianism, in line with the orthodox condemnation of Erasmus.

[33] The reforming decrees of the twenty-second session of the Council of Trent (1562) proscribed luxury, feasting, dancing, gambling, sports and other 'crimes and secular pursuits' for the clergy only (*Canons and Decrees*, p. 153).

on a lay reformation of manners for the advancement of the commonwealth; the humanist exaltation of the *vita activa* has given way to a new stress on contemplative virtues; the ideal of the godly living out the gospel in the market-place under the guidance of informed conscience has been replaced with an insistence on lay obedience to clerical instruction. The works of devotion most popular among Elizabethan English Catholics– Parsons' *Christian Directory*, Southwell's *Short Rule of a Good Life*, Loarte's *Exercise of a Christian Life*, and Lascelle's *Little Way How to Heare Masse* – all enjoin a regularity of sacramental practice which necessitated a resident chaplain. They foster a notion of the godly life as one of intense, directed, contemplative spirituality for the educated, and one of correct, rather mechanical performance of rituals and rote prayers for the less sophisticated, but all under the strict oversight of a clergyman.[34] The remedy prescribed at Trent for the ills of Christendom was not the reformism of Christian humanists, but the conformism of the *zelanti*. Clerical abuses were to be purged, under strict episcopal supervision; the laity were enjoined not to analyze and criticize, but to obey. In the humanist scheme, the godly layman was responsible for social diagnosis as well as critical self-examination. The objective of the Counter-Reformation was to restore the clerical estate to a position of moral superiority and absolute authority, and society properly regulated was portrayed as society clerically dominated.

Decades of theological controversy had taken their toll on the social vision of Roman Catholicism. While social theory was hardly the main focus of the Council of Trent, the social implications of Christian humanism were no more immune from censure than were its religious and theological proposals. To the extent that elements of the humanist social critique were adaptable to the objectives of the Counter-Reformation, they would be retained– the clearest case being that of welfare reform. This was a highly selective retention, however. Rejection of the underpinning of Erasmian reformism is much more noticeable, both in the Tridentine decrees and in the social ideology of Counter-Reformation Catholics. In a religious society, religious conservatism does not easily co-exist with social reformism; in the interests of self-preservation, sixteenth-century Catholicism necessarily rejected the preponderance of Erasmian social theory as part and parcel of humanist anticlericalism.

That Erasmian social theory was more than an incidental casualty

[34] Christopher Haigh, 'From Monopoly to Minority: Catholicism in Early Modern England,' *TRHS*, 5th ser., 31 (1981), 129–48, p. 138; J. C. H. Aveling, 'Catholic Households in Yorkshire, 1580–1603,' *Northern History*, 16 (1980), 85–101, esp. p. 96.

of the Counter-Reformation is perhaps nowhere more apparent than in the anti-humanist social vision of the Elizabethan Jesuit Robert Parsons. Parsons' *Memorial for the Reformation of England* (1596) is a proposal for the re-structuring of English society after its projected return to the true faith (presumably by Spanish arms). It is in a sense a vision of a Utopia, but a very different one from that envisaged by More and approved by Erasmus, for its overriding feature is clerical domination. The monastic ideal is there re-affirmed, and monastic lands are restored in Parsons' Utopia; a clerical Council of Reform is to oversee legal reform (including the re-institution of canon law) and social welfare; and the Roman office of censor is to be revived and assigned not to the reforming lay magistrate, as in Vives' scheme, but to the clergy.[35] The censors, moreover, are to concern themselves less with the behavior of the commons (the main responsibility of Vives' censors) than with their doctrinal conformity. Collegiate instruction is to be abolished, since it is less susceptible to centralized oversight than are university lectures, and grammar schools, universities and the Inns of Court are all to be subject to frequent visitations by bishops and clerical commissioners to insure their orthodoxy.[36] A national Synod is to enforce the decrees of Trent, and the council of Reform is to be succeeded by an English Inquisition. As his critics aptly charged, Parsons' desire was to establish 'an *ecclesiastical* Utopia'.[37] His social ideal was blatantly clericalist and theocratic. Social order was to be insured by deference to a divinely ordained hierarchy rather than by individual moral reformation guided by personal confrontations with the demands of Scripture. The ultimate aim of Parsons' social order was a conformity to dogmatic orthodoxy; accordingly, the primary emphasis in his instructions to householders, teachers and magistrates is on obedience to constituted authority. Parsons is typical of the post-Tridentine Catholic clergy in that when he addressed social issues at all, his overriding concern was with ecclesiastical control.

The Counter-Reformation's repudiation of Christian humanist social theory left protestants to carry on the Erasmian vision of

[35] Parsons, *Memorial*, pp. 89–90; Scarisbrick, *passim*.   [36] Scarisbrick, pp. 25–6.
[37] Parsons, *Memorial*, pp. 220–4, 256–7; A. Copley, *An answere to a letter of a Jesuited gentleman* (1601), cited in Scarisbrick, p. 34 (emphasis mine); Scarisbrick, p. 39. Scarisbrick notes the similarity of Parsons' to Genevan government by elders; however, the puritan/humanist regard for individual conscience and their demands for social reformation through lay education, religious instruction and discipline in families, and the restructuring of secular institutions are noticeably absent.

social change, and in England, protestants of all liturgical persuasions took up the cause with zeal during the sixteenth and early seventeenth centuries. Accordingly, in the foregoing three chapters the opinions of Elizabethan and Jacobean conformists have frequently been cited along with those of puritans in support of the thesis of a protestant consensus on the nature of the social order which was drawn from Christian humanism. But the English hierarchy was no less aware than the Tridentine of the potential dangers of the reformist position, and when those dangers began to be actualized in the closing decades of the sixteenth century, the conformist clergy began to retreat from humanist social theory in the same direction as their Catholic counterparts had taken at Trent. Elizabethan and early Stuart puritanism posed for the English hierarchy a similar threat to that of Lutheranism for Catholics. It was a threat which had social and political overtones not to be ignored by supporters of the established order – the danger posed by autonomous individual conscience to the authority vested in clerical hierarchy. The elevation of biblically informed conscience and the critique of the Great Chain of Being which puritans had adopted from Christian humanism presented the same threat to the protestant as to the Catholic hierarchy, and called forth from them a similar revival of Aristotelian doctrines of natural hierarchy and a parallel demand for obedience and conformity. It is not altogether surprising that when the Jesuit Martin Becanus sought English support for his opposition to the popular availability of the vernacular Scriptures, he found it in Richard Hooker's argument for clerical authority over personal conviction:

Yea, as a Protestant of great name, well acquainted with the proceedings of their churches, complains, 'This conceit hath made thousands so headstrong, even in gross and palpable errors, that a man whose capacity will scarce serve him to utter five words in a sensible manner blusheth not in any doubt concerning matter of Scripture to think his own bare *Yea* as good as the *Nay* of all the wise, grave, and learned judgments that are in the whole world, which indolency must be repressed, or it will be the bane of the Christian religion.' Thus he.[38]

In fact, the demise of the Great Chain of Being had all along implied a decrease in clerical authority. While humanists and puritans saw the role of the clergy in guiding men to a knowledge of God and right behavior as important, they agreed that the priest

[38] Martinus Becanus, *A Treatise of the Judge of Controversies*, tr. W. W[right] ([St Omer], 1619), Preface, *et passim*.

does not have 'a sovereign power of making laws, but a power of giving judgment of controversies' according to Scripture. Clerical judgment, Perkins said, does not 'constrain conscience ... [since] the sovereign power of binding and loosing is not belonging to any creature, but is proper to Christ... As for the power of the Church, it is nothing but a ministry of service.'[39] Perkins was here defining the difference between protestant and Catholic casuistry, but he had witnessed the parallel controversy between presbyterians and bishops within the English church, and the implications of his arguments were not lost on his puritan readers in the 1590s.

In the reformist tradition of individual moral involvement, the cleric was a guide, not a spiritual magistrate, a functionary, not an intermediary. The common weal was assured when each person became his own casuist. It was when they realized that this theoretical limitation of the authority of the clerical hierarchy was combined with searching scrutiny and criticism of the behavior of bishops as well as princes, that elements of the English protestant hierarchy finally began to turn away from reformist social ideology. The lines were drawn when the puritan William Tay compared bishops whose orders failed to meet the requirements of Scripture and conscience with the apostates of Jude's epistle who preferred 'their political, carnal, human jurisdiction and hierarchy before the spiritual and heavenly ordinance of the Lord.'[40] Convinced that their ecclesiastical 'jurisdiction and hierarchy' were in fact the only possible guarantee of social order, and seeing the reformist disdain for that hierarchy as evidence of the imminent onset of social chaos, Anglican conformists opted as their Tridentine counterparts had to seek order through conformity and obedience, if necessary even at the expense of lay moral reformation.

It is true that the lines were not as clearly drawn in Elizabethan England as they had been at Trent. Royal headship of the church complicated the hierarchical arrangement of cleric over prince to which the Counter-Reformation was dedicated; and the shared theology of Anglicans and puritans prevented many of the more extreme lengths to which Catholics had been willing to go to restore clericalism. The comparison is a relative one. There were Anglican attempts to strengthen clericalism, most notably in the 1604 canons, but even earlier in Whitgift's efforts to strengthen the ju-

[39] William Perkins, *A Discourse of Conscience*, ed. T. F. Merrill in *William Perkins: His Pioneer Works on Casuistry* (The Hague, 1966), p. 23.
[40] *Minute Book of the Dedham Classis, 1582–1589*, in *The Presbyterian Movement in the Reign of Queen Elizabeth*, ed. R. G. Usher (1905), pp. 86–7.

dicial arm of the church by a resort to High Commission and his purging of the Canterbury diocesan commission of its lay members.[41] But these lacked the ferocity of the Counter-Reformation orders and methods of enforcement, partly due to the theological unity of puritans and conformists at that point on the issues of predestination and free will.[42] Consensus if possible, compromise if necessary, were the order of the day in the Jacobean church, and departures from the order were relatively few.

Still, the discrepancies which did develop between Anglican and puritan approaches to and involvement with social reform in the seventeenth century must not be ignored in our acceptance of relative Jacobean stability and our pursuit of the theme of intellectual continuity. Such data as striking differences in the subject matter of seventeenth-century Anglican and puritan publications demand an explanation: if the humanist consensus continued in full force at the turn of the century, why do the published works of conformists evince relatively little concern with such issues as family government and the use of wealth[43] – issues which had occupied Erasmus and continued to obsess puritans? By the 1630s, moreover, divergence of Anglican and puritan views of the social order had become more than a matter of Anglican omission. Jacobean Anglicans for the most part seem not to have disagreed with reigning protestant opinion about the need to train and discipline the poor, for instance, or about the household as a spiritual unit; they simply devoted less attention to these subjects in their published sermons than puritans did, and perhaps progressively less attention to them as their concern with clerical authority and the problem of nonconformity increased. But in the era of Laud's ascendancy, substantial conformist departures from the time-honored humanist understanding of social order are impossible for the historian to avoid.

---

[41] Peter Clark, *English Provincial Society* (Hassocks, Sussex, 1977), pp. 182–183.

[42] Nicholas Tyacke has argued that Calvinism 'helped to reconcile the differences' between Anglicans and puritans until the 1620s; only then did many (although by no means all) Anglicans embrace Arminianism and thereby add a basic theological issue to the puritans' grievances against them: 'puritanism, Arminianism and Counter-Revolution,' in *The Origins of the English Civil War*, ed. Conrad Russell (London, 1973), pp. 121, 119–43; Tyacke, 'Arminianism in England, in Religion and Politics, 1604–1640' (unpublished D.Phil thesis, University of Oxford, 1968). For a recent critique of Tyacke's view, see Peter White, 'The Rise of Arminianism Reconsidered,' *P&P*, 101 (1983), 34–54.

[43] Joseph Hall seems to have been the only bishop of this period to have dealt at length with these subjects and other ethical issues, in, for example, his *Salomons Divine Arts* (1609).

The explanation must lie in the fact that despite the restraint offered by theological cohesion, episcopal reaction to puritanism first opened and then widened the gap between conformist and puritan social ideology. If Anglican rejection of Erasmianism was more selective than that of the cardinals at Trent, with Anglicans retaining, for instance, humanist scholarly and exegetical innovations, some departure from the social thought of Christian humanism was mandated by episcopal fear of disorder arising from dissent and the growing conviction of the established hierarchy that order must be imposed from above. In other words, the shifts away from humanist reformism which begin to emerge in Anglican approaches to social problems in the early Stuart period can best be explained by acknowledging those common elements in Tridentine Catholicism and clericalist Anglicanism which most actively militated against the earlier understanding of social order. In light of this suggestion, it is not so surprising that the English bishops' drive for order and control drew many in the 1630s perilously close to arguing the necessity of priestly mediation between the individual and God, the validity of a life of religious retirement from the world, and the social and political danger of widespread lay Bible reading. Hooker's earlier warnings about the effects of religious education on the common sort presaged the opinions of many seventeenth-century Anglican clerics whose concern for conformity overcame their commitment to reform. [44] As for the contemplative life, George Meriton told King James in 1606 that the highest form of nobility is 'neglecting mortal things' to 'aspire unto the heavenly.' The active public life of a mayor or a JP, he said, 'cannot sort so well with noble estate, as *Priesthood* may.' [45] And from the presumed superiority of the clerical estate followed such positions as Bancroft's and Donne's that priests, bishops and archbishops stand between the laity and God. [46] Such sentiments sound popish indeed, suggesting that to the extent that Anglican departures from humanist social thought parallel, if not equal, those of Tridentine Catholics, surely the explanation for the divergence is to be found in their common inclination to

[44] Richard Bancroft, *Tracts*, ed. A. Peel (Cambridge, 1953), p. 118; e.g., John Donne, *Sermons*, 10 vols, ed. G. R. Potter and E. M. Simpson (Berkeley, 1957), vol. 1, p. 255.

[45] Meriton, *A Sermon of Nobilitie* (1607), sigs. Civ, Eii *verso*-Eiii. A priestly life is described as one of retirement from the cares of this world to the haven of study (sigs. Eiii–Eiii, *verso*). While this strong conviction was not altogether characteristic of Anglicanism, it is visible in a significant strand of the conformist contingency and was tolerated by the more activist clergy; moreover, it is all but impossible to find, even stated less vehemently, in puritan sermons.

[46] Bancroft, p. 118; Donne, *Sermons*, vol. 4, p. 312.

respond to dissent with an insistence on conformity and obedience
to an authoritarian clericalist hierarchy.

The culmination of this conservative movement occurred during
the archbishopric of William Laud, with results that lend credibility
to the judgment that what we now call Laudianism, if not Laud himself, was 'the greatest calamity ever visited upon the English
Church.'[47] Puritanism had become enough of a force for reform,
both social and religious, by the 1630s, that the repression of
theological dissent and the enforcement of outward assent to
ceremonies, vestments, and episcopal government became very
nearly the sole concerns of the Laudian hierarchy.[48] In the climate of
compromise and consensus which had for the most part characterized the Jacobean church, a climate in which puritan and
conformist alike had held to Erasmian ideals of family religion and
labor discipline and moral education, the ascendancy of William
Laud came like a destroying wind, shattering the social vision along
with the theological cohesion of the religion of protestants. If official endorsement of Arminian doctrine and the inauguration of the
first serious repression of puritan preachers since the Elizabethan
anti-presbyterian campaigns were not enough, Laud showed himself
'nearly as hostile to social puritanism as he was to the clerical non-
conformity with which it was often associated.'[49] In social as well as
theological and ecclesiological terms, 'it is almost impossible to
overestimate the damage caused by the Laudians.'[50]

The reforged Chain of Being which had appeared with increasing
frequency in Anglican thought with the rising threat of puritan protest in the 1620s became the basis in Laudian England of a conserva-

[47] Collinson, *Religion of Protestants*, p. 90. Christopher Haigh's criticism of Collinson's
statement, *EHR*, 50 (1985), 840–3, 'Where, in the integrated and stable Jacobean
Church, can Laud have come from? – and Andrewes, Buckeridge, Harsnet,
Howson, Neile and Overall?', gives rise to my substitution of 'Laudianism' for
Laud. The roots of the '-ism' are to be found in conformist fear of puritans from
Whitgift, Bancroft and Hooker on; in light of Laud's renewed and fierce enforcement of ceremonialism and his patronage of anti-predestinarian theology, it seems
appropriate to give the -ism his name.
[48] Local studies have shown that relatively little repression of puritanism was carried
out by an Elizabethan hierarchy concerned more with Catholic recusancy than
with protestant non-conformity. The concern to establish a preaching ministry
drove such Anglican bishops as Cox of Ely to appoint to livings men like Richard
Greenham who would later refuse to conform to Whitgift's Articles: Margaret
Spufford, *Contrasting Communities* (Cambridge, 1974), p. 259, *cf.* 256–265; Ronald A.
Marchant, *The Puritans and the Church Courts in the Diocese of York, 1560–1642*
(London, 1960); William Hunt, *The Puritan Moment* (Cambridge, Mass., 1983).
[49] Hunt, p. 253.
[50] John S. Morrill, 'The Religious Context of the English Civil War,' *TRHS*, 5th ser.,
34 (1984), 155–78.

tive social theory very close to that of Trent. The English church under Laud, like the Catholic church at Trent, was split by a 'fundamental political difference between those to whom a priest was an official invested with authority from above, without regard to merit or capacity, and those to whom he was a minister appointed by the community to assist them in the realisation of their own powers.'[51] The Laudian hierarchy appropriated the Tridentine solution for internal dissension by affirming, in John Cosin's words, that 'we are to honour, reverence, and obey, in the very next degree unto God, the voice of the Church of God wherein we live.'[52] The *jus divinum* of bishops (and tithes) and the 'sacredness of the clergy' were staples of Laudian dialogue.[53] The position of the clergy in the Chain of Being provided the apologetic for unquestioning obedience by the laity.

For Laud, as for the Tridentine fathers, the clergy were to be the sole arbiters of matters of faith. The layman was by nature ill-equipped for theological discussion; lest he usurp clerical authority, therefore, he was told to leave religious controversies to the judgment of a superior estate. Donne had argued in 1617 that subtleties of biblical interpretation, 'every artificer's wearing now,' should not be 'served in every popular pulpit to curious and itching ears, [and] least of all made table-talk, and household discourse.' Ten years later, when Cosin compiled his visitation articles for the archdeaconry of the East Riding in Yorkshire, he excluded Erasmus' *Paraphrases* on the New Testament and his *Paraclesis* from the volumes to be made available in parish churches, presumably because they encouraged just the sort of lay discussion which fed puritan discontent with the established religious order.[54] One historian has concluded that most Anglican divines thought that 'private judgment. . . was of no value, whereas the verdict of the Church fell only just short of inerrancy.'[55] What was required of the godly layman was not theological understanding and religious self-analysis based on personal Bible-reading, but conformity to dogmatic and liturgical orthodoxy enforced from above. Laud's notorious dislike of the vestry, with its

[51] H. R. Trevor-Roper, *Archbishop Laud* (Hamden, Conn., 1962), pp. 45–6.
[52] John Cosin, *Works* (Oxford, 1845), vol. 1, p. 172.
[53] Schwarz, p. 2; Patrick Collinson, *The Religion of Protestants* (Oxford, 1982), discusses earlier seventeenth-century versions of divine right episcopacy, but the culmination of this development was clearly Laudian, and in combination with Laudian enforcement of ceremonies and Arminianism, it was bound to prove intolerable.
[54] Donne, *Sermons*, vol. 1, p. 255; Cosin, *Works*, vol. 2, pp. 3–4.
[55] James T. Addison, 'Early Anglican Thought, 1559–1667,' *Historical Magazine of the Protestant Episcopal Church*, 22 (1953), 248–369, p. 260.

mutually dependent ministry and laity, is a logical corollary, and one which helped to mobilize and radicalize puritan opposition to Lambeth. The radical potential inherent in the humanist view of social order had lain as dormant in puritans as in Erasmus himself until the Laudian era, but systematic repression of individual conscience and of lay participation in church government was too great a departure from both traditional English anticlericalism and humanist exaltation of individual judgment to go unopposed. And within the Erasmian scheme of social order were the seeds of a truly radical opposition. There is good reason to agree with William Hunt that 'the credit for transforming social puritanism into a revolutionary force belongs very largely to William Laud,'[56] but it is essential to recognize that English protestants had a theoretical underpinning for their radicalism in their humanism.

It should be noted that puritans were not the only critics of the new clericalism. There were among Anglican laity such opponents of Laudianism as Falkland, who told the Long Parliament that Laud and his cohorts wanted 'a blind dependence of the people upon the clergy, and of the clergy upon themselves.' But it is surely no accident that Falkland's editor identified Erasmus as 'a person much esteemed by Falkland,' and that the viscount's writings are replete with references to the humanist.[57]

Whether Falkland can in any case be considered representative of Anglican lay opinion is debatable, but his conclusions about the nature of Laudian clericalism stand.[58] To the extent that Laud's views were espoused in the Stuart church, autonomous individual conscience was dethroned. 'No school can teach conscience but the Church of Christ,' according to Laud, so that despite one interpreter's insistence that Anglicans, in contrast to puritans, 'urged all men to evaluate the results of their actions in terms of the public peace,' in fact this characterization more nearly describes the puritan plea.[59] Anglicans preferred that men should not evaluate

---

[56] Hunt, p. 253.
[57] Schwarz, pp. 3, 15, quoting first Lucius Cary, Viscount Falkland, *A Speech Made to the House of Commons concerning episcopacy* (1641), and then the Dedicatory Epistle to Falkland's *Discourse and Reply* (1651).
[58] Much more work needs to be done on lay Anglican opinion before full credence can be given to Schwarz's thesis that 'the new model Anglicanism erected by archbishop Laud and his supporters was . . . a jerry built facade, a cadre of generals without battalions, a clerical elite without a lay following' (p. 1). Falkland, on whom Schwarz depends heavily, is an exception to many rules.
[59] William Laud, *Works* (Oxford, 1842), vol. 1, p. 112; cf. J. Sears McGree, *The Godly Man in Stuart England: Anglicans, Puritans, and the Two Tables, 1620–1640* (New Haven, 1976), p. 169.

their own social ethics at all. Evaluation was not the responsibility of
the individual, but of the hierarchy. The pious conforming layman
would do well to limit both his ethical and his theological speculation and concentrate instead on the rather ethereal, pietistic
devotional activities recommended in orthodox manuals. Puritans,
of course, were by no means free of pietism – witness the popularity
of Edmund Bunny's edition of Parsons' intensely devotional
Resolutions; but when taking their spiritual temperatures, they
measured not only their emotional fervor during spiritual contemplation, but also, and perhaps to an even greater extent, the degree
to which their behavior in market-place and household conformed
to the detailed instructions meted out by the preachers.[60] The image
to which they most closely conformed was that of Erasmus' godly
youth.[61]

Puritan obsession with 'cases of conscience,' practical theology
and regular self-examination by the godly layman thus contrasts
markedly to Laudian preoccupation with authority and obedience.
Both puritans and Anglicans were striving for an ideology of social
control, but by Laud's time they were approaching the problem
from precisely opposite directions. Laudian bishops were no longer
calling for the achievement of social order through a reformation of
lay manners; their desire was simply for conformity to rules handed
down from above. Their instructions were addressed to subjects, not
citizens, and the concerns were conformist, not reformist. Their sermons and treatises are preoccupied not with domestic conduct,
acquisition and proper use of material goods, control of frivolity and
drunkenness, and the inculcation of self-discipline, but rather with
explicating 'the beauty of holiness' and demanding obedience to
episcopal authority.[62] The visitation articles of Bishops Wren and
Neile emphasize lay opinion and liturgical conformity, not lay social
behavior; they require presentation of those who criticize episcopacy, refuse to conform to liturgical requirements, and attend

[60] Among countless examples are the diaries of Richard Rogers and Samuel Ward, in
Two Elizabethan Puritan Diaries, ed. M. M. Knappen (Gloucester, Mass., 1966); *The
Diary of Lady Margaret Hoby*, ed. D. M. Meads (1930); and the commonplace book
of Nehemiah Wallington (BL, Add. MS 40883), discussed by Paul Seaver,
Wallington's World (Stanford, 1985). cf. Edmund Bunny, *A book of christian exercise
appertaining to Resolution By R. P[arsons]* (n.p., 1585), and Bunny, *A briefe answer unto
those idle quarrels of R. P. against the late edition of the Resolution* (n.p., 1589).
[61] *Confabulatio pia* (1522), *Coll.*, pp. 30–41, discussed in chapter 2 above.
[62] Hunt notes that opposition to Laud in Essex can also be traced to the *expense* of the
'beauty of holiness' in the midst of the economic hardships of the 1630s. John
Bastwick was arrested in Colchester in 1634 for charging the bishops with, among
other things, 'wasteful extravagance and neglect of the duties of charity'
(p. 261).

unlawful sermons.[63] Laud's attempts to control the Merchant Adventurers were aimed at censorship of reading material, the structure and services of chapels, and the opinions of their deputies, not at the ethics of their mercantile endeavors or their familial and public responsibilities.[64] While Laud and his cohorts required an ascetic behavioral standard for clerics (including university students), their overriding policy of parochial conformity meant that their attempts to deal with popular profanity failed to go beyond mere formality.[65] A double standard of behavior for clergy and laity, not inconsistent with the hierarchical social theory of the Laudians, effectively undermined puritan efforts at reforming manners by making the easy prelates preferable to the exacting preachers in the lukewarm popular mind.[66] The re-issue and enforced reading of the Book of Sports in 1633, which puritans saw as undercutting the authority of householders as well as encouraging profanation of the sabbath, is a good indicator of Laudian priorities. The reformation of manners had clearly gone by the board in favor of the campaign for conformity.

For Laudian Anglicans, as for other upholders of the Chain of Being, an important device for social control was the use of ceremony to reinforce hierarchical distinctions. It was in the context of an argument that 'Christ shall make master and servant equal, but not yet, not here' that Donne insisted on the setting apart of holy places and the use there of signs of reverence. The puritans' failure to 'distinguish places,' he said, was concomitant to their denial of 'distinctions of persons.'[67] Bishop Cosin redefined 'godly discipline' in purely ceremonial terms, and the social ideology underlying his

---

[63] Spufford, pp. 266–7; R. C. Richardson, *Puritanism in North-West England* (Manchester, 1972), p. 22.   [64] Trevor-Roper, pp. 253–4.

[65] Trevor-Roper has noted that 'the asceticism ... which the Anglican and the Catholic confined to the clergy, was, by the puritan, demanded of all the godly, whatever their profession' (p. 155). Among Laud's complaints of the extravagant and frivolous activities of Oxford students are a 1634 letter to the Warden of All Souls (*Works*, vol. 6, pp. 387–8); however, he agreed with Charles' reissue of the Book of Sports, with its rejection of strict sabbatarianism and its allowance of maypoles, church ales, etc. (Trevor-Roper, p. 158). The 1617 Declaration of Sports, it should be noted, was written by Bishop Morton, the first Bishop of Chester (1616–19) to perceive the preachers as a bigger threat to order in that diocese than the Catholic recusants (Richardson, p. 21). Cosin's practice followed Laud's principle: while he demanded only avoidance of disobedience and criticism by the laity, he required ministers in the East Riding to renounce the use of 'dice, cards, tables, or other idle and unlawful games,' hunting, hawking, dancing and swearing (*Works*, vol. 2, p. 15).

[66] Keith Wrightson's observation in 'The Puritan Reformation of Manners with special reference to the Counties of Lancashire and Essex, 1640–1660,' p. 128.

[67] Donne, *Sermons*, vol. 4, pp. 377–8.

position is abundantly clear in his 1633 warning that those who oppose formal distinctions of times and places 'will not only shake the universal fabric of all government and authority, but instantly open a gap, nay set open the flood gates to all confusion and anarchy.'[68] He was not far wrong: the Essex radicals who destroyed the chancel window in the Chelmsford church after the church-wardens had removed its religious pictures but left the escutcheons of its gentle benefactors were indeed challenging a 'monument to social subordination.'[69] Their social iconoclasm was a logical exten-sion of their vision of a godly commonwealth ordered on virtuous behavior. When another Essex puritan, John Gibson, had been pros-ecuted a few years earlier for 'teaching scholars in church,' it was likewise his humanistic combination of stressing popular education and scoffing at 'popish' ceremonial distinctions which drew the wrath of his Laudian opponents; he was supported by the puritan villagers who were concerned more with the reformation of behavior through godly instruction than with conformity to epis-copal 'superstition'.[70]

Laudians, puritans and humanists agreed that education was important; however, their varying approaches to establishing social order are reflected in their disagreements not only about the prop-riety of using churches as classrooms, but also about the educational process itself and the manner in which it was to benefit church and society. For Christian humanists and puritans, popular education was a means to individual moral reformation, a process by which one could attain virtue and be prepared for service to and reformation of the commonwealth. For the Laudians, on the other hand, the pur-pose of education was to reinforce the existing order, to instill into the individual the importance of obedience. When educational institutions failed to perform this function, they were uncom-promisingly suppressed. While Christian humanists had responded to the ills of grammar school and university instruction in their day by introducing gradual but significant reforms in methods and curricula, archbishop Laud responded to Strafford's difficulties in controlling Irish schools by assenting to 'the prohibiting of the teaching of arts abroad in the country . . . and the sooner it be done

---

[68] Cosin, *Works*, vol. 1, pp. 51, 170.
[69] Recounted by Hunt, p. 292.
[70] Keith Wrightson and David Levine, *Poverty and Piety in an English Village: Terling, 1525–1700* (New York, 1979), pp. 146–7.

the better.'[71] In Salisbury, the Laudian Recorder, Robert Hyde, took the extreme position of 'being against the breeding of poor men's children to learning.'[72]

On the university scene, Laud's drive for central control and the suppression of dissent is visible as early as 1616, when, as Neile's chaplain, he accompanied the king to Scotland and returned with royal instructions for the regulation of studies at Oxford. Later, as Chancellor of that university (from 1629), he was responsible for a code of statutes which 'show Laud's primary concern with externals – with the details of conduct and discipline,' with reverence and ceremony over preaching, with the imposition of 'uniformity and order in externals' from above by central authority as the solution to the problem of ill discipline in the university.[73] It is true that the Laudian statutes did go beyond mandating ceremonial conformity and attendance at newly-ordered Latin prayers in St Mary's in their quest for order: they were concerned, too, with a *reformatio morum* for students, the details of which were not objectionable to puritans.[74] The similarity of Laud's and puritans' demands for moral discipline in the university simply show that they were on some issues still thinking within the same conceptual space, one defined in part by Christian humanism, whether that debt was acknowledged or not. But there were significant differences between puritan humanism and these unacknowledged survivals of Renaissance moralism in Laud: the Chancellor's reformation of manners was not extended beyond the university and the clergy, and its mode of implementation rested on the assumption that reform is best achieved not so much by exhortations to pious self-examination and education for virtue as by requiring obedience of a code imposed and enforced by central authority at the expense of collegiate autonomy. While we must grant a recent commentator's affirmation that the Oxford of

---

[71] Laud, *Works*, vol. 6, p. 356; *cf.* Wentworth to Laud (1633) in *The Earl of Strafforde's Letters and Dispatches*, ed. William Knowler (Dublin, 1740), vol. 1, p. 188. It was an extreme reaction to the problem of popish influence in grammar schools: it is difficult to imagine humanists or puritans closing the schools altogether rather than launching into a reform program. Presumably some of the protestant schoolmasters who might have filled the gap were disqualified by non-conformity – a greater concern for Laud and Strafford than the teaching of grammar.

[72] Derek Hirst, *The Representative of the People?* (Cambridge, 1975) p. 206. Hyde was also known for his opposition to preaching and for his punitive approach to poor relief.

[73] Kevin Sharpe, 'Archbishop Laud and the University of Oxford,' in *History and Imagination*, ed. H. Lloyd-Jones, V. Pearl and B. Worden (New York, 1981), 146–64, pp. 156, 161.   [74] Sharpe, p. 153 *et passim*.

Laud was not the Salamanca of Philip II (the encouragement of new scientific speculation in Laudian Oxford is evidence enough[75]), Laud's high-handed dealing with the heads of colleges– eventually at both universities– his insistence on recognition of his authority, and above all his apparent approval of Neo-scholastic studies suggest that the difference is one of degree.[76]

In regard to curriculum, Laud's forward-looking foundation of lectureships in Arabic and Hebrew and his fostering of the new science were offset by his reinstituting the study of unabridged texts of the Schoolmen and of continental Neo-scholastics.[77] It was under Laud's oversight that Wren upheld scholastic theology in the 1631 dispute with Ganning.[78] The statutes of 1636 included administrative changes designed to increase control over collegiate instruction to enforce this conservative curriculum, and Laud attempted to visit both universities metropolitically to impose his statutes and these texts on the institutions which had by then produced Hampden and Pym, Oliver St John, Lord Saye and Sele, John Selden, and Sir Henry Vane the Younger.[79] Scholastic curricula in Oxford and Cambridge were doubtless intended to serve the same functions for Laudians in the 1630s that they had in continental Catholic universities since it had first been realized that humanist reformism threatened constituted authority. In fact, so similar were Laud's concerns and activities to those of Tridentine Catholics that the Earl of Arundel thought the Archbishop 'a fitting instrument for the advancement of the Roman faith'; in 1633 Laud was twice offered a cardinal's hat.[80]

Anglican support for the Great Chain of Being was not limited to arguments for lay obedience to the clerical estate. The social order which they wished to uphold included kings as well as clerics, and Thomas Cartwright's judgment that monarchy is as superfluous as

---

[75] Nicholas Tyacke, 'Science and Religion at Oxford before the Civil War,' in *Puritans and Revolutionaries*, ed. D. Pennington and K. Thomas (Oxford, 1978), pp. 73–93.

[76] Sharpe, pp. 150, 155–6; BL, Add. MS 32,093, fol. 140 (Cambridge heads to Laud, 19 December 1635); CUL, Add. MS 40(C),2 (Samuel Ward to Archbishop Ussher, 24 May 1637).

[77] Trevor-Roper, pp. 45, 49; Hugh Kearney, *Scholars and Gentlemen* (London, 1970), pp. 94–6; *cf.* Tyacke, 'Science and Religion,' and Sharpe, p. 162.

[78] SP 16/193/91, described in chapter 3 above.

[79] Mark Curtis, *Oxford and Cambridge in Transition* (Oxford, 1959), p. 277. On the proposed visitation of Cambridge, see CUL, MSS Add. 22, fols. 115 ff, CUR 6.1, items 41–6, CUR 78, items 28–58; BL, MS Add. 32,093, fol. 140; and my ' "An Act of Discretion": Evangelical Conformity and the Puritan Dons,' *Albion*, 18 (1986), 581–99.   [80] Trevor-Roper, p. 307.

archbishops had forewarned them (and James I) of what would result
should they fail to revive popular adherence to the medieval
hierarchy of essence and degree.[81] The warning was apparently
heeded by Matthew Wren when, as Master of Peterhouse, he led the
opposition in 1627–8 to the puritan Lord Brooke's first history lecturer at Cambridge: Dr Dorislaus had, it seems, spoken much too
positively about ancient Roman consular government for Wren's
taste, and Wren complained to Bishop Laud that 'he seemed to acknowledge no right of kingdoms.' According to another auditor,
Dorislaus 'was conceived of by some to speak too much for the
defense of the liberties of the people'; clearly he was putting classical
learning to a use unforeseen by clericalist supporters of monarchy.
The support given Dorislaus by the puritan heads on the Cambridge
consistory must have made the whole situation even more alarming.[82] In buttressing the authority of the church in society, the
Laudians were compelled to invoke the Chain of Being in all its
facets, from its immutable rankings of angels to its foundation of the
commonwealth not so much on responsible citizenship as on
hereditary monarchy and aristocracy.[83]

While the followers of Erasmus had urged obedience to the king
on the basis of his own merit and virtuous activity in defense of the
realm, the Anglican Roger Mainwaring sought to instill obedience
by pointing out the king's position in the cosmological hierarchy:
'Relations and respects [not behavior] challenge duties correspon-
dent.' It should not be surprising that he quoted Aristotle in
medieval exegetical fashion by way of St Thomas, and drew support
for social degree from the works of Suarez.[84] An Anglican student at
Balliol drew on the same sources in his contemporary comparison of
the hereditary monarch to 'the sun in the firmament, from whom the
other stars receive their light.' Because 'from him it is that the others
move . . . one must out of duty and for conscience' sake, be subject
and obey.'[85] However faulty his astronomy, this student was well

[81] Quoted in Trevor-Roper, p. 4.
[82] Wren's letter to Laud is transcribed in J. B. Mullinger, *The University of Cambridge*
(Cambridge, 1911), vol. 3, pp. 84ff. Wren was supported by Eden, a fellow-
Laudian, and opposed by the puritan master of Sidney Sussex, Samuel Ward.
Ward's account of Dorislaus' lecture is included in a letter to Archbishop Ussher
of Armagh complaining about the trouble caused in Cambridge by the Laudian
heads: *The Whole Works of the Most Rev. James Ussher* (Dublin, 1843), vol. 15, pp.
402–3 (16 May 1628).
[83] Jeremy Taylor, *Works*, ed. R. Heber (London, 1828), vol. 4, p. 151; Laud, *Works*,
vol. 1, pp. 85–6 (a Parliament sermon of 1625); Richard Hooker, *Laws of Ecclesiastical Polity*, ed. R. A. Houk (New York, 1931), Book VIII, p. 168.
[84] Roger Mainwaring, *Religion and Allegiance* (London, 1627), pp. 2, 8.
[85] Balliol, MS 337 (n.f.).

aware that the royal prerogative which he saw as the source of social harmony was best defended by affirming the Chain of Being. At the episcopal level, Thomas Morton's *Causa regia, sive, de authoritate, et dignitate principum christianorum*, directed against Bellarmine's theories of resistance in 1620, was easily adapted later to address English puritan opposition to monarchy as *The necessity of Christian subjection. Demonstrated, and proved . . . that the power of the King is not of humane, but of divine right*.[86]

Seventeenth-century conformists saw birth as the proper determinant of the status and authority of the aristocracy as well as of the monarchy: George Meriton told James I that true nobility may be possessed by one whose behavior is immoral, simply by virtue of his birth. Arguing against the intellectual heroes of both Christian humanists and earlier protestants, the Stoics, 'the old brokers of parity,' Meriton asserted that nobility of birth is the 'image and splendor of God's divinity' in this world.[87] Nobility of birth is superior to that nobility of virtue which humanists and puritans had regarded as the only true nobility. In fact, however, nobles seldom beget immoral children, since 'it may not be denied, but that the pure naturals in some are better than in others, for the procreation of moral or civil virtues.' A more anti-humanist attitude than Meriton's denial that *Nobilitas sola est animum quae moribus ornat* is difficult to imagine.[88] And he, like Mainwaring, quoted Aristotle in defense of a natural hierarchy of being.[89] John Donne similarly returned to the principles of the Chain of Being when he argued in a 1622 sermon that nobles are 'types' of God, as the king's court is a type of the court assembled around God's throne. While Erasmus and his protestant progeny in the sixteenth century had noticed the poverty and ignoble birth of Jesus, the saints, and the Apostles, Donne went to the extreme of asserting John the Baptist's fitness to be a witness of Christ on the basis of his noble birth. The Baptist's

---

[86] *The necessity of subjection* was published in 1643, probably in London.
[87] George Meriton, *A Sermon of Nobilitie* (1607), sigs. Cii, Biii, Div. That opposition to Stoic notions of equality is not related to theological position, as Walzer would have it, is demonstrated by the Calvinist Bishop Joseph Hall's belief that equality will have no more place in heaven than on earth: *Works* (Oxford, 1837), vol. 8, pp. 366–7. While few puritans actively opposed hereditary aristocracy, none offered such an extreme theoretical defense of it as Meriton. Until the 1640s, the concern for social order which they shared with Anglicans (and with their humanist forbears) prevented puritans from acknowledging the logical implications of the doctrines of spiritual equality and the superiority of virtue to pedigree as a determinant of status.
[88] Meriton, sigs. Ciiii, Cii *verso*–Ciii. *cf.* Sig. Eiiii, on the superiority of inherited to elective kingship.   [89] Meriton, sigs. Biiii, Ci *verso*.

nobility he extrapolated inventively from the fact that his father was a priest, and 'in all well policed states . . . they have ever thought it fittest to employ [as priests] persons of good families, and of noble extraction.'[90] Later in the same year he preached against those [puritans] who dared subject even the king to their 'censures and corrections.'[91] Respect must be given to each man in his place, he insisted, 'for in the chain of order, every link depends upon one another.'[92] Archbishop Laud's patronage of the Calvinist Joseph Hall may be less mysterious if we consider Hall's commitment not only to *jure divino* episcopacy and the suppression of religious dissent, but also to the notion that that land is blessed whose rulers are 'not of any servile condition,' but sons of nobles. 'It is a monster in a state,' Hall goes on, 'to see servants ride on horses and princes (of blood) to walk as servants on the ground; neither more monstrous, than intolerable,' since 'as his blood is heroical, so his disposition.'[93] Richard Hooker had laid the theoretical foundations for this position when he had opposed the presbyterian discipline's disregard of social estate with the principle that it is 'repugnant to the majesty and greatness of English nobility' to bring 'equally high and low unto parish churches.'[94] In the century which followed *Utopia* and the *Adages*, in the six or seven decades since Dering had castigated the sins of princes and magistrates, a reversal had taken place: order was to be sought not so much in reform, as in a recognition of the inherent superiority and authority of the well-born.[95]

It was on the basis of this inherent authority of the upper echelons of the medieval hierarchy – lay and clerical – that Anglicans focused their demand for obedience regardless of the leanings of the conscience. For Mainwaring, religion was 'the stay of the polity' not as the agent of individual moral reform, but as the teacher of obedience. Thus narrowly did Anglicans conceive of religion as 'the

---

[90] Donne, *Sermons*, vol. 4, pp. 146, 177.
[91] *Ibid.*, vol. 4, p. 250; *cf.* vol. 1, p. 183, vol. 2, p. 303, Vol. 4, pp. 240–1, and Laud, *Works*, vol. 1, pp. 16ff, arguing that the puritan William Gouge's criticism of the sins of the prince reveal him as anti-monarchical and therefore heretical. Gouge's self-defense is in the preface to his commentary on Hebrews (1655).
[92] Donne, *Sermons*, vol. 4, p. 316. He also used the Chain of Being image in a 1617 sermon at Paul's Cross (vol. 1, p. 208).
[93] Joseph Hall, *Salomons Divine Arts* (1609), pp. 109–10; T. F. Kinloch, *The Life and Works of Joseph Hall, 1574–1656* (1951), pp. 32–5.   [94] Hooker, vol. 2, p. 475.
[95] There are, of course, exceptions. Arthur Lake was still even-handed in his denunciation of the sins of rulers, railing in a sermon on Psalm 82, for example, against magistrates who 'understand not, consider not, walk on in darkness' to the danger of state (*Ten Sermons* (London, 1640), p. 110, *cf.* pp. 119–20). The development being described here was gradual, and it did not culminate until Laud rose to power. What we are attempting to trace is a process of change.

foundation of the well-ordered commonwealth,' since it was obedience to a code of externals, rather than reformation of internal attitudes and inclinations, which would produce social order.[96] John Carpenter actually traced the roots of social restlessness to the reforming spirit; accusing his opponents of desiring social and political, as well as religious reformation, he pictured them as perfectionists, 'dreaming of Plato's commonwealth. . . In the pride of their hearts, [they] imagine themselves to be rather kings reigning with God in heaven, than men living among men on earth.'[97] Puritans, in the humanist tradition, are here justly portrayed as enemies of the Chain of Being, if inaccurately as proponents of social disorder; order was in the last analysis the aim of their appeals to conscience. Anglicans did not deny a role to conscience, but they changed its functions drastically: for Archbishop Laud, concerned above all else with the enforcement of conformity, the function of conscience was not to determine right, but under the direction of the Church to accord obedience.[98]

Perceiving the threat posed to the existing system by the humanist/puritan program of control through reform, Anglicans had deliberately repudiated much of the sixteenth-century consensus for the protection offered by a traditional social ideology. They in effect fled in the face of the reformist assault to the haven of a rigid hierarchical structure, a divinely-ordered system of social degree reflective of the cosmic hierarchy of planets and spheres, angels and heavenly principalities, before whose innate authority disobedience was out of the question. Being, not action, was to determine status; estate of birth rather than devotion to the common weal evinced right to rule. The institutions of monarchy and episcopacy were givens; princes and bishops were not subject to review. The extent to which social reform was perceived as no threat to ecclesiastical conformity would determine the point to which the bishops would accept Christian humanist social ideology. It was at the point where reform challenged conformity that they would repudiate humanist presuppositions. When reformist predilections came into conflict with hierarchical interests, the choice had to be made between repression and reform.

The outcome of the conflict in England did not become apparent

---

[96] Mainwaring, pp. 4–5; McGee (pp. 142–70) has amply documented this insistence on unquestioning obedience, although his interpretation of it is debatable.

[97] John Carpenter, *A Preparative to Contentation* (1597), sig. Kiiii.

[98] Laud, *Works*, vol. 1, p. 112. Jeremy Taylor followed suit in seeing no sin more heinous than disobedience (*Works*, vol. 4, p. 150).

until the Civil War, when conscience enthroned finally succeeded in casting down the actuality, as well as the theory, of the traditional hierarchy. The war can thus be interpreted as in part an ideological dispute over the relative authority of individual lay conscience and established hierarchy.[99] Behind this dispute, however, lay the struggle between two groups equally concerned with the imposition of order on society, but in disagreement as to whether that order was best achieved from the top, by demanding unquestioning obedience or by means of a grass roots approach, a reformation of manners directed toward the realization of a well-ordered commonwealth. The same choice had confronted the delegates at Trent; the same conflict is represented in Contarini's opposition to Carafa. The same resolution was made at Trent as at Lambeth, with many of the same effects on social theory.

It was the decision first of the Tridentine cardinals and later of the Anglican hierarchy to realize social order through enforced conformity rather than humanist reform that explains the divergence of Catholic from protestant, puritan from Anglican household theory. William Perkins dated the shift in Catholic thinking about the family quite accurately when he associated the popish belief 'that this secret coming together of man and wife [is] filthiness' with the judgment of the Council of Trent.[100] It was at Trent, he charged, 'after that marriage was condemned by them, [that] some began to detest and hate women.'[101] The puritan John Dod was similarly perceptive when he criticized the Jesuits, who 'so straightly tie the women to wheel and spindle, as they do cut them off and bar them from all conference touching the word of God, as absurd and far unbeseeming their sex.'[102] By the time Perkins and Dod were writing, there was indeed a sharp contrast between protestant and papist household theory, a contrast which goes far toward explaining the emphasis of historians on the unique character of protestant domestic conduct theory.

---

[99] Seeing the Civil War in terms of conflicting social ideology helps to explain why English 'Catholic commitment to armed support of the King was all out of proportion to the size of the community as such, and was, furthermore, most marked in the upper echelons of the army in terms of rank, and in the elite arm, the cavalry.' P. R. Newman, 'Catholic Royalists of Northern England, 1642–1645,' *Northern History*, 15 (1979), 88–95, p. 88.

[100] Perkins, *Works* (Cambridge, 1618), vol. 3, p. 689. Joseph Hall concurred in *The Honor of the Married Clergie Mayntayned* (1620), Dedicatory Epistle.

[101] Perkins, vol. 3, pp. 669ff, 689.

[102] John Dod, *Bathshebaes Instructions to her Sonne Lemuel* (1614), pp. 61–2; *cf.* pp. 1–3, 64.

It has been argued above that the pre-eminent concern of the
Council of Trent was with doctrinal uniformity. The practice of
religious education and discipline in the household was seen by the
Council as liable to threaten the spiritual authority of the official
hierarchy by replacing it with the quasi-priestly position of parents.
Participation in household religion was viewed as incompatible with
conformity to strictly orthodox doctrine and practice: 'in the
Counter-Reformation hierarchy the notion of the nuclear family as
an autonomous entity inspired indifference or distaste ... The
Counter-Reformation hierarchy seems to have taken it for granted
that a household religion was a seed-bed of subversion.'[103] The solution of the fathers at Trent was to enforce parochial conformity at
the expense of familial autonomy. The Tridentine canons and
decrees accordingly gave bishops, and not fathers and mothers, the
responsibility to provide catechism for children; unauthorized
teaching was prohibited, and parental religious responsibilities are
conspicuous by their absence.[104] In England, where the families that
sheltered outlawed priests had to be considered coterminous with
parochial units, the Jesuits campaigned to transform households
into clerically-dominated seminaries. Richard Smith's biography of
Lady Montague gives no indication that lay members of her
household had anything but a passive role in household religion, and
Parsons' *Booke of the Christian Exercise* (1582), a very popular guide for
Christian living, contains no reference to the religious responsibilities of lay heads of households.[105] In fact, the publications most
encouraged by Jesuits and seminarists to guide the spiritual lives of
English families – works like Parsons', Southwell's and Lascelles',
noted earlier, and Peter Canisius' *Little Catechism*, Gaspar de Loarte's
Exercise of a Christian Life and his *Spiritual Combat*, Luis de Granada's
Spiritual Doctrine Containing a Rule to Live Well and his *Excellent Treatise
of Consideration and Prayer* – stress 'the worldliness and manifold dis-
tractions of ordinary family life and the absolute need for devout
individuals ... to go aside from family commitments, to make their
souls under clerical direction.'[106] Aveling notes that 'Catholic cleri-

[103] John Bossy, 'The Counter-Reformation and the People,' *P&P*, 47 (1970),
51–70, p. 68.
[104] *Canons and Decrees*, pp. 26, 196; *cf.* Bossy, 'The Character of Elizabethan
Catholicism,' in *Crisis in Europe, 1560–1660*, ed. Trevor Aston (1965), pp. 229–35,
and *The English Catholic Community 1570–1850* (Oxford, 1976), chs. 1–3.
[105] Smith, *The Life of the Most Honourable and Vertuous Lady, the La. Magdalen Viscountesse
Montague*, tr. J. C. Fursdon (1627), *passim*; Robert Parsons, *The First Booke of the
Christian Exercise, appertayning to resolution* (1582), *passim*.
[106] Aveling, p. 101; *cf.* Haigh, p. 138, commenting that the 'intense family religiosity'
enjoined by these works centered around a resident chaplain and regular
sacramental practice.

cal writers, for their part, did their best to suppress Erasmus' writings and forget More's liberalism.'[107] Accordingly, when the Yorkshire gentlewoman Mary Ward attempted in 1610 to launch her own female missionary endeavor to guide married women in the religious instruction of their households, she found her efforts engulfed in 'a wave of hysterical agitation . . . [by the clergy, and] suppressed by the papacy before the close of the 1620s.'[108] The Jesuits' ' "monastic" tradition of spirituality [had] prevailed over tendencies toward "devout humanism".'[109]

Not only did Tridentine Catholicism deprive householders of a religious role, it also affirmed the inferiority of the married state to that of virginity. A canon adopted by the twenty-fourth session of the council declared that 'if anyone says that the married state excels the state of virginity or celibacy and that it is better and happier to be united in matrimony than to remain in virginity or celibacy, let him be anathema.'[110] Ignatius Loyola told readers of his *Spiritual Exercises* 'to praise much religious orders, virginity and continence, and not so much marriage as any of these.'[111] Parsons regarded virginity as a superior state and vigorously criticized Edmund Bunny's protestantized edition of his *Christian Exercise* for its omission of all references to virginity: 'he maketh me to speak like a good minister of England.'[112] Smith recorded of Lady Montague, 'Albeit she chose not the highest degree of chastity, which is virginity, that perhaps may rather be ascribed to want of advice and counsel, whereof she often lamented to have been destitute in her youth, than of desire to follow the best.'[113] This devaluation of marriage clearly contributed to the Counter-Reformation goal of returning religious authority to the priesthood: if husbands and wives are spiritually inferior beings, then their potentially subversive religious teaching is likely to be disregarded in favor of the orthodox doctrine of the celibate priest. Thus, the Tridentine concern for parochial conformity led to the demise of the family as a primary religious institution in Catholic teaching.

The same conviction can be seen at work in the Laudian Church of England, although in a less extreme version and ultimately with less

---

[107] Aveling, p. 100.
[108] Bossy, *English Catholic Community*, pp. 160, 282. The general misogyny of the Council of Trent has been illuminated by Joan Morris, *Against Nature and God* (1974), pp. 150–8. Abbesses were for the first time subjected to episcopal or general chapter supervision by the twenty-fifth session (1563) of the Council (*Canons and Decrees*, pp. 223–4).   [109] Aveling, p. 101.   [110] *Canons and Decrees*, p. 182.
[111] *Spiritual Exercises*, sec. 356, 4th rule, p. 230.
[112] Parsons, *Christian Exercise*, fols. 13, 9. Bunny was chaplain to the Archbishop of York and later minister at Bolton.   [113] R. Smith, p. 31.

success, when doctrinal and liturgical uniformity came to be seen as a primary goal of the ecclesiastical institution. Laud's visitation articles are reminiscent of the Tridentine decrees in that the only religious responsibility assigned to parents is that of sending their children to church for catechism by the priest. In 1636, Bishop Wren of Norwich actually instructed churchwardens to present laymen who presumed to discuss religion in their families.[114] The dearth of domestic conduct manuals among Anglican treatises and the absence of practical advice to parents in their sermons are evidence of an attempt to replace the spiritual autonomy of families with a clerically dominated, conformist religion. Even John Cosin, who sometimes condoned household religion, showed signs of ambivalence toward the spiritualized household in his notion that 'single life be a thing more angelical and divine' than marriage; had Christ not attended the wedding at Cana, he said, men might have ceased marrying at all, since 'married life itself seems to be but an imperfect state; the state of perfection is virginity, so much commended by our Saviour, so highly esteemed by St. Paul.'[115] Donne's view of the family was similarly equivocal. He actually rearranged the three ends of marriage, placing companionship last, and in a 1619 sermon he interpreted the death of children as God's way of showing us 'the sinful voluptuousness in which they were begotten and conceived.' As for women, puritan patriarchy was tame by comparison with Donne's assertion, 'We are sure women have souls as well as men, but yet it is not so expressed, that God breathed a soul into woman as he did into man.' The political parallel which he immediately drew – that while all governments have 'soul,' God 'breathed it more manifestly into monarchy' – clarifies the extent of his patriarchalism, the conservatism of his political theory, and the dependence of both on the Great Chain of Being.[116] It is this divergence of both Catholic and conformist Anglican doctrine from the humanist/puritan consensus in the late sixteenth and early seventeenth century which has resulted in the misleading emphasis of historians on the innovative character of puritan household theory.

Much the same phenomenon can be seen in the area of economic doctrines and poor relief schemes, although here the utility of many

---

[114] Laud, *Works*, vol. 5, p. 446; Wren's position is noted by Hill, *Society and Puritanism*, p. 468.
[115] Cosin, *Works*, vol. 1, pp. 48, 56. These statements were made in a wedding sermon! It should be noted that the household religion which he commended was preferably to follow the authorized catechism and the Prayer Book (vol. 2, pp. 8–10).   [116] *Ibid.*, vol. 4, p. 241.

aspects of Christian humanist thought for proponents of a strictly controlled society qualified both Tridentine and (to a greater extent) Laudian rejection of humanist innovations. Tridentine Catholics upheld medieval views of religious poverty and of the intrinsic merit of almsgiving, however indiscriminate. But they accepted the humanist innovation of workhouses, although modifying them in a penal direction into mechanisms for the enforcement of conformity. The adaptability of the workhouse to their drive for control made it the one exception to the Tridentine/Laudian tendency to oppose innovation and uphold tradition as the foundation of social order.

The importance attached by orthodox Catholics to the spiritual character of poverty and almsgiving had always presented a problem for humanist opponents of mendicity, religious or otherwise. According to traditional Catholic doctrine, the poor are representative of Christ on earth, and every Christian ought to dispense charity both out of regard for this religious significance inherent in poverty and as a necessary means of attaining eternal salvation. Humanist schemes to eliminate begging and ultimately poverty itself were seen as a barrier to the realization of this soteriological imperative, but in a more immediate sense, they were interpreted as an obvious criticism of religious mendicity. Accordingly, Vives' plan for Ypres was labeled heretical and Lutheran by the vicar of the Bishop of Tournai in 1527 and by the mendicant orders of Ypres in the 1530s, and in 1531 the Sorbonne responded to it by ruling against any prohibition of public begging and almsgiving.[117] The Lyon Aumône-Générale likewise drew the wrath of Dominicans and of the Inquisition in the 1530s, as did Francis I's Bureau Général des Pauvres in the 1540s.[118] With the solidification of the Counter-Reformation at the Council of Trent, opposition to humanist

---

[117] Natalie Davis, *Society and Culture in Early Modern France* (Stanford, 1975), p. 17; Linda Martz, *Poverty and Welfare in Hapsburg Spain* (Cambridge, 1983), pp. 7, 13. It should be noted, however, that the mendicant orders did not always oppose the humanist drive to eliminate begging. Franciscan reformers, particularly in the New World, frequently patronized Vivesian schemes. See John Leddy Phelan, *The Millennial Kingdom of the Franciscans in the New World* (Berkeley, 1956), on Geronimo de Mendieta; Bataillon, vol. 2, pp. 435–54; Lewis Hanke, *The First Social Experiments in America* (Cambridge, Mass., 1935). Opposition to these New World reforms from Dominican inquisitors was in part an aspect of traditional inter-order rivalry.

[118] Davis, p. 17; Howard M. Solomon, *Public Welfare, Science and Propaganda in Seventeenth Century France: The Innovations of Theophraste Renaudot* (Princeton, 1972), p. 27. The Bureau did not prohibit begging, but did attempt to separate deserving poor from rogues and establish *ateliers*. Its primary offenses in clerical eyes were lay administration and discriminate, indirect distribution: 'by policing the poor, it removed from circulation the vessel through which the Christian became Christ-like' (p. 32).

attitudes toward poverty and its relief intensified, despite the apparent successes of the humanist reforms in Ypres and Lyon. By the 1540s it was apparent to the Catholic hierarchy that the Vivesian scheme threatened not only the theological foundations of the mendicant orders and the doctrine of the necessity of works for salvation, but also clerical control over a traditionally ecclesiastical function, the relief of poverty. It was clearly perceived as a facet of Erasmian anticlericalism, and its opponents were henceforth led by the same Dominican and Jesuit *zelanti* who were responsible for the revival of Thomism, the establishment of the Roman Inquisition, the inclusion of Erasmus on the Index and the dogmatism of the Tridentine decrees.

Thus, among Cardinal Pole's quarrels with the hard-liners at Trent were his objections to Seripando's draft decree on justification (1546), which stressed the need for expiatory almsgiving.[119] He was overruled by a Council intent on re-affirming traditional doctrine, with the end result that the 'motive of self-sanctification' remained an important and openly-avowed precept of Catholic charity in the sixteenth and seventeenth centuries.[120] By 1568, Nicholas Sander's assertion that 'our daily sins and inward uncleanness are made clean by almsdeeds' was an articulation of typically Catholic opinion.[121] The only other English Catholic to write in any detail about poor relief after Trent, Robert Parsons, likewise focused his work on the salutary functions of charity for the penitent benefactor. While he accepted several aspects of the humanist welfare program (including no- or low-interest loans to poor artisans and job training for poor children), it was always with the assumption that all such programs would be under strict episcopal control and that they would thereby enable benefactors to contribute to their own salvation and simultaneously augment the authority of the ecclesiastical hierarchy.[122] In the seventeenth century, English Jesuits would be less qualified in their condemnation of humanist poor relief: Edward Knott described the discriminating, indirect almsgiving of protestant England as 'Charity Mistaken.'[123]

---

[119] Fenlon, *Heresy and Obedience*, p. 163. This document was repudiated by Pole (p. 164).
[120] Brian Pullan, 'Catholics and the Poor in Early Modern Europe,' *TRHS* 5th Ser., 26 (1976), 15–34, p. 27, noting the opinion of the Bavarian Jesuit Jerome Drexel that alms do not lose their merit in unworthy hands.
[121] Nicholas Sander, *A briefe Treatise of Usurie* (Louvain, 1568), sig. Bii, *verso*.
[122] Parsons, *Memorial*, pp. 86–7, 256–61.
[123] Edward Knott [alias Matthew Wilson], *Charity Mistaken* (1630); *Mercy and Truth maintained by Catholics* (1634), *passim*.

In Spain, it was the Neo-scholastic theologian of Salamanca, Domingo de Soto, who quashed the humanist poor relief plan of Juan de Robles (1545) because its 'removal of the indigent from the streets would result in grave spiritual harm by denying the faithful the opportunity of practicing charity,' and because its involvement of secular magistrates would reduce clerical control over social order.[124] Juan de Robles had insisted that alms given indiscriminately were not meritorious (denying de Soto's distinction between mercy and justice), but that involuntary charity could be (allowing the possibility of a rate). He went along with his enemy in departing from Vives on only one point, that relief should be administered by ecclesiastics. Beyond this, he was a thoroughgoing humanist: it is not without significance that when he died in 1572, he left a Spanish translation of the New Testament unpublished, 'possibly because he feared the adverse judgement of the Inquisition.' De Soto, by contrast, was sent to the Council of Trent in 1545 and contributed there to the legislation on justification.[125]

De Soto's opposition to Vives, like Knott's, was unqualified; moreover, in Spain it was relatively effective.[126] A 1557 edict of Philip II reversed the magisterial reforms of Bruges by allowing the poor to beg; in 1559 Philip sponsored a propaganda campaign headed by the Augustinian preacher Lorenzo de Villevicencio against any secular authority attempting to forbid begging or administer charity; and the 1565 poor law for the Spanish Empire decreed a licensed begging system, outlawed a rate, and made no provision for educating the poor.[127] When a humanist-inspired movement to rationalize relief emerged from the followers of Juan de Ávila at the University of Baeza, it was suppressed by 'the unfavorable judgment of the Inquisition,' including Ávila's imprisonment

---

[124] Martz, pp. 2, 22–9, discussing de Soto's *Deliberación en la causa de los pobres* (1545); William J. Callahan, 'The Problem of Confinement: An Aspect of Poor Relief in Eighteenth Century Spain,' *Hispanic American Historical Review*, 51 (1971), p. 4. See also Robert Jütte, 'Poor Relief and Social Discipline in 16th-Century Europe,' *European Studies Review*, 11 (1981), 25–52. So important was direct, personal almsgiving to de Soto that he even opposed the use of a servant as an intermediary (Callahan, p. 5, n. 18). It should be noted, however, that most Spanish welfare reformers supported some limitation on public mendicity; even Loyola had persuaded the council of his home town of Azpeitia in 1535 to eliminate public begging and encourage the moral reformation of the poor (Martz, pp. 2, 14–15).

[125] Martz, pp. 25–9.

[126] The only point that de Soto lost in the 1565 Poor Law of Philip II related to the law's requirement that the poor confess and communicate before receiving relief (Martz, pp. 33–4).

[127] Martz, pp. 31–3. Lorenzo de Villevicencio's explicit criticism of Vives is embodied in his *De oeconomia sacra circa pauperum curam a Christo institutam* (Paris, 1564).

for 'suspicious practices and preaching.'[128] Later in the century, when municipalities attempted to confine the poor in beggars' hospitals, their attempts were generally short-lived, partly because of opposition from conservative theologians to enclosure and limits on begging.[129] Moreover, the relative absence of regular employment and educational schemes in Spanish poor relief even in the era of reform so ably described by Linda Martz is striking in comparison with the welfare systems of countries and municipalities not affected by the Roman Index and the Tridentine decree. In the New World, the end of the humanist Zumárraga's utopian educational schemes for poor Indians came in the 1550s when the Montúfar Inquisition, in good Dominican fashion, condemned his works 'with the firm conviction that Zumárraga's Erasmianism was heretical.'[130] Not until the eighteenth-century Enlightenment revived the works of Vives were any further attempts made by secular Spanish authorities to limit begging, define the deserving poor, and establish reforming institutions for the indigent. It is interesting to note that it was a staunch opponent of the Jesuits, Fabian y Fuero, who in 1781 financed the first Spanish edition of Vives' *De Subventione Pauperum* since the sixteenth century, and the pattern subsequently followed by the Spanish government was that of sixteenth-century Ypres and Lyon.[131]

Post-Tridentine Catholic poor relief was thus a return to the medieval tradition of direct distribution of alms to groups of beggars in the streets, with the inadvertent result that when Pierre de l'Estoile visited Rome in 1596 he found that 'the crowds of poor in the street were so great that one could not pass through,' and in 1607 a traveler reported that 'in Rome one sees only beggars.'[132] The

---

[128] Martz, p. 39. Many of the Baeza publications were put on the Index of 1559 by Inquisitor Fernando Valdes, who called them 'books of contemplation for carpenters' wives,' underlining the clericalism and the misogyny of the Counter-Reformation.

[129] The great institutional reform of sixteenth-century Spanish relief was hospital consolidation, which was accompanied by administrative changes allowing stricter episcopal supervision of charitable institutions (Martz, pp. 34–59, 64, 71–6, 119–58).

[130] Richard E. Greenleaf, *Zumárraga and the Mexican Inquisition* (Washington, DC, 1961), p. 39.   [131] Callahan, pp. 3, 8–9.

[132] Henry Kamen, *The Iron Century: Social Change in Europe, 1550–1660* (New York, 1971), p. 387. On the decay of sixteenth-century municipal charity in France, see Emmanuel Chill, 'Religion and Mendicity in Seventeenth Century France,' *International Review of Social History*, VII (1960), 400–25, pp. 403–4. An exception to this rule is found in Venice, where humanist innovations survived the Tridentine period, no doubt in part because of traditional Venetian anti-papalism. Even here, however, begging was not entirely eliminated: see Brian Pullan, 'Catholics and the Poor,' p. 24, and *Rich and Poor in Renaissance Venice* (Cambridge, Mass., 1971), pp. 363, 369–71.

severity of the problem finally demanded of Catholics some attempt at a new solution, and lest secular princes and magistrates return in desperation to the lay-administered Vivesian scheme, the church finally recognized the need to adopt those humanist institutions which could both control the proliferation of the poor and be easily modified and overseen by the clerical hierarchy.[133] The campaign to eliminate begging thus found sponsors like Carlo Borromeo, Archbishop of Milan, and many Jesuits returned to their founder's opposition to begging.[134] The solution which was appropriated, moreover, was the workhouse. However the Counter-Reformation version of this institution was not the reform-oriented combination of school and manufactory described by Vives, but a quasi-penal structure in which the poor could be confined and controlled, and from which in some cases they could beg, although only under strict supervision.

An anonymous *Mémoire concernant les pauvres qu'on appelle enfermés* (1617), together with the writings produced by the Company of the Holy Sacrament to establish the pattern for the *hôpitaux généraux* of seventeenth-century France, are representative of what became Counter-Reformation poor relief theory.[135] The members of the Company of the Holy Sacrament, a powerful, secret group of devout laymen and priests founded in the 1620s by St François de Sales and Pierre Berulle, were responsible for most of what are in fact the relatively few works of Tridentine social thought providing any detail at all on the structure, intent, and administration of relief institutions.[136] The distinctive features of the ideal *hôpital général* or

[133] The response of secular magistrates in Catholic Europe seems in fact to have been brutally repressive, with the exception of the humanist-inspired municipal relief programs which had managed to survive Tridentine oppression. See I. A. A. Thompson, 'A Map of Crime in Sixteenth Century Spain,' *Economic History Review*, 2nd Ser., 21 (1969), 244–67, p. 245; Maria Jiménez Salas, *Historia de la asistencia social in España* (Madrid, 1958), pp. 127, 139; Michel Foucault, *Madness and Civilization*, tr. Richard Howard (New York, 1965), pp. 38–64 (on the royal Hôpital Général of Paris, pp. 46–7); Solomon, p. 33.
[134] Pullan, 'Catholics and the Poor,' p. 24.
[135] The *Mémoire* is included in *Archives Curieuses de l'histoire de France*, ed. M. L. Climber and F. Danjou (Paris, 1837) Ier Série, 15, pp. 248–69. The *Annales de la Compagnie du St-Sacrement*, collected in the seventeenth century by Comte René de Voyer d'Argenson, have been edited by H. Beauchet-Filleau (Marseille, 1900); the Company's plan for Toulouse, *L'Aumône Générale*, is reproduced in A. August, *La Compagnie du Saint-Sacrement à Toulouse* (Paris, 1913), pp. 47–59.
[136] While St François de Sales was heavily involved in the administration of ecclesiastical charity, his views on the subject must be deduced from the documents of the company of the Holy Sacrament, since his major treatises, the *Treatise on the Love of God*, tr. Henry Benedict Mackey (Westminster, Md., 1949), and the *Introduction à la Vie dévote* (1608), ed. Robert Morel (Haute Provence, 1963), have little to say about poverty (beyond a commendation of voluntary poverty and of contentment with involuntary poverty in the *Introduction*, pp. 186–95), and less to say about charity

hôtel-dieu described in their schemes and the *Mémoire*, in comparison with the system proposed by Christian humanists, are strict episcopal oversight, the enforcement of religious asceticism on inmates, and the application of a punitive discipline to all the poor, whatever the nature and causes of their poverty. The seventeenth-century *dévots* emphasized the effects, not the sources, of destitution, and addressed themselves not to changing social institutions which contributed to poverty, but to isolating the poor from society. The theory of the *hôpitaux généraux*, as of the contemporary *hospicios* of Spain, saw internment and repression as the only way to address the poverty problem, and order was linked with asceticism imposed from above.[137] Accordingly, while the humanist scheme for Rouen had encouraged relief of the poor at home in 1534, by the early seventeenth century the assumption of clerics and laymen alike was that forcible incarceration of the poor was the only way to impose order.[138] The *Mémoire* demanded incarceration of the poor in *ateliers*, where they were to be subjected to 'harsh, vexatious, and difficult employments' designed to chasten them.[139] As a result, the general hospitals established under post-Tridentine ecclesiastical auspices have been described as '*prisons des pauvres*,' '*institutions repressives*,' 'fundamentally disciplinarian and penal in spirit,' differing from medieval institutions in their harsh demands upon the poor and in their 'bureaucratic rationality.'[140]

The *Annales* specified that charity was to be provided not by the secular government, but by ecclesiastical agencies, and only when

(other than the approval of direct, personal benevolence given in the *Introduction*, p. 191). St Vincent de Paul, another member of the company, wrote voluminous letters of advice to the missionaries and charitable societies administering poorhouses and foundling homes in mid-seventeenth-century France; however, it is significant that these letters focus to a much greater extent on the missionaries' spiritual status and attitudes toward the poor they served, and on their *religious* responsibilities toward inmates, than on plans to reform and rehabilitate the poor and idle: e.g., *Correspondance, Entretiens, Documents*, ed. Pierre Coste, 14 vols (Paris, 1925), vol. 9, pp. 5, 249, 253, 593; vol. 10, pp. 679–80; vol. 11, pp. 32, 381–4, 392; vol. 12, pp. 74, 87, 470, 473; vol. 13, pp. 761–820 (instructions to the Dames de la Charité of the Paris Hôtel-Dieu).

[137] *Mémoire, passim; Annales, passim*; Chill, pp. 400–25; *cf.* Solomon, p. 12, and Foucault, p. 62. The *hospicios* of Tridentine Spain were ecclesiastically dominated and were openly admitted, even by advocates of confinement of the poor, to be penal in nature, toward both able-bodied idlers and the truly impotent poor (Callahan, p. 15).

[138] Jean-Pierre Gutton, *La Société et les pauvres: L'exemple de la généralite de Lyon, 1534–1789* (Paris, 1971), pp. 295–6, 298–9, 305–6, 314. Internment of the poor began at Rouen in 1613 and in Lyon in 1614, based on a plan of 1591.

[139] *Mémoire*, p. 248. The ultimate objective of the Company for the poor, according to Gutton, was the 'désolation des âmes,' and their methods became steadily more punitive after the 1640s: *Lyon*, pp. 324–5.

'the interest of religion' would thereby be served.[141] That the interest of religion was not necessarily that of the poor themselves was all too evident in the Spanish *hospicios* where the clerical staff were so busy saying masses for the dead that the inmates were deprived of all priestly services; in France, even in the theory of Vincent de Paul the same priorities are reflected – 'The Daughters of the Hôtel-Dieu,' he said, 'have as their end *first* their own perfection and *then* the relief of the sick.'[142] The nature of that 'interest of religion' is further clarified in the plans developed by the *dévots* for the treatment of the recipients of charity. Brian Pullan has argued that while protestants changed the monastery into a hospital or a school, Tridentine Catholics extended monasticism and imposed it on the poor under the oversight of those lay brother- and sisterhoods, 'clerically inspired and bent on self-sanctification.'[143] According to the *Annales*, the poor were to be forcibly incarcerated in order to subject them to strict church oversight and control. Inmates of an *hôpital*, whether rogues or *bons pauvres*, were to be subjected to a rigorous time and work regimen, frequent prayers and masses – ceremonial reinforcers of ecclesiastical authority – and the regular exercise of harsh discipline.[144] In France as in Spain, the work which went on in the workhouse was seen as punishment, and in both countries this

---

[140] Chill, pp. 418–19, 421; Gutton, *Lyon*, pp. 295, 301. In practice, protestant workhouses doubtless occasionally degenerated into quasi-penal institutions as well; however, they had to depart from their theoretical foundations in order to do so. That this was not the case for Catholic *hôpitaux* implies a resultant difference in the degree, and perhaps in the nature, of actual repression of the poor in protestant and Catholic institutions. Even in an article intended to demonstrate the continuity between protestant and Catholic welfare reform in the early modern period, Brian Pullan admits that 'when it came to the correction of the homeless poor by means of internment, hard labour, corporal punishment, and compulsory piety, there can have been few English bridewells to compare in scope or scale with the motley complex of barrack-like hospitals and dungeons controlled by the governors of Hôpital Général in seventeenth-century Paris' (Catholics and the Poor,' p. 19).

[141] *Annales*, pp. 120, 127; *cf.* Robert M. Kingdon, 'Social Welfare in Calvin's Geneva,' *American Historical Review*, 76 (1971), 50–69, p. 66.

[142] *Conferences of St. Vincent de Paul to the Sisters of Charity*, tr. J. Leonard (1938), vol. 3, p. 98 (1655), emphasis mine; Martz, p. 84.

[143] Pullan, 'Catholics and the Poor,' pp. 32, 34. He compares the *hôpital-général* of seventeenth-century France to a 'penal monastery' (p. 32); Gutton, *Lyon*, p. 296, compares the children's Hôpital de la Trinité in Paris to a convent and notes that the *enfermés* had no contact with the outside world; their day was a round of religious exercises and work.

[144] *Mémoire*, pp. 260, 269; *L'Aumône Générale*, pp. 54, 56; St Vincent de Paul, vol. 11, pp. 381–4 and vol. 12, p. 87; Pullan, 'Catholics and the Poor,' pp. 29–33; Pullan, *Rich and Poor*, pp. 362–70; Gutton, *Lyon*, pp. 295 ff; *cf.* Foucault, pp. 38–64. Foucault emphasizes that Counter-Reformation theory perceived work as punishment, *askesis* (pp. 59–60).

attitude became more pronounced, the treatment of beggars grew harsher and punishments were more severe as the seventeenth century progressed – 'an expression of the *nouvelle vague* of Counter-Reformation charity that permeated much of Catholic Europe,' according to a recent interpreter.[145] As for reformation through education, while instruction in literacy and religious catechism was recommended by the Company's plan for Toulouse, the reformist intent of Vives' education schemes for the poor is not visible: the plan makes no provisions for vocational training, apprenticeship or other devices to move the poor out of the institution and establish them as productive members of the community.[146] In any case, by the end of the century, the workshops themselves had disappeared from the general hospitals, and schools for the poor in France were few and far between.[147] The most negative aspects of the static social theory of the Middle Ages are evident in the Company's conviction that, in the words of the Toulouse scheme, 'the poor, who *by birth* should serve the rich,' are not susceptible to improvement, whether by education or by labor discipline, but only to control.[148]

That control, finally, must be strictly clerical: Vincent de Paul's preoccupation with priestly oversight of the *hôpitaux* and the women who frequently ran them is a strikingly recurrent theme of his letters; his goal, like that of the Council of Trent and of other members of the Company, was ecclesiastical control of the social order in the

[145] *cf.* with the *Annales* and the *Mémoire* Cristobal Perez de Herrera's *Amparo des pobres* (n.p., 1598), disussed by Martz, pp. 86–7; the quote is from Martz, p. 158.
[146] *L'Aumône Générale*, pp. 56 *et passim*; *cf.* St Vincent de Paul, vol. 10, pp. 381–2, vol. 12, pp. 74, 470, 473.
[147] Gutton makes this last observation for France and Venice and points out that those that did exist frequently admitted paying students to the exclusion of the poor; neither masters nor parents showed excessive zeal for the admission of poor children free. He also notes the frequency with which elementary schools degenerated into Sunday catechism classes (*La Société et les pauvres en Europe*, p. 155).
[148] *L'Aumône Générale*, pp. 48–9 (emphasis mine); *cf.* Richard C. Trexler, 'Charity and the Defense of Urban Elites in the Italian Communes,' in *The Rich, the Well Born, and the Powerful: Elites and Upper Classes in History*, ed. Frederic Cople Jaher (Urbana, Illinois, 1973), pp. 64–109, arguing the thesis that sixteenth-century Italian charity administered by religious confraternities 'aimed at preserving corporate identification, not at fostering interclass mobility' (p. 69). The innovations proposed by Renaudot to improve the situation of the poor, including the establishment of a job bureau for the unemployed of Paris (the Bureau d'Adresse, founded with royal approval in 1628), was an exception to the seventeenth-century Catholic rule. It should be noted, however, that Renaudot was of Huguenot extraction – he converted to Catholicism in 1625 to facilitate royal acceptance of his schemes for social improvement – and that the Bureau was a secular institution. In any case, by 1639 even this progressive plan was transformed into a repressive institution when registration by the jobless was made mandatory (Solomon, pp. 14–21, 35–52).

name of Catholic orthodoxy. It was partly in protest against the confinement of the poor by secular authorities that Vincent de Paul
refused the spiritual services of his priests to the Hôpital Général de
Paris.[149] And the confraternities which ran the hospitals of seventeenth-
century France were more closely tied to the administrative structure and oversight of the church than their early sixteenth-century
counterparts had been.[150] But the primacy of the Company's concern with conformity, even at the expense of the poor, is nowhere
more apparent than in their campaign to destroy Huguenot *hôpitaux*,
however desperate the plight of their inmates, in order to combat
heresy.[151] In the final analysis, then, the social welfare projects of the
Counter-Reformation for the most part 'obeyed the limits marked
out by the pessimistic spirituality of the . . . Counter Reformation,'
and the Company of the Holy Sacrament was entirely typical in that
its 'bureaucratic, disciplinarian tendency, its passion for religious
decorum, its flair for systematic and rational means derived, not
from new needs or from a rational program or conception of society,
but rather from ascetic impulses turned in a socially repressive direction and colored by a profound conformism to the existing
order.'[152]

English protestant conformists did not face the theological dilemmas which Christian humanist ideas about poverty and charity
posed for Catholics; therefore, they are frequently found in substantial agreement with puritans on much of their poor relief theory. But
the areas of disagreement reveal the extent to which conformism
had replaced humanist reformism in their social theory; and these
areas of disagreement expanded in direct proportion to Laudian
opposition of individual nonconformity.

Anglicans tended to agree with humanist/puritan ambivalence
toward wealth, but also with the Erasmian denial of sanctity in
poverty. Exceptions can, of course, be found. Laud's close friend
Henry Hammond saw poverty as a clear punishment for sin, and he
viewed ambition and covetousness as less serious sins than did
puritans or humanists.[153] But at the same time John Normanton of

---

[149] Gutton, *La Société et les pauvres en Europe*, p. 144.
[150] Pullan, 'Catholics and the Poor,' p. 20; Bossy, 'Counter-Reformation and the
People,' pp. 59–60.
[151] Vincent de Paul, vol. 2, p. 92; vol. 9, pp. 50, 661; vol. 10, pp. 205, 304, 313; vol. 12,
pp. 377, 387, 393–7. *Annales*, p. 154.   [152] Chill, p. 423.
[153] Henry Hammond, *Works* (Oxford, 1853), vol. 1, p. 268; Timothy H. Breen, 'The
Non-Existent Controversy: Puritan and Anglican Attitudes on Work and Wealth,
1600–1640,' *CH*, 35 (1966), 273–87 (on Hammond, pp. 281, 286–7). Breen notes
that Hammond was 'the only pre-Civil War divine who developed these ideas so
completely' (p. 281).

Caius articulated a view of poverty of which any Counter-Reformation Catholic would have approved:

Happy... were those ancient heroes... those ancient fathers of the church that have been hermits, anchorites, and monastic men that have refused, scorned, condemned, and trampled on the world, and have given away all to follow Christ and his disciples... Happy were those kings and princes that have left their glittering palaces for a gloomy and melancholic cell. Amongst hundreds of examples, that of Charles the fifth is the most eminent.[154]

Neither Hammond nor Normanton, however, can be described as typically Anglican on these points. Rather, agreement of Anglicans and puritans is much more noticeable than their divergence on the nature of wealth and poverty.[155]

Anglicans likewise found the humanist distinction between deserving poor and idle rogues perfectly admissible, and, as has been argued at length earlier, they sponsored along with their puritan opponents the poor relief legislation for which puritans have received so much credit. In this area, however, exceptions to the rule are more numerous and are perhaps significant demonstrations of the Anglican tendency to affirm traditional values in defense of established social order. While many Anglicans shared Robert Sanderson's harsh attitude toward the undeserving poor, both Donne and Cosin spoke approvingly of public acts of personal, indiscriminate charity.[156] The ultra-royalist cleric Clement Paman found merit in almsgiving 'even to the loose and impious,' and Neile was known to stop his carriage in poor towns to distribute alms to all and sundry.[157] Such acts by clerics and by the well-born naturally tended to reinforce the essential hierarchy which Anglicans supported, and clerical approval of them should probably be interpreted in this light. But the Laudian hierarchy never went so far as to condone begging itself or to denounce discriminate relief programs; on the

---

[154] Sidney Sussex, Ward MS F, fol. 103v. Normanton also told the Vice-Chancellor's court that the increase of poverty in the realm was due to the pulling down of monasteries by the Tudor forerunners of the puritans (fol. 194v).

[155] Breen, *passim*; Donne, *Sermons*, vol. 2, p. 214, vol. 3, pp. 53–5 (on the temptations of riches), 58, 65 (on using wealth for commonwealth), vol. 4, pp. 172 (recommending mediocrity in material possessions), 189 (on celestial usury), 318 (on causes of poverty), vol. 5, p. 203 (on luxury); Humphrey Sydenham, *The Rich Mans Warning-peece* (1630), pp. 11–18 (citing Seneca and Vives on moderation).

[156] Robert Sanderson, *XXXIV Sermons* (London, 1661), p. 108, 251; *cf.* Fuller, *Works*, ed. G. M. Walter (New York, 1938), vol. 2, p. 154; Lancelot Andrewes, *Works* (Oxford, 1854), vol. 5, p. 43. On the other side, Cosin, *Works*, vol. 1, p. 27; Donne, *Sermons*, vol. 5, p. 154.

[157] H. Jenkins, *Edward Benlowes* (1952), quoting Paman (p. 159); Trevor-Roper, p. 143.

contrary, the weight of their arguments lies on the side of discriminate charity.

Work, too, had value for Anglicans as for humanists and puritans, although it must be admitted that Laudians expressed less approval of the equal sanctity of secular and clerical callings than did Erasmians. Here, obviously, their tendency to exalt clerical authority as a means of establishing social order provides the explanation for their divergence.[158] But the difference is one of degree, rather than kind, and as a means of dealing with the poor, work was advised no less by Anglicans than by puritans.[159]

There is perhaps no better illustration of the selective but substantial survival of humanist social ideology in seventeenth-century Anglicanism than in the joint sponsorship of the Books of Orders of 1630–1 by the most staunchly conformist of the hierarchy and the most zealous of puritans. The conciliar orders mandated setting on work for the masterless poor, forced labor for able vagrants, the apprenticeship of young children and stricter control of alehouses – all measures which Vives or More or Starkey would approve.[160] And at the county level they were 'generally well enforced... and opposition was fairly small scale' and based on localist resentment of centralized political authority rather than on rejection of the content of the Orders.[161] While traditionally the Books of Orders have been seen as part of the Laudian policies of 'Thorough,' recent research reveals that the primary influences on their formulation were the king's Huguenot physician Sir Theodore de Mayerne and the

---

[158] *cf.* Sidney Sussex, Ward MS F, fol. 103v (quoted above) and Sanderson's defense of ancient monastic retirement from the world (p. 247) with Donne, *Sermons*, vol. 1, p. 207, vol. 3, pp. 68, 196, 232–4, vol. 4, pp. 160, 272, 304, 318–19. In all fairness to Sanderson, it should be pointed out that he denounced 'present day monks' with their 'lean skulls and... fat paunches' (p. 247) and strongly upheld the intrinsic value of productive labor (pp. 239–46).

[159] Sanderson, pp. 107, 246, 249, 251; Breen, *passim*; Sir John Oglander, *A Royalist's Notebook*, ed. Francis Bamford (London, 1936), p. 204. C. John Sommerville, 'The Anti-Puritan Work Ethic,' *JBS*, 20 (1981), 70–81, has found stronger Anglican than dissenter support for a Weberian work ethic after 1660; by this time, of course, puritans had largely given up their vision of social reform in the face of political defeat, whereas, as Sommerville remarks, Anglicans had developed theologically in a more semi-pelagian direction and socially into a more self-conscious, 'denominational' group (pp. 77–8). Sommerville also sees Anglican development of a work ethic as in part a response to their own perceived failure to govern society effectively (pp. 80–1).

[160] In fact, an official handbook for the magistrates who were to enforce the orders reprinted much of the Elizabethan legislation on vagrancy and poor relief, part of which was of course Vivesian in inspiration: *Certaine Statutes... to be carefully put in execution by all Justices* (1630).

[161] Clark, *English Provincial Society*, p. 352.

zealously puritan Earl of Manchester, Henry Montagu.[162] Moreover, it has been suggested that part of the reason the orders were relatively well-enforced is that they had already been substantially implemented in counties like Somerset and Kent and Essex long before the 1630s.[163] In Essex, the orders were most vigorously enforced by the Earl of Warwick, Sir Thomas Barrington and Sir William Masham – all puritans, and all militant Parliamentarians when the war came. In the Book of Orders, as William Hunt comments, the 'Privy Council merely generalized the techniques that had been implemented over the previous half-century by parochial, municipal, and county elites, especially by those of a godly persuasion.'[164] But if primary credit cannot, after all, be given to Laud and Wentworth, still their agreement with the tenor of the conciliar orders at the beginning of the Personal Rule attests to the continued influence of humanist-inspired reforms even after those in authority had launched their campaign against many of the most potentially subversive aspects of Erasmian humanism, such as its criticism of hereditary nobility and its advocacy of household religion.

Perhaps the most significant Anglican departure from the sixteenth-century consensus on poor relief is not so much a disagreement with the substance of the consensus as a matter of omission: the small degree to which the conformist clergy concerned themselves with the issue at all is a stark contrast to the volumes of practical advice on wealth and charity preached and published by puritans. In this area of social theory, as in that of domestic conduct, most Stuart Anglicans simply had little or nothing to say. Their concerns lay elsewhere – with doctrinal, liturgical and ecclesiological questions. To preach conformity to orthodox instructions in these areas would in the Laudian framework do more for social order than would sermons on social issues. As a result, Laudian theories of poor relief (with the notable exceptions of Hammond's and Sanderson's) must be deduced from passing statements in sermons on less practical topics, and little detail is ever provided of specific proposals for

---

[162] Paul Slack, 'Books of Orders: The Making of English Social Policy, 1577–1631,' *TRHS*, 5th ser., 30 (1980), 1–22, pp. 1, 8, 14.

[163] T. G. Barnes, *Somerset, 1625–1640* (Oxford, 1961); Clark, p. 351; Hunt, pp. 248–9.

[164] Hunt, pp. 248–50, quote from 250. Hunt goes on to say that the program envisioned by the Book of Orders 'could never be implemented under the regime of William Laud. Laud's ecclesiastical policies alienated those very social groups whose cooperation was essential to the success of Stuart paternalism: ministers, vestrymen, and noble professors.'

the relief of poverty or the disciplining of the idle.[165] Frequently, Anglican sermons which initially appear to concern themselves with poverty and benevolence turn out to be spiritualizations of the concept of charity. Donne, for example, defined charity in spiritual terms, and identified the 'best charity' as prayer.[166] And when economic issues arise in private correspondence, advice on the proper use of wealth is similarly lacking.[167] In comparison with Erasmian and puritan theory, Anglican poor relief ideas are infrequent and sparse.

The same generalization applies to a comparison of Anglican with puritan charitable activities. In actuality, as in theory, the nature and extent of Anglican participation in poor relief reflects the conformists' pre-eminent concern with ecclesiastical control and doctrinal uniformity rather than with individual and social reformation. However generous Archbishop Laud himself was to the poor of his home town, Laudians generally come off badly in comparison with non-Laudian benefactors in terms of amounts given to reformist institutions. Laud's support of apprenticeship programs for poor children, provisions of work for the able poor, and municipal education, might better be explained in terms of his own social origins and mobility than as an example of Anglican generosity to institutions designed along humanist lines to improve the prospects of the poor and unemployed.[168] In any case, in analyzing Laud's attitudes toward poor relief, these personal bequests must be weighed against his overriding preoccupation with church control of charitable institutions and against the sort of advice which he gave to

[165] Sanderson is in many ways an intermediate figure, difficult to place theologically as well as ideologically: G. R. Cragg, *From Puritanism to the Age of Reason* (Cambridge, 1966), pp. 22–9. Examples of Anglican failure to provide any details of briefly mentioned welfare plans include Donne, *Sermons*, vol. 4, p. 272 (on the Virginia plantations as bridewells); Cosin, *Works*, vol. 2, p. 118; Sydenham, *passim*.

[166] Donne, *Sermons*, vol. 5, pp. 278–9. McGee's thesis that puritans were more concerned with First Table duties, Anglicans with practical works of piety is difficult to see in a comparison of Donne and Perkins on poor relief.

[167] Laud, writing to Wentworth 24 October 1637 concerning a charge made against his remarkable economic good fortune in Ireland, reported the king's approval of his increasing wealth, 'with a profession of much joy, that any of his good servants should in honourable ways grow and increase in his service.' (Laud, *Works*, Vol. VI, p. 509). The opportunity which would have been eagerly seized by More or Perkins or Greenham to warn against the potential dangers of wealth and exhort to righteous acquisition and use of riches is pointedly ignored by Laud.

[168] *The Benefactions of William Laud to the County of Berkshire*, ed. John Bruce (1841), *passim*, and especially pp. 21–8, 55–66; Laud, *Works*, vol. 3, p. 220, vol. 4, p. 445, vol. 5, p. 108, vol. 6, pp. 318, 420, 470–1, 578, 586; Trevor-Roper, pp. 340, 341–84.

Bishop Williams in 1635 permitting a drastic reduction in the proportion of clerical income traditionally regarded as owed to the poor.[169] Certainly other conformists were not as generous as was the archbishop or as able as were Christian humanists and puritans at encouraging charitable endeavors by their parishioners: charitable giving in England fell during the Laudian decade from its early Stuart peak, and it was not to rise significantly again until the puritan ascent to power in the Interregnum.[170] During that pre-Laudian peak period, moreover, the majority of charitable donations went to education and other charities aimed at individual reformation; it was educational giving which underwent the most marked decline during the 1630s, reflecting both the reluctance of puritans to give to institutions coming increasingly under Laudian control and the deemphasis of the Anglican hierarchy on reformist charity.[171]

The obvious charitable option for benefactors concerned with religious uniformity consisted in those institutions which symbolized the authority of the hierarchy. A 1619 sermon on charity by Donne accordingly exhorted the godly to donate to the building of houses of worship as a means of easing their way to heaven. And in a list of Cosin's benefactions totalling £3,151, only £366 is designated for the poor; the majority of the remaining £2,785 was for the beautification of cathedrals, the construction of other church buildings and the purchase of altar ornaments.[172]

Finally, conformist Anglicans diverged from the humanist/ puritan conviction that the poor were to be reformed and equipped

---

[169] Bruce, *Benefactions*, pp. 22, 26–7; W. K. Jordan, *Philanthropy in England, 1480–1660: A Study of the Changing Patterns of English Social Aspirations* (New York, 1959), pp. 133–5 (on attempts by Laudians to centralize control over local relief); Laud, *Works*, vol. 6, pp. 427–31. Laud concluded his advice to Williams,

> as the chargeableness of the times now are, and the many contributions by subsidies to shipping, and otherwise, which the Clergy in those [patristic] ages and places felt not, and the great difference in housekeeping, between the diet and manner of living in those hotter countries and these of ours, that it will be best, till it shall please God better to furnish this Church with means, to leave the Clergy free masters of their own charity. (p. 431)

[170] Jordan, pp. 245, 183; H. R. Trevor-Roper, *Historical Essays*, pp. 127–8; A. L. Beier, 'Poor Relief in Warwickshire 1630–1660,' *P&P*, 35 (1966), 78–99, p. 83, Table III. Jordan's failure to take inflation into account weakens the impact of his figures, but does not invalidate his observation of decline in the 1630s. For criticism of Jordan's figures, see W. Bittle and R. Lane, 'Inflation and Philanthropy in England,' *EcHR*, 29 (1976), 203–10, and D. C. Coleman, 'Philanthropy Deflated: A Comment', *EcHR*, 31 (1978), 105–28.

[171] Jordan, pp. 283–96. Jordan comments that early Stuart donors' 'educational interests were in large part derived from the humanistic' influence of the Renaissance (p. 287). Nearly all of the grammar schools established during this period gave free tuition to poor boys (p. 290).

[172] Donne, *Sermons*, vol. 2, pp. 213, 215–22, 234; Cosin, *Works*, vol. 1, pp. xxxi–xxxii. Again, note Anglican stress on First Table duties.

to be self-supporting, rather than isolated, confined and subjected to punitive discipline.[173] Like the Tridentine hierarchy, they transformed the theoretical aim of the workhouse from the reformation of the individual to the enforcement of obedience. Henry Hammond demanded a tough, quasi-penal labor discipline in workhouses, a position logically required by his view of poverty as punishment for sin.[174] Robert Sanderson exhorted his auditors, 'Let us harden our hearts against' the idle poor 'and not spare them . . These ulcers and drones of the Common-wealth are ill worthy of any honest man's alms, of any good magistrate's protection.'[175] The sentiment may not be much of a departure from Vives' or Perkins', but the language is, and the optimistic humanist assumption that the idle can be trained in self-discipline and job skills and so reformed is missing altogether. Rather, 'he that helpeth one of these sturdy beggars to the stocks and the whip and the house of correction not only deserveth better of the commonwealth, but doth a work of greater charity in the sight of God than he that helpeth him with meat and money and lodging.'[176] More significant is the extension of this attitude to the impotent poor by those in authority during the Laudian years and after the Restoration. It has been observed that 'rarely was there a hint of sympathy for the poor' in the Caroline orders, and that during the 1630s, examples can be found of the poor being persecuted merely because of their indigence, regardless of its causes.[177] Post-Restoration institutions for the poor reflect the triumph of the conformist position in their de-emphasis on education and in the increasingly punitive approach to the poor which gave late seventeenth-century workhouses the reputation which survives in popular literature.[178]

The conformists' suppression of some of the more innovative attempts to train and reform the poor can be interpreted as concomitant with their assumption that a change in behavior and mode

[173] *cf.* Sydenham's thesis that poverty is to be accepted unquestioningly (p. 19) with the humanist assumption that it is to be eliminated.

[174] Hammond, *Works*, vol. 1, pp. 200, 207, 299.   [175] Sanderson, p. 108.

[176] *Ibid.*, p. 251; *cf.* p. 107; Barnes, *Somerset*, pp. 189–90, remarks on the harshness with which vagrants were repressed during the Personal Rule in that county.

[177] Beier, p. 99.

[178] Valerie Pearl, 'Puritans and Poor Relief: The London Workhouse, 1649–1660,' *Puritans and Revolutionaries*, ed. Donald Pennington and Keith Thomas (Oxford, 1978), p. 230, comments that the workhouses of Middlesex and Westminster, established in 1664 and 1666 respectively, 'did not operate with the earlier [puritan] emphasis on education and both were markedly unsuccessful.' The reestablished Corporation of the Poor (1698) added in 1700 a vagrants' wing which was 'run like a house of correction,' a phenomenon which Pearl comments that she does not find in the London of the Interregnum.

of life is neither possible nor the proper concern of the authorities. In Salisbury, it was the dean and chapter who opposed aldermanic financing of work for the poor and training for poor children with a municipal brewhouse; the ecclesiastical authorities held that poverty is properly controlled by a penal workhouse, and that the innovations of the lay magistrates were evidence of 'inconformity to the state government and of puritanism and the like.'[179] Under their increasing influence in the 1630s, the municipal workhouse was enlarged, the inmates were more strictly segregated from the community and more harshly disciplined, employment opportunities for poor children were eliminated, outside relief for those able to contribute toward their own maintenance at home was abolished, and the idle were routinely whipped when sent to the workhouse, there 'to be kept as prisoners.' In Laudian Salisbury, as in Tridentine France and Spain, 'the ambition that outdoor employment and relief might lead to the gradual abolition of all but minimal poverty was tacitly abandoned, to be replaced by this quasi-penal incarceration of the poor.'[180]

When control and conformity became the order of the day, the Christian humanist hope for social transformation through individual reformation was repudiated. The Anglican social order, like the Tridentine, was a system of enforced obedience to a set of behavioral and ceremonial expectations imposed from above. Puritanism, continuing the Erasmian insistence on the rule of individual conscience, lay self-examination and social analysis based on direct confrontation with Scripture, household religious teaching and discipline, and rational, secular schemes to eliminate poverty through education, could only be seen as a threat to the strictly hierarchical, descending authority of the clerical and aristocratic estates. This is not to deny that there was in early Stuart England a spectrum of opinion – there were moderate Anglicans interested in social reform, and there were moderate puritans willing to compromise more or less with established authority. To have described here the polarities is not to say that a middle ground did not exist; it is merely an attempt to clarify the options open to early modern Englishmen concerned with social order.

By 1640 the polarities were becoming more obvious than the middle ground, and Englishmen were being confronted with

[179] Paul Slack, 'Poverty and Politics in Salisbury, 1597–1666,' in *Crisis and Order in English Towns 1500–1700: Essays in urban history*, ed. Peter Clark and Paul Slack (Toronto, 1972), 164–203, p. 188.   [180] *Ibid.*, p. 192; *cf.* pp. 186–91.

demands to ally themselves with one system of social order or the other. Puritans, who had been left to carry the banner of Erasmian reformism alone, carried it at last into the Civil War. Having hung in the balance during the course of that struggle, Erasmian social theory at last emerged as the dominant approach to order in the commonwealth. The victory of puritanism in the 1640s meant the victory, too, of Erasmian humanism in the area of social reform; the execution of Laud symbolized the existence at long last of an opportunity for the Christian humanist social vision to be carried out by the hotter sort unopposed by the upholders of tradition. Of course, the rulers of the new commonwealth were faced with political, religious, and diplomatic problems as well as social ones, so that their implementation of humanist social theory during the Interregnum was at best partial and seldom firmly enough established to weather the storms of the Restoration. But credit must be given to the enthusiastic endeavors of Parliamentarians and local magistrates, preachers and projectors, parents and educators, to realize the Erasmian Golden Age, or in their terms, the New Jerusalem.

In the order established by victorious puritanism, the spiritualized household was enjoined by law, not merely idealized by preachers and presbyters. The 1645 Directory for Public Worship called newlyweds to be diligent in family Bible-reading and prayer, and in 'watching over and provoking each other to love and good works.'[181] Legislation passed under the Protectorate required free consent to marriage by both parties and ended the sexual double standard, at least in the eyes of the law.[182] The conjugal family unit was to be indeed the church and commonwealth writ small which Erasmus and More had envisioned a century and a half earlier; and it was to be hedged by the stricter legislation against adultery for which puritans had been agitating for decades: the Adultery Act of 1650 followed the advice of More and other humanists in making adultery a capital offense.[183]

The sobriety of Utopian life and the pietism of Erasmus' Christian knight were also in effect legislated by puritan Parliaments, in the name of that same biblicism which had inspired the Christian humanists. While the Interregnum prohibitions of drunkenness, gambling, frivolity and extravagant living were not in most cases

---

[181] F&R, vol. 1, p. 600; *cf. Minutes of the Manchester Presbyterian Classis*, ed. W. A. Shaw (Chetham Society, 1890), pp. 117, 400.   [182] *F&R*, vol. 2, pp. 388, 717.
[183] Keith Thomas, 'The Puritans and Adultery: The Act of 1650 Reconsidered,' *Puritans and Revolutionaries*, ed. Donald Pennington and Keith Thomas (Oxford, 1978), pp. 257–81.

acknowledged as Erasmian by their authors, the puritans' intellectual debt to the Christian humanist social vision is reflected by the striking similarities of these laws to those recommended by Erasmus to Charles V, by Starkey to Henry VIII, and by Bucer to Edward VI.[184] Cromwellian laws against drunkenness and other forms of self-indulgence were passed not only to eliminate the dishonor to God which accompanied such activities, but also because they 'do often produce the ruin of persons and their families' – they were recognized as secondary causes of poverty.[185] Sabbatarian legislation, moreover, was designed not only to encourage worship of God and regard for First Table duties, but also to subject the poor, the idle and the frivolous to the moral instructions being meted out from the pulpit.[186] Preaching was encouraged by law as a means whereby God would be glorified, and in the process, society would be reformed by persuasion of individual conscience.[187]

Innovative educational schemes flourished during the Interregnum as never before. Legal encouragement was given by Parliament to the foundation of new schools wherein persons of 'piety and learning . . . employ themselves in the education of children in piety and good literature' and of new, puritan-sponsored universities (Dublin and Durham) designed to produce both learned ministers and able public servants.[188] Reformers like William Petty, John Dury and Samuel Hartlib, critical of scholasticism, traditional academic exercises and metaphysics, projected new schools with more practical curricula.[189] Petty's suggestion of 'literary workhouses' for all children over seven, including the poor, would have delighted Erasmus and Vives; he aimed to change a social order in which 'many are now holding the plough, which might have been made fit to steer the state.'[190] Foundlings in London (girls as well as boys) were routinely given Bibles and other books, and 8s per annum was spent on each

[184] Cromwellian injunctions against drunkenness include F&R, vol. 2, pp. 940–2, 1050, 1132; against gambling, vol. 2, p. 1250; and against plays as encouragers of vice, vol. 1, pp. 1027, 1070–1071. 'Pastimes' were no more legitimate in puritan than in humanist eyes (vol. 2, p. 1249); however, recreation *per se* was not condemned: regular days of recreation were established in 1647 (vol. 1, p. 954).
[185] F&R, vol. 2, pp. 345, 861.
[186] F&R, vol. 1, pp. 420–2; *cf.* vol. 1, pp. 23, 81, and vol. 2, pp. 384–5, 1167. The ineffectiveness of this legislation is discussed by John Morrill, 'The Church in England, 1642–9,' *Reactions to the English Civil War* (New York, 1983), pp. 89–109. [187] F&R, vol. 1, p. 830.
[188] F&R, vol. 2, p. 345; Charles Webster, *The Great Instauration: Science, Medicine and Reform 1626–1660* (New York, 1975), pp. 224–42.
[189] Webster, pp. 199–202, 207–20. Dury's *The Reformed School* advocated education for girls as well as boys (Webster, p. 219).
[190] William Petty, *Advice . . . for Advancement of . . . Learning* (London, 1648), p. 4.

one's education in the 1640s and 1650s.[191] Hartlib's apologetic for the London Corporation of the Poor explained that the corporation would take in hand the children of the poor 'to civilize and train them up, in their books, and so by degrees to trades, that so they may be fit servants for the Commonwealth'; his aim was thus a far cry from that of the French *dévots* who merely isolated poor children from the larger society.[192] Pullan's remark following his account of the pre-occupation of early modern English philanthropy with the foundation of grammar schools, that 'It is hard to find anything exactly comparable in sixteenth century Venice,' is a telling comment on the Counter-Reformation's approach to social reform.[193] An iconoclastic attitude toward scholasticism prevailed in the universities during the 1650s, and university reforms under Parliament and the army 'created conditions favorable to intellectual experiment' there.[194]

At the Restoration, Durham University was suppressed, Dublin and many other projects stillborn, and educational revenues rechanneled to ecclesiastical uses. The educational workhouses of the puritan commonwealth were replaced in 1660 by workhouses 'motivated by purely economic considerations, rather than by a genuine humanitarian belief in the value of education,' and the conformist charity schools of the later seventeenth century, 'designed to instil the basic literacy needed for moral and religious conformity,' have been described as 'a return to attitudes of the Laudian period.'[195] As noted earlier, those attitudes also diminished the educational offerings of workhouses and turned them into semipenal institutions more akin to the *hospicios* of Hapsburg Spain than the training grounds envisioned by Vives.

As for poor relief, puritan reinforcement during the Interregnum of discrimination between the impotent poor and rogues, of strict lay oversight of relief, and of ambitious work projects for the idle and unemployed have been mentioned in an earlier chapter, as has puritan generosity toward charities aimed at reforming the poor and equipping them for self-support.[196] Puritan workhouses were far

[191] Pearl, 'Social Policy in Early Modern London,' in *History and Imagination*, ed. H. Lloyd-Jones, V. Pearl and B. Worden (New York, 1981), 115–31, p. 126.
[192] Pearl, 'Puritans and Poor Relief,' p. 219, quoting *Londons Charitie* (1649), *et passim.* [193] Pullan, *Rich and Poor*, p. 401; *cf.* pp. 401–5.
[194] Webster, p. 144, *cf.* pp. 129–44, 178–90. [195] *Ibid.*, pp. 244–5.
[196] F&R, vol. 1, pp. 1042–5, vol. 2, pp. 104–10, 252, 1019–25, 1098; Pearl, 'Puritans and Poor Relief,' *passim*, focusing on the puritan-founded Corporation of the Poor; E. M. Hampson, *The Treatment of Poverty in Cambridgeshire, 1597–1834* (Cambridge, 1934), p. 44; Beier, pp. 95–7; see chapter 5 above.

from the *prisons des pauvres* of the Company of the Holy Sacrament: residence (or incarceration) was not a prerequisite for assistance, either for adults or for children, and the objective of work was vocational rehabilitation so that inmates could hope to become productive citizens.[197] Pearl has concluded that the London Corporation of the Poor, a representative puritan institution in the Interregnum, was 'a pioneering education and workhouse foundation rather than the prison for vagrants into which it was turned by historians of our own day.'[198] Such efforts as these reflect the Vivesian assumptions which guided puritan legislators, perhaps unconsciously, and which had been largely absent from or penally interpreted by their Laudian predecessors, as they would be by their Restoration successors.[199] In addition, while Hill has charged that 'humanitarianism was irrelevant to those who believed in the fixed decrees,' puritan legislators of the Commonwealth and Protectorate were responsible for orders to supply the London poor with fuel during the wartime crisis ('the poor sort of every parish to be first served, and after the other degrees and ranks of people'), for the release from prison of debtors unable to pay their creditors, and for designating portions of the royal estates 'the poors' ground.'[200] In 1649, the Council of State formed a committee to 'consider what is fit to be done for abating the price of corn, and for setting the poor at work,' and the decision in the same year to drain the Fens professed as one of its objectives the creation of employment for the poor.[201] On a local level, orders for the correction of vagrants and rogues in Warwickshire aimed at 'positive, preventative measures, and punitive ones took second place.'[202] In London, publically-financed wage supplements to the under-employed were substantial, and managers made risky investments in public real estate to house the poor, successfully raising capital loans from parishioners. It is clear that there was in fact a 'growing sense of communal responsibility [which] . . . increased, rather than diminished, in the century of Puritanism.'[203]

---

[197] Pearl, pp. 221, 224–5. Provision was made for parish pensioners to walk poor children to the workhouse each morning and home at the end of the day.
[198] 'Puritans and Poor Relief,' p. 230.
[199] Christopher Hill, *Society and Puritanism* (New York, 1964), p. 295, observes that 'serious attempts to set the poor on work were abandoned' after the Restoration, when state policy 'concentrated on restricting the mobility of labour' instead.
[200] *Ibid.*, p. 287. On fuel provisions, F&R, vol. 1, p. 303, *cf.* pp. 304–5, 481–2; on poor debtors, vol. 2, pp. 240–1, 321–4, 378–9, 582; on common land for the poor, vol. 2, p. 785.
[201] *CSPD*, 22 November 1649, ed. M. A. E. Green (1875), p. 402; F&R, vol. 2, pp. 130–9. [202] Beier, p. 99. [203] Pearl, 'Social Policy,' pp. 115–31, quote from p. 131.

In this reforming legislation, in the republican experiment itself,[204] in the content of puritan sermons and treatises and in the activities of puritan householders, can be seen the survival of Christian humanist social theory in the Interregnum. Undeniably the puritan Erasmianism of the seventeenth century had undergone significant sea changes – shifts in emphasis and context sufficient to obscure considerably its true identity (particularly to historians intent on saddling puritans with Victorian morality and profiteering). Except in the area of social thought and textual exegesis, the humanism of the puritans was indeed altered almost beyond recognition. It was cluttered with dogmatic quarreling with which Erasmus would have had little sympathy. It was, in the Interregnum, re-shaped by millenarianism, which, while not altogether dissimilar to utopianism, did shift the emphasis in a more exclusive, spiritually elitist direction than the humanists had had in mind. Carried into battle with the black and gold of Parliament, the humanist banner wound up waving over acts of political radicalism and violence which would have appalled Erasmus and More, and, indeed, most of their Elizabethan and Jacobean followers. The humanism of seventeenth-century puritans had also lost Erasmus' elegance of language and urbanity of wit – no small loss to modern students who find it hard to turn from the *Moriae Encomium* to Perkins' sermons.

All this is surely to be expected, for the Erasmian tradition was no more stagnant than any other intellectual development in history. By its very nature Christian humanism would manifest itself differently in 1650 from in 1520: it was, after all, a set of assumptions about the nature of man and society which would itself pave the way for changes scarcely foreseen by its first authors, even in their most radical visions. Protestantism injected different nuances, and social conditions and political change reshaped the details of its projected reforms, but humanism was *per se* an ethic of change.

The fact remains that even in protestant dress and in the midst of civil war, the social goal of the hotter sort remained that of Erasmus and Vives, More and Whitforde, Starkey and Lupset – to transform medieval social stasis into a progressive, sober, hard-working, disciplined order. The new order was to be imposed by godly, educated

[204] Blair Worden, 'Classical Republicanism and the Puritan Revolution,' in *History and Imagination*, ed. H. Lloyd-Jones, V. Pearl and B. Worden (New York, 1981), pp. 182–200, finds the republicanism of the Interregnum rooted in the classical literature with which puritans were so familiar. But he sets this classicism in the tradition of Renaissance humanism (p. 193).

laymen, but imposed not through demands for outward conformity to authorized ritual and dogma, but through the training of individual conscience in pious self-control, in an industrious mode of living for the common good, in the practical morality of the *philosophia Christi*. The social order of Erasmus and Perkins was not secular; it was a sanctification of the *seculum*. Household and market-place, political forum and village school were the proper fields of Christian activity, and it was the hope of Cromwellian magistrates no less than of Christian humanist educators that biblically-inspired activism on these fronts would realize Utopia.

BIBLIOGRAPHY

MS NOTEBOOKS OF MEMBERS OF OXFORD AND CAMBRIDGE COLLEGES[1]

COLLEGE	AUTHOR	DATE	DESCRIPTION	MS LOCATION[2]/ REFERENCE NO.
Broadgates Hall	[Carnsew brothers][3]	1573–4	Fragmentary remains of academic diary	PRO/SP 46/15
Corpus Christi, Oxford	John Rainolds	1573–8	Lectures on Aristotle	Queen's, Oxford/354
Christ Church	John Stone	1576–85	Notes on theology, sermons and orations, Scripture, recent historical events	Bodl/Rawl. D.273
Christ Church	Anthony Parker	1581	Theological notebook	BL/Harl. 4048
Brasenose, University College	Robert Batti	1581–4	Lecture notes; verses; letter book	Bodl/Rawl. D.985
Christ's, Cambridge	Arthur Hildersham	1582–1614	Theological notebook	BL/Harl. 3230
[Emmanuel]	Anon.	1583–1628	Notes on history and theology	CUL/Gg.1.29
Oriel	John Day	1589	Notes on Aristotle	Bodl/Rawl. D.274
[Cambridge]	Anon.	ca. 1590	Greek text of Demosthenes with Latin commentary	CUL/Add. 6314
Pembroke, Cambridge	Anon.	1590–2	Commonplaces; lecture and disputation notes	LC II.164
Christ's, Cambridge	Samuel Ward	1590	Commonplace book	Sidney MS 44
Trinity, Dublin	Lucas Challoner	1595–ca.1612	Commonplace book	TCD MS 357
Christ's, Cambridge	Samuel Ward	1595–9	Diary (some later entries dated 1601, 1621, 1625, 1629)	Sidney MS 45
University College	Alexander Cooke	1596	Theological notebook	BL/Harl. 5247
Christ's, Cambridge	Samuel Ward	1596–9	Primarily lists of book loans; logic notes	Sidney Sussex/Ward A[4]
King's, Cambridge	Anon.	1597	Commonplace book	Bodl/Rawl.
Queens', Cambridge	Richard Morton	ca. 1600	Notes on natural philosophy	Horne 43
[Emmanuel]	Anon.	ca. 1600	Theology and sermon notes	CUL/Dd.3.85.5
Emmanuel	Samuel Ward	ca.1600–10	Theological notebooks; notes on grammar, logic,	Sidney/Ward B, C, D, E, F, G, H, I

COLLEGE	AUTHOR	DATE	DESCRIPTION	MS LOCATION[2]/ REFERENCE NO.
			history; F and I have some later entries (1635–42)	
St John's, Oxford	[John English]	1601	Commonplace book	Bodl/Rawl. D.1423
Trinity, Cambridge	Robert Boothe	*ca.* 1605	Aristotelian logic/ physics	BL. Harl. 5356
Corpus, Oxford	Daniel Featly	1606–22	Notes on theology, sermons; letter book	Bodl/Rawl. D.47
Sidney Sussex	Samuel Ward	*ca.*1610–1630	Theological note-books; notes on Synod of Dort	Sidney/Ward J, K, L, M, O[5]
Exeter	Anon.	1615	Lecture, disputation and sermon notes; Scripture commentary	BL/Harl. 977
Balliol	Thomas Laurence	1615–17	Letter and common-place book; notes on ancient authors	Balliol/438
[Queen's, Oxford]	Edmund Sheapheard	1617	Notes on Aristotle	Queen's, Oxford/437
St John's, Cambridge	Simonds D'Ewes	1618	*Collectanea philosophia*	BL/Harl. 190
—	—	1618	Commonplace book	BL/Harl. 182
—	—	1619	Aristotelian logic	BL/Harl. 191
—	—	1619	Notes on history	BL/Harl. 192
Pembroke, Cambridge	Alexander Bolde	1620	Commonplaces; sermon notes; verses	St John's, Cambridge/ S.34
Oriel	[Thomas Kearn]	*ca.* 1620	Commonplace book	Bodl/Rawl. D.947
Wadham	[Richard Seymes]	1622	Commonplace book; notes on ancient authors	Queen's, Oxford/438
St John's, Cambridge	Simonds D'Ewes	1622–3, 1646	Commonplaces; notes on history, genealogy	BL/Harl. 186
Queen's, Oxford	Anon.	1623	Crackenthorpe's *Logic*	Queen's, Oxford/196
Emmanuel	William Sancroft	1620–40	Notes in philosophy; logic disputation notes (by both the later Archbishop Sancroft and his uncle)	Bodl/Sancroft 25
Trinity, Cambridge	Anon.	post-1629	Theological commonplaces	St John's, Cambridge/ S.18
Emmanuel	William Sancroft	1630–40	Commonplaces; logic notes (the latter certainly by the archbishop)	Bodl/Sancroft 87
Emmanuel	William Sancroft	1630–40s	Letter book; notes on ancient authors	Bodl/Tanner 467
Oriel; Jesus, Oxford	Henry Vaughan	1634–9	Commonplace book; notes on ancient history, rhetoric	St John's, Cambridge/ K.38
Pembroke, Cambridge	Anon.	post-1631	Commonplaces; ancient authors	LC II.16
Oxford	Anon.	1635–6	Commonplace book; notes on theology and Scripture	St John's, Cambridge/ S.44
[Christ Church]	Anon.	1635–53	Notebook and letter book	Bodl/Add. B.109
Balliol	Francis Boughley	1637	Disputation notes	BL/Harl. 1779
St John's, Cambridge	Thomas Baker	post 1637	Notes on university history	BL/Harl. 7033
Emmanuel	William Bright	1644–61	Sermon and historical notes; theological commonplaces	CUL/Add. 6160

COLLEGE	AUTHOR	DATE	DESCRIPTION	MS LOCATION²/ REFERENCE NO.
Queen's, Oxford	Thomas Brathwaite	1642	Theological notes; commonplaces	CUL/Dd.12.57
Trinity, Cambridge	Daniel Foote	1646	Aristotelian ethics, physics	BL/Sloane 586
University College	[William Johnson]	1650–7	Commonplaces, poems, accounts; notes on ancient history	St John's, Cambridge/ O.64
Balliol	Anon.	1656	Transcription of Brierwood's *Logic*	Balliol/399
Trinity, Cambridge	James Duport	1660	'Rules for Students'	O.10A.33
—	Isaac Newton	1660	Book list; expenses	R.4.48d
Pembroke, Cambridge	Anon.	1672–3	Sermon and theological notes	LC II.14
Queen's, Oxford	Nehemiah Rogers	1675	Aristotelian logic notes; poems	BL/Harl. 5043

UNDATED EARLY TO MIDDLE SEVENTEENTH CENTURY STUDENT NOTEBOOKS

COLLEGE	AUTHOR	DESCRIPTION	MS LOCATION/ REFERENCE NO.
Trinity, Cambridge	Edward Palmer	Massive commonplace book; notes on ancient authors	R.16.6
—	Anon.	Commonplace book, similar to above	R.16.7
—	Anon.	Commonplace book with Hebrew glossary and pronunciation guide; Greek grammar	R.16.8
—	Anon.	Commonplace book, similar to R.16.6	R.16.9
—	Anon.	Commonplace book, similar to R.16.6	R.16.10
—	Edward Palmer	Commonplace book, Greek and Latin	R.16.11
—	[Palmer]	Commonplace book, frequently citing Ovid and Martial (less Greek than above)	R.16.12
—	[Palmer]	Commonplace book, heavily Greek	R.16.13
—	Anon.	Commonplace book, similar to R.16.13 but in different hand; heavily patristic, Stoic, indebted to Vives	R.16.14
—	Anon.	Commonplace book, smaller and less neatly kept than R.16.6–14	R.16.15
—	Anon.	Commonplace book, smaller and less neatly kept than R.16.6–14	R.16.16
—	Anon.	Commonplace book, similar to R.16.13	R.16.17
—	Anon.	Commonplace book, similar to R.16.6, 7, 9, 10	R.16.18
—	"W. Ga."	Philosophical commonplace book, predominantly Aristotelian	R.16.19
Pembroke, Cambridge	Nicholas Felton	Notes on scholastic metaphysics	LC II.5⁶
Pembroke, Cambridge	Anon.	Verses; notes on the *Iliad*	LC II.11
Pembroke, Cambridge	Anon.	Theology notebook	LC II.12
Pembroke, Cambridge	Anon.	Transcript of Matthew Wren's commentary on Scripture	LC II.133, 134
St John's, Cambridge	Anon.	Commonplace book	St John's, Cambridge/I.34
St John's, Cambridge	Simonds D'Ewes	Theological observations	BL/Harl. 227

COLLEGE	AUTHOR	DESCRIPTION	MS LOCATION/ REFERENCE NO.
Cambridge	Anon.	Logic notebook, 'Notae . . . Burgersdicii'	BL/Sloane 600
Cambridge	Anon.	Aristotelian logic notebook	CUL/Dd.5.47
(Unknown)	Anon.	Notes on Aristotle	BL/Sloane 1981
(Unknown)	Anon.	Aristotelian logic notebook	BL/Lansdowne 797
Balliol	[Joseph Bussard]	Theological commonplace book	Balliol/337
Queens', Cambridge	[John Eames or Thomas Lovering]	Theological commonplace book; sermon notes	Horne 41

MS NOTEBOOKS FROM NON-ENGLISH UNIVERSITIES

COLLEGE	DATE	DESCRIPTION	MS LOCATION/ REFERENCE NO.
Cagliari	*ca.* 1575–1600	Transcript of Aristotle's *Logic* with Thomistic commentary	Balliol/322[7]
Rome	1623	Notes on scholastic philosophy	St John's, Cambridge/I.37
Salamanca	1652	Notes on Aristotelian logic	CUL/Add. 4359

OTHER MANUSCRIPTS CONSULTED

Part I: Sixteenth Century

MS LOCATION/ REFERENCE NO.	AUTHOR	DESCRIPTION	DATE
Balliol/354	Richard Hill	Commonplace book; family records	1518–27
BL/Royal 17.1.XLIX	Thomas Lumley	Abstract of Erasmus' *Institutes of a christen prince*	1550
BL/Royal 18.C.VI	Anon.	Treatise on poor relief	1531
BL/Royal 12.A.I–IV	Lady Mary Fitzalan	Translations of various Greek authors	
BL/Arundel 73	Nicholas Harpsfield	*Ecclesiastical History* to 1522	post-1522
BL/Vespasian F.III. No. 35	Catherine Parr	Correspondence to Princess Mary regarding Erasmus	
BL/Lansdowne 95, 3	[Thomas Smith]	Treatise on poor relief	1580
Bodleian/Auct. S.2.29	John Rainolds	Aristotle's *De arte dicendi libri tres* (Paris, 1562), interleaved in and bound with MS commentary in Rainolds' hand; presumably his lectures at Corpus	1572–78
CUL/Add. 7197	Anon.	Ridley's sermons, compiled for a Cambridge scholar	1529
Cambridge U.		Booklists from Wills and	1520–1660

MS LOCATION/ REFERENCE NO.	AUTHOR	DESCRIPTION	DATE
Archives		Inventories in Chancellor's Court Registers	
Oxford U. Archives		Booklists from Wills and Inventories in Chancellor's Court Registers	1527–1653

Part 2: Seventeenth Century

MS LOCATION/ REFERENCE NO.	AUTHOR	DESCRIPTION	DATE
BL/Harl. 118–21	Simonds D'Ewes	School notebooks	1615–17
BL/Add. 25, 285	Oliver St John	Commonplace book	
BL/Add. 21, 935	Nehemiah Wallington	Historical notes and meditations	1630–49
BL/Add. 40883	—	Diary	1641–3
CUL/Dd. 3.85, 18	Lancelot Andrewes	Treatise against re-marriage after divorce	1601
CUL/Dd. 3.85, 10	Anon.	Treatise dedicated to Andrewes	
CUL/Dd. 3.83, 19	Thomas Gataker	Letter of pastoral counsel	1631
CUL/Add. 84	John Patrick	Book catalogue	1630–50
CUL/Add. 6867	John Walker	Commonplace and letter book	1632–55
CUL/Add. 3102	Anon	Book catalogue; the names of Sir John Hare and Anthony Thomas appear on the flyleaf	*ca.* 1650
CUL/Add. 40(C), 2	Samuel Ward	Letter to Ussher	1637
CUL/Add. 22		Documents concerning university affairs	16th–17th C.
CUL/CUR 6.1		Documents concerning religious conflict in Cambridge	16th–17th C.
CUL/CUR 78		Documents concerning religious conflict in Cambridge	16th–17th C.
CUL/VC Ct. I.49, I.8 and Com.Ct. I.18		Vice-Chancellor's court registers, Cambridge	early 17th C.
Lambeth Palace/MS 2086	William Rawley	Commonplace book	1626–44
Nottingham U. MS, Box 166	Brilliana Conway (later Harley)	Commonplace book	1622
PRO/SP 16/193/91	E. Duncan	Letter to Mr Querles concerning a controversy at Corpus Christi College	1631
St John's, Cambridge/U.5	Anon.	Catalogue of books given to St John's [by Bishop John Williams?]	
St John's, Cambridge/0.65	Matthew Robinson	*Strena Poetica* (to his tutor, Zachary Cawdrey)	
Sidney Sussex/ Ward R	Anon.	Debate between William Ames and Thomas Gataker on lots, with letters from Ames to Samuel Ward and [Matthew] Stonam	1626
Emmanuel/I.2.27	Richard Holdsworth	Directions for students in the universities	1630s

Notes to Ms Bibliography

1 Order of arrangement is roughly chronological, 1570–1675; notebooks from continental universities (kept by presumably Catholic English students) and undated notebooks are listed separately. Notebooks of fellows and masters of colleges, as well as of undergraduate students, are included.
2 If other than college listed in first column.
3 Brackets indicate uncertain identification.
4 Classification of the Ward manuscripts is found in Margo Todd, 'The Samuel Ward Papers at Sidney Sussex College, Cambridge,' *Transactions of the Cambridge Bibliographical Society*, 8 (1985), 582–92.
5 Listed by manuscript location.
6 This and the foregoing fourteen manuscripts are in early seventeenth-century hands.
7 Described by R. A. B. Mynor's *Catalogue of the MSS of Balliol College, Oxford* (Oxford, 1963) as by 'A professor in the Jesuit College at Cagliari.'

SELECT PRINTED WORKS

1 Primary sources

Abstracts from the Wills and Testamentary Documents of Printers, Binders, and Stationers of Cambridge from 1504 to 1699, ed. G. J. Gray and W. M. Palmer, London, 1915.

Acts and Ordinances of the Interregnum, ed. C. H. Firth and R. S. Rait, London, 1911.

The 'Adages' of Erasmus, trans. Margaret Mann Phillips, Cambridge, 1964.

Allen, Robert, *A Treatise of Christian beneficence*, London, 1600.

Ames, William, *Conscience with Power and the Cases Thereof*, London, 1639.
　The Marrow of Theology, trans. and ed. John Eusden, Boston, 1968.

Andrewes, Lancelot, *Works*, Oxford, 1854.

Annales de la Compagnie du St-Sacrement, ed. H. Beauchet-Filleau, Marseille, 1900.

Aquinas, St Thomas, *Summa theologiae*, trans. Fathers of the English Dominican Province, London, 1913–42.

Archives Curieuses de l'histoire de France, ed. M. L. Cimber and F. Danjou, Paris, 1837.

Arthington, Henry, *Provision for the Poore*, London, 1597.

Ascham, Roger, *Toxophilus*, London, 1545.

Autobiography and Correspondence of Sir Simonds D'Ewes, ed. J. O. Halliwell, London, 1845.

Bacon, Francis, *Works*, ed. James Spedding, London, 1868.

Bale, John, *Select Works*, ed. Henry Christmas, Cambridge, 1849.

Ball, John, *The Power of Godliness*, London, 1657.

Bancroft, Richard, *Dangerous Positions*, London, 1593.

Tracts, ed. Albert Peel, Cambridge, 1953.

[Barlow, Thomas], '*A Library for Younger Schollers*' *Compiled by an English Scholar-Priest about 1655*, ed. Alma Dejordy and H. F. Fletcher, Urbana, Illinois, 1961.

Batty, Bartholomew, *The Christian mans Closet*, trans. William Lowth, London, 1581.

Baxter, Richard, *The Reformed Pastor*, London, 1656.

Christian Directory, London, 1673.

The Catechising of Families, London, 1683.

Autobiography, ed. J. Lloyd Thomas, London, 1931.

Becanus, Martinus, *A Treatise of the Judge of Controversies*, trans. W. W[right], [St Omer], 1619.

Becon, Thomas, *The Jewel of Joy*, London, 1560.

Catechism, ed. John Ayre, Cambridge, 1844.

Bedel, Henry, *A sermon exhortyng to pitie the poore*, London, 1572.

Bedell, William, *The ABC. or, the institution of a Christian*, Dublin, 1631.

Bellarmine, Robert, *De ascensione mentis in Deum per scalas creaturarum...A most learned and pious treatise framing a ladder whereby our mindes may ascend to God*, Douai, 1616.

Opera Omnia, ed. Justin Fèvre, Paris, 1870–4.

The Benefactions of William Laud to the County of Berkshire, ed. John Bruce, London, 1841.

Bolton, Robert, *Instructions for a Right Comforting Afflicted Consciences*, London, 1631.

Brierwood, Edward, *Elementa logicae*, London, 1614.

Bucer, Martin, *A Treatise How by the Worde of God, Christian mens Almose ought to Be distributed*, London [1557].

De Regno Christi, trans. Wilhelm Pauck and Paul Larkin in *Library of Christian Classics*, vol. 19, *Melanchthon and Bucer*, Philadelphia, 1969.

Bullinger, Heinrich, *The Christen state of Matrimonye*, trans. Miles Coverdale, London, 1541.

Bunny, Edmund, *A book of christian exercise appertaining to Resolution By R. Parsons*, n.p., 1585.

A briefe answer unto those idle quarrels of R. P. against the late edition of the Resolution, London, 1589.

Calvin, John, *Commentary on Seneca's De Clementia*, trans. Ford Lewis Battles and Andre Malan Hugo, Leiden, 1969.

Cambridge Transactions during the Puritan Controversies, eds. J. Heywood and T. Wright, Cambridge, 1854.

Canons and Decrees of the Council of Trent, trans. and ed. H. J. Schroeder, St Louis, 1941.

Carpenter, John, *A Preparative to Contentation*, London, 1597.

Cartwrightiana, ed. Albert Peel and Leland H. Carson, London, 1951.

Chaderton, Laurence, *An Excellent and godly Sermon... preached at Paules Crosse the xxvi daye of October, An. 1578*, London, 1578.

[Cheke, Sir John], *The Hurt of Sedicion howe Greveous it is to a Commune Welth*, London, 1549.

Cleaver, Robert and John Dod, *A Godly Forme of Householde Government,* London, 1598.
Clinton, Elizabeth, *The Countess of Lincolns Nurserie,* London, 1622.
Colet, John, *Enarratio in Primam Epistolam S. Pauli ad Corinthios,* trans. J. H. Lupton, London, 1874.
Collected Works of Erasmus, various editors, Toronto, 1974–
The Colloquies of Erasmus, trans. Craig R. Thompson, Chicago, 1965.
The Complete Works of St Thomas More, vol. 4, *Utopia,* ed. Edward Surtz and J. H. Hexter, New Haven, 1965.
The Correspondence of Sir Thomas More, ed. E. F. Rogers, Princeton, 1947.
Cosin, John, *Works,* ed. John Henry Parker, Oxford, 1843–5.
Crackenthorpe, Richard, *Introductio in metaphysicam,* Oxford, 1619.
 Logicae libri quinque, London, 1622.
Dent, Arthur, *Plaine mans Pathway to Heaven,* London, 1601.
de Sales, François, *Treatise on the Love of God,* trans. Henry Benedict Mackey, Westminster, Maryland, 1949.
 Introduction à la Vie dévote, ed. Robert Morel, Haute Provence, 1963.
Desiderius Erasmus: Christian Humanism and the Reformation, ed. John C. Olin, Gloucester, Massachusetts, 1973.
D'Ewes, Sir Simonds, *The Journals of all the Parliaments during the Reign of Queen Elizabeth,* London, 1682.
The Diary of Lady Margaret Hoby, ed. Dorothy M. Meads, London, 1930.
Dod, John, *Bathshebaes Instructions to her Sonne Lemuel,* London, 1614.
 and Robert Cleaver, *A Godly Forme of Householde Government,* London, 1598.
Donne, John, *Sermons,* ed. G. R. Potter and E. M. Simpson, Berkeley, 1957.
The Earl of Strafforde's Letters and Dispatches, ed. William Knowler, Dublin, 1740.
Elyot, Sir Thomas, *The Boke Named the Governour* (1531), ed. S. E. Lehmberg, London, 1962.
England in the Reign of King Henry the Eighth, ed. Sidney J. Herrtage, London, 1878.
Erasmi opuscula, ed. Wallace K. Ferguson, The Hague, 1933.
Erasmus, Desiderius, *Apophthegmes,* trans. Nicholas Udall, London, 1542.
 The Censure and judgement . . . Whyther dyvorsemente betwene man and wyfe stondeth with the lawe of God, trans. Nycolas Lesse, London, [1550].
 Comparation of a vyrgin and a martyr, trans. Thomas Paynell, London, 1537.
 Complaint of Peace, trans. Thomas Paynell, London, 1559; Scholars' Facsimiles, Delmar, New York, 1946.
 De Civilitate Morum Puerilium . . . A lytell booke of good manners for chyldren, trans. Robert Whittington, n.p., 1532.
 De Contemptu mundi, trans. Thomas Paynell, London, 1533.
 Dicta sapientū . . . Very necessary and profitable for children to lerne . . . , London [1527].
 The Education of a Christian Prince (Institutio Principis Christiani), trans. and ed. L. K. Born, New York, 1936.

Enchiridion militis Christiani, trans. and ed. Paul Himelick, Bloomington, Indiana, 1963.

An Exhortation to the diligent studye of scripture, n.p., 1529.

A playne and godly exposytion or declaratiõ of the comune Crede and of the X. comaundementes, London, 1533.

The Praise of Folly, trans. and ed. Betty Radice, New York, 1971.

Proverbes or adagies with newe addicions gathered out of the Chiliades of Erasmus by Richard Taverner, London, 1539.

A ryght frutefull Epystle devysed by the moste excellent clerke Erasmus in laude and prayse of matrymony, trans. Richard Taverner, n.p., n.d. [1531].

A Sermon . . . in the seconde chaptyre of the Gospell of saynt Johan, n.p., n.d.

Erasmus and Cambridge: The Cambridge Letters of Erasmus, trans. and ed. D. F. S. Thomson and H. C. Porter, Toronto, 1963.

The Essential Erasmus, trans. John P. Dolan, New York, 1964.

The First Tome or Volume of the Paraphrase of Erasmus upon the Newe Testamente, London, 1548; Scholars' Facsimiles, Gainesville, Florida, 1975.

Fish, Simon, *The Supplication of Beggars*, London, 1524.

The Forme and Maner of Subvētion or Helping for Pore People devysed and practysed ĩ the Cytie of Hypres in Flanders (Forma Subventionis Pauperum), trans. William Marshall, London, 1535.

Forrest, Sir William, *Pleasaunt Poesye of Princelie Practise*, London, 1548.

Fuller, Thomas, *Church History*, ed. J. S. Brewer, London, 1868.

Works, ed. M. G. Walter, New York, 1938.

A Garden of spirituall Flowers Planted by Ri. Rogers, Will Perkins, Ri. Greenham, M. M., & Geo. Webbe, London, 1610.

Gataker, Thomas, *A Good Wife Gods Gift*, London, 1623.

Certaine sermons, London, 1637.

Gouge, William, *Of Domesticall Duties*, London, 1622.

Greenham, Richard, *Workes*, London, 1601.

Griffith, Matthew, *Pharisaisme and Christianity*, London, 1608.

Bethel, London, 1633.

Hall, Joseph, *The Honor of the Married Clergie Mayntayned*, London, 1620.

Works, Oxford, 1837.

Hamilton, John, *Catechism*, Edinburgh, 1552.

Hammond, Henry, *Sermons*, London, 1695.

Works, Oxford, 1853.

Harpsfield, Nicholas, *The life and death of Sir Thomas Moore . . . written in the tyme of Queene Marie*, ed. E. V. Hitchcock, London, 1932.

Hill, Robert, *The Pathway to Prayer and Pietie*, London, 1613.

Hooker, Richard, *Of the Laws of Ecclesiastical Polity*, ed. P. G. Stanwood, Cambridge, Massachusetts, 1981.

Hull, William, *Repentance not to be Repented Of*, London, 1612.

Hutchinson, Lucy, *Memoires of the Life of Colonel Hutchinson*, ed. Julius Hutchinson, London, 1822.

Jones, William, *A Briefe Exhortation to all men to set their houses in order*, London, 1612.

A pithie & short treatise whereby a godly christian is directed how to make his last will, London, 1612.

Keckerman, Bartholomew, *Systema Systematum*, ed. J. H. Alsted, Hanover, 1613.

Knott, Edward, *Charity Mistaken*, London, 1630.

Mercy and Truth maintained by Catholics, London, 1634.

Lake, Arthur, *Ten Sermons*, London, 1640.

Langland, Stephen, *The Vision of Piers Plowman*, ed. Arthur Burrell, London, 1949.

Latimer, William, *Sermons*, ed. G. E. Corrie, Cambridge, 1844.

Laud, William, *Works*, Oxford, 1842.

Leigh, Dorothy, *The Mother's Blessing: Or, the Godly Counsaile of a Gentlewoman . . . for her children*, London, 1621.

The Letter-Book of Gabriel Harvey, 1573–1580, ed. E. J. L. Scott, London, 1884.

The Letters of Stephen Gardiner, ed. J. A. Muller, Cambridge, 1933.

The Library of Sir Simonds D'Ewes, ed. Andrew G. Watson, London, 1966.

Lupset, Thomas, *Works*, ed. J. A. Gee, New Haven, 1928.

Luther, Martin, *Works*, ed. J. Pelikan and S. Lehmann, Philadelphia, 1955.

Mainwaring, Roger, *Religion and Alegiance*, London, 1627.

Melville, James, *Diary, 1556–1601*, Edinburgh, 1844.

Meriton, George, *A Sermon of Nobilitie*, London, 1607.

Milton, John, *Complete Prose Works*, ed. D. M. Wolfe, New Haven, 1953.

Morison, Richard, *An Exhortation to styire all Englishmen to the defence of theyr countreye*, London, 1539.

An Invective agenste the great and detestable vice, treason, London, 1539.

A Remedy for Sedition, London, 1536; ed. E. M. Cox, London, 1933.

Morton, Thomas, *The necessity of Christian subjection*, London, 1643.

Mum and the Sothsegger, ed. M. Day and R. Steele, London, 1936.

Nowell, Alexander, *A Catechisme or First Instruction*, trans. Thomas Norton, London, 1570; Scholars' Facsimiles, Delmar, New York, 1975.

Oglander, Sir John, *A Royalist's Notebook*, ed. Francis Bamford, London, 1936.

Opus Epistolarum Des. Erasmi Roterodami, ed. P. S. Allen, H. M. Allen and H. W. Garrod, Oxford, 1906–58.

Opus Sancti Patris Francisci, Quaracchi, 1904.

Original Letters, and Other Documents, relating to the benefactions of William Laud to the County of Berkshire, ed. John Bruce, London, 1841.

Parker, Archbishop Henry, *Dives et Pauper*, n.p., 1493; Scholars' Facsimiles, Delmar, New York, 1973.

Parker, Henry, *A Discourse Concerning Puritans*, n.p., 1641.

Parsons, Robert, *The First Booke of the Christian Exercise, appertayning to resolution*, London, 1582.

Memorial for the Reformation of England, n.p., 1590.

Second Part of the Booke of Christian exercise. . . Or a Christian directorie, London, 1591.

A Treatise of Three Conversions of England, St Omer, 1604.

Perkins, William, *Workes*, London, 1616.

Petty, William, *Advice . . . to Samuel Hartlib for Advancement of . . . Learning*, London, 1648.

The Poems of George Herbert, ed. F. E. Hutchinson, Oxford, 1961.

The Presbyterian Movement in the Reign of Queen Elizabeth, as Illustrated by the Minute Book of the Dedham Classics, 1582–1589, ed. R. G. Usher, London, 1905.

The Privileges of the University of Cambridge, ed. George Dyer, London, 1824.

Ramus, Petrus, *Commentariorum de religione Christiana*, Frankfurt, 1576.

Randolph, Thomas, *Aristippus or the Jovial Philosopher*, London, 1630.

Rochfort, Luke, *An antidot for laziness*, Dublin, 1624.

Rogers, Daniel, *Matrimonial Honour*, London, 1642.

Rogers, Francis, *A sermon preached on September the 20th 1632 . . . at the Funerall of William Proud*, London, 1633.

Sander, Nicholas, *A briefe Treatise of Usurie*, Louvain, 1568.

Sanderson, Robert, *Logicae artis compendium*, London, 1618.

XXIV Sermons, London, 1661.

Works, ed. Jacobson, Oxford, 1854.

Sandys, Edwin, *Sermons*, London, 1585.

Sermons and Homilies Appointed to be Read in the Churches in the Time of Queen Elizabeth, London, 1840.

Seton, John, *Dialectica*, London, 1545.

Sherry, Richard, *A Treatise of Schemes and Tropes*, London, 1550; Scholars' Facsimiles, Gainesville, Florida, 1961.

Sibbes, Richard, *Light from Heaven . . . in foure Treatises*, London, 1638.

Beames of divine light . . . XXI Sermons, London, 1639.

Smith, Henry, *Preparative to Marriage*, London, 1591.

The Poore Mans Teares, London, 1592.

Sermons, London, 1593.

Smith, Richard, *The Life of the Most Honourable and Vertuous Lady, the La. Magdalen Viscountesse Montague*, trans. John Cuthbert Fursdon, London, 1627.

Smith, Sir Thomas, *A Discourse of the Commonweal of this Realm of England*, ed. Mary Dewar, Charlottesville, Virginia, 1961.

Some Early Tracts on Poor Relief, ed. F. R. Salter, London, 1926.

Starkey, Thomas, *A Dialogue between Reginald Pole and Thomas Lupset*, ed. K. M. Burton, London, 1948.

Statuta Antiqua Universitatis Oxoniensis, ed. Strickland Gibson, Oxford, 1931.

Statutes of the Colleges of Oxford, Oxford, 1853.

Sydenham, Humphrey, *The Rich Mans Warning-peece*, London, 1630.

Taylor, Jeremy, *Works*, ed. R. Heber, London, 1828.

Tilney, Edmund, *A brief . . . discourse of duties in Marriage, called the Flower of Friendshippe*, London, 1568.

Tudor Constitutional Documents, ed. J. R. Tanner, Cambridge, 1948.

Tudor Economic Documents, ed. R. H. Tawney and Eileen Power, London, 1924.

Two Elizabethan Puritan Diaries by Richard Rogers and Samuel Ward, ed. M. M. Knappen, Gloucester, Massachusetts, 1966.

Vincent de Paul, *Correspondance, Entretiens, Documents*, ed. Pierre Coste, Paris, 1925.

Vives, Juan Luis, *Opera,* Basel, 1555.

    On Education (De tradendis disciplinis), trans. Foster Watson, Cambridge, 1913.

Vives and the Renascence Education of Women, ed. Foster Watson, New York, 1912.

Ward, Samuel, *A Balme from Gilead to Recover Conscience*, London, 1612.

    The wonders of the load-stone, London, 1640.

Webster, John, *Academiarum Examen*, London, 1654.

Whitforde, Richard, *The werke for housholders*, n.p., 1537.

William Perkins: His Pioneer Works on Casuistry. Ed. Thomas F. Merrill. The Hague, 1966.

Wilson, Thomas, *A Discourse upon Usury*, London, 1572.

Zwingli, Ulrich, *Of the Upbringing and Education of Youth in Good Manners and Christian Discipline*, trans. G. W. Bromiley in *Library of Christian Classics*, vol. 24, *Zwingli and Bullinger*, Philadelphia, 1953.

2 Secondary sources

Adams, Robert P., 'Designs by More and Erasmus for a New Social Order,' *Studies in Philology*, 42 (1945), 131–46.

Auguste, A., *La Compagnie du Saint-Sacrement à Toulouse*, Paris, 1913.

Baldwin, John Welsey, *The Medieval Theories of the JustPrice: Romanists, Canonists and Theologians, in the Twelfth and Thirteenth Centuries*, Philadelphia, 1959.

    Masters, Princes and Merchants: The Social Views of Peter the Chanter and his Circle, Princeton, 1970.

Barnes, Thomas Garden, *Somerset 1625–1640*, Cambridge, Mass., 1961.

Bataillon, Marcel, *Érasme et l'Espagne*, Paris, 1937.

Battles, F. L., *New Light on Calvin's Institutes*, London, 1966.

Baumer, Franklin Le Van, *The Early Tudor Theory of Kingship*, New Haven, 1940.

Beer, Barrett L., *Rebellion and Riot: Popular Disorders in England during the Reign of Edward VI*, Kent, Ohio, 1982.

Beier, A. L., 'Poor Relief in Warwickshire 1630–1660,' *P&P*, 35 (1966), 77–100.

    'Vagrants and Social Order in Elizabethan England,' *P&P*, 64 (1974), 3–29.

Bindoff, S. T., *Ket's Rebellion, 1549*, London, 1949.

Bolgar, R. R., *The Classical Heritage and its Beneficiaries*, Cambridge, 1958.

    'Education and Learning,' in *The Counter-Reformation and Price Revolution*, ed. R. B. Wernham, vol. 3 of *The New Cambridge Modern History*, Cambridge, 1968.

Borah, Woodrow, 'Social Welfare and Social Obligation in New Spain: A tentative assessment,' *XXXVI Congresso Internacional de Americanistas, Seville, 1964* (Seville, 1966), 45–57.

Bossy, John, 'The Character of Elizabethan Catholicism,' in *Crisis in Europe, 1560–1660*, ed. Trevor Aston (London, 1965), 223–46.

'The Counter-Reformation and the People,' *P&P*, 47 (1970), 51–70.

'The Social History of Confession in the Age of the Reformation,' 5th ser., 25 (1975), 21–38.

The English Catholic Community 1570–1660, Oxford, 1976.

'Holiness and Society,' *P&P*, 75 (1977), 119–37.

Bouwsma, William, 'The Two Faces of Humanism: Stoicism and Augustinianism in Renaissance Thought,' in *Itinerarium Italicum*, ed. Heiko Oberman and Thomas A. Brady, Jr. (Leiden, 1975), 3–60.

Breen, T. H., 'The Non-Existent Controversy: Puritan and Anglican Attitudes on Work and Wealth, 1600–1640,' *CH*, 35 (1966), 273–87.

Burke, Peter, *Popular Culture in Early Modern Europe*, London, 1978.

Callahan, William J., 'The Problem of Confinement: An Aspect of Poor Relief in Eighteenth Century Spain,' *Hispanic American Historical Review*, 51 (1971), 1–24.

Caspari, Fritz, 'Erasmus on the Social Functions of Humanism,' *JHI*, 8 (1947), 78–106.

Humanism and the Social Order in Tudor England, Chicago, 1954.

Chénon, Émile, *Histoire Générale du Droit Français Public et Privé*, Paris, 1926.

Chill, Emmanuel, 'Religion and Mendicity in Seventeenth Century France,' *International Review of Social History*, 7 (1962), 400–25.

Christianson, Paul, *Reformers and Babylon*, Toronto, 1978.

'Reformers and the Church of England under Elizabeth I and the Early Stuarts,' *J E H*, 31 (1980), 463–82.

Clark, Peter, *Provincial Society from the Reformation to the Revolution*, Brunswick, NJ, 1977.

and Paul Slack, eds., *Crisis and Order in English Towns 1500–1700*, London, 1972.

Clebsch, William, *England's Earliest Protestants*, New Haven, 1964.

Collinson, Patrick, 'The Beginnings of English Sabbatarianism,' *Studies in Church History*, 1 (1964), 207–21.

The Elizabethan Puritan Movement, Berkeley, 1967.

Archbishop Grindal, Berkeley, 1979.

'A Comment: "Concerning the Name Puritan",' *JEH*, (1980), 483–8.

The Religion of Protestants, Oxford, 1982.

English Puritanism, London, 1983.

Godly People, London, 1983.

Coolidge, John S., *The Pauline Renaissance in England*, Oxford, 1970.

Coppens, J. J., ed., *Scrinium Erasmianum*, 2 vols., Leiden, 1969.

Costello, William J., *The Scholastic Curriculum at Early Seventeenth Century Cambridge*, Cambridge, Mass., 1958.

Cragg, G. R., *From Puritanism to the Age of Reason: A Study of Changes in Religious*

Thought within the Church of England 1660–1700, Cambridge, 1966.

Cressy, David, *Education in Tudor and Stuart England*, London, 1975.

Literacy and the Social Order, Cambridge, 1980.

Cross, Claire, *The Puritan Earl: The Life of Henry Hastings, Third Earl of Huntingdon*, London, 1966.

Curtis, Mark H., *Oxford and Cambridge in Transition, 1558–1642*, Oxford, 1959.

Dainville, François de, *La Naissance de l'humanisme moderne*, Paris, 1940.

L'éducation des jésuites, Paris, 1978.

Davies, C. S. L., 'Slavery and the Protector Somerset; The Vagrancy Act of 1547,' *Economic History Review*, 2nd ser., 19 (1966), 533–49.

Davies, Kathleen M., 'The Sacred Condition of Equality – How Original were Puritan Doctrines of Marriage?', *Social History*, 5 (1977), 563–80.

Davis, Natalie, *Society and Culture in Early Modern France*, Stanford, 1975.

Delattre, Pierre, *Les Établissements des Jésuites en France dupuis quatre siècles*, Enghien, 1940.

Dent, C. M., *Protestant Reformers in Elizabethan Oxford*, Oxford, 1983.

Dewar, M., *Sir Thomas Smith: A Tudor Intellectual in Office*, London, 1964.

Duhamel, P., 'The Oxford Lectures of John Colet,' *JHI*, 14 (1953), 493–510.

Elton, G. R., *Reform and Reformation*, Cambridge, Mass., 1973.

Reform and Renewal: Thomas Cromwell and the Common Weal, Cambridge, 1973.

Feingold, Mordechai, *The Mathematicians' Apprenticeship*, Cambridge, 1984.

Fenlon, D. B., *Heresy and Obedience in Tridentine Italy: Cardinal Pole and the Counter Reformation*, Cambridge, 1972.

'The Counter Reformation and the Realisation of *Utopia*,' in *Historical Studies: Papers Read at the Ninth Conference of Irish Historians*, ed. J. Barry, Dublin, 1973.

'England and Europe: *Utopia* and its aftermath,' *TRHS*, 5th ser., 25 (1975), 115–36.

Ferguson, Arthur B., 'The Tudor Commonweal and the Sense of Change,' *JBS*, 3 (1963), 11–35.

The Articulate Citizen and the English Renaissance, Durham, NC, 1965.

Clio Unbound: Perception of the Social and Cultural Past in Renaissance England, Durham, NC, 1979.

Ferguson, Wallace K., *Renaissance Studies*, New York, 1970.

Fideler, Paul A., 'Christian Humanism and Poor Law Reform in Early Tudor England,' *Societas*, 4 (1974), 269–86.

Findlayson, Michael, *Historians, Puritanism and the English Revolution*, Toronto, 1983.

Fletcher, A., *The Outbreak of the English Civil War*, London, 1981.

Fletcher, H. F., *The Intellectual Development of John Milton*, Urbana, Illinois, 1961.

Foucault, Michel, *Madness and Civilization*, trans. Richard Howard, New York, 1965.

Fowler, T., *History of Corpus Christi College*, Oxford, 1893.

Fulbrook, Mary, *Piety and Politics: Religion and the Rise of Absolutism in England, Wurtemberg and Prussia*, Cambridge, 1983.

George, Charles H., 'Social Interpretation of English Puritanism,' *JMH*, 25 (1953), 327–42.

'The Making of the English Bourgeoisie, 1500–1750,' *Science and Society*, 35 (1971), 385–412.

and Katherine George, *The Protestant Mind of the English Reformation, 1570–1640*, Princeton, 1961.

Greaves, Richard, *Society and Religion in Elizabethan England*, Minneapolis, 1981.

'The Puritan-Nonconformist Tradition in England, 1560–1700,' *Albion*, 17 (1985), 449–86.

Green, Robert W., ed., *Protestantism and Capitalism*, Boston, 1959.

Greenleaf, Richard E., ed., *Zumárraga and the Mexican Inquisition, 1536–1543*, Washington, DC, 1961.

The Roman Catholic Church in Colonial Latin America, New York, 1971.

Gutton, Jean-Pierre, *La Société et les pauvres: L'éxemple de la généralité de Lyon, 1534–1789*, Paris, 1971.

La Société et les pauvres en Europe, Vendôme, 1974.

Haigh, Christopher, *Reformation and Resistance in Tudor Lancashire*, Cambridge, 1975.

'From Monopoly to Minority: Catholicism in Early Modern England,' *TRHS*, 5th ser., 31 (1981), 129–48.

ed., *The Reign of Elizabeth I*, Athens, Georgia, 1985.

Hall, Basil, 'Puritanism: The Problem of Definition,' *Studies in Church History*, 2 (1965), 283–96.

Haller, William, *The Rise of Puritanism*, New York, 1938.

and Malleville Haller, 'The Puritan Art of Love,' *HLQ*, 5 (1942), 235–72.

Hampson, E. M., *The Treatment of Poverty in Cambridgeshire, 1597–1834*, Cambridge, 1934.

Hanke, Lewis, *The First Social Experiments in America*, Cambridge, Mass., 1935.

Henderson, R. W., 'Sixteenth Century Community Benevolence: An Attempt to Resacralize the Secular,' *CH*, 38 (1969), 421–8.

Hexter, J. H., *More's 'Utopia': The Biography of an Idea*, Princeton, 1952.

Reappraisals in History, New York, 1961.

The Vision of Politics on the Eve of the Reformation, New York, 1973.

Hill, Christopher, *Puritanism and Revolution*, London, 1958.

'Protestantism and the Rise of Capitalism,' in *Essays in the Economic and Social History of Tudor and Stuart England in honour of R. H. Tawney*, ed. F. J. Fisher (Cambridge, 1961), 15–39.

'Puritans and "the Dark Corners of the Land",' *TRHS*, 5th ser., 13 (1963), 77–102.

Society and Puritanism, New York, 1964.

Intellectual Origins of the English Revolution, Oxford, 1965.

The World Turned Upside-Down, New York, 1972.
Milton and the English Revolution, New York, 1977.
The Experience of Defeat, New York, 1984.
Hirst, Derek, *The Representative of the People?*, Cambridge, 1975.
Authority and Conflict, Cambridge, Mass., 1986.
Hogrefe, Pearl, *Women of Action in Tudor England*, Ames, Iowa, 1977.
Hooykaas, R., *Humanisme, science et réforme: Pierre de la Ramée (1515–1572)*, Leyden, 1958.
Religion and the Rise of Modern Science, Grand Rapids, Michigan, 1972.
Howell, W. S., *Logic and Rhetoric in England, 1500–1700*, Princeton, 1956.
Huizinga, Johan, *Erasmus and the Age of Reformation*, New York, 1924.
Hunt, William, *The Puritan Moment*, Cambridge, Mass., 1983.
Hyma, Albert, *The Life of Desiderius Erasmus*, Assen, The Netherlands, 1972.
James, Margaret, *Social Problems and Policy during the Puritan Revolution*, London, 1930.
Jardine, Lisa, 'The Place of Dialectic Teaching in Sixteenth Century Cambridge,' *Studies in the Renaissance*, 21 (1974), 31–62.
Jayne, Sears, *John Colet and Marsile Ficino*, Oxford, 1963.
Johnson, James T., 'Ends of Marriage,' *CH*, 38 (1969), 429–36.
Jordan, W. K., *The Development of Religious Toleration in England*, London, 1932–6.
Philanthropy in England 1480–1660, London, 1959.
Jütte, Robert, 'Poor Relief and Social Discipline in Sixteenth-Century Europe,' *European Studies Review*, 11 (1981), 25–52.
Kamen, Henry, *The Iron Century: Social Change in Europe, 1550–1660*, New York, 1971.
Kearney, Hugh, 'Puritanism, Capitalism and Scientific Revolution,' *P&P*, 28 (1964), 81–101.
Scholars and Gentlemen, London, 1970.
Kendall, R. T., *Calvin and English Calvinism to 1649*, Oxford, 1979.
Kiernan, V., 'Puritanism and the Poor,' *PEP*, 3 (1953), 45–53.
Kingdon, Robert M., 'Social Welfare in Calvin's Geneva,' *American Historical Review*, 76 (1971), 50–69.
Knappen, M. M., *Tudor Puritanism*, Chicago, 1939.
Köhls, Ernst-Wilhelm, *Die Theologische Lebensaufgabe des Erasmus und die Oberrheinischen Reformatoren*, Stuttgart, 1969.
Kristeller, P. O., *Renaissance Thought*, New York, 1961.
Kruger, F., *Bucer und Erasmus*, Wiesbaden, 1970.
Lake, Peter, 'Matthew Hutton– A Puritan Bishop?', *History*, 64 (1979), 182–204.
Moderate Puritans and the Elizabethan Church, Cambridge, 1982.
'Puritan Identities,' *JEH*, 35 (1984), 112–23.
Land, Stephen K., *Kett's Rebellion: The Norfolk Rising of 1549*, Ipswich, 1977.
Lang, August, *Puritanismus und Pietismus*, Neukirchen, 1941.
Leites, Edmund, 'The Duty to Desire: Love, Friendship, and Sexuality in

Some Puritan Theories of Marriage,' *Journal of Social History*, 15 (1979), 383–408.

Lindberg, Carter, ' "There Should Be No Beggars Among Christians": Karlstadt, Luther and the Origins of Protestant Poor Relief,' *CH*, 46 (1977), 313–34.

Linder, Robert D., 'Calvinism and Humanism: The First Generation,' *CH*, 44 (1975), 167–81.

Littell, F. H., 'New Light on Butzer's Significance,' in *Reformation Studies in Honor of Roland Bainton* (Richmond, Virginia, 1962), 145–67.

Little, Lester, K., 'Evangelical Poverty, The New Money Economy and Violence,' in *Poverty in the Middle Ages*, ed. David Flood, Werl, Westphalia, 1975.
Religious Poverty and the Profit Economy in Medieval Europe, Ithaca, New York, 1978.

Lloyd-Jones, H., V. Pearl and B. Worden, eds., *History and Imagination*, New York, 1981.

Lockhart, James, *Spanish Peru, 1532–1560*, Madison, Wisconsin, 1968.

Lovejoy, Arthur O., *The Great Chain of Being*, Cambridge, Mass., 1936.

MacCulloch, Diarmaid, 'Kett's Rebellion in Context,' *P&P*, 84 (1979), 36–59.

Macfarlane, Alan, *The Family Life of Ralph Josselin*, Cambridge, 1979.

McConica, James K., *English Humanists and Reformation Politics under Henry VIII and Edward VI*, Oxford, 1965.
'The Prosopography of the Tudor University,' *Journal of Interdisciplinary History*, 3 (1973), 543–55.
'Social Relations in Tudor Oxford,' *TRHS*, 5th ser., 27 (1977), 115–34.
'Humanism and Aristotelianism in Tudor Oxford,' *EHR*, 94(1979), 291–317.
'The Patrimony of Thomas More,' in *History and Imagination*, ed. Hugh Lloyd Jones, Valerie Pearl and Blair Worden (New York, 1981), 56–71.

McGee, J. Sears, *The Godly Man in Stuart England: Anglicans, Puritans, and the Two Tables, 1620–1670*, New Haven, 1976.

McGregor, J. F. and B. Reay, eds., *Radical Religion in the English Revolution*, Oxford, 1984.

McLean, Antonia, *Humanism and the Rise of Science in Tudor England*, New York, 1972.

Mallet, C. E., *A History of the University of Oxford*, Oxford, 1924–7.

Manning, Roger B., *Religion and Society in Elizabethan Sussex: A study of the Enforcement of the Religious Settlement 1558–1603*, Leicester, 1969.

Marchant, Ronald A., *The Puritans and the Church Courts in the Diocese of York, 1560–1642*, London, 1960.
The Church under the Law, Cambridge, 1969.

Marshall, Gordon, *Presbyteries and Profits*, Oxford, 1980.

Martz, Linda, *Poverty and Welfare in Hapsburg Spain*, Cambridge, 1983.

Maurer, Wilhelm. *Das Verhältnis des Staates zur Kirche nach humanistischer*

Anschauung, vornehmlich bei Erasmus, Giessen, 1930.

Miller, Perry, *Errand into the Wilderness*, Cambridge, Mass., 1956.

Mollat, Michel, ed., *Études sur l'histoire de la pauvreté*, Paris, 1974.

Morey, Adrian, *The Catholic Subjects of Elizabeth I*, London, 1978.

Morgan, Irvonwy, *Prince Charles's Puritan Chaplain*, London, 1957.

The Godly Preachers of the Elizabethan Church, London, 1978.

Morgan, John, *Godly Learning: Puritan Attitudes towards Reason, Learning, and Education, 1540–1640*, Cambridge, 1986.

Morison, Samuel Eliot, *The Intellectual Life of Colonial New England* Ithaca, NY, 1936.

Morrill, J. S., *Cheshire 1630–1660*, Oxford, 1974.

The Revolt of the Provinces: Conservatives and Radicals in the English Civil War 1630–1650, London, 1976.

'The Church in England 1642–9', in *Reactions to the English Civil War*, ed. J. S. Morrill (London, 1983), 89–114.

'The Religious Context of the English Civil War,' *TRHS*, 5th ser., 34 (1984), 155–78.

'Sir William Brereton and England's Wars of Religion,' *Journal of British Studies*, 24 (1985), 311–32.

Morris, Joan, *Against Nature and God*, London, 1974.

Mullinger, J. B., *The University of Cambridge from the Earliest Times to the Decline of the Platonist Movement*, Cambridge, 1873–1911.

O'Connell, Laura Stevenson, 'Anti-Entrepreneurial Attitudes in Elizabethan Sermons and Popular Literature,' *JBS*, 15 (1976), 1–20.

Olin, John C., *Six Essays on Erasmus*, New York, 1979.

Ong, Walter, J., *Ramus, Method, and the Decay of Dialogue*, Cambridge, Mass., 1983 (first edn., 1958).

'Tudor Writings on Rhetoric,' *Studies in the Renaissance*, 15 (1968), 39–69.

Ozment, Steven, *When Fathers Ruled*, Cambridge, Mass., 1983.

Parker, Kenneth, 'Thomas Rogers and the English Sabbath: The Case for a Reappraisal,' *CH*, 53 (1984), 332–47.

Parker, T. M., 'Arminianism and Laudianism in Seventeenth Century England,' *Studies in Church History*, 1 (1964), 20–34.

Pearl, Valerie, 'Puritans and Poor Relief: The London Workhouse, 1649–1660,' in *Puritans and Revolutionaries*, ed. Donald Pennington and Keith Thomas (Oxford, 1978), 206–32.

Pearson, Scott, *Thomas Cartwright*, Cambridge, 1925.

Peile, John, *Biographical Register of Christ's College*, Cambridge, 1910.

Peremans, Nicole, *Érasme et Bucer d'après leur correspondance*, Paris, 1979.

Peters, Robert, 'Erasmus and the Fathers: Their Practical Value,' *CH*, 36 (1967), 254–61.

Phelan, John Leddy, *The Millennial Kingdom of the Franciscans in the New World*, Berkeley, 1956.

Phythian-Adams, Charles, *Desolation of a City: Coventry and the Urban Crisis of the Late Middle Ages*, Cambridge, 1979.

Pocock, J. G. A., 'Working on Ideas in Time,' in *The Historian's Workshop*, ed. L. P. Curtis (New York, 1970), 151–66.

Politics, Language, and Time, London, 1972.

The Machiavellian Moment: Florentine Political Thought and The Atlantic Republican Tradition, Princeton, 1975.

Porter, H. C., *Reformation and Reaction in Tudor Cambridge*, Cambridge, 1958.

Powell, Chilton, *English Domestic Relations, 1487–1653*, New York, 1917.

Pullan, Brian, *Rich and Poor in Renaissance Venice*, Cambridge, Mass., 1971.

Reay, B., 'Radicalism and Religion in the English Revolution,' in *Radical Religion in the English Revolution*, ed. B. Reay and J. F. McGregor (Oxford, 1984), 1–21.

Renaudet, A., *Études Érasmiennes*, Paris, 1939.

Richardson, R. C., *Puritanism in North-west England*, Manchester, 1972.

Rosenthal, Joel T., *The Purchase of Paradise: Gift Giving and the Aristocracy, 1307–1485*, Toronto, 1972.

Rupp, E. G., *Studies in the Making of the English Protestant Tradition*, Cambridge, 1949.

Russell, Elizabeth, 'The Influx of Commoners into the University of Oxford before 1581: An Opitcal Illusion?', *EHR*, 92 (1977), 721–45.

Scarisbrick, J. J., 'Robert Parsons's Plans for the "true" Reformation of England,' in *Historical Perspectives: Studies in English Thought and Society in Honour of J. H. Plumb*, ed. Neil McKendrick (London, 1974), 19–42.

The Reformation and the English People, Oxford, 1984.

Schmitt, Charles B., *Aristotle and the Renaissance*, Cambridge, Mass., 1983.

John Case and Aristotelianism in the Renaissance, Montreal, 1983.

Schnucker, Robert V., 'The English Puritans and Pregnancy, Delivery, and Breast Feeding,' *History of Childhood Quarterly*, 1 (1974), 639–58.

'Elizabethan Birth Control and Puritan Attitudes,' *Journal of Interdisciplinary History*, 5 (1975), 655–67.

Schoell, F. L., *Études sur l'humanisme continental en Angleterre à la fin de la Renaissance*, Paris, 1926.

Schücking, Levin L., *The Puritan Family*, trans. B. Battershaw, New York, 1970.

Scott-Giles, C. W., *Sidney Sussex College*, Cambridge, 1975.

Seaver, Paul S., *The Puritan Lectureships*, Stanford, 1970.

'The Puritan Work Ethic Revisited,' *JBS*, (1980), 35–53.

Wallington's World, Stanford, 1985.

Sharpe, Kevin, 'Archbishop Laud and the University of Oxford,' in *History and Imagination*, ed. Hugh Lloyd-Jones, Valerie Pearl and Blair Worden (New York, 1981), 146–64.

Seigel, Jerrold E., *Rhetoric and Philosophy in Renaissance Humanism*, Princeton, 1968.

'Archbishop Laud,' *History Today*, (1983), 26–30.

Siegel, Paul, 'Milton and the Humanist Attitude toward Women,' *JHI*, 11 (1950), 42–53.

Simon, Joan, *Education and Society in Tudor England*, Cambridge, 1966.

Skinner, Quentin, 'Meaning and Understanding in the History of Ideas,' *History and Theory*, 8 (1969), 3–53.

'Motives, Intentions, and the Interpretation of Texts,' *New Literary His-*

tory, 3 (1971), 393–408.

'Some Problems in the Analysis of Political Thought and Action,' *Political Theory*, 2 (1974), 277–303.

The Foundations of Modern Political Thought, Cambridge, 1978.

Slack, Paul, 'Poverty and Politics in Salisbury, 1597–1666,' in *Crisis and Order in English Towns 1500–1700*, ed. Peter Clark and Paul Slack (Toronto, 1972), 164–203.

'Book of Orders: The Making of English Social Policy, 1577–1631,' *TRHS*, 5 th ser., 30 (1980), 1–22.

'Poverty and Social Regulation in Elizabethan England,' in *The Reign of Elizabeth I* (Athens, Georgia, 1985), 221–41.

Smith, Preserved, *Erasmus*, New York, 1923.

Solomon, Howard M., *Public Welfare, Science, and Propaganda in Seventeenth Century France: The Innovations of Theophraste Renaudot*, Princeton, 1972.

Sommerville, C. John, 'Religious Typologies and Popular Religion in Restoration England,' *CH*, 45 (1976), 32–9.

'The Anti-Puritan Work Ethic,' *JBS*, 20 (1981), 70–81.

Spufford, Margaret, *Contrasting Communities: English Villagers in the Sixteenth and Seventeenth Centuries*, Cambridge, 1974.

Stone, Lawrence, 'The Ninnyversity?', *NYRB*, 28 January 1971.

ed., *The University in Society*, Princeton, 1974.

The Family, Sex and Marriage in England, New York, 1977.

Strype, John, *Life of Cheke*, Oxford, 1821.

Tawney, R. H., *Religion and the Rise of Capitalism*, New York, 1926.

Thirsk, Joan, *Economic Policy and Projects*, Oxford, 1979.

Thomas, Keith, 'Women and the Civil War Sects,' *P&P*, 13 (1958), 42–62.

'Double Standard,' *JHI*, 20 (1959), 195–216.

'The Social Origins of Hobbes' Political Thought,' in *Hobbes Studies*, ed. K. C. Brown, Cambridge, Mass., 1965.

'The Puritans and Adultery: The Act of 1650 Reconsidered,' in *Puritans and Revolutionaries*, ed. Donald Pennington and Keith Thomas (Oxford, 1978), 257–81.

Tierney, Brian, *Medieval Poor Law: A Sketch of Canonical Theory and its Application in England*, Berkeley, 1959.

Todd, Margo, 'Seneca and the Protestant Mind: The Influence of Stoicism on Puritan Ethics,' *Archive für Reformationsgeschichte*, 74 (1983), 182–99.

'The Samuel Ward Papers at Sidney Sussex College, Cambridge,' *Transactions of the Cambridge Bibliographical Society*, 8 (1985), 582–92.

' "An Act of Discretion": Evangelical Conformity and the Puritan Dons,' *Albion*, 18 (1986), 581–99.

Tomlinson, Howard, *Before the English Civil War*, New York, 1984.

Tracey, James D., *The Politics of Erasmus*, Toronto, 1978.

Trevor-Roper, H. R., *Historical Essays*, London, 1957.

Archbishop Laud 1573–1645, Hamden, Connecticut, 1962.

Trexler, Richard C., 'Charity and the Defense of Urban Elites in the Italian

Communes,' in *The Rich, the Well Born, and the Powerful*, ed. Frederic Cople Jaher (Urbana, Illinois, 1973), 64–109.

Trinkaus, Charles, and Heiko A. Oberman, eds., *The Pursuit of Holiness in Late Medieval and Renaissance Religion*, Leiden, 1974.

Trinterud, Leonard J., 'Origins of Puritanism,' *CH*, 20 (1951), 37–57.

Tyacke, Nicholas, 'Puritanism, Arminianism and Counter-Revolution,' in *The Origins of the English Civil War*, ed. Conrad Russell (London, 1973), 119–43.

'Science and Religion at Oxford before the Civil War,' in *Puritans and Revolutionaries*, ed. Donald Pennington and Keith Thomas (Oxford, 1978), 73–93.

Ullmann, Walter, *Medieval Foundations of Renaissance Humanism*, Ithaca, NY, 1977.

Venn, John and J. A., *Alumni Cantabrigiensis*, Cambridge, 1922.

Wallace, Dewey, *Puritans and Predestination: Grace in English Protestant Theology, 1525–1695*, Chapel Hill, NC, 1982.

Walzer, Michael, *The Revolution of the Saints*, New York, 1972.

Warren, F. Benedict, 'The Idea of the Pueblos of Sante Fe,' in *The Roman Catholic Church in Colonial Latin America*, ed. Richard E. Greenleaf, New York, 1971.

Watson, Foster, *The English Grammar Schools to 1660*, Cambridge, 1908.

Weber, Max, 'Die protestantische ethik und der geist des kapitalismus,' in *Gesammelte aufsätze zur religionssoziologie*, Tubingen, 1922.

Webster, Charles, *The Great Instauration: Science, Medicine, and Reform 1626–1660*, New York, 1975.

White, Helen C., *Social Criticism in Popular Religious Literature of the Sixteenth Century*, New York, 1944.

White, Peter, 'The Rise of Arminianism Reconsidered,' *P&P*, 101 (1983), 34–54.

Whitelocke, R. H., *Memoires of Bulstrode Whitelocke*, London, 1860.

Williams, A. M., *Conversations at Little Gidding*, Cambridge, 1970.

Woodhouse, A. S. P., *Puritanism and Liberty*, London, 1938.

Wright, Louis B., *Middle-Class Culture in Elizabethan England*, Ithaca, NY, 1935.

'William Perkins: Elizabethan Apostle of "Practical Divinity",' *Huntington Library Quarterly*, 3 (1940), 171–96.

Wrightson, Keith, *English Society, 1580–1680*, New Brunswick, NJ, 1982.

and David Levine, *Poverty and Piety in an English Village: Terling, 1525–1700*, New York, 1979.

Zavala, Silvio, 'The American Utopia of the Sixteenth Century,' *Huntington Library Quarterly*, 10 (1947), 337–47.

'Sir Thomas More in New Spain,' in *Essential Articles for the Study of Thomas More*, ed. R. S. Sylvester (Hamden, Connecticut, 1977), 302–11.

Zeeveld, Gordon, *Foundations of Tudor Policy*, Cambridge, Mass., 1948.

THESES AND UNPUBLISHED PAPERS

Bauckham, Richard, 'The Career and Thought of Dr. William Fulke' (unpublished Ph.D., University of Cambridge, 1972).

Huppert, George, 'Social Functions of Classical Education in Renaissance France,' Paper read at the Sixteenth Century Studies Conference, 25 October 1980.

Tyacke, N. R. N., 'Arminianism in England, in Religion and Politics, 1604–1640' (unpublished D.Phil., University of Oxford, 1968).

Wrightson, Keith E., 'The Puritan Reformation of Manners with special reference to the Counties of Lancashire and Essex 1640–1660' (unpublished Ph.D., University of Cambridge, 1974).

INDEX